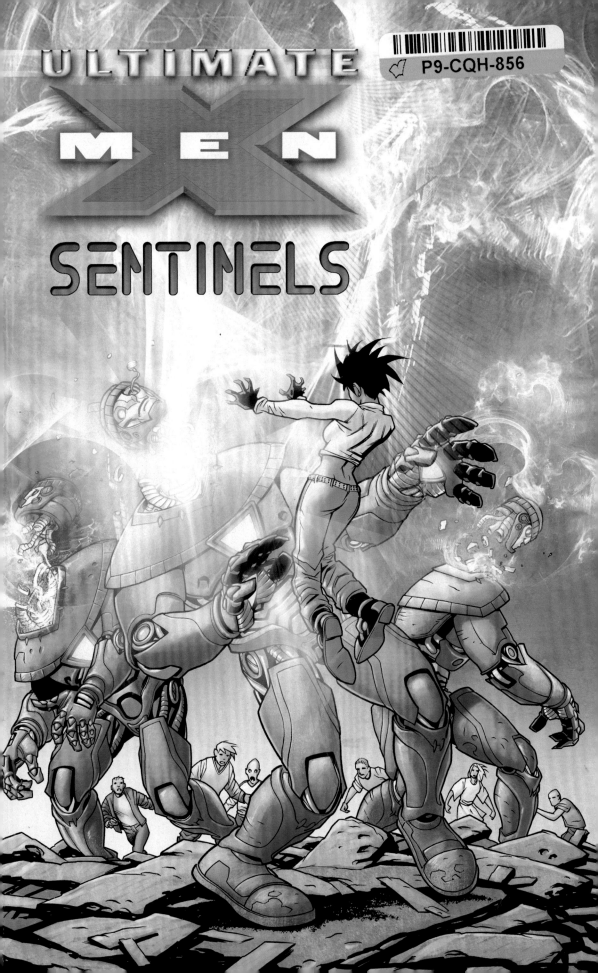

ULTIMATE X-MEN

SENTINELS

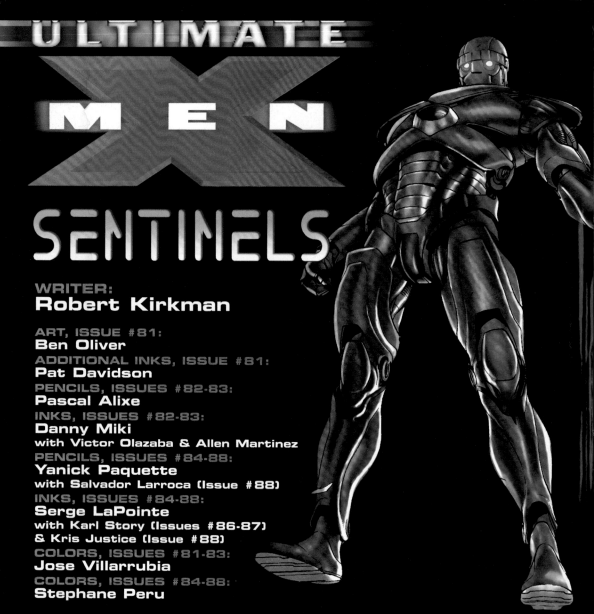

ULTIMATE X MEN

SENTINELS

WRITER:
Robert Kirkman

ART, ISSUE #81:
Ben Oliver
ADDITIONAL INKS, ISSUE #81:
Pat Davidson
PENCILS, ISSUES #82-83:
Pascal Alixe
INKS, ISSUES #82-83:
Danny Miki
with Victor Olazaba & Allen Martinez
PENCILS, ISSUES #84-88:
Yanick Paquette
with Salvador Larroca (Issue #88)
INKS, ISSUES #84-88:
Serge LaPointe
with Karl Story (Issues #86-87)
& Kris Justice (Issue #88)
COLORS, ISSUES #81-83:
Jose Villarrubia
COLORS, ISSUES #84-88:
Stephane Peru

LETTERS:
Virtual Calligraphy's Joe Caramagna with Cory Petit
COVERS:
Yanick Paquette, Serge LaPointe & Stephane Peru
ASSISTANT EDITOR:
Lauren Sankovitch
EDITORS:
John Barber & Bill Rosemann
SENIOR EDITOR:
Ralph Macchio

COLLECTION EDITOR:
Jennifer Grünwald
ASSISTANT EDITORS:
Cory Levine & John Denning
ASSOCIATE EDITOR:
Mark D. Beazley
SENIOR EDITOR, SPECIAL PROJECTS:
Jeff Youngquist
SENIOR VICE PRESIDENT OF SALES:
David Gabriel

EDITOR IN CHIEF:
Joe Quesdada
PUBLISHER:
Dan Buckley

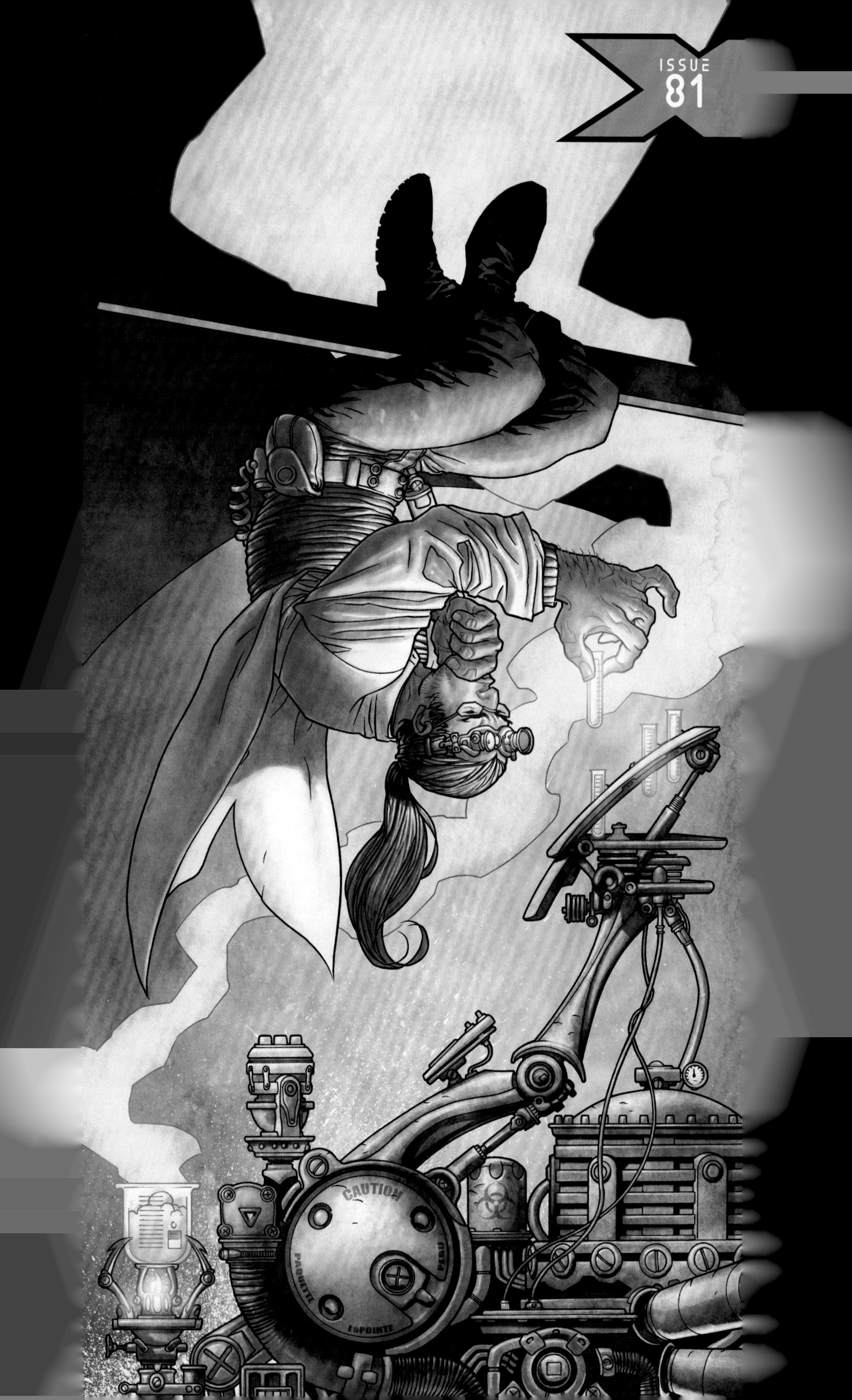
ISSUE
81
CAUTION
PAQUETTE
PERU
LaPOINTE

PREVIOUSLY IN
ULTIMATE X-MEN:

Born with strange and amazing abilities, the X-Men are young mutant heroes, sworn to protect a world that fears and hates them.

After a series of blows to the team's morale, a man called CABLE attacked the X-Mansion. His mission: KILL CHARLES XAVIER.

He has succeeded. Professor Charles Xavier is dead. His dream for a peaceful coexistence between humans and mutants may have died with him.

As a result of Xavier's death, Scott Summers has disbanded the X-Men.

CLIFFHANGERS

The Triskelion.
Headquarters of The Ultimates and also a superhuman penitentiary housing some of the most dangerous super-criminals and mutants known to man.

Crap.

Yeah.

What the *hell* is going on here?!

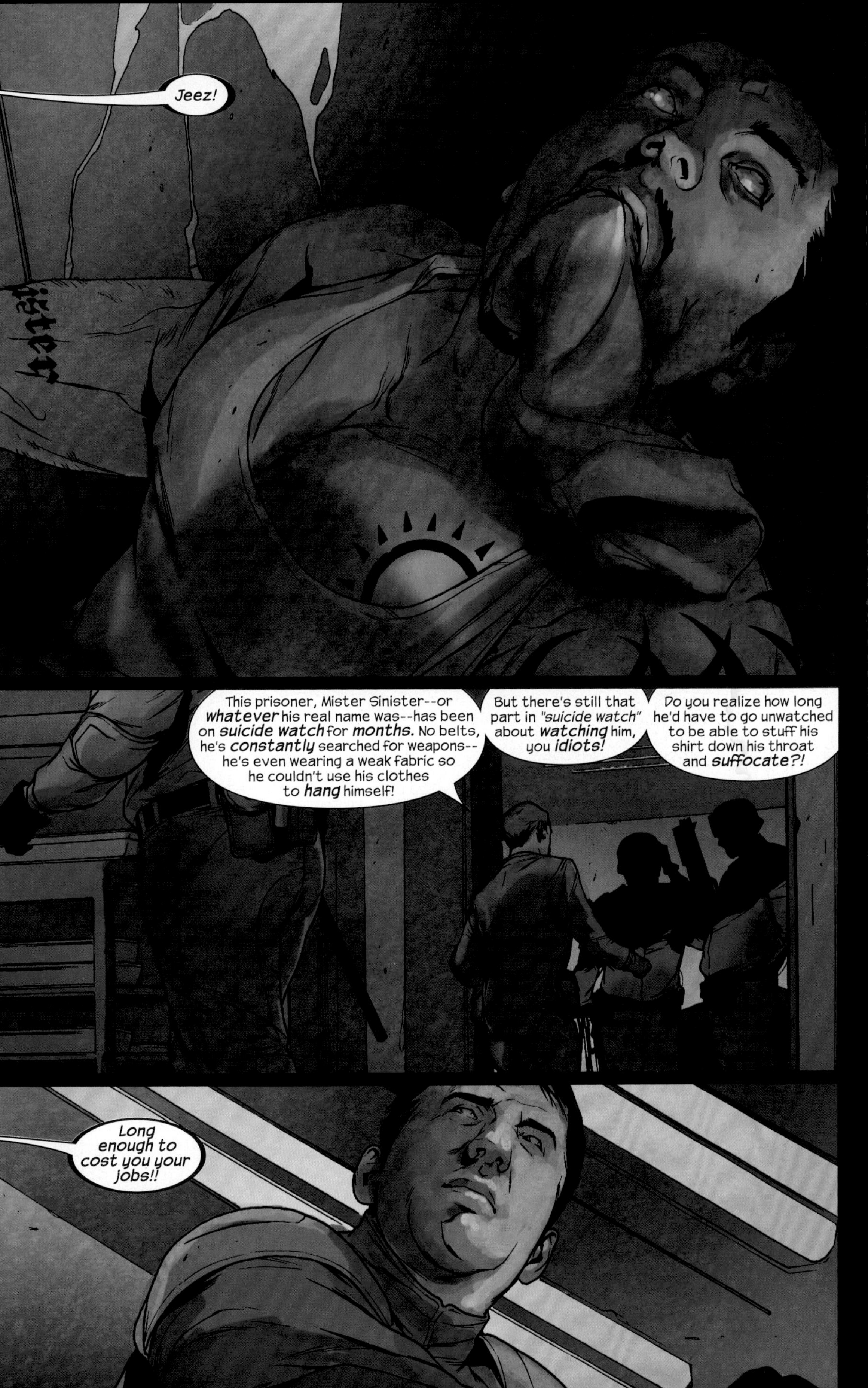

Jeez!
This prisoner, Mister Sinister--or whatever his real name was--has been on suicide watch for months. No belts, he's constantly searched for weapons--he's even wearing a weak fabric so he couldn't use his clothes to hang himself!
But there's still that part in "suicide watch" about watching him, you idiots!
Do you realize how long he'd have to go unwatched to be able to stuff his shirt down his throat and suffocate?!
Long enough to cost you your jobs!!

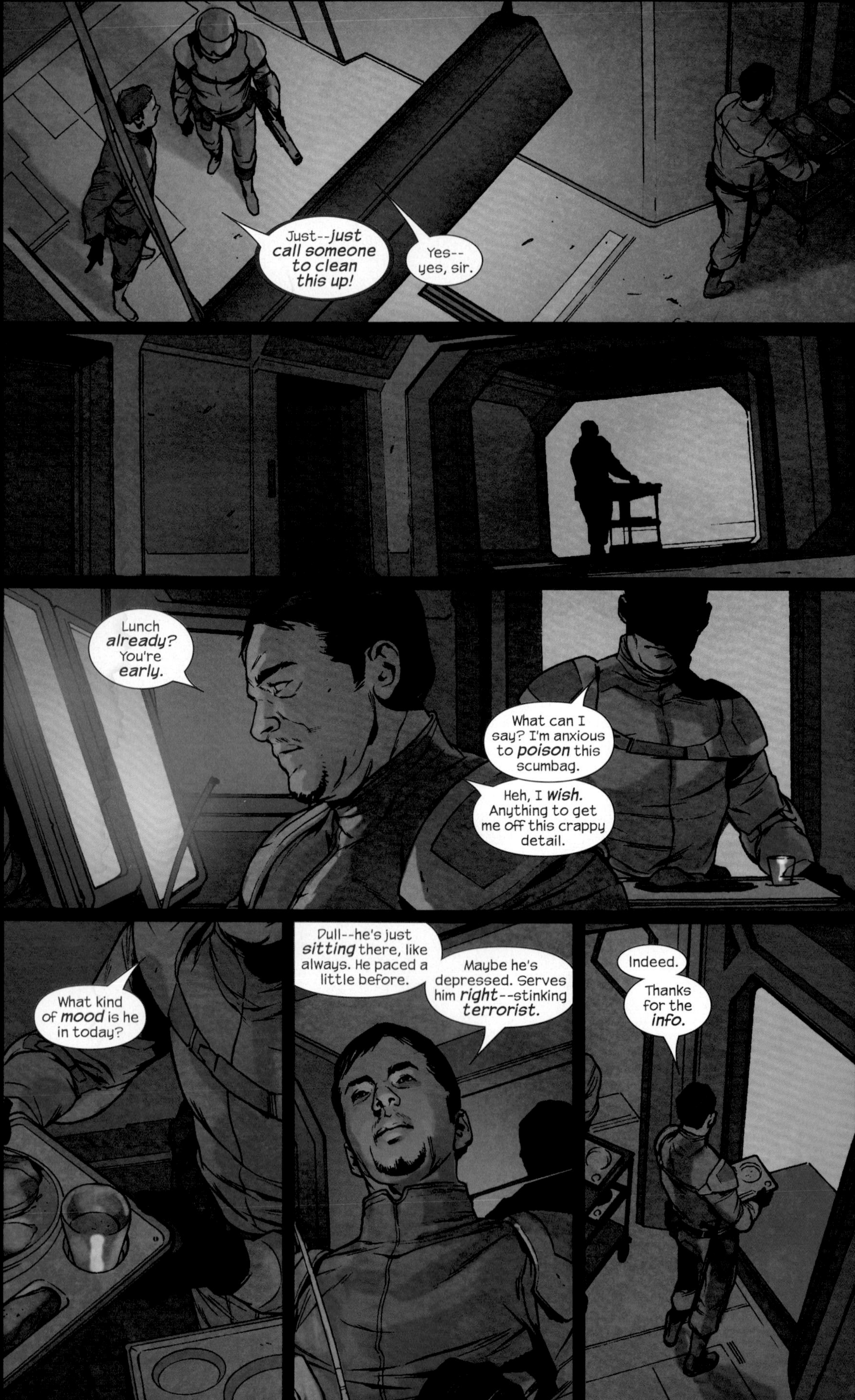
Just--just call someone to clean this up!
Yes-- yes, sir.
Lunch already? You're early.
What can I say? I'm anxious to poison this scumbag.
Heh, I wish. Anything to get me off this crappy detail.
What kind of mood is he in today?
Dull--he's just sitting there, like always. He paced a little before.
Maybe he's depressed. Serves him right--stinking terrorist.
Indeed.
Thanks for the info.

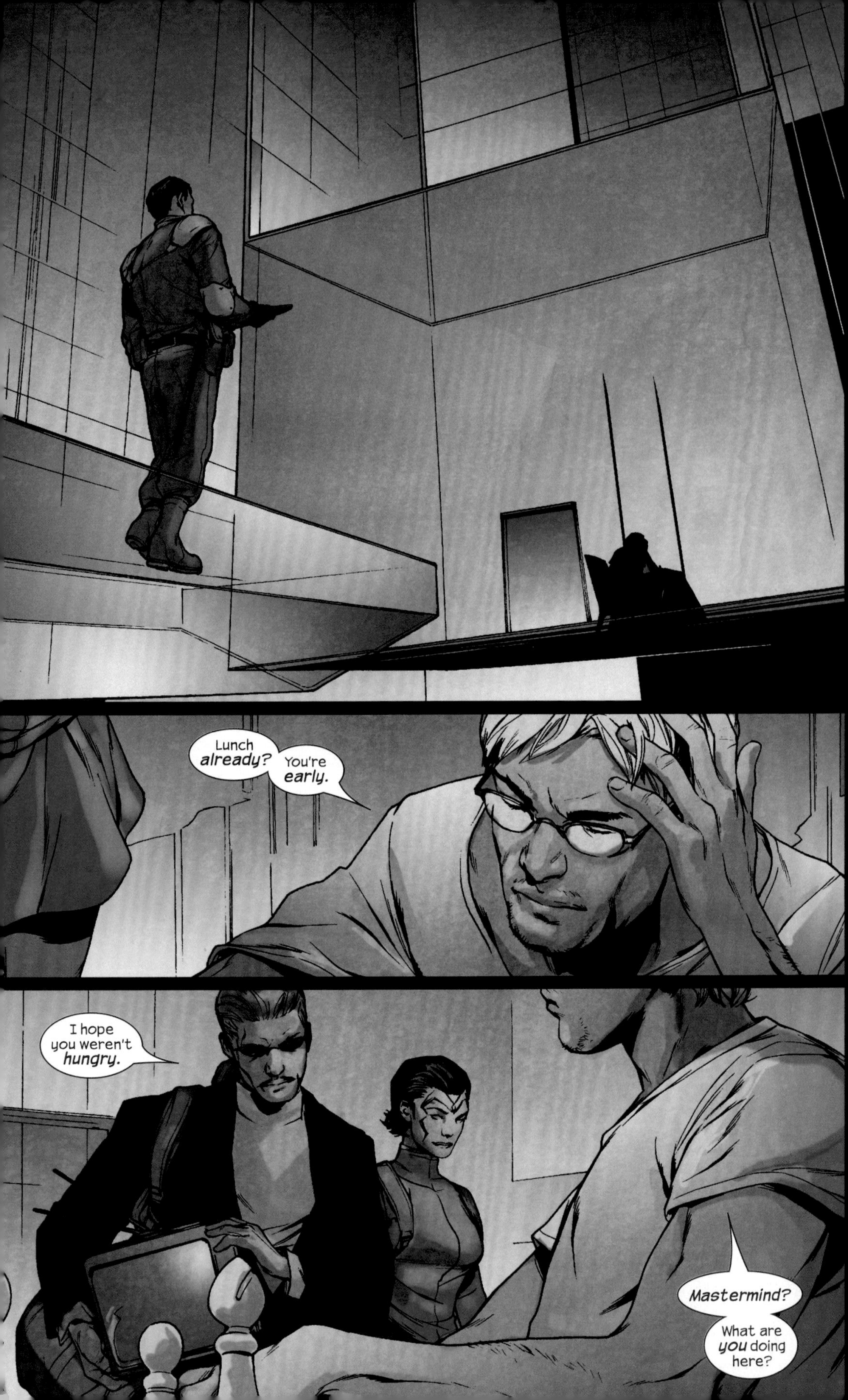
Lunch already?
You're early.
I hope you weren't hungry.
Mastermind?
What are you doing here?

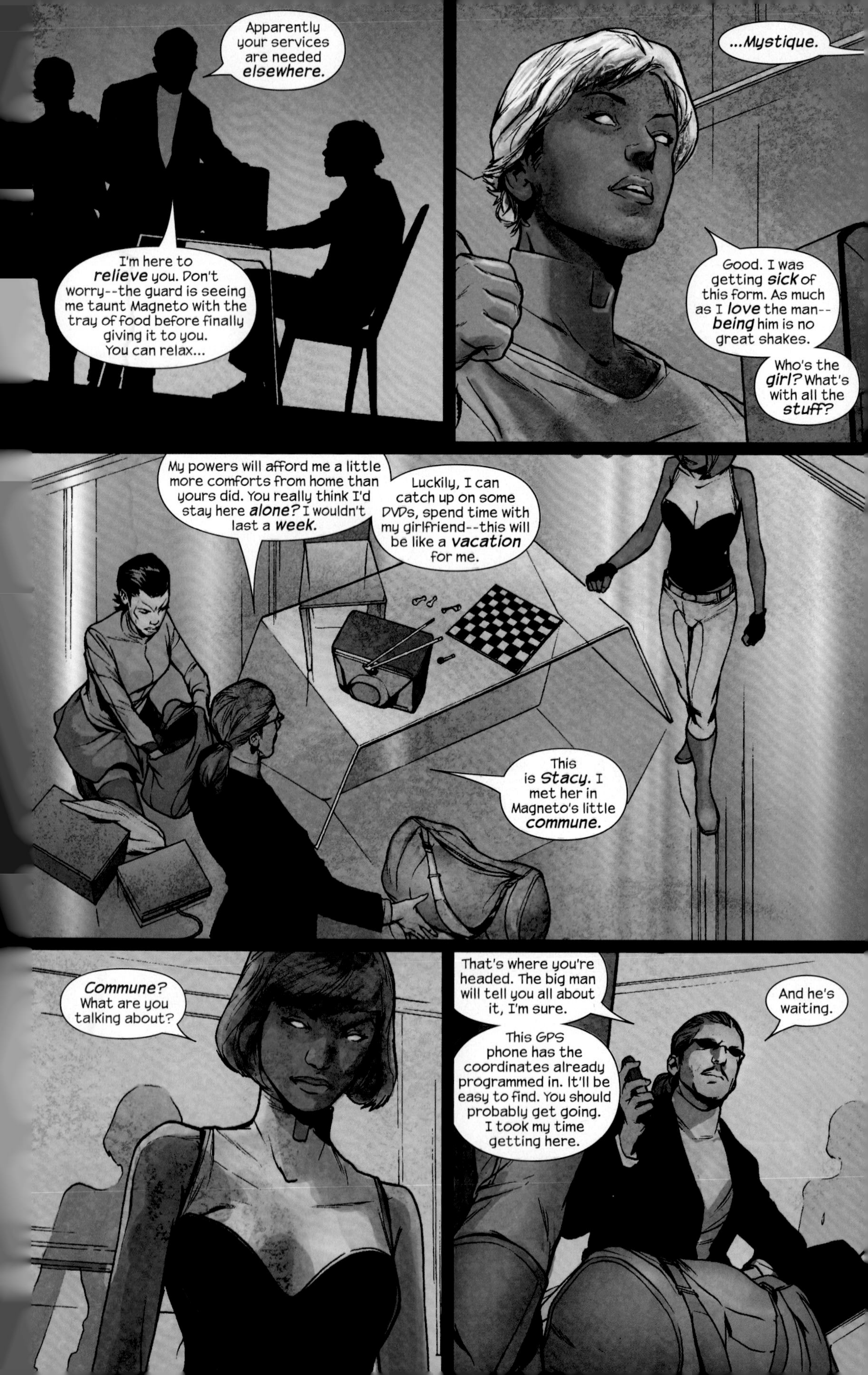
Apparently your services are needed elsewhere.
I'm here to relieve you. Don't worry--the guard is seeing me taunt Magneto with the tray of food before finally giving it to you. You can relax...
...Mystique.
Good. I was getting sick of this form. As much as I love the man-- being him is no great shakes.
Who's the girl? What's with all the stuff?
My powers will afford me a little more comforts from home than yours did. You really think I'd stay here alone? I wouldn't last a week.
Luckily, I can catch up on some DVDs, spend time with my girlfriend--this will be like a vacation for me.
This is Stacy. I met her in Magneto's little commune.
Commune? What are you talking about?
That's where you're headed. The big man will tell you all about it, I'm sure.
This GPS phone has the coordinates already programmed in. It'll be easy to find. You should probably get going. I took my time getting here.
And he's waiting.

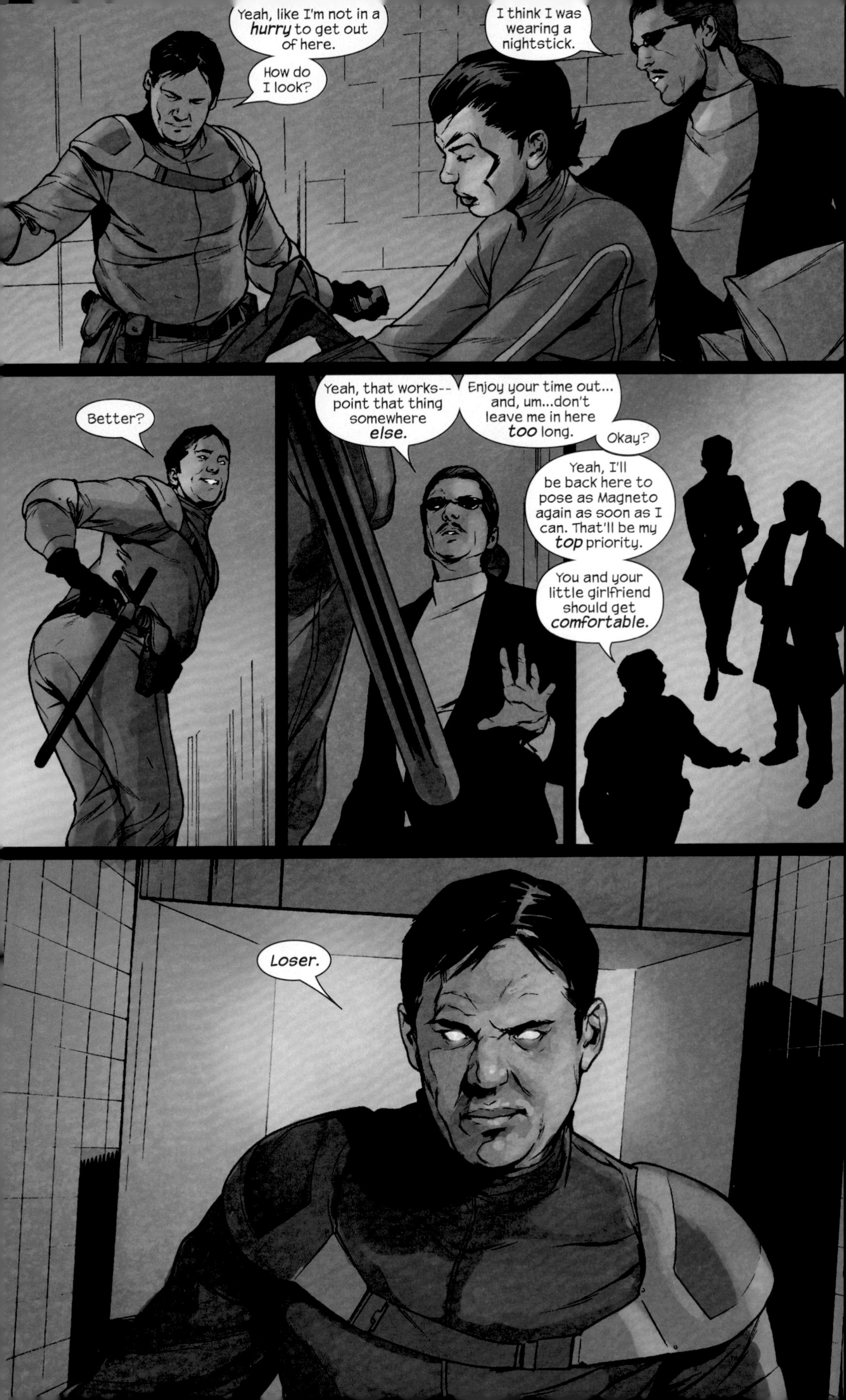
Yeah, like I'm not in a *hurry* to get out of here.
How do I look?
I think I was wearing a nightstick.
Better?
Yeah, that works-- point that thing somewhere *else*.
Enjoy your time out... and, um...don't leave me in here *too* long.
Okay?
Yeah, I'll be back here to pose as Magneto again as soon as I can. That'll be my *top* priority.
You and your little girlfriend should get *comfortable*.
Loser.

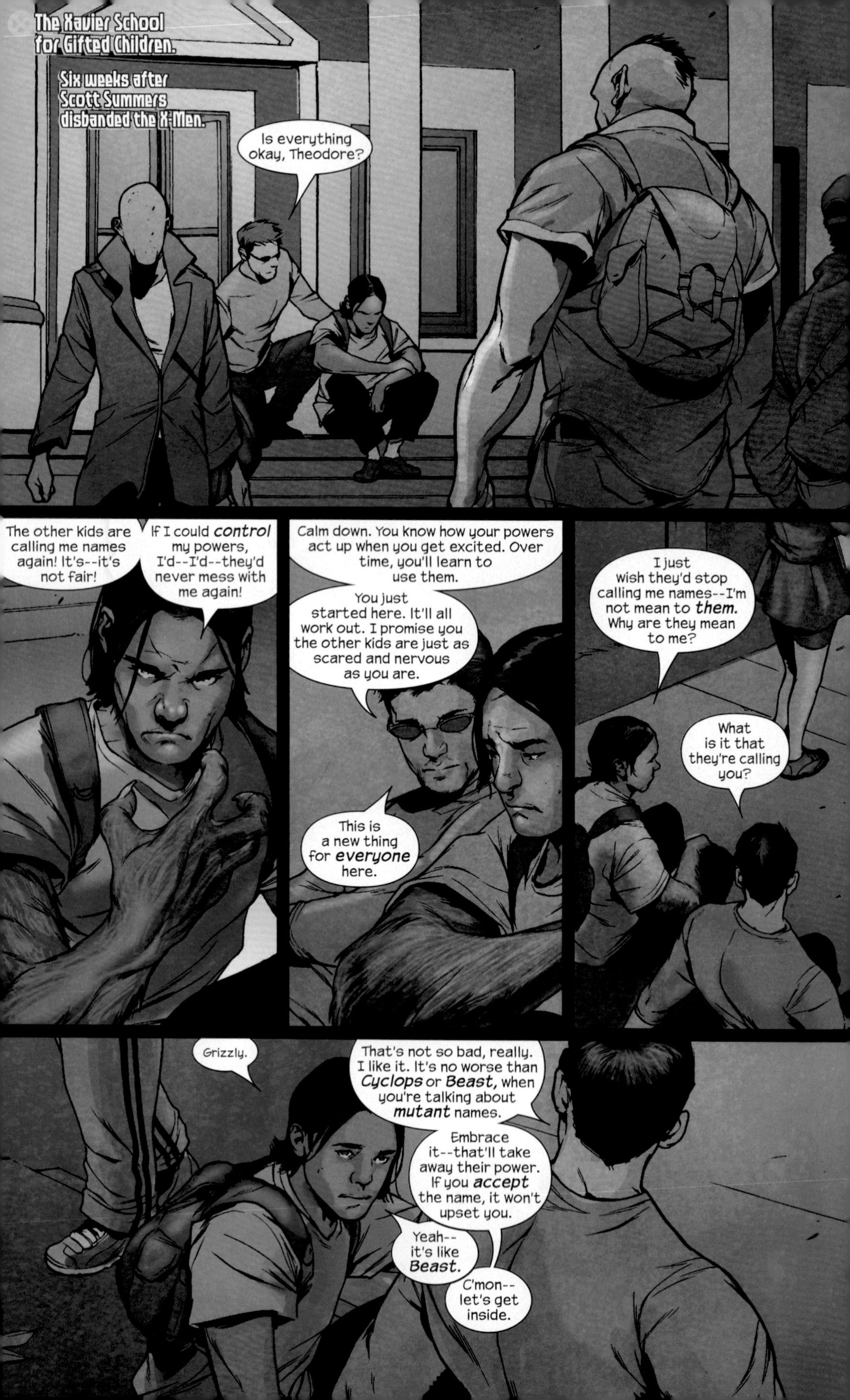
The Xavier School for Gifted Children.
Six weeks after Scott Summers disbanded the X-Men.
Is everything okay, Theodore?
The other kids are calling me names again! It's--it's not fair!
If I could *control* my powers, I'd--I'd--they'd never mess with me again!
Calm down. You know how your powers act up when you get excited. Over time, you'll learn to use them.
You just started here. It'll all work out. I promise you the other kids are just as scared and nervous as you are.
This is a new thing for *everyone* here.
I just wish they'd stop calling me names--I'm not mean to *them.* Why are they mean to me?
What is it that they're calling you?
Grizzly.
That's not so bad, really. I like it. It's no worse than *Cyclops* or *Beast,* when you're talking about *mutant* names.
Embrace it--that'll take away their power. If you *accept* the name, it won't upset you.
Yeah-- it's like *Beast.*
C'mon-- let's get inside.

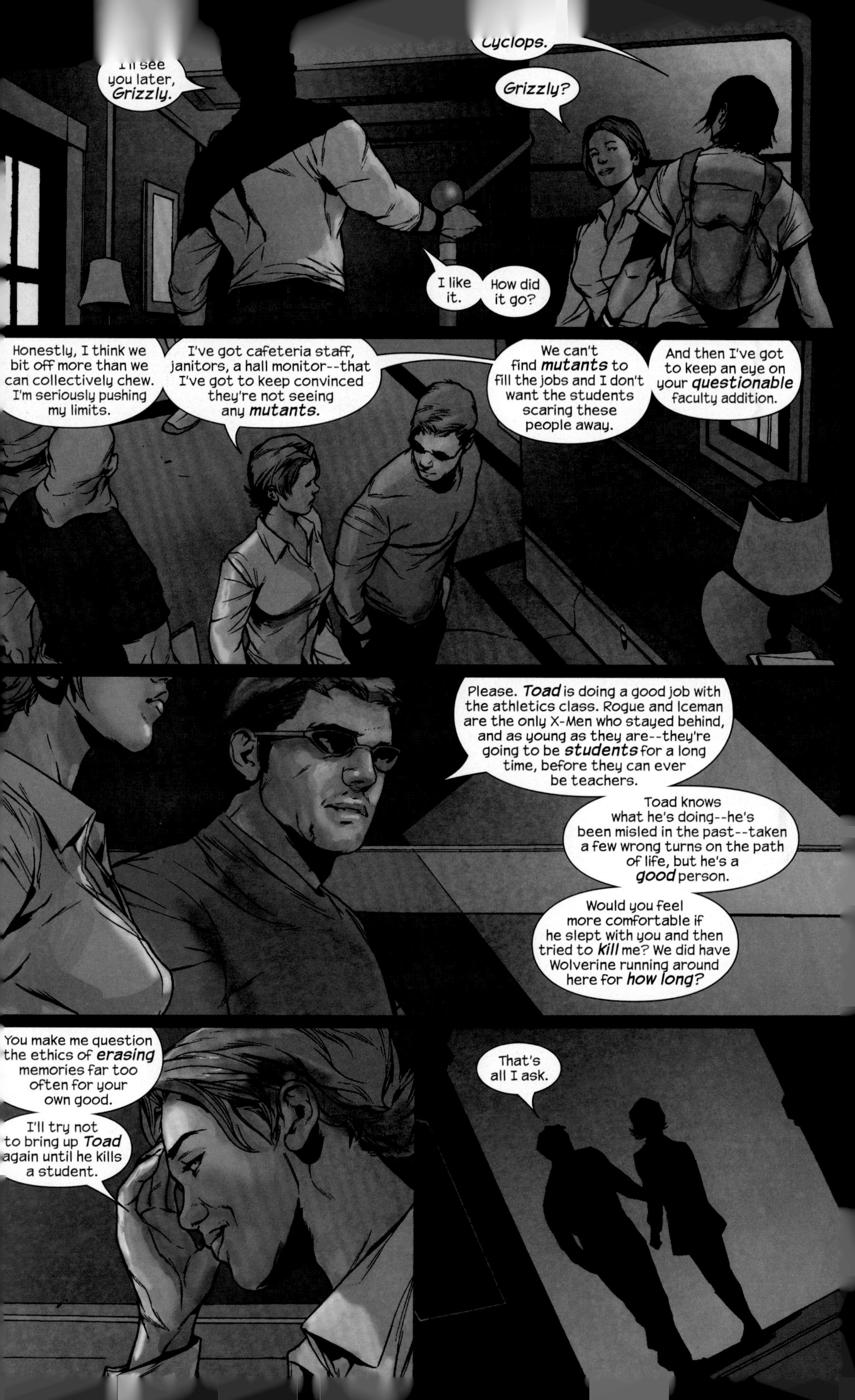

you later, Grizzly.
Cyclops.
Grizzly?
I like it.
How did it go?
Honestly, I think we bit off more than we can collectively chew. I'm seriously pushing my limits.
I've got cafeteria staff, janitors, a hall monitor--that I've got to keep convinced they're not seeing any *mutants.*
We can't find *mutants* to fill the jobs and I don't want the students scaring these people away.
And then I've got to keep an eye on your *questionable* faculty addition.
Please. *Toad* is doing a good job with the athletics class. Rogue and Iceman are the only X-Men who stayed behind, and as young as they are--they're going to be *students* for a long time, before they can ever be teachers.
Toad knows what he's doing--he's been misled in the past--taken a few wrong turns on the path of life, but he's a *good* person.
Would you feel more comfortable if he slept with you and then tried to *kill* me? We did have Wolverine running around here for *how long?*
You make me question the ethics of *erasing* memories far too often for your own good.
I'll try not to bring up *Toad* again until he kills a student.
That's all I ask.

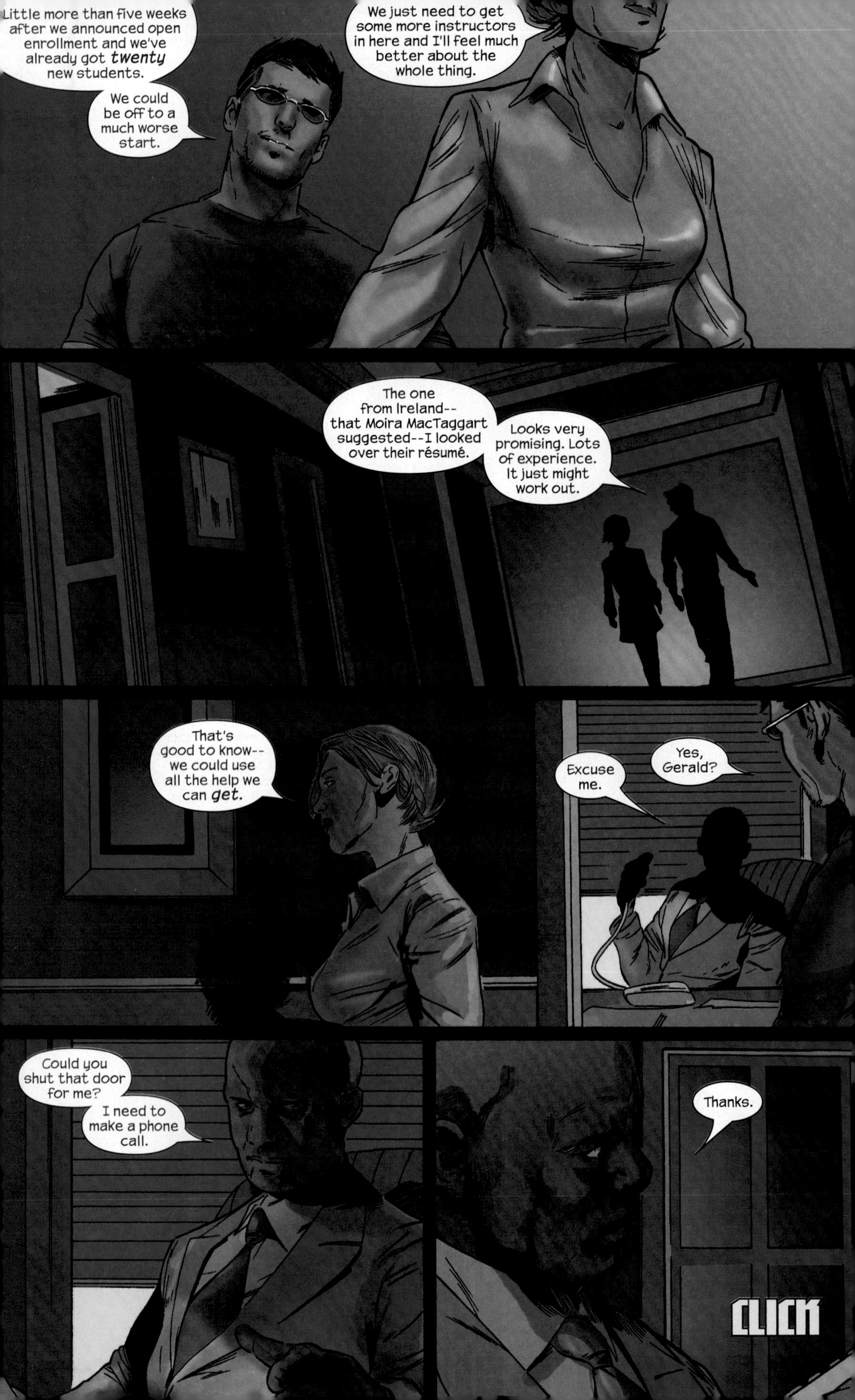
Little more than five weeks after we announced open enrollment and we've already got *twenty* new students.
We could be off to a much worse start.
We just need to get some more instructors in here and I'll feel much better about the whole thing.
The one from Ireland--that Moira MacTaggart suggested--I looked over their résumé.
Looks very promising. Lots of experience. It just might work out.
That's good to know--we could use all the help we can *get.*
Excuse me.
Yes, Gerald?
Could you shut that door for me?
I need to make a phone call.
Thanks.
CLICK

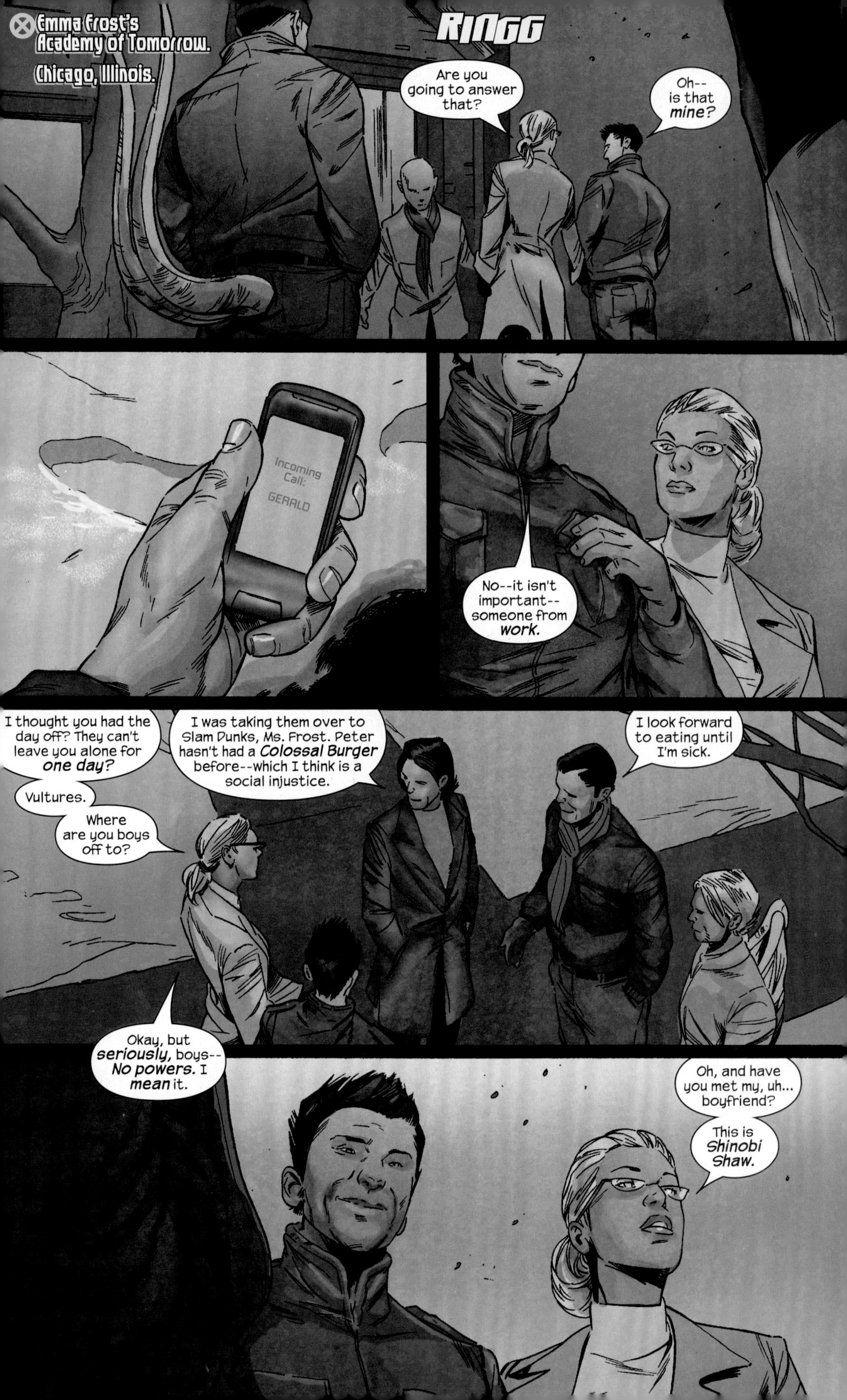
Emma Frost's Academy of Tomorrow.
Chicago, Illinois.
RINGG
Are you going to answer that?
Oh-- is that *mine*?
Incoming Call: GERALD
No--it isn't important-- someone from *work.*
I thought you had the day off? They can't leave you alone for *one day?*
Vultures.
Where are you boys off to?
I was taking them over to Slam Dunks, Ms. Frost. Peter hasn't had a *Colossal Burger* before--which I think is a social injustice.
I look forward to eating until I'm sick.
Okay, but *seriously,* boys-- *No powers.* I *mean* it.
Oh, and have you met my, uh... boyfriend?
This is *Shinobi Shaw.*

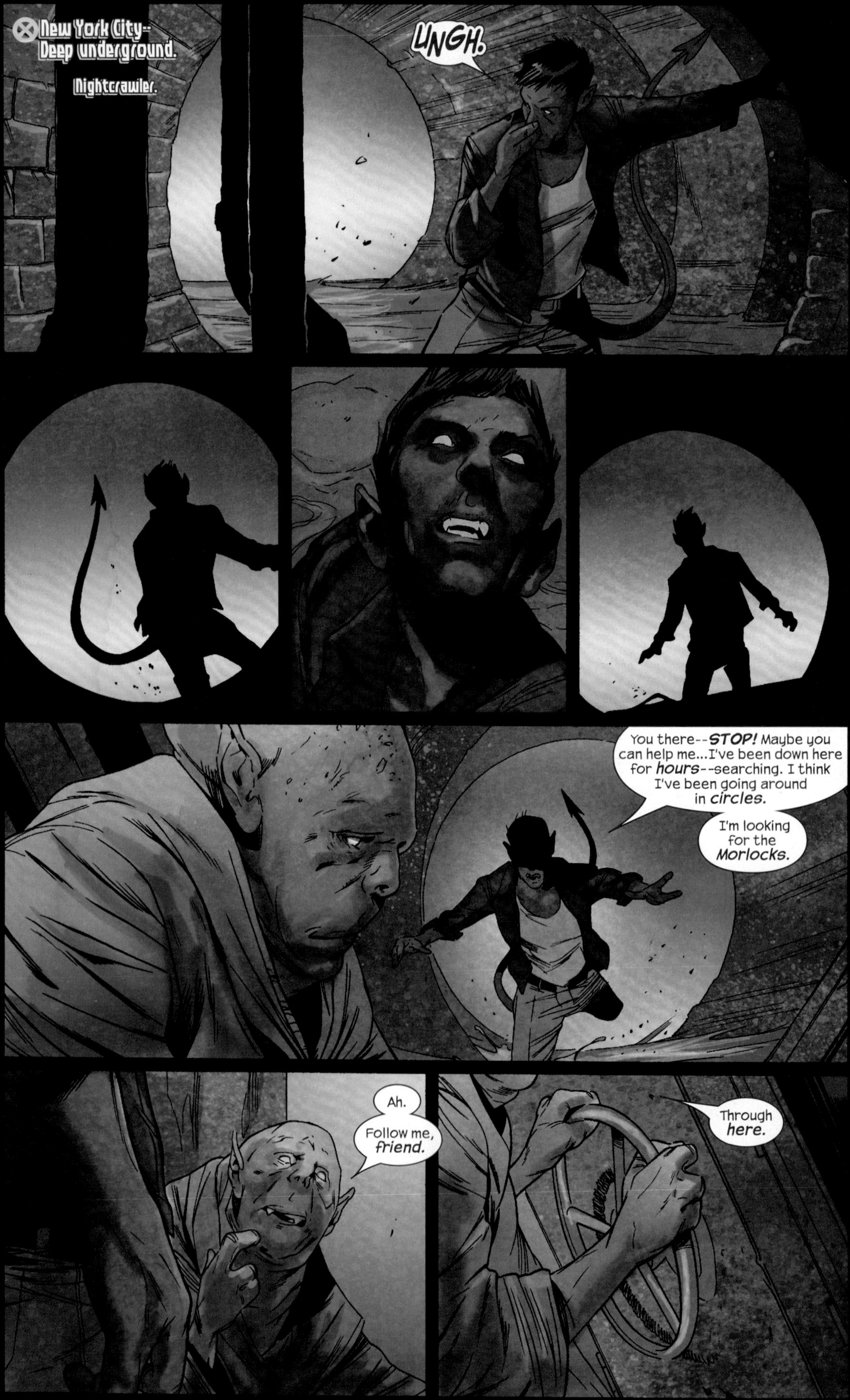
New York City--
Deep underground.
Nightcrawler.
UNGH.
You there--STOP! Maybe you can help me...I've been down here for hours--searching. I think I've been going around in circles.
I'm looking for the Morlocks.
Ah.
Follow me, friend.
Through here.

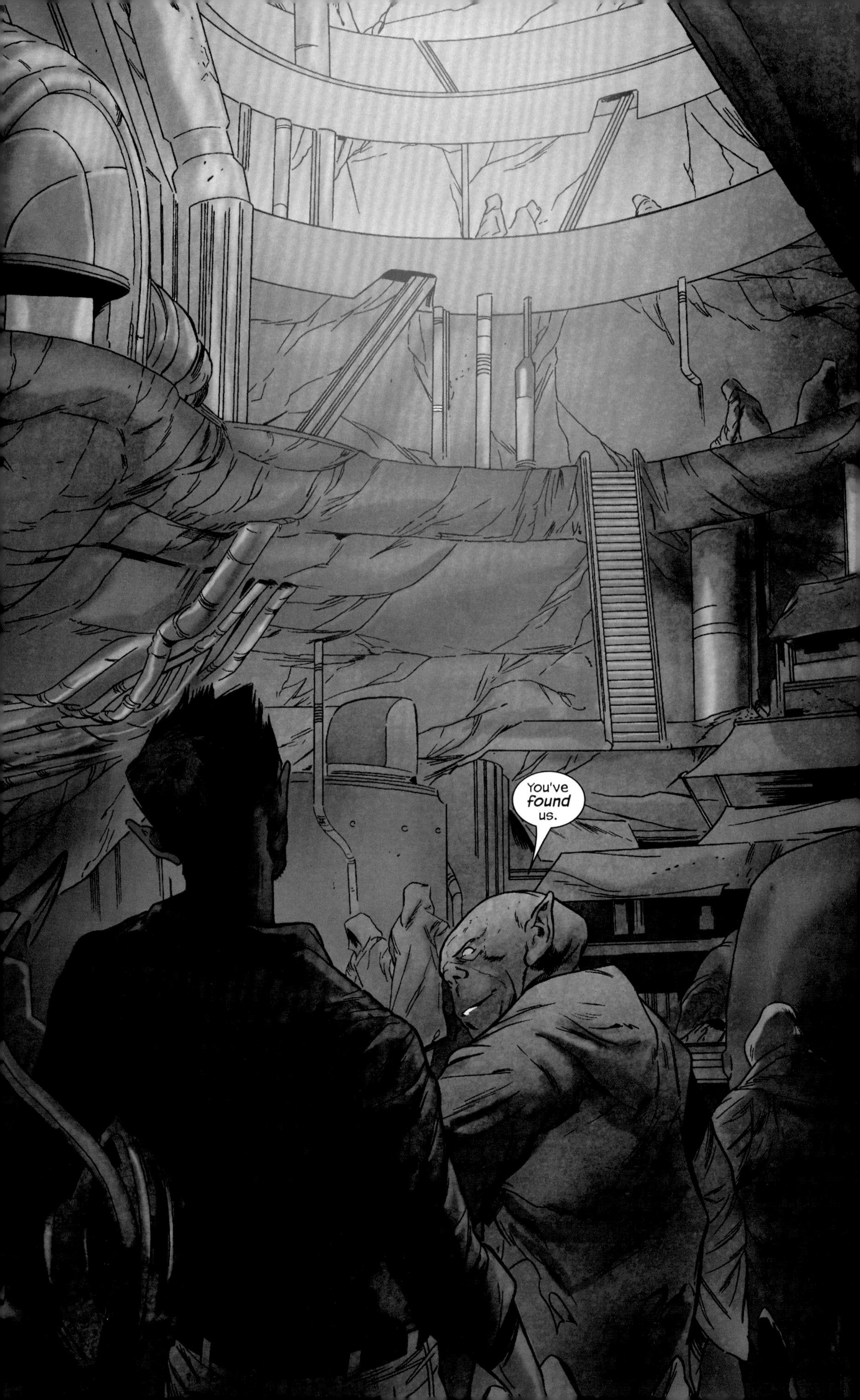
You've found us.

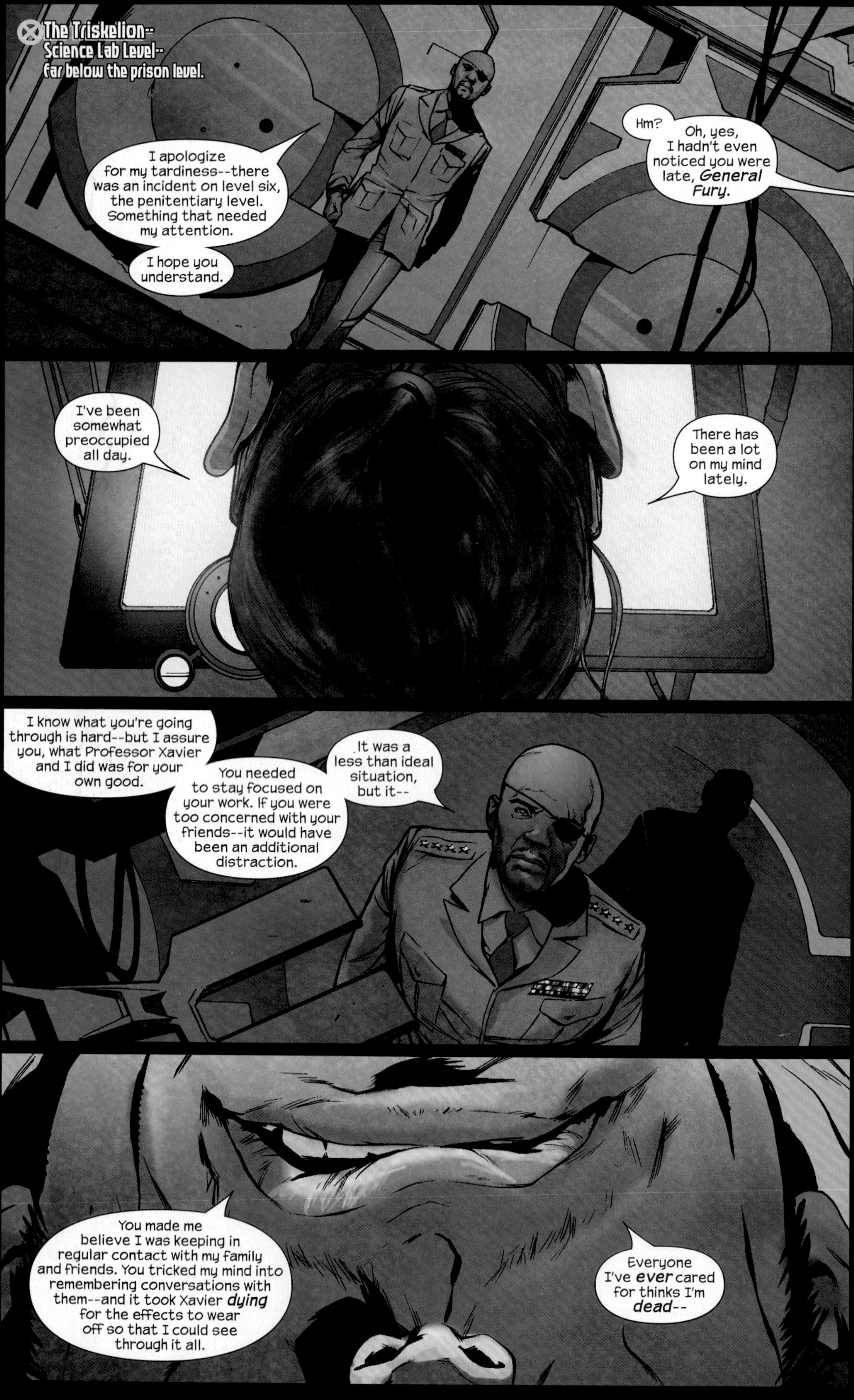
The Triskelion--
Science Lab Level--
Far below the prison level.
I apologize for my tardiness--there was an incident on level six, the penitentiary level. Something that needed my attention.
I hope you understand.
Hm?
Oh, yes, I hadn't even noticed you were late, General Fury.
I've been somewhat preoccupied all day.
There has been a lot on my mind lately.
I know what you're going through is hard--but I assure you, what Professor Xavier and I did was for your own good.
You needed to stay focused on your work. If you were too concerned with your friends--it would have been an additional distraction.
It was a less than ideal situation, but it--
You made me believe I was keeping in regular contact with my family and friends. You tricked my mind into remembering conversations with them--and it took Xavier dying for the effects to wear off so that I could see through it all.
Everyone I've ever cared for thinks I'm dead--

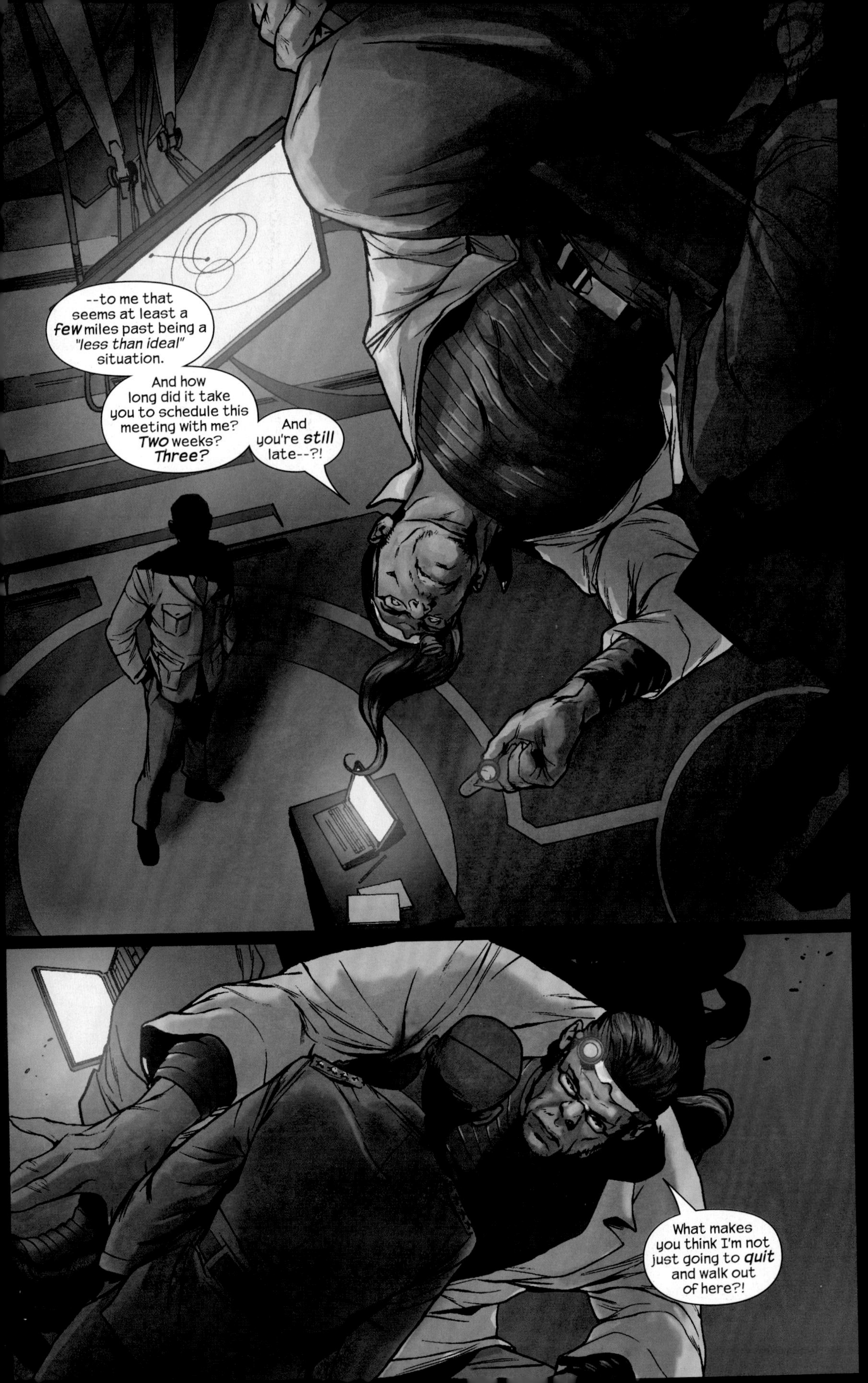
--to me that seems at least a few miles past being a "less than ideal" situation.
And how long did it take you to schedule this meeting with me? TWO weeks? Three?
And you're still late--?!
What makes you think I'm not just going to quit and walk out of here?!

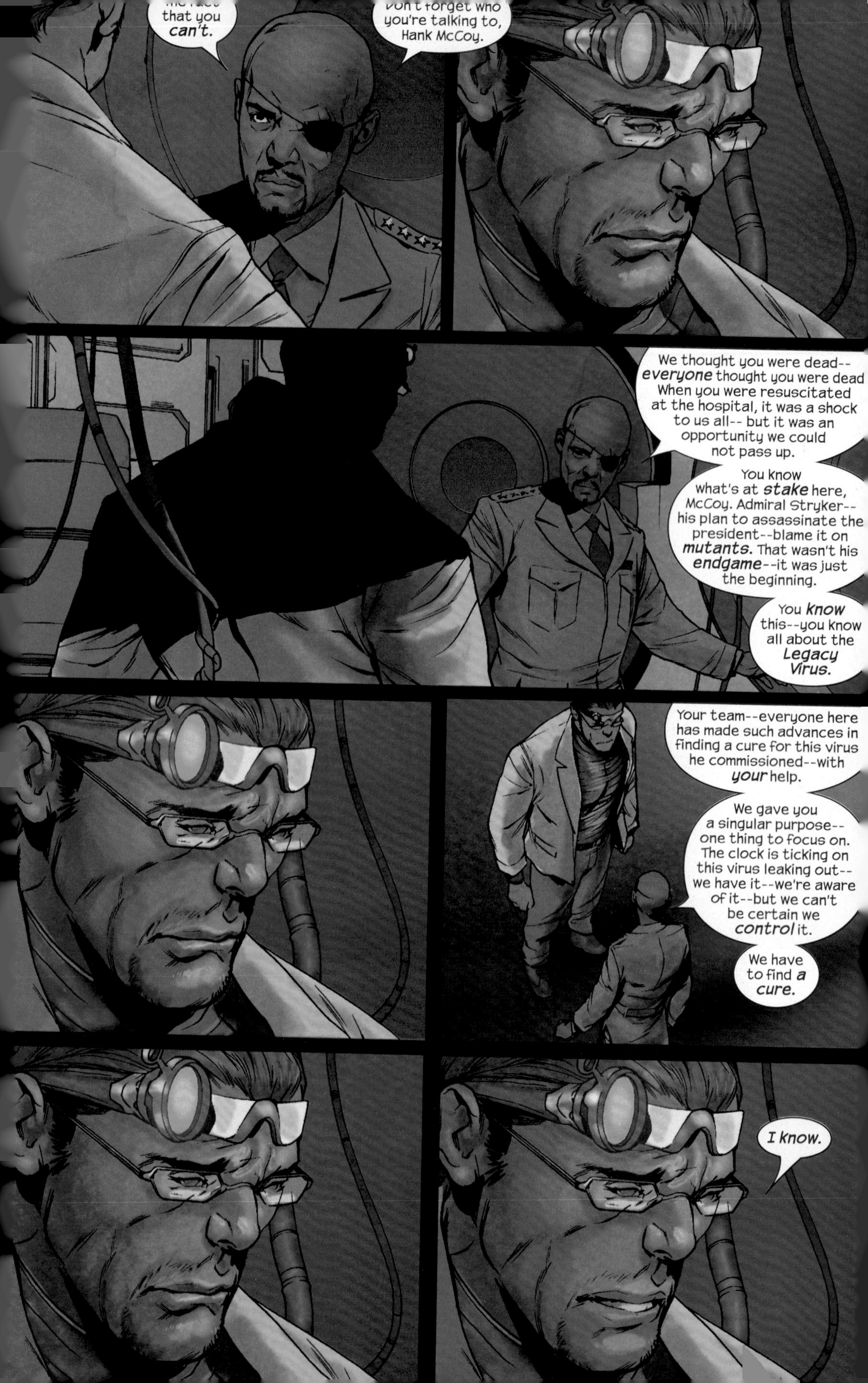

that you can't.
Don't forget who you're talking to, Hank McCoy.
We thought you were dead-- everyone thought you were dead When you were resuscitated at the hospital, it was a shock to us all-- but it was an opportunity we could not pass up.
You know what's at stake here, McCoy. Admiral Stryker--his plan to assassinate the president--blame it on mutants. That wasn't his endgame--it was just the beginning.
You know this--you know all about the Legacy Virus.
Your team--everyone here has made such advances in finding a cure for this virus he commissioned--with your help.
We gave you a singular purpose--one thing to focus on. The clock is ticking on this virus leaking out--we have it--we're aware of it--but we can't be certain we control it.
We have to find a cure.
I know.

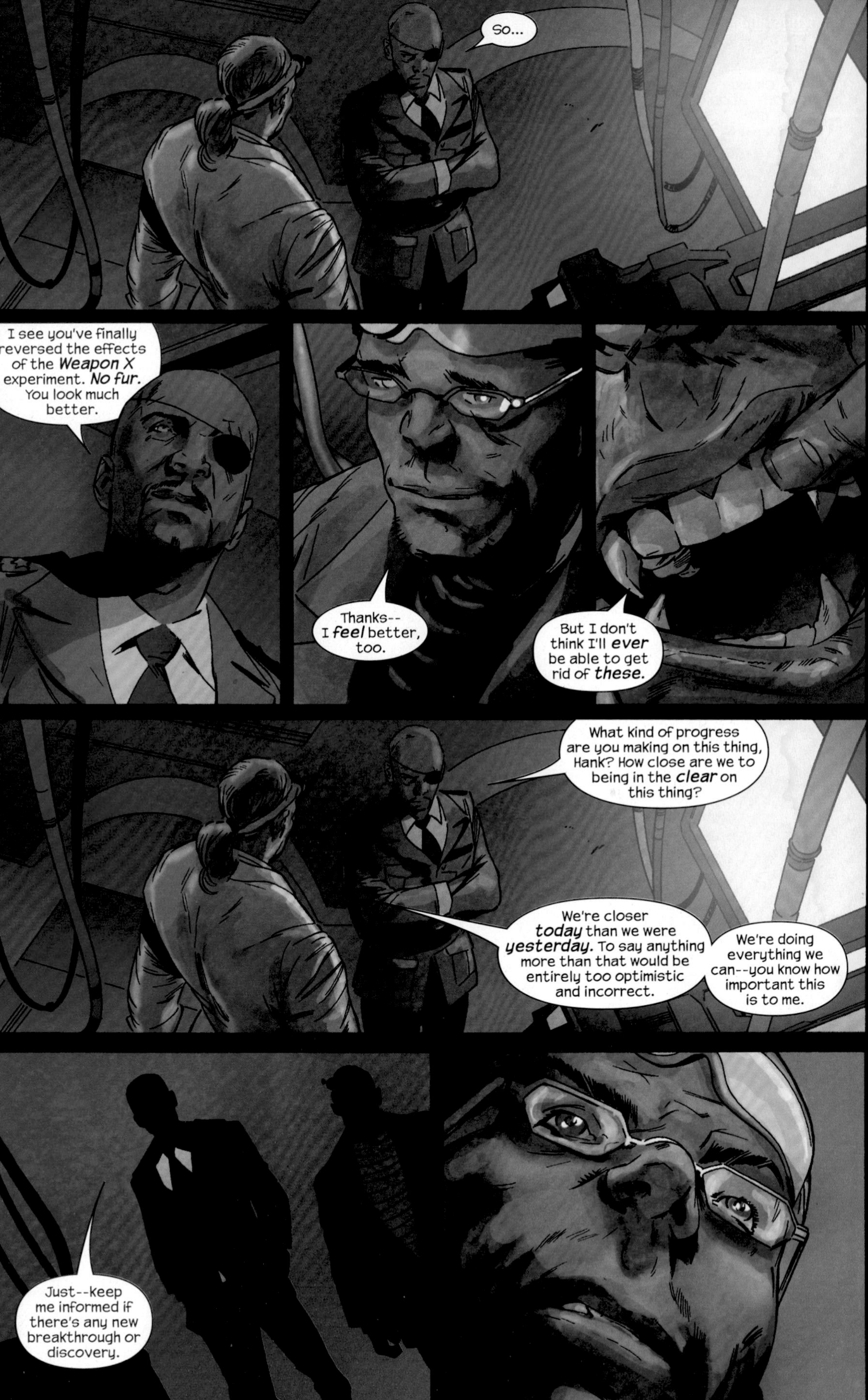
So...
I see you've finally reversed the effects of the *Weapon X* experiment. *No fur.* You look much better.
Thanks-- I *feel* better, too.
But I don't think I'll *ever* be able to get rid of *these.*
What kind of progress are you making on this thing, Hank? How close are we to being in the *clear* on this thing?
We're closer *today* than we were *yesterday.* To say anything more than that would be entirely too optimistic and incorrect.
We're doing everything we can--you know how important this is to me.
Just--keep me informed if there's any new breakthrough or discovery.

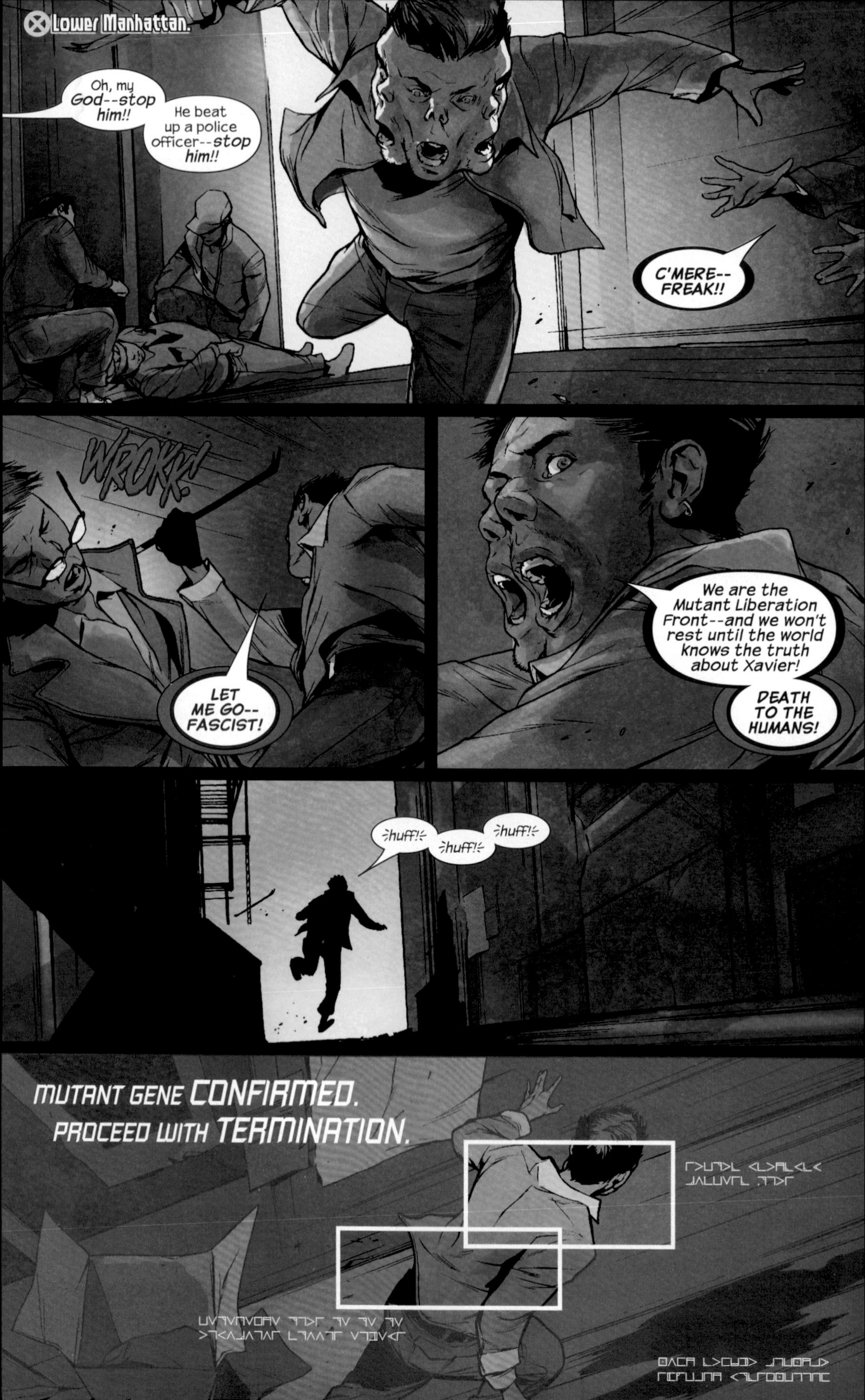
Lower Manhattan.
Oh, my God--stop him!!
He beat up a police officer--stop him!!
C'MERE--FREAK!!
WROKK!
LET ME GO--FASCIST!
We are the Mutant Liberation Front--and we won't rest until the world knows the truth about Xavier!
DEATH TO THE HUMANS!
huff!
huff!
huff!
MUTANT GENE CONFIRMED.
PROCEED WITH TERMINATION.

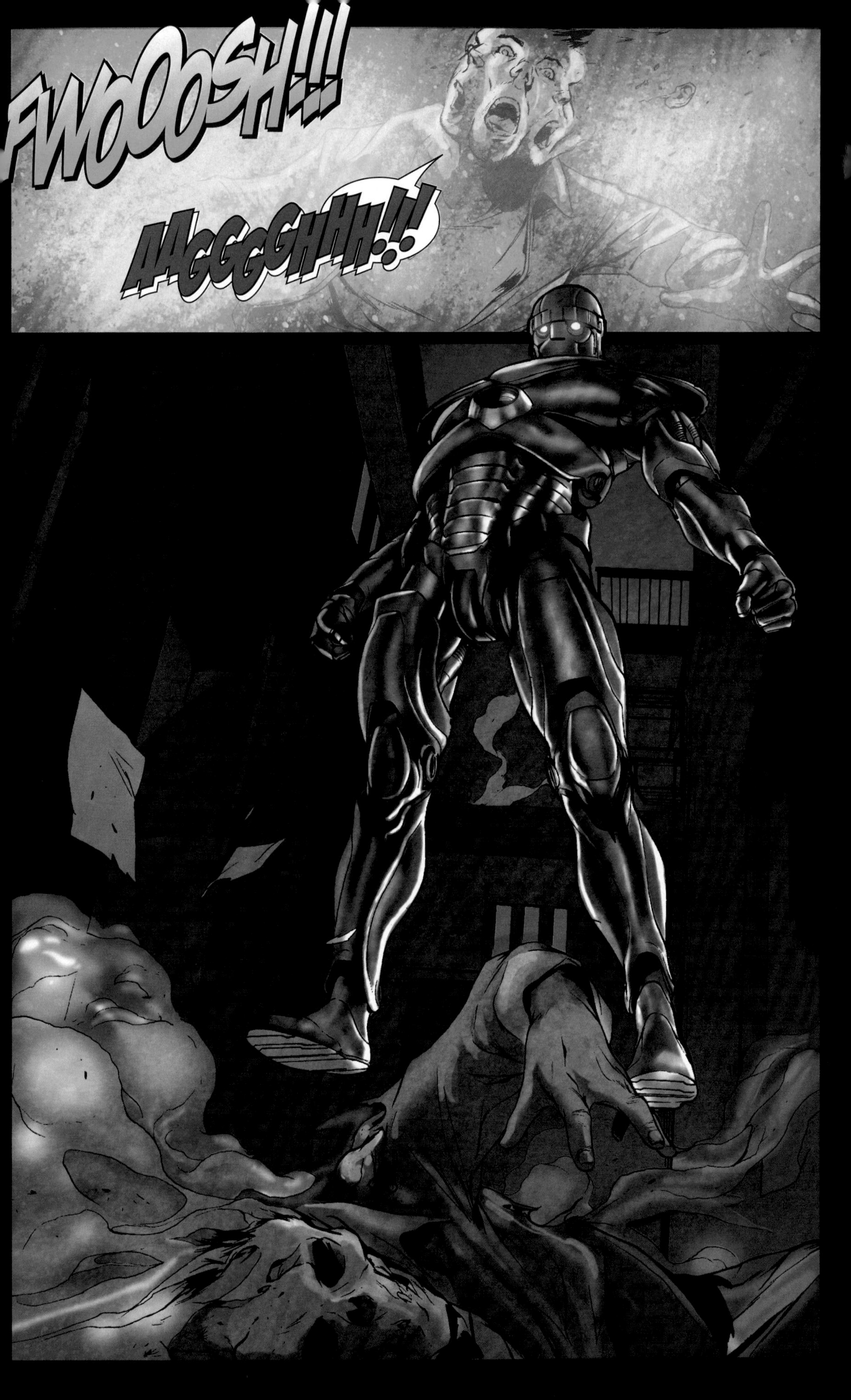
FWOOOSH!!!
AAGGGGHHH!!!

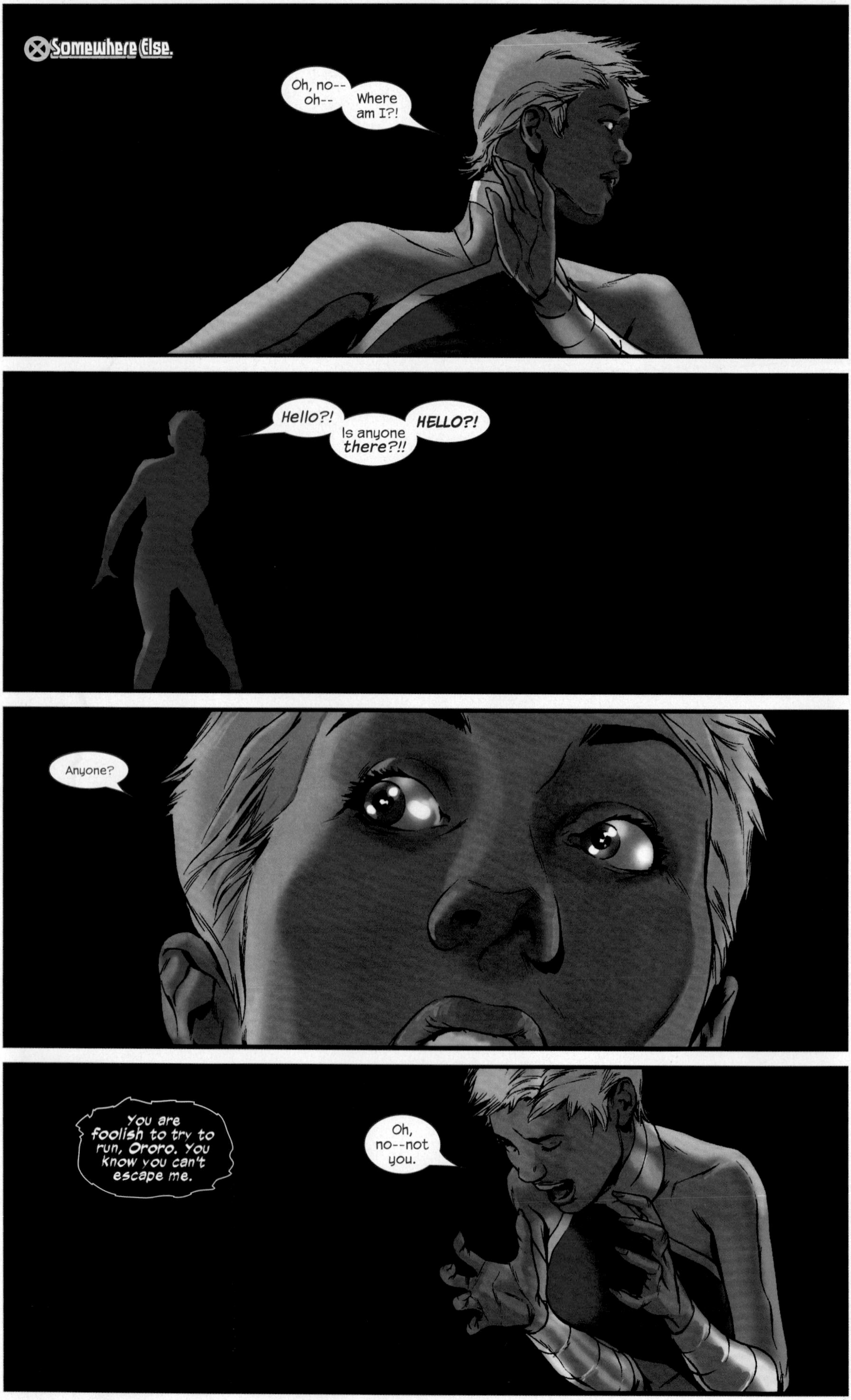
Somewhere Else.
Oh, no-- oh--
Where am I?!
Hello?!
Is anyone there?!!
HELLO?!
Anyone?
You are foolish to try to run, Ororo. You know you can't escape me.
Oh, no--not you.

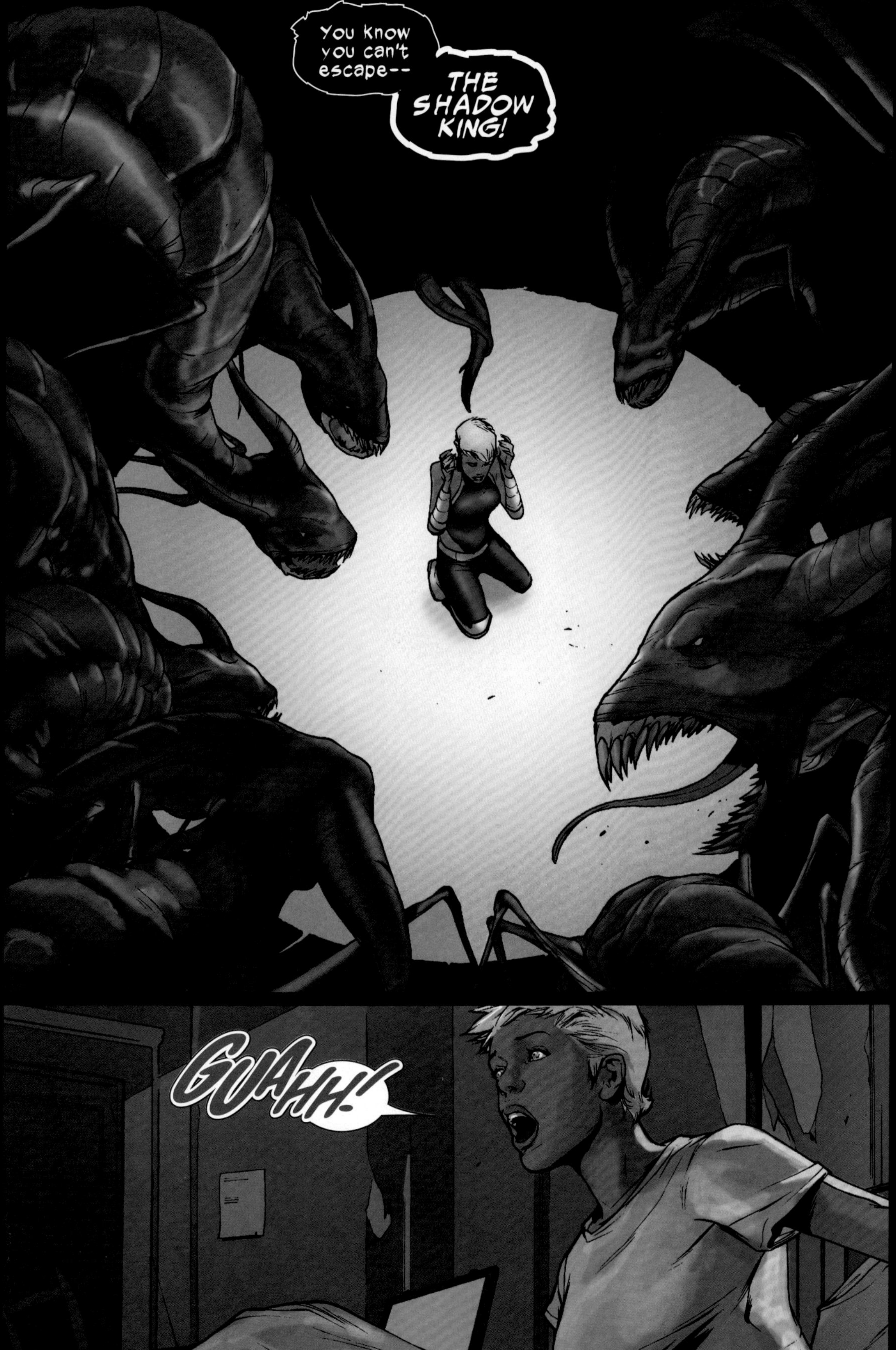
You know you can't escape--
THE SHADOW KING!
GUAHH!

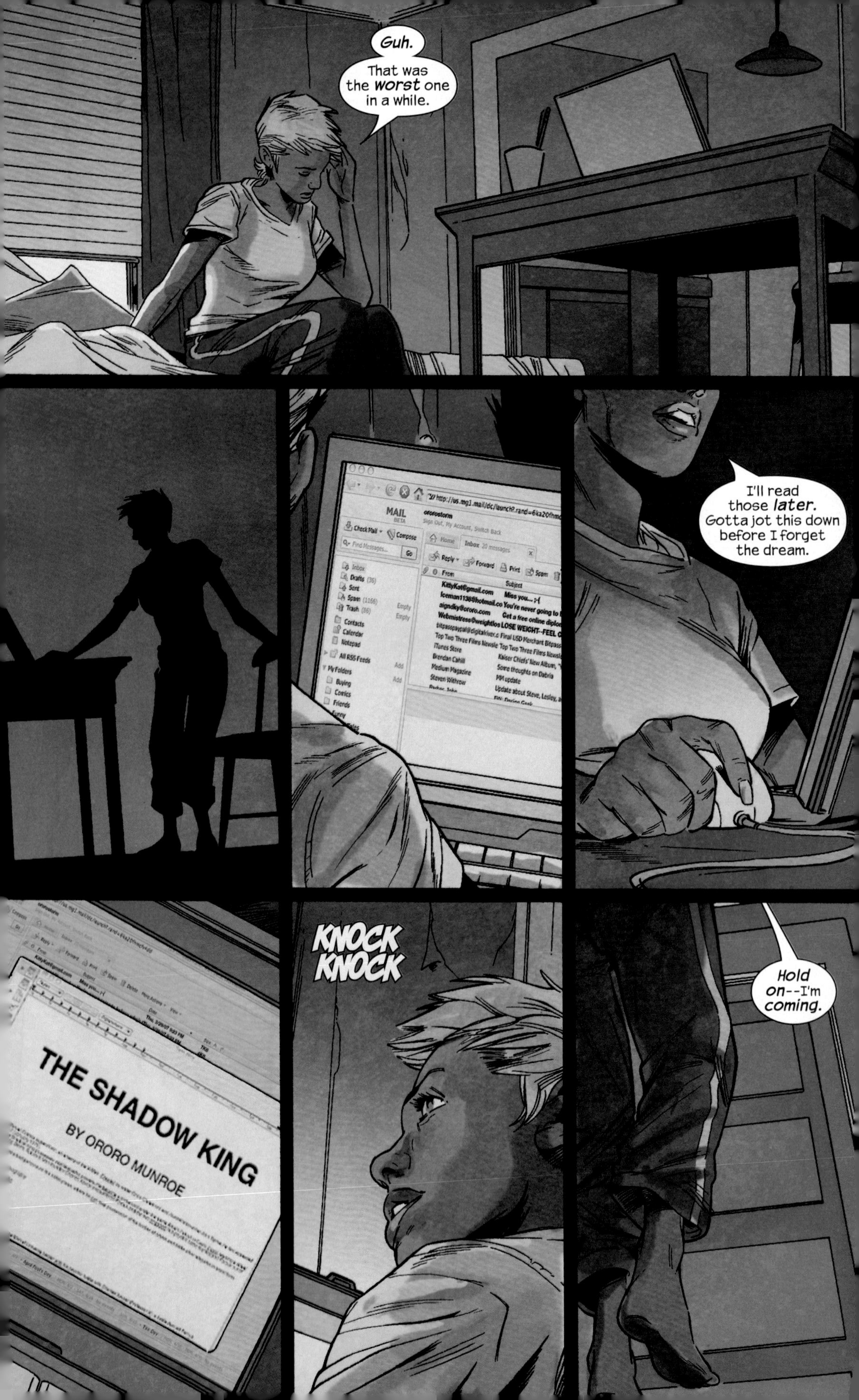

Guh.
That was the worst one in a while.
I'll read those later. Gotta jot this down before I forget the dream.
THE SHADOW KING
BY ORORO MUNROE
KNOCK KNOCK
Hold on--I'm coming.

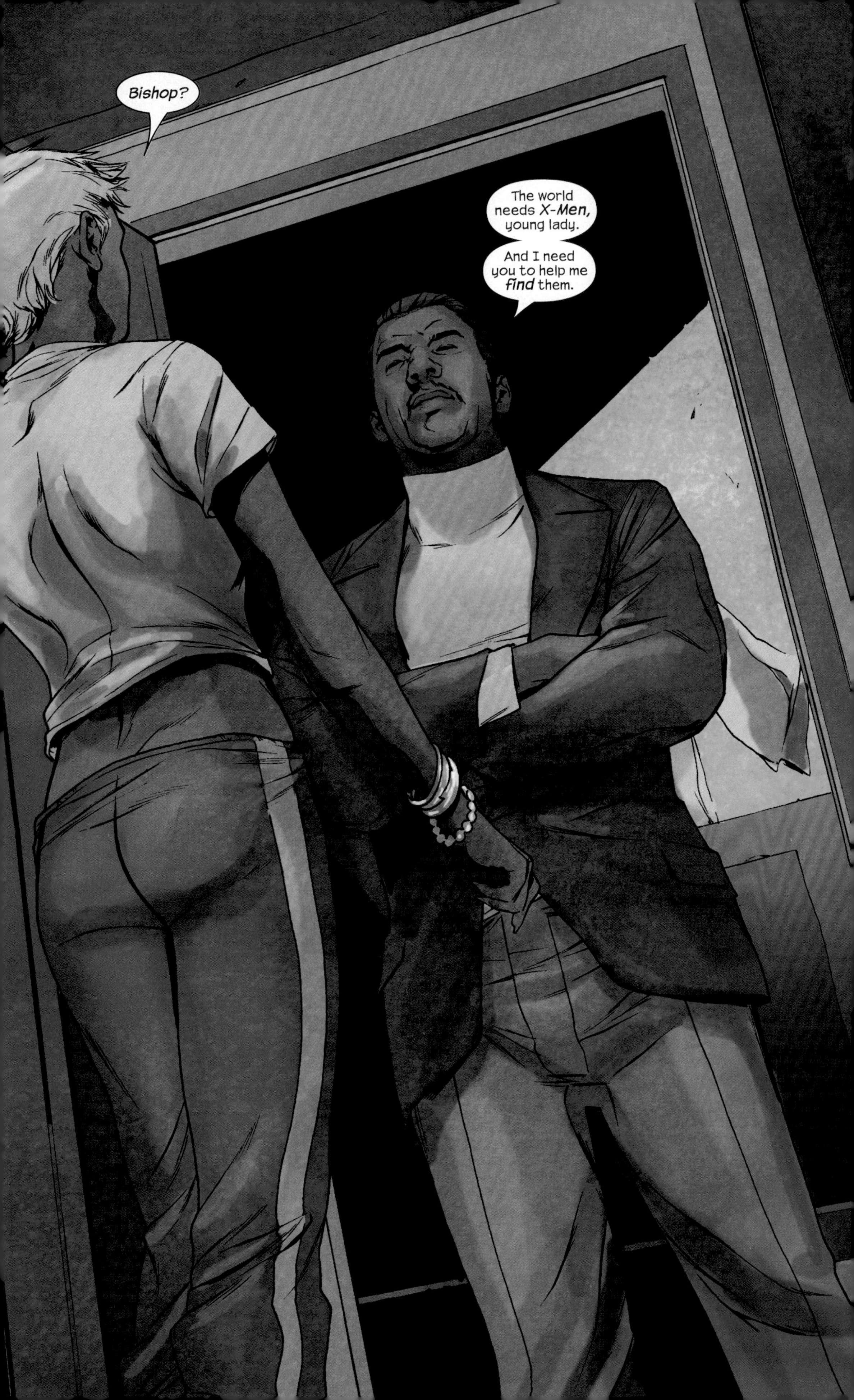
Bishop?
The world needs X-Men, young lady.
And I need you to help me find them.

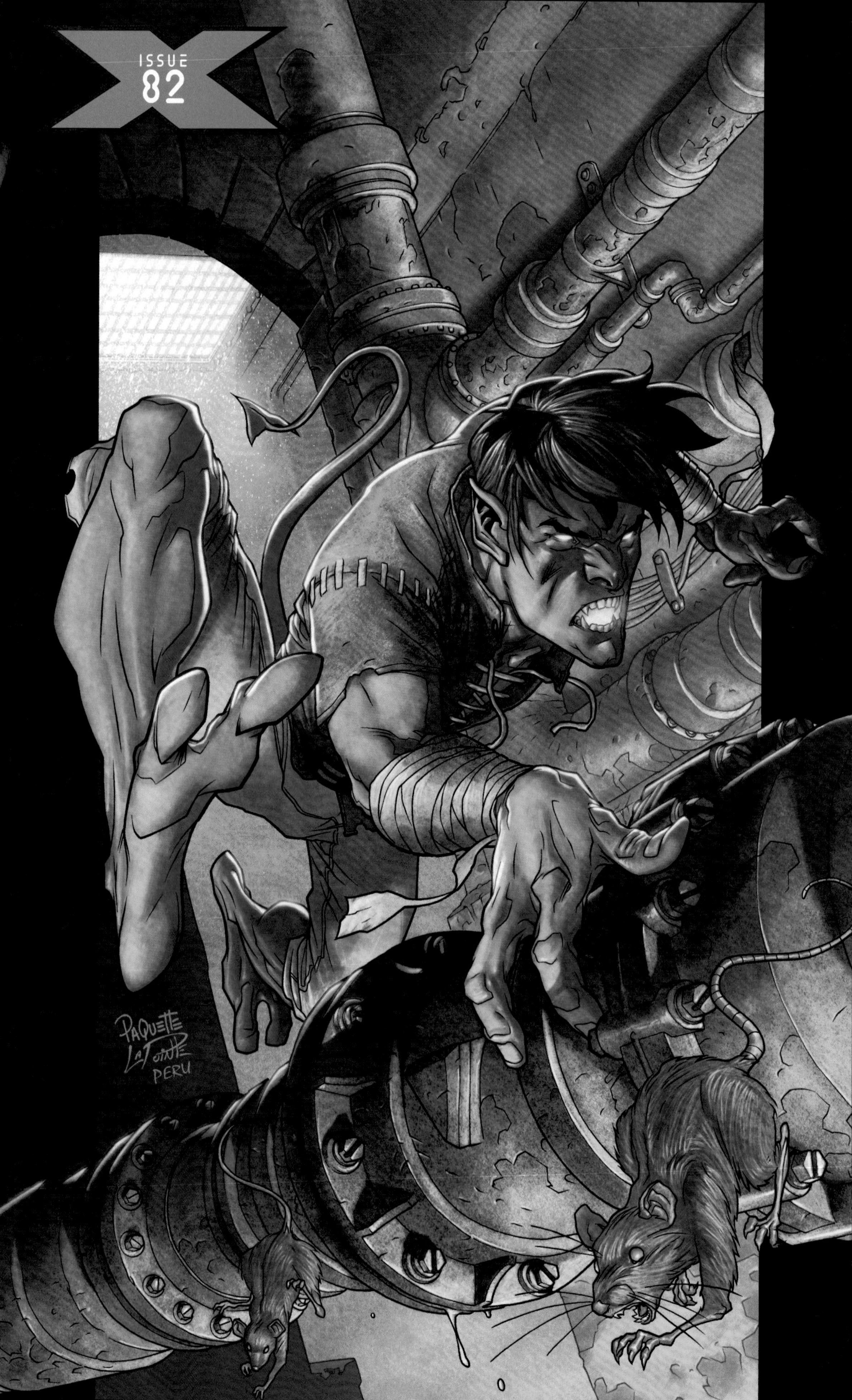
ISSUE
82
PAQUETTE
LAPOINTE
PERU

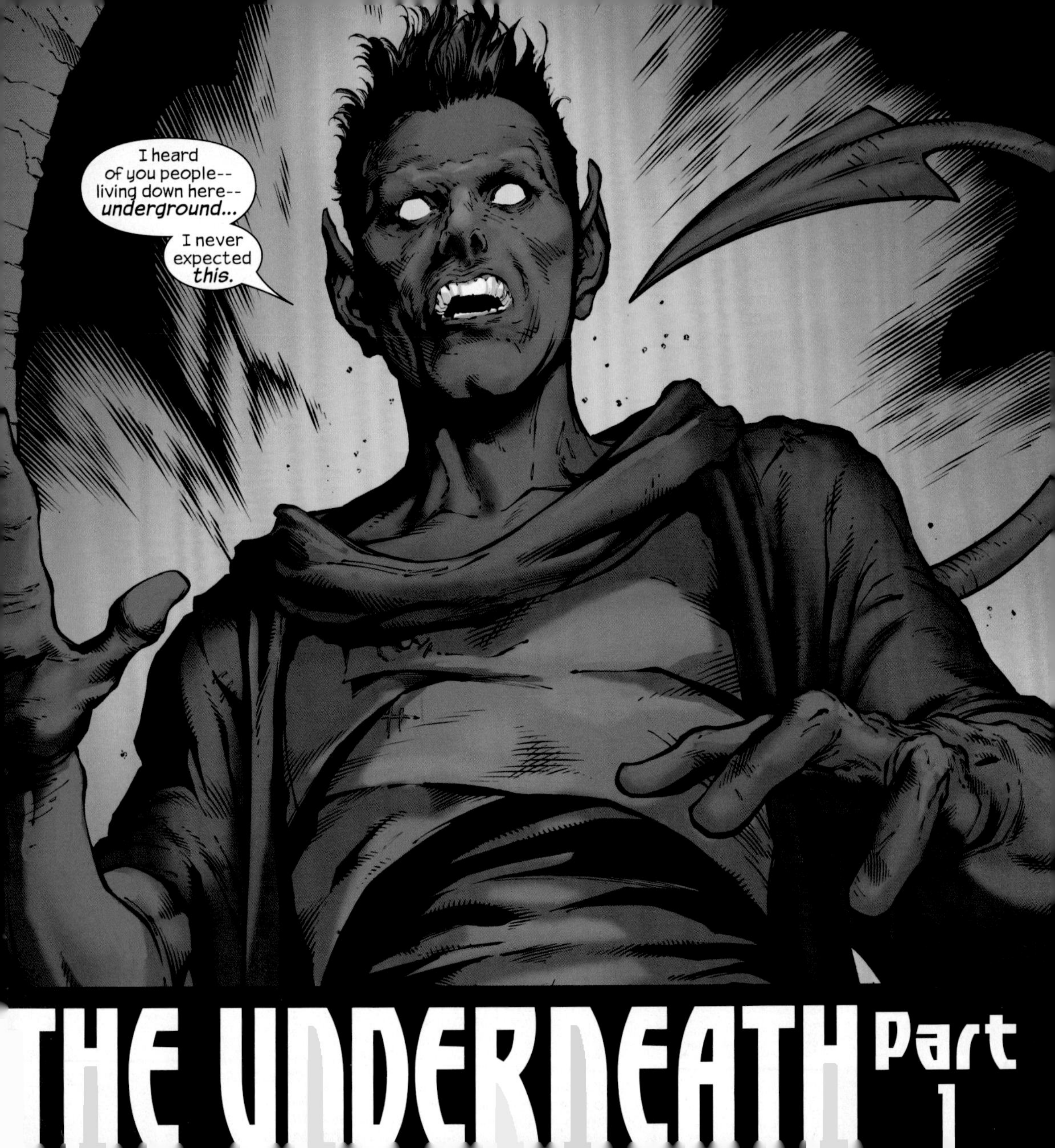
I heard of you people-- living down here-- *underground...*
I never expected *this.*
THE UNDERNEATH Part 1

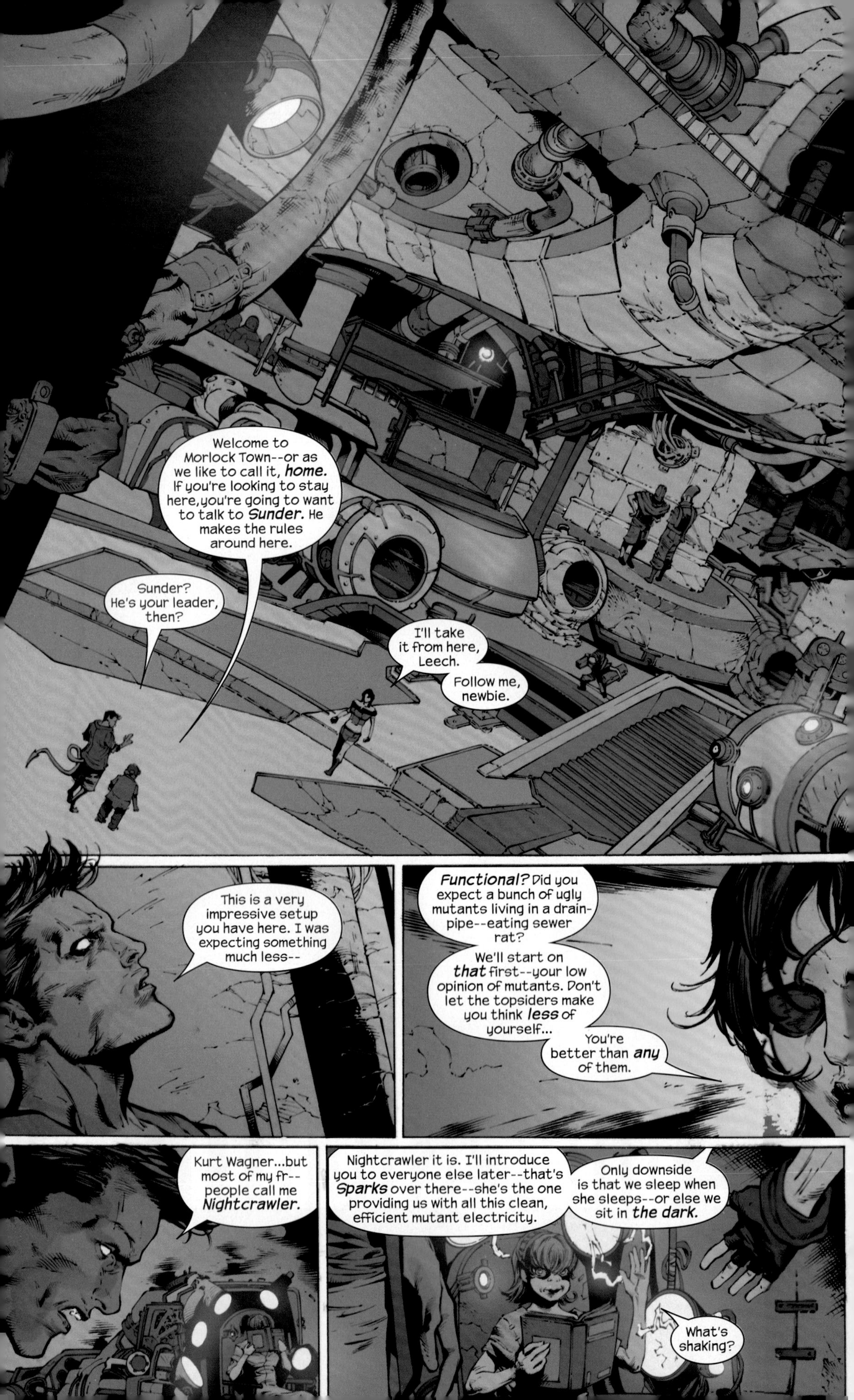
Welcome to Morlock Town--or as we like to call it, home. If you're looking to stay here, you're going to want to talk to Sunder. He makes the rules around here.
Sunder? He's your leader, then?
I'll take it from here, Leech.
Follow me, newbie.
This is a very impressive setup you have here. I was expecting something much less--
Functional? Did you expect a bunch of ugly mutants living in a drain-pipe--eating sewer rat?
We'll start on that first--your low opinion of mutants. Don't let the topsiders make you think less of yourself...
You're better than any of them.
Kurt Wagner...but most of my fr-- people call me Nightcrawler.
Nightcrawler it is. I'll introduce you to everyone else later--that's Sparks over there--she's the one providing us with all this clean, efficient mutant electricity.
Only downside is that we sleep when she sleeps--or else we sit in the dark.
What's shaking?

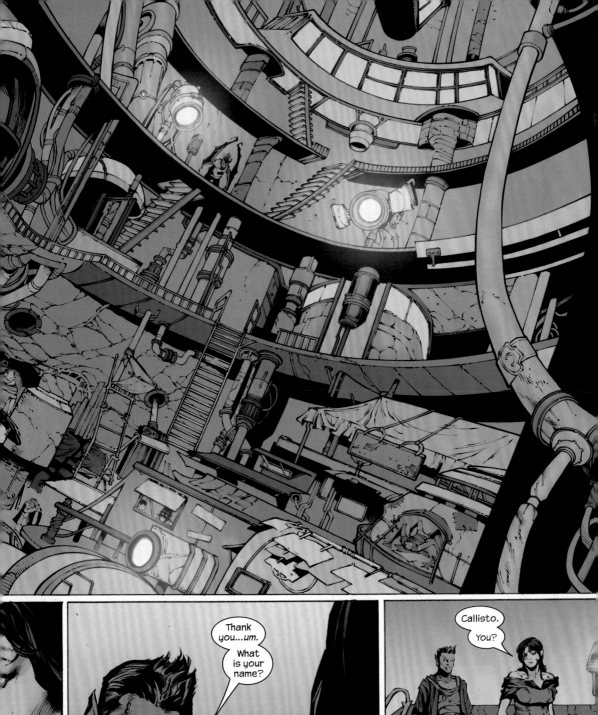

Thank you...*um.*
What is your name?

Callisto. You?

But we get along pretty well down here. We're mostly vegetarians-- we've got hydroponics gardens, we can grow our own food down here. We make our own clothes--we're pretty much on our own.

Everyone is welcome here until they prove otherwise. Think you'd like to stay here with us?

Yes-- very much so.

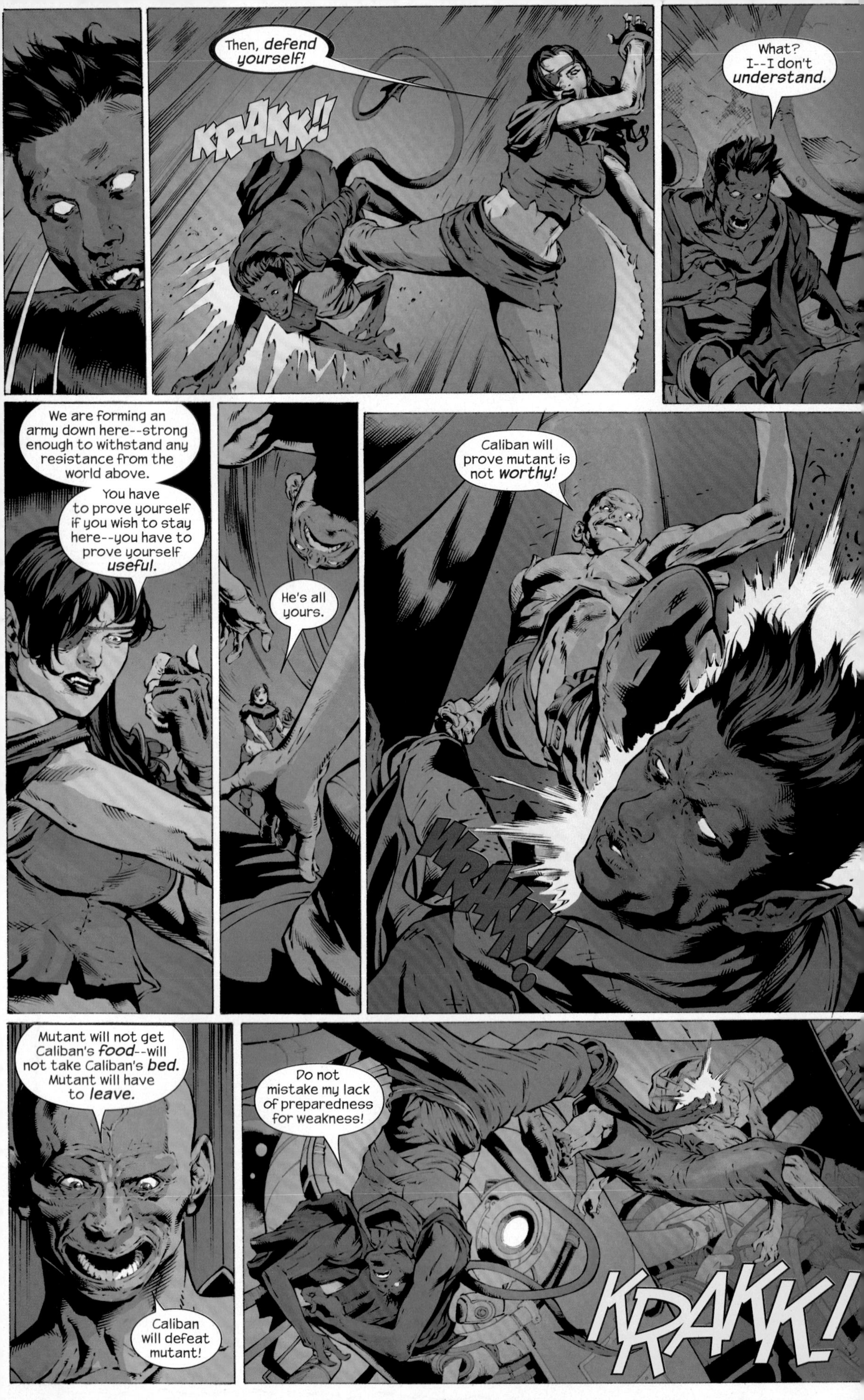

Then, *defend yourself!*
KRAKK!!
What? I--I don't **understand.**
We are forming an army down here--strong enough to withstand any resistance from the world above.
You have to prove yourself if you wish to stay here--you have to prove yourself ***useful.***
He's all yours.
Caliban will prove mutant is not *worthy!*
WRAKK!!
Mutant will not get Caliban's *food*--will not take Caliban's *bed.* Mutant will have to *leave.*
Caliban will defeat mutant!
Do not mistake my lack of preparedness for weakness!
KRAKK!

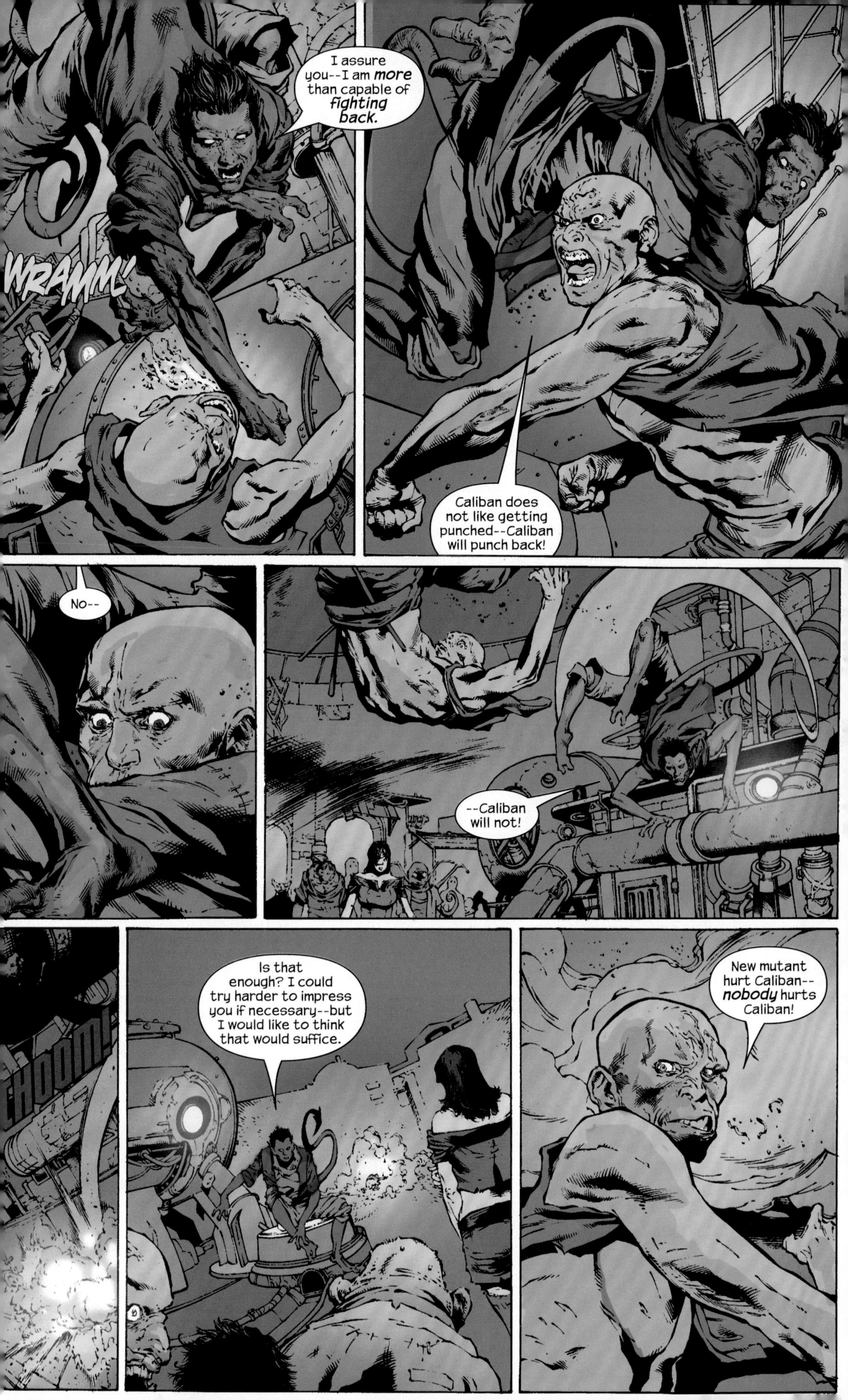
I assure you--I am more than capable of fighting back.
WRAMM!
Caliban does not like getting punched--Caliban will punch back!
No--
--Caliban will not!
CHOOM!
Is that enough? I could try harder to impress you if necessary--but I would like to think that would suffice.
New mutant hurt Caliban--nobody hurts Caliban!

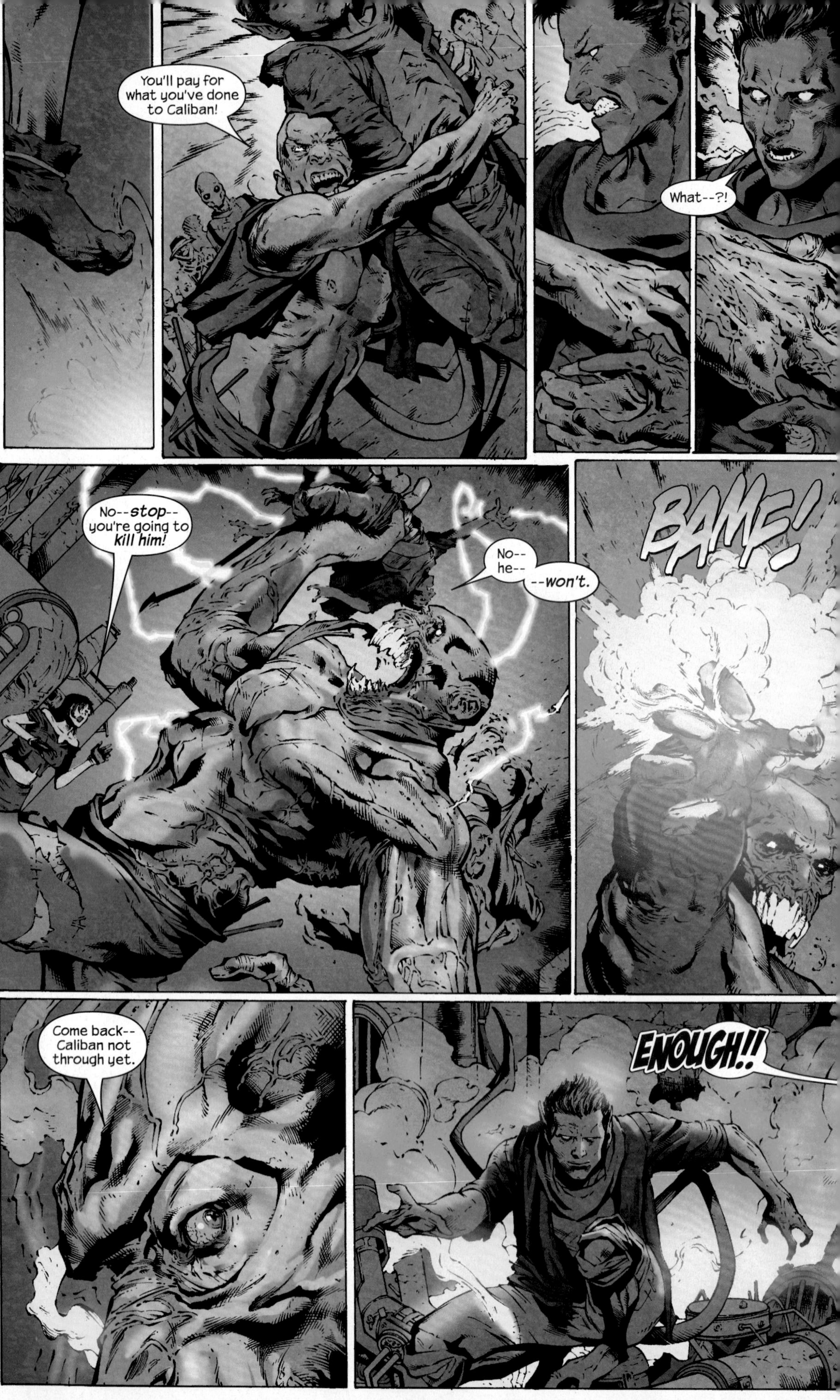
You'll pay for what you've done to Caliban!
What--?!
No--*stop*--you're going to *kill him!*
No--he--
--*won't.*
BAMF!
Come back--Caliban not through yet.
ENOUGH!!

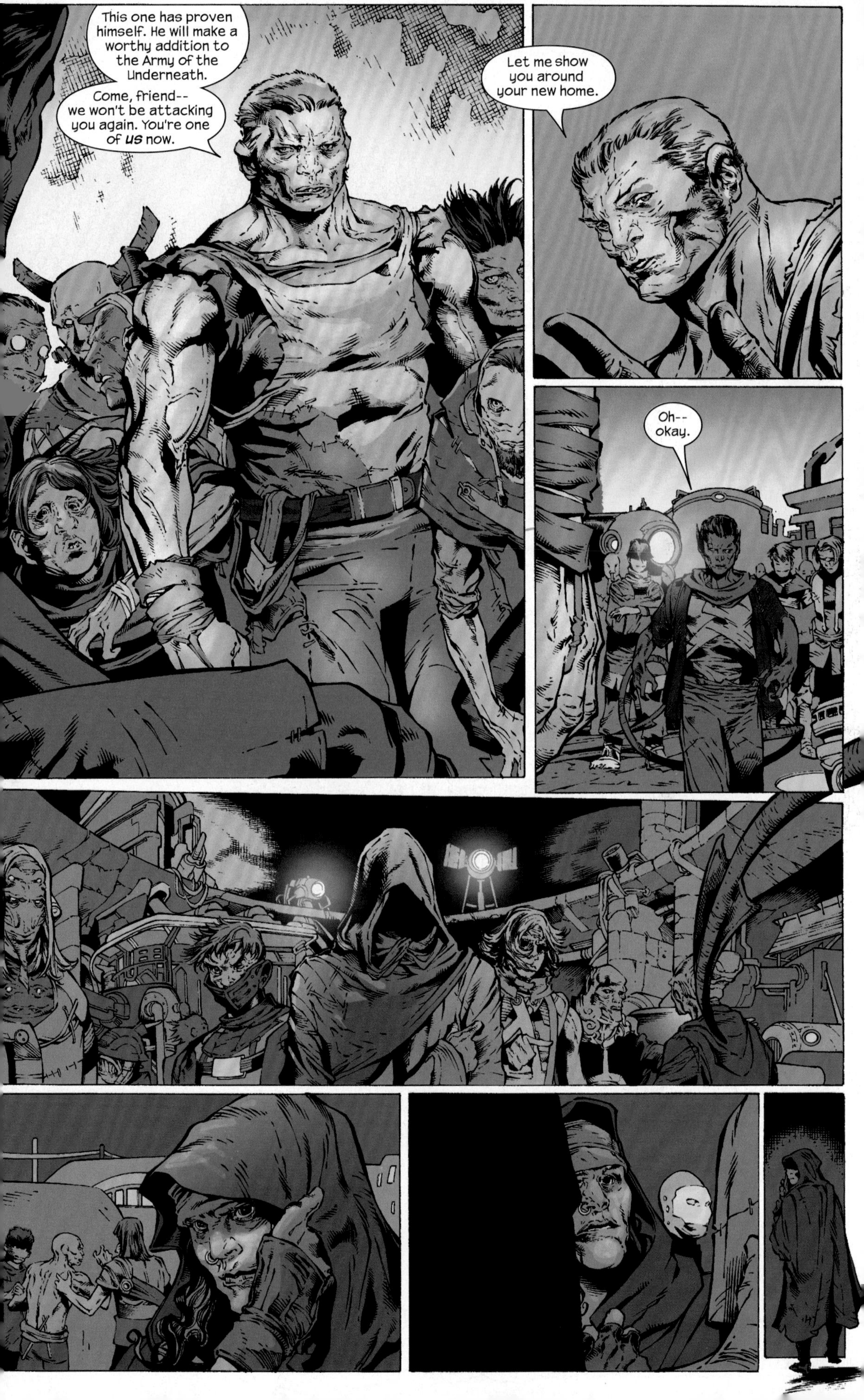
This one has proven himself. He will make a worthy addition to the Army of the Underneath.
Come, friend-- we won't be attacking you again. You're one of US now.
Let me show you around your new home.
Oh-- okay.

Xavier's Institute for Gifted Youngsters.

You're sending him on *missions,* now?

We're not the X-Men anymore, Jean--we don't have *"missions"* any more.

What do you call it then?

We have a faculty member who is on a recruiting assignment.

I can't *believe* you couldn't wait two weeks before sending him out into the world, representing this school. I don't *trust* Toad, Scott.

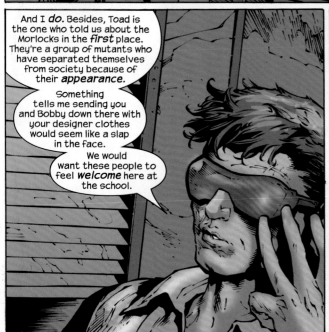

And I *do.* Besides, Toad is the one who told us about the Morlocks in the *first* place. They're a group of mutants who have separated themselves from society because of their *appearance.*

Something tells me sending you and Bobby down there with your designer clothes would seem like a slap in the face.

We would want these people to feel *welcome* here at the school.

I never said you didn't have a good reason. I'm just worried about the amount of *trust* you're already giving Toad.

And I *don't* wear designer clothes.

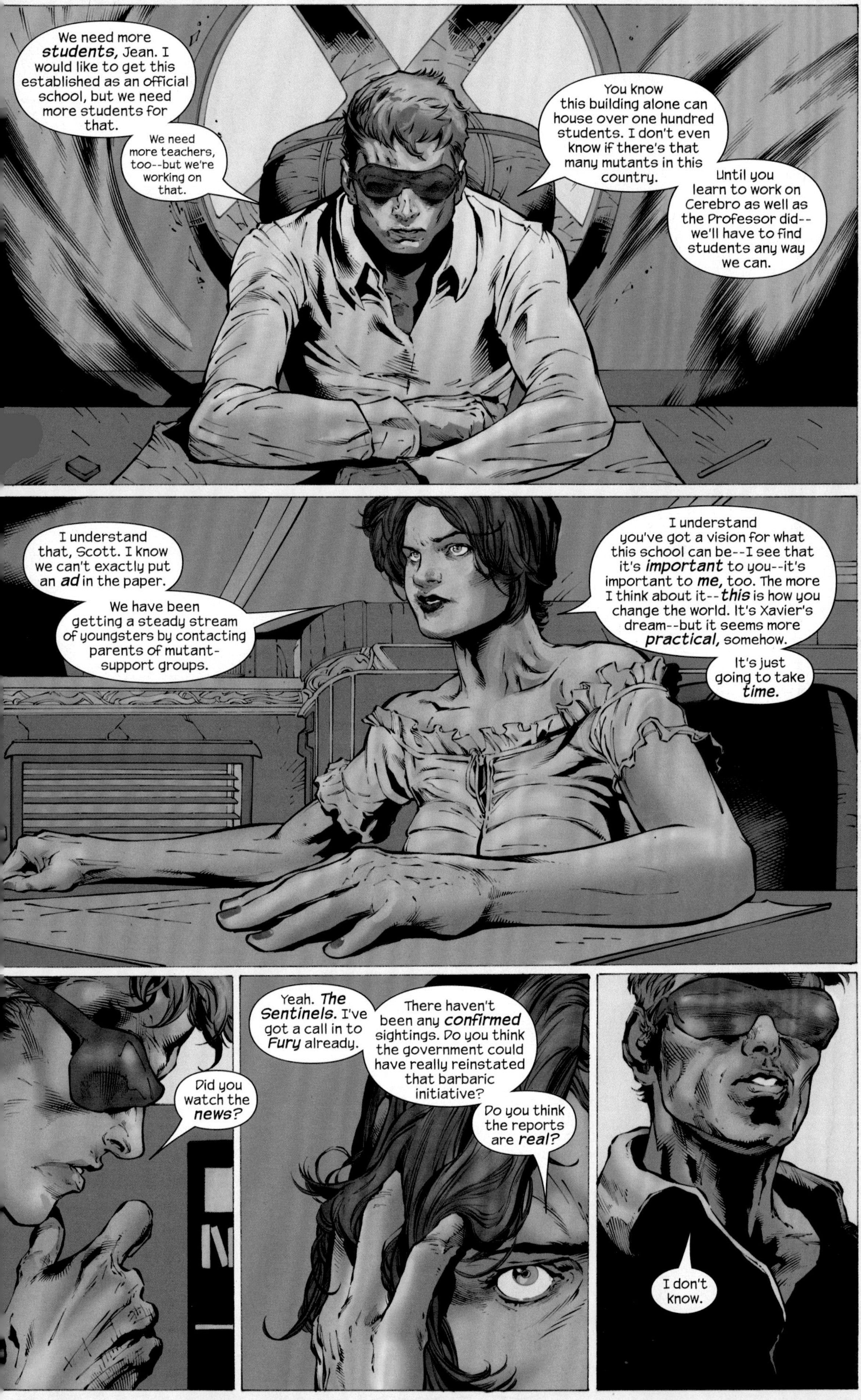
We need more students, Jean. I would like to get this established as an official school, but we need more students for that.
We need more teachers, too--but we're working on that.
You know this building alone can house over one hundred students. I don't even know if there's that many mutants in this country.
Until you learn to work on Cerebro as well as the Professor did--we'll have to find students any way we can.
I understand that, Scott. I know we can't exactly put an ad in the paper.
We have been getting a steady stream of youngsters by contacting parents of mutant-support groups.
I understand you've got a vision for what this school can be--I see that it's important to you--it's important to me, too. The more I think about it--this is how you change the world. It's Xavier's dream--but it seems more practical, somehow.
It's just going to take time.
Did you watch the news?
Yeah. The Sentinels. I've got a call in to Fury already.
There haven't been any confirmed sightings. Do you think the government could have really reinstated that barbaric initiative?
Do you think the reports are real?
I don't know.

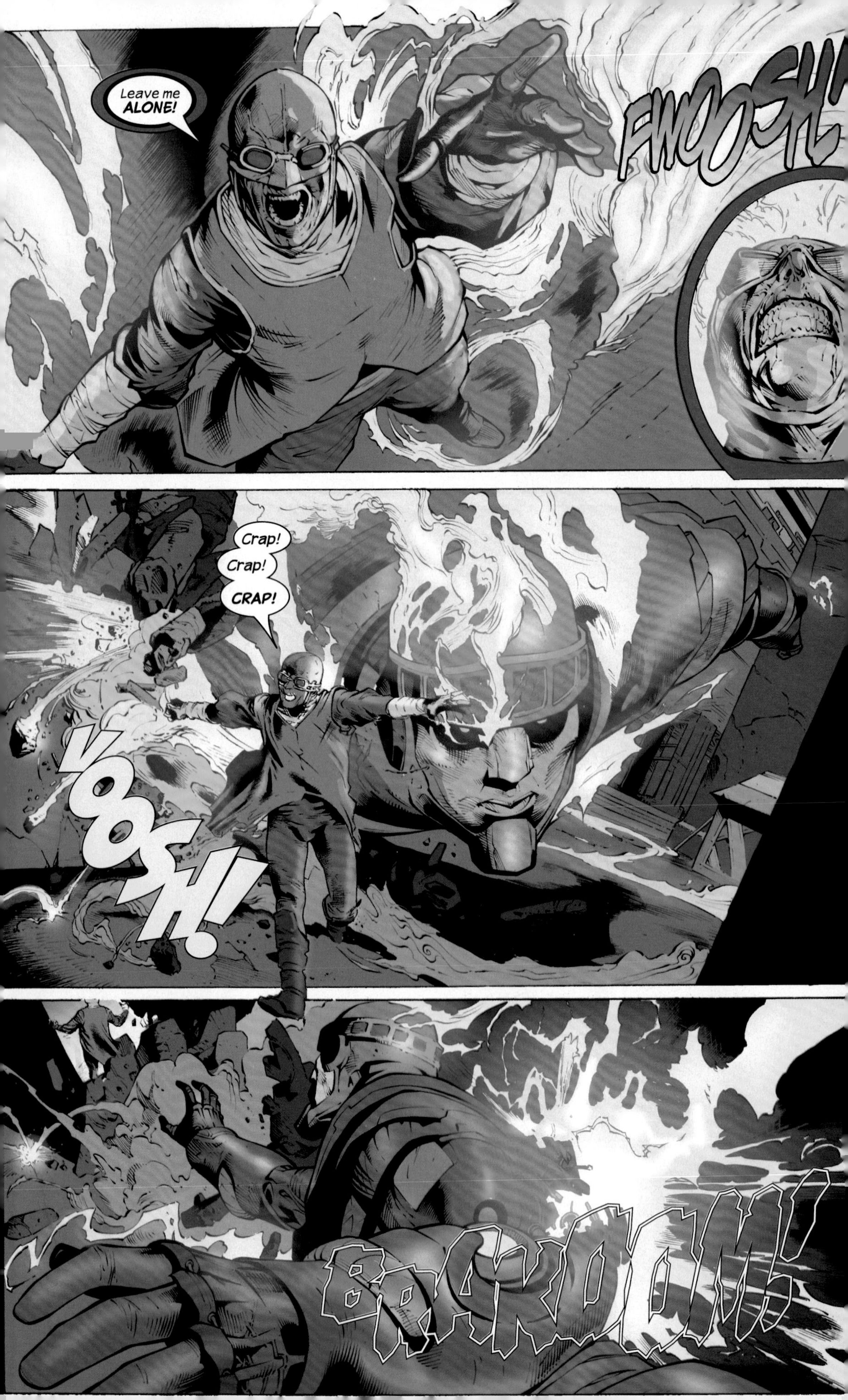

Leave me ALONE!
FWOOSH!
Crap!
Crap!
CRAP!
VOOSH!
BRAKOOM!

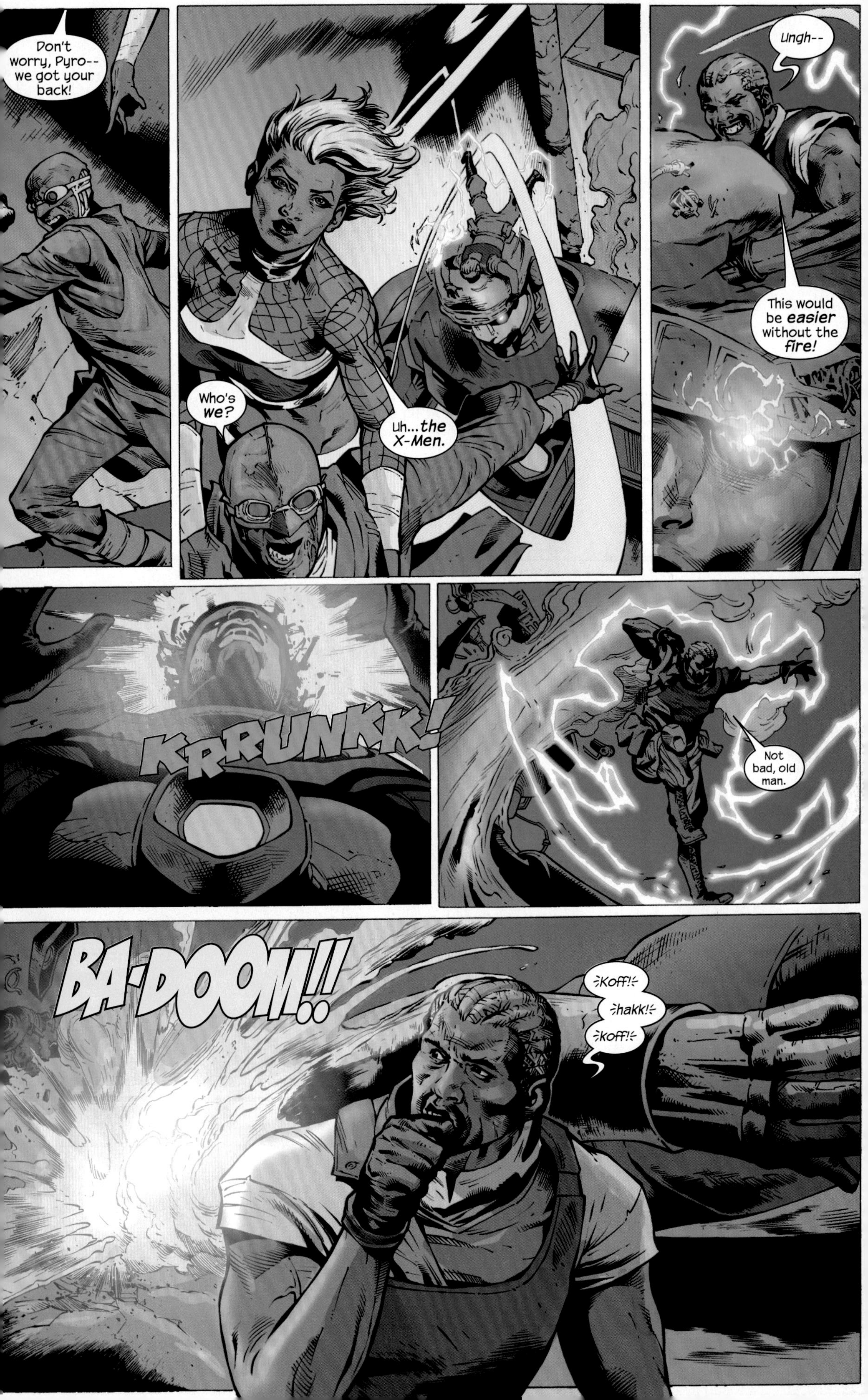
Don't worry, Pyro-- we got your back!
Who's we?
Uh...the X-Men.
Ungh--
This would be easier without the fire!
KRRUNKK!
Not bad, old man.
BA-DOOM!!
-Koff!-
-hakk!-
-koff!-

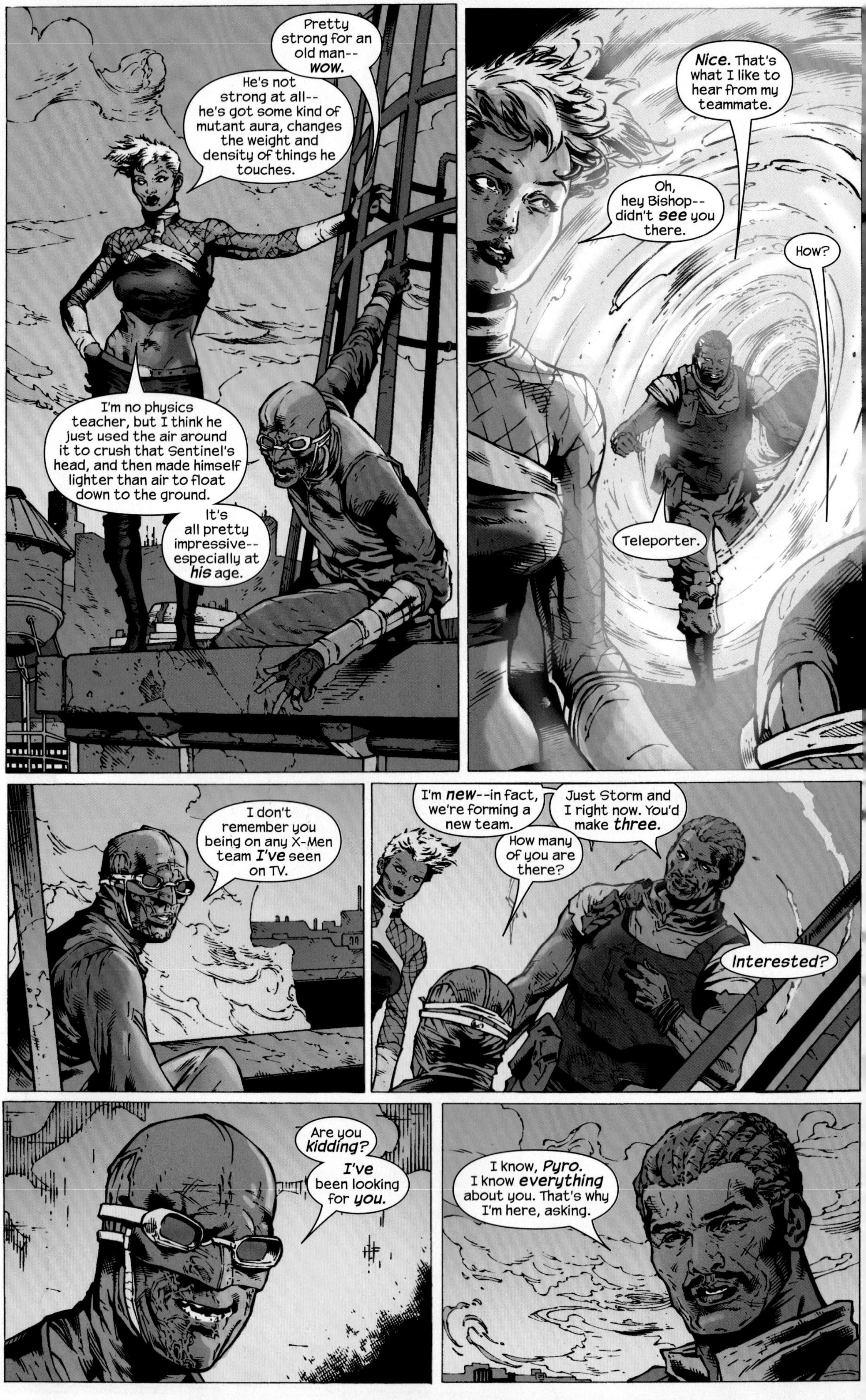

Pretty strong for an old man-- *wow.*
He's not strong at all-- he's got some kind of mutant aura, changes the weight and density of things he touches.
I'm no physics teacher, but I think he just used the air around it to crush that Sentinel's head, and then made himself lighter than air to float down to the ground.
It's all pretty impressive-- especially at *his* age.
Nice. That's what I like to hear from my teammate.
Oh, hey Bishop-- didn't *see* you there.
How?
Teleporter.
I don't remember you being on any X-Men team *I've* seen on TV.
I'm *new*--in fact, we're forming a new team.
How many of you are there?
Just Storm and I right now. You'd make *three.*
Interested?
Are you *kidding?*
I've been looking for *you.*
I know, *Pyro.* I know *everything* about you. That's why I'm here, asking.

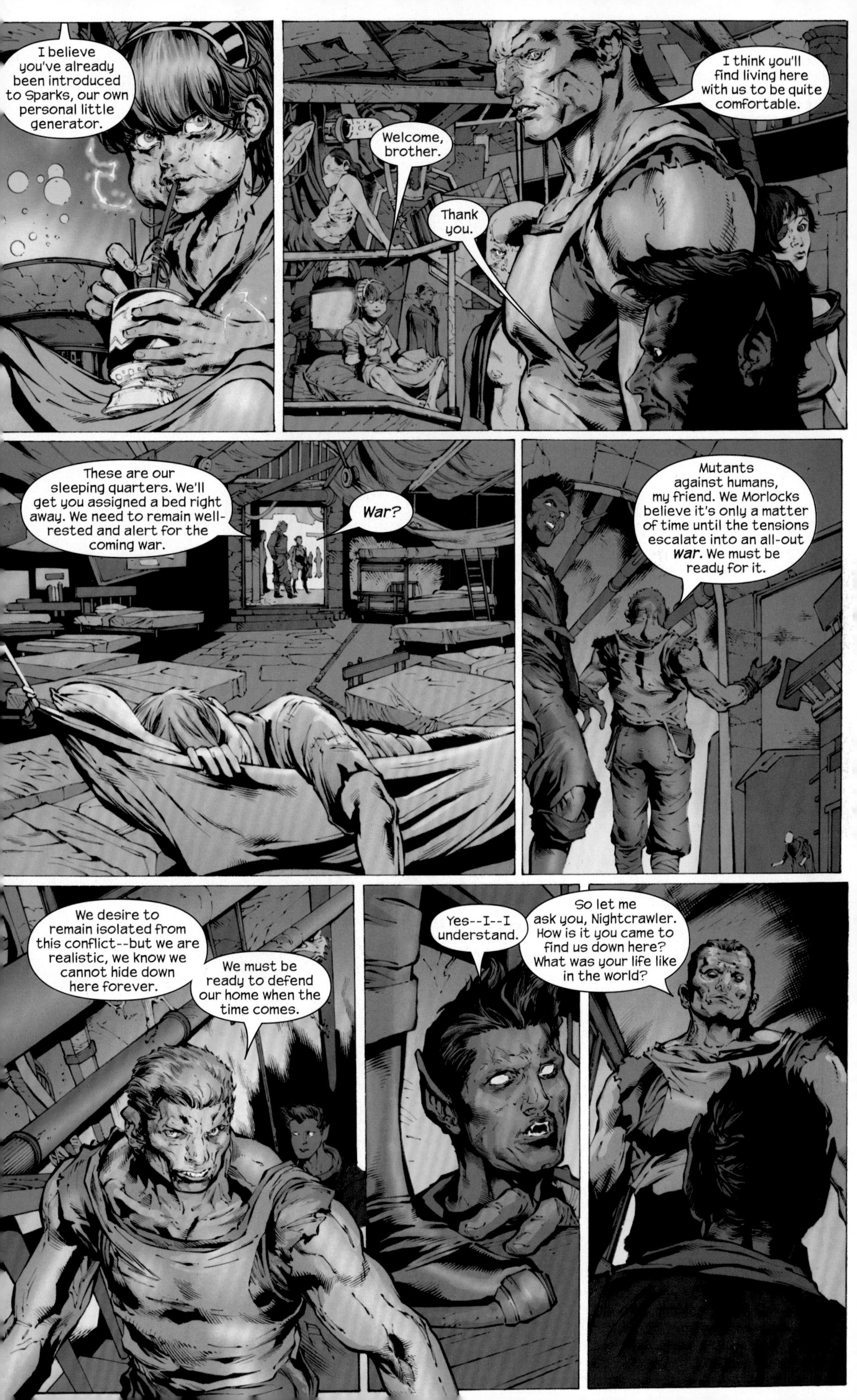
I believe you've already been introduced to Sparks, our own personal little generator.
I think you'll find living here with us to be quite comfortable.
Welcome, brother.
Thank you.
These are our sleeping quarters. We'll get you assigned a bed right away. We need to remain well-rested and alert for the coming war.
War?
Mutants against humans, my friend. We Morlocks believe it's only a matter of time until the tensions escalate into an all-out war. We must be ready for it.
We desire to remain isolated from this conflict--but we are realistic, we know we cannot hide down here forever.
We must be ready to defend our home when the time comes.
Yes--I--I understand.
So let me ask you, Nightcrawler. How is it you came to find us down here? What was your life like in the world?

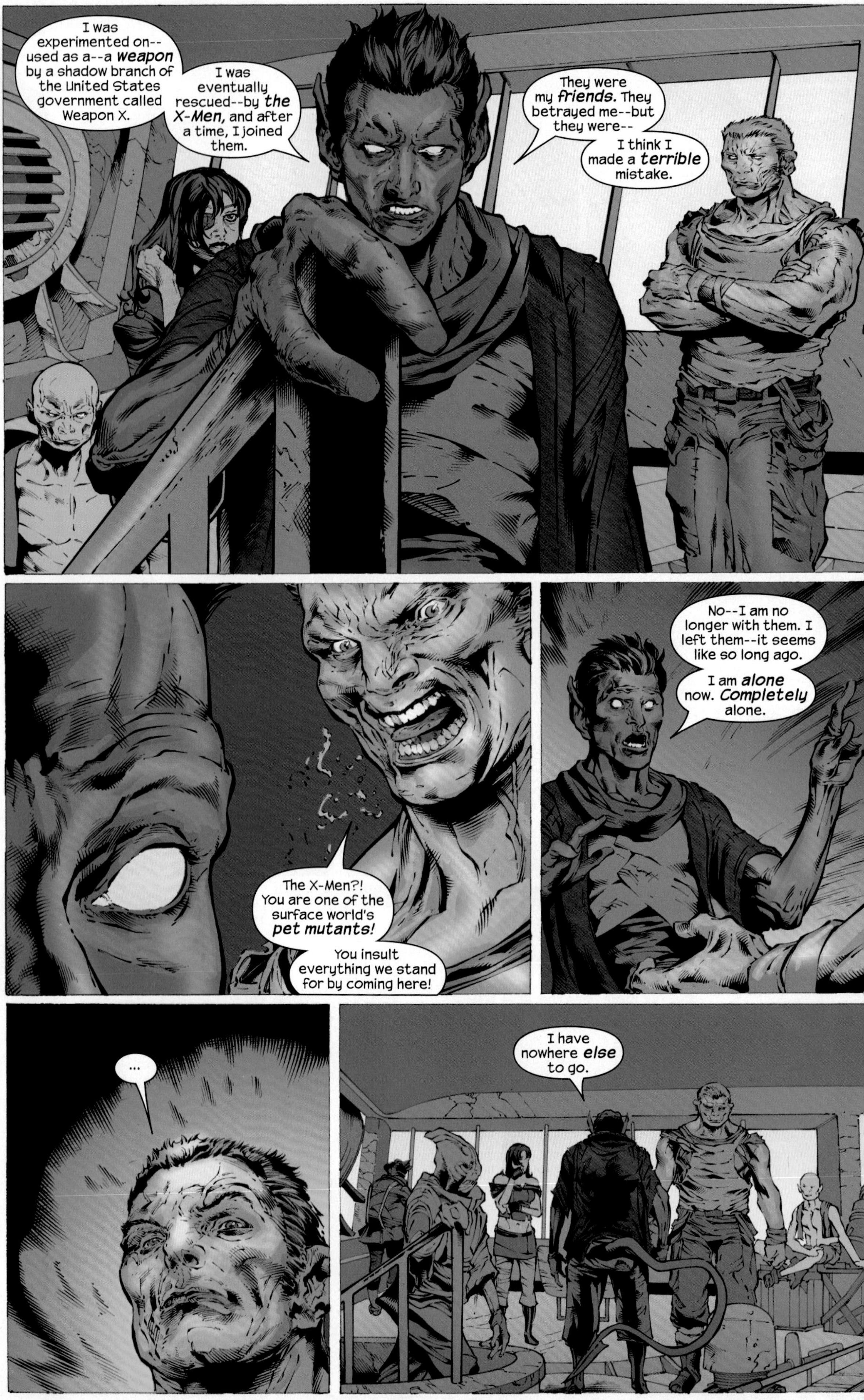
I was experimented on--used as a--a *weapon* by a shadow branch of the United States government called Weapon X.
I was eventually rescued--by *the X-Men,* and after a time, I joined them.
They were my *friends.* They betrayed me--but they were--
I think I made a *terrible* mistake.
The X-Men?! You are one of the surface world's *pet mutants!*
You insult everything we stand for by coming here!
No--I am no longer with them. I left them--it seems like so long ago.
I am *alone* now. *Completely* alone.
...
I have nowhere *else* to go.

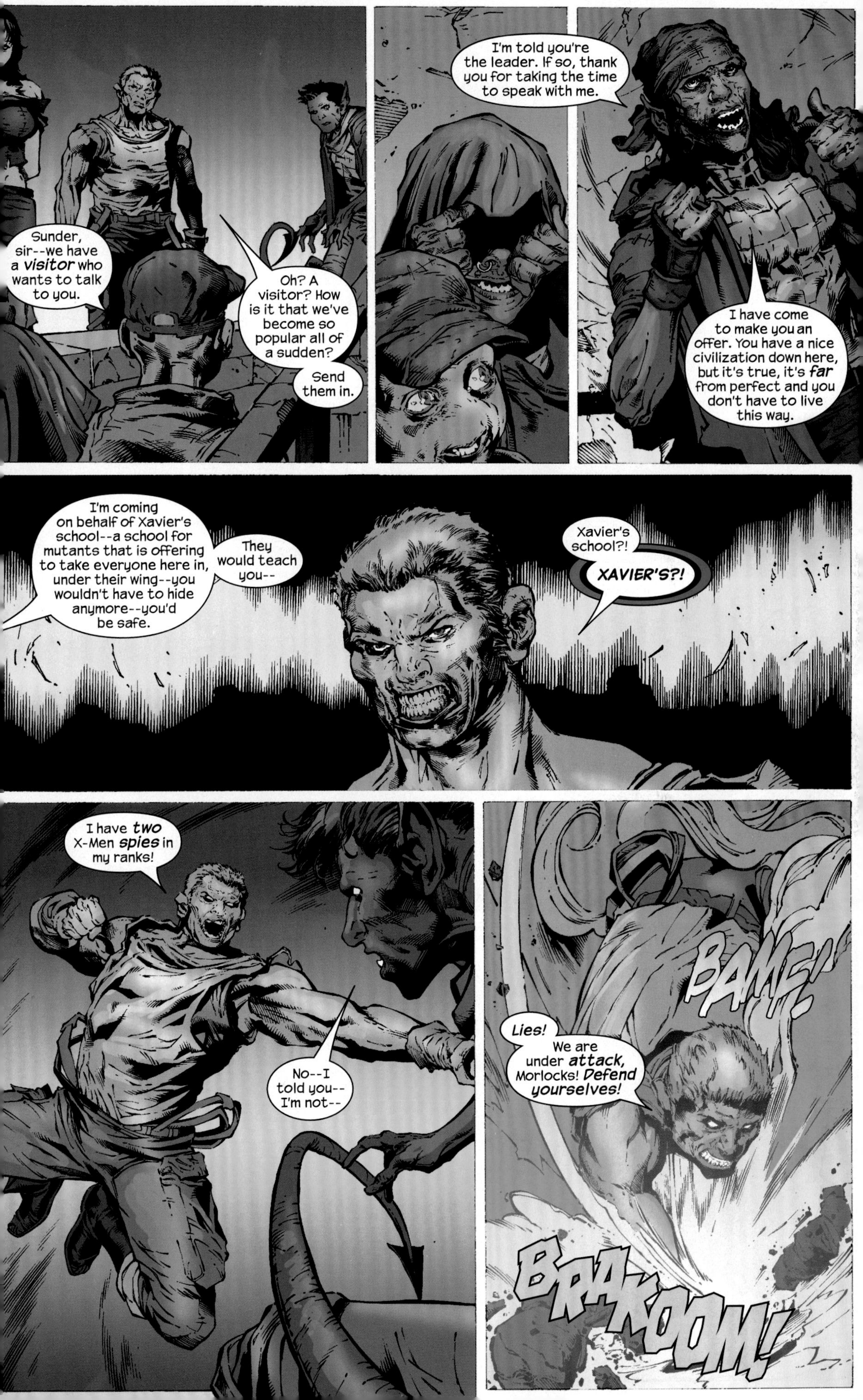

Sunder, sir--we have a **visitor** who wants to talk to you.
Oh? A visitor? How is it that we've become so popular all of a sudden?
Send them in.
I'm told you're the leader. If so, thank you for taking the time to speak with me.
I have come to make you an offer. You have a nice civilization down here, but it's true, it's **far** from perfect and you don't have to live this way.
I'm coming on behalf of Xavier's school--a school for mutants that is offering to take everyone here in, under their wing--you wouldn't have to hide anymore--you'd be safe.
They would teach you--
Xavier's school?!
XAVIER'S?!
I have **two** X-Men **spies** in my ranks!
No--I told you-- I'm not--
BAMF!
Lies!
We are under **attack**, Morlocks! **Defend yourselves!**
BRAKOOM!

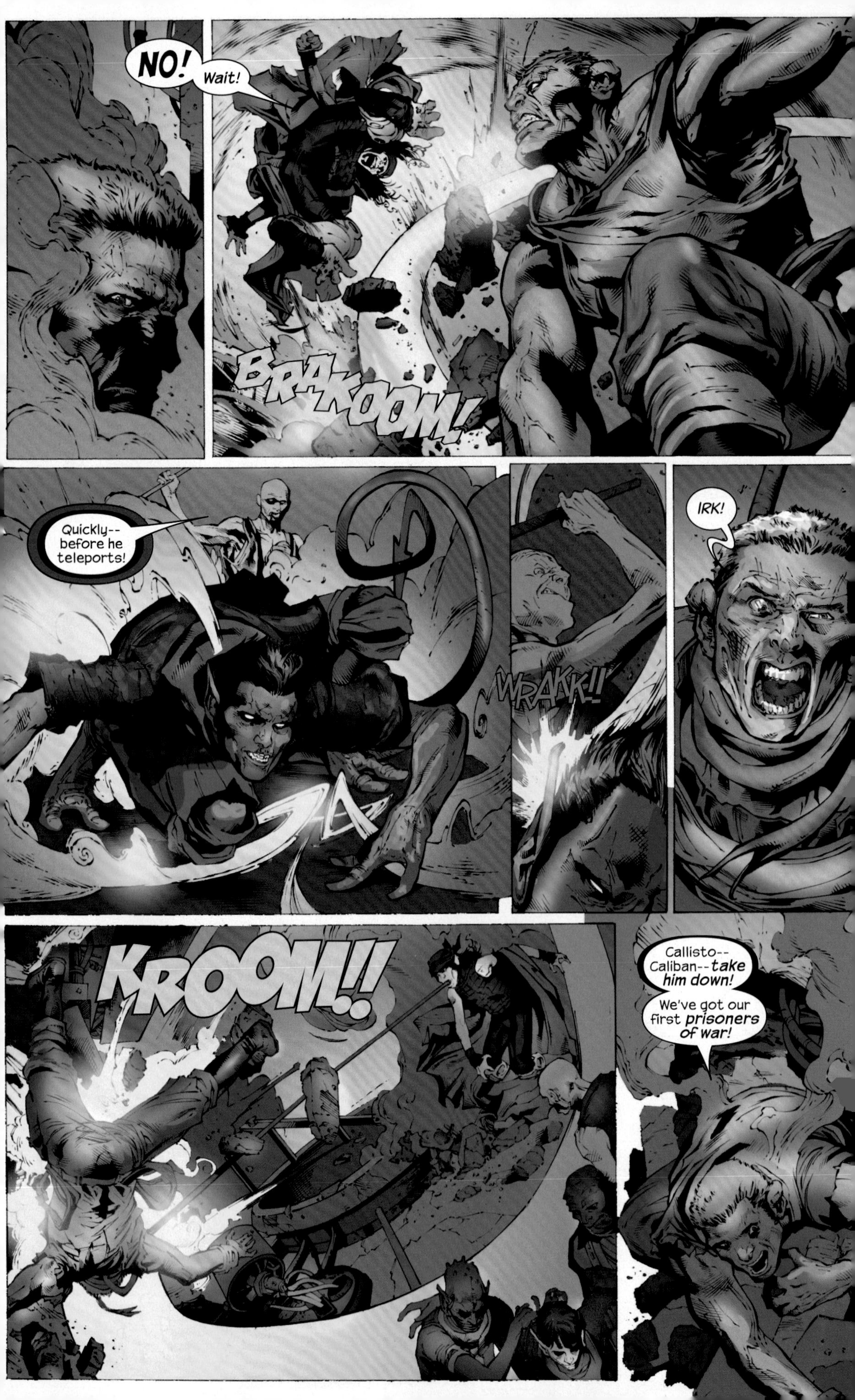
NO! Wait!
BRAKOOM!
Quickly-- before he teleports!
WRAKK!!
IRK!
KROOM!!
Callisto-- Caliban--take him down!
We've got our first prisoners of war!

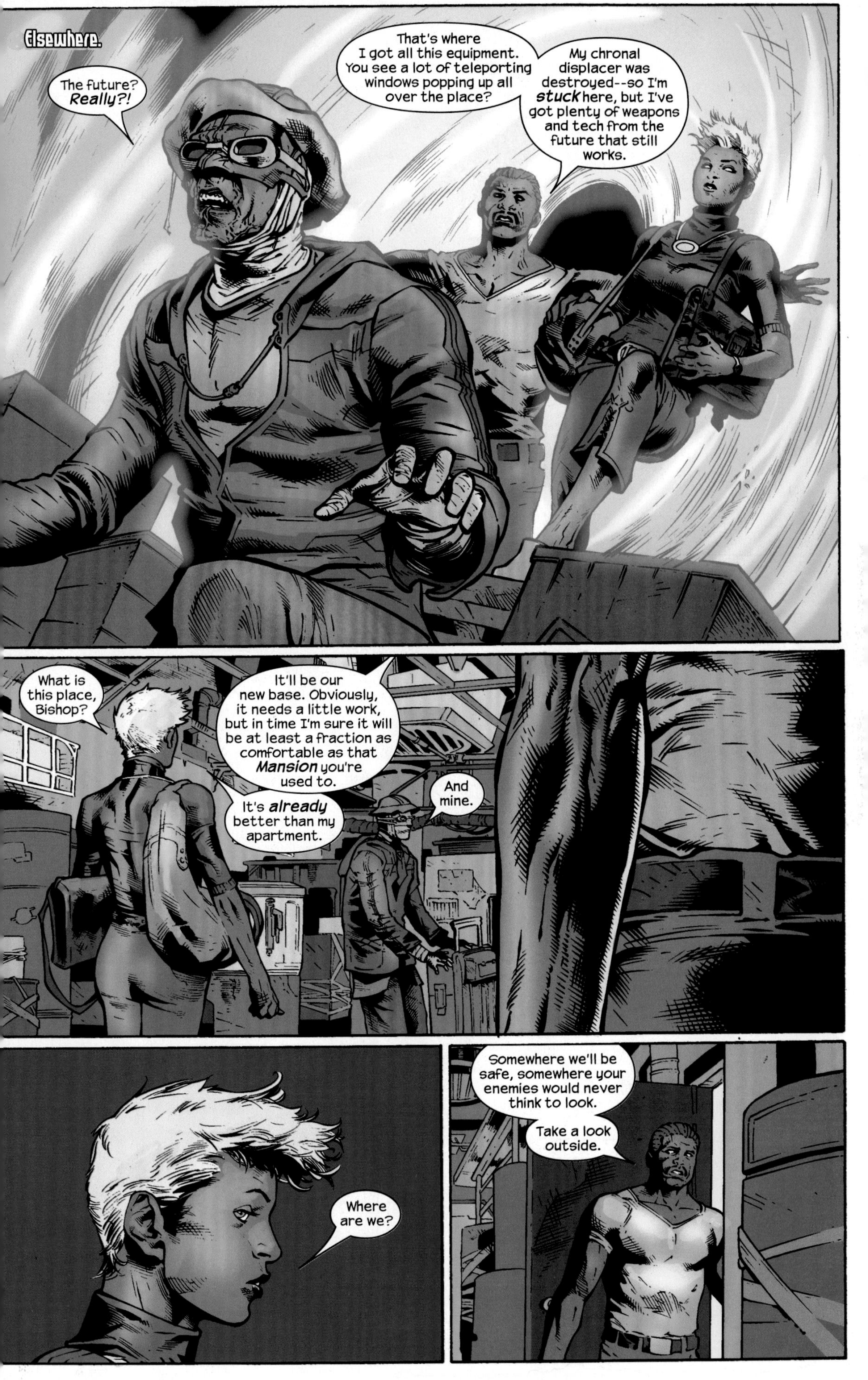
Elsewhere.
The future? Really?!
That's where I got all this equipment. You see a lot of teleporting windows popping up all over the place?
My chronal displacer was destroyed--so I'm stuck here, but I've got plenty of weapons and tech from the future that still works.
What is this place, Bishop?
It'll be our new base. Obviously, it needs a little work, but in time I'm sure it will be at least a fraction as comfortable as that Mansion you're used to.
It's already better than my apartment.
And mine.
Where are we?
Somewhere we'll be safe, somewhere your enemies would never think to look.
Take a look outside.

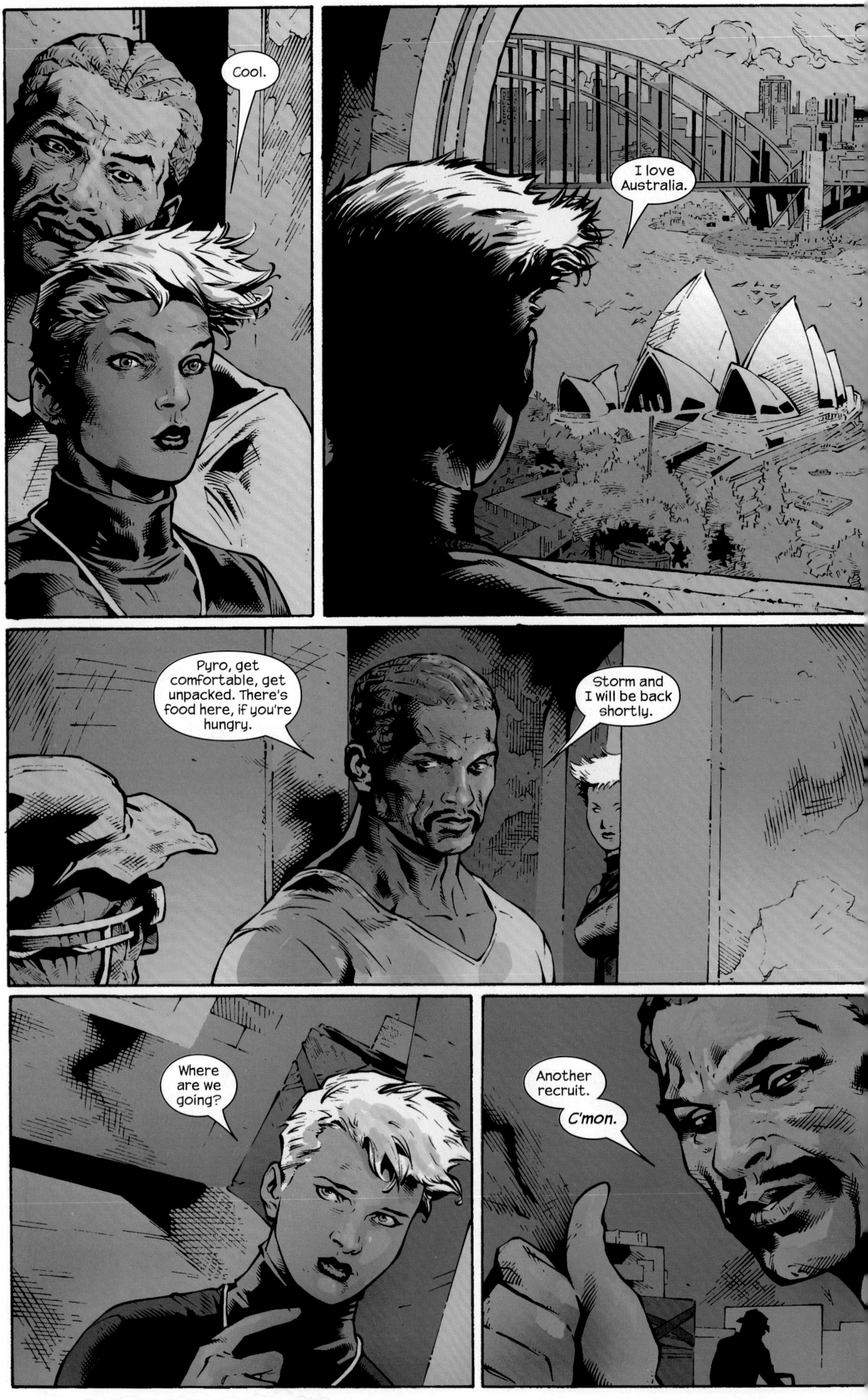
Cool.
I love Australia.
Pyro, get comfortable, get unpacked. There's food here, if you're hungry.
Storm and I will be back shortly.
Where are we going?
Another recruit.
C'mon.

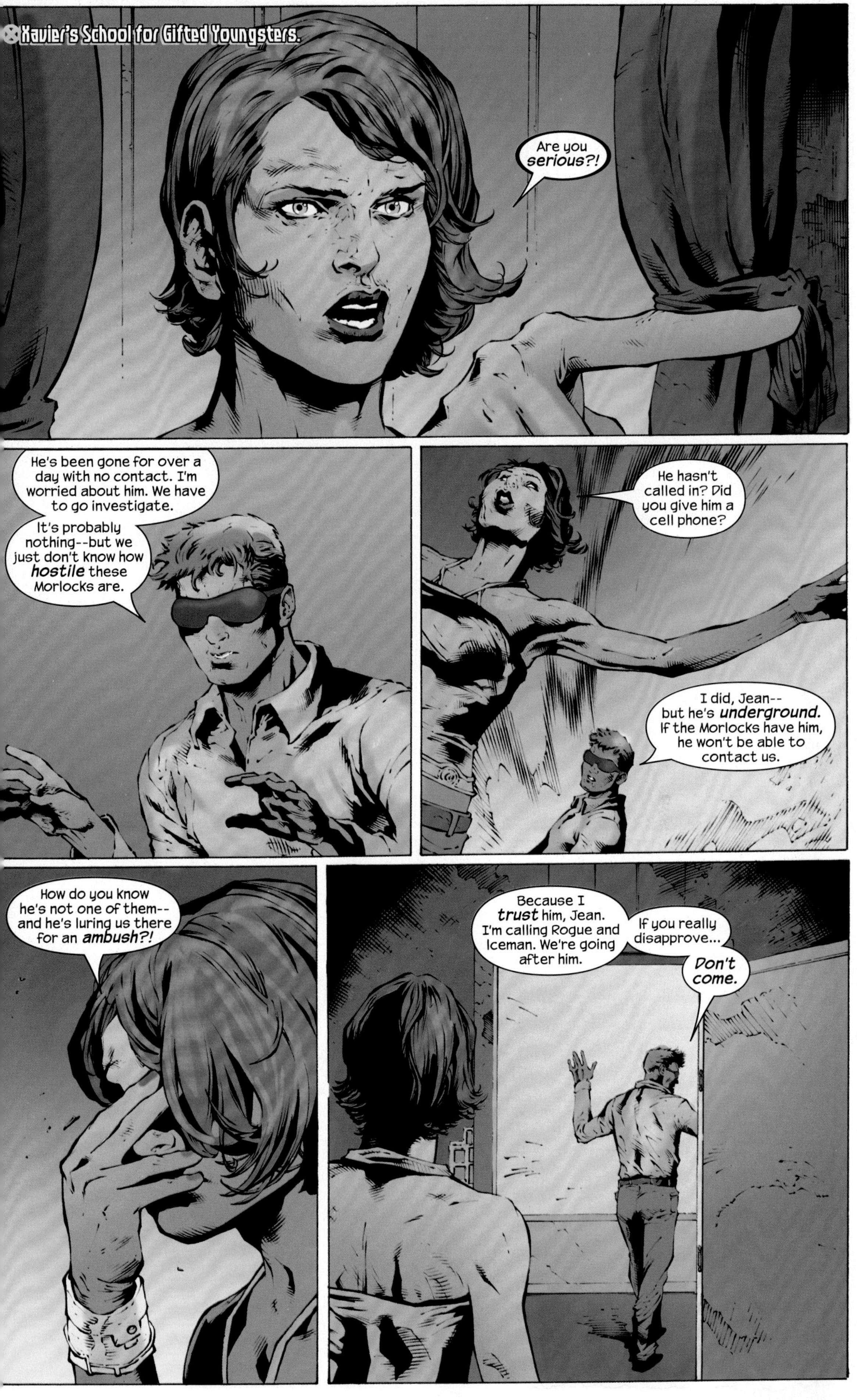
Xavier's School for Gifted Youngsters.
Are you serious?!
He's been gone for over a day with no contact. I'm worried about him. We have to go investigate.
It's probably nothing--but we just don't know how hostile these Morlocks are.
He hasn't called in? Did you give him a cell phone?
I did, Jean--but he's underground. If the Morlocks have him, he won't be able to contact us.
How do you know he's not one of them--and he's luring us there for an ambush?!
Because I trust him, Jean. I'm calling Rogue and Iceman. We're going after him.
If you really disapprove...
Don't come.

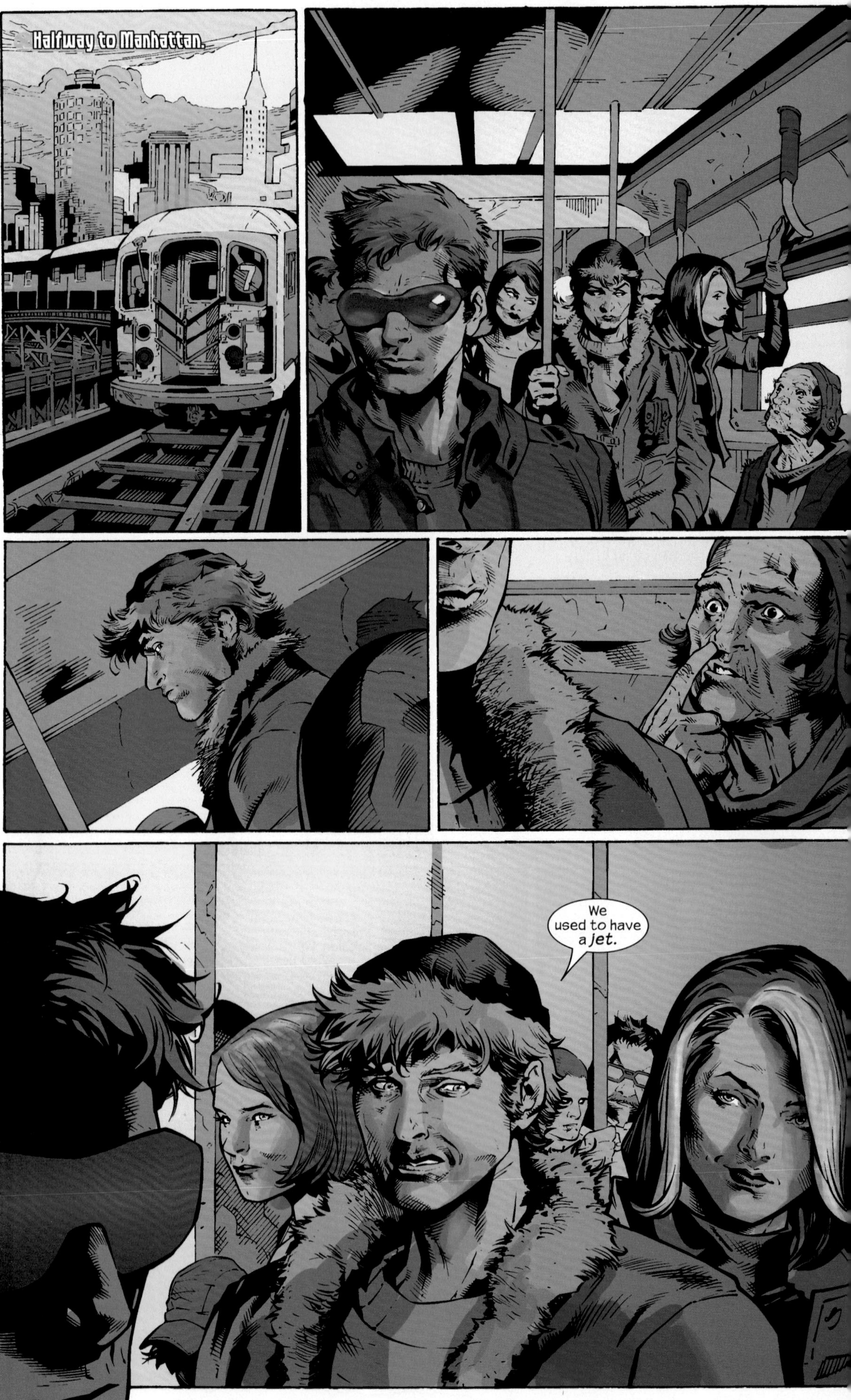
Halfway to Manhattan.
7
We used to have a jet.

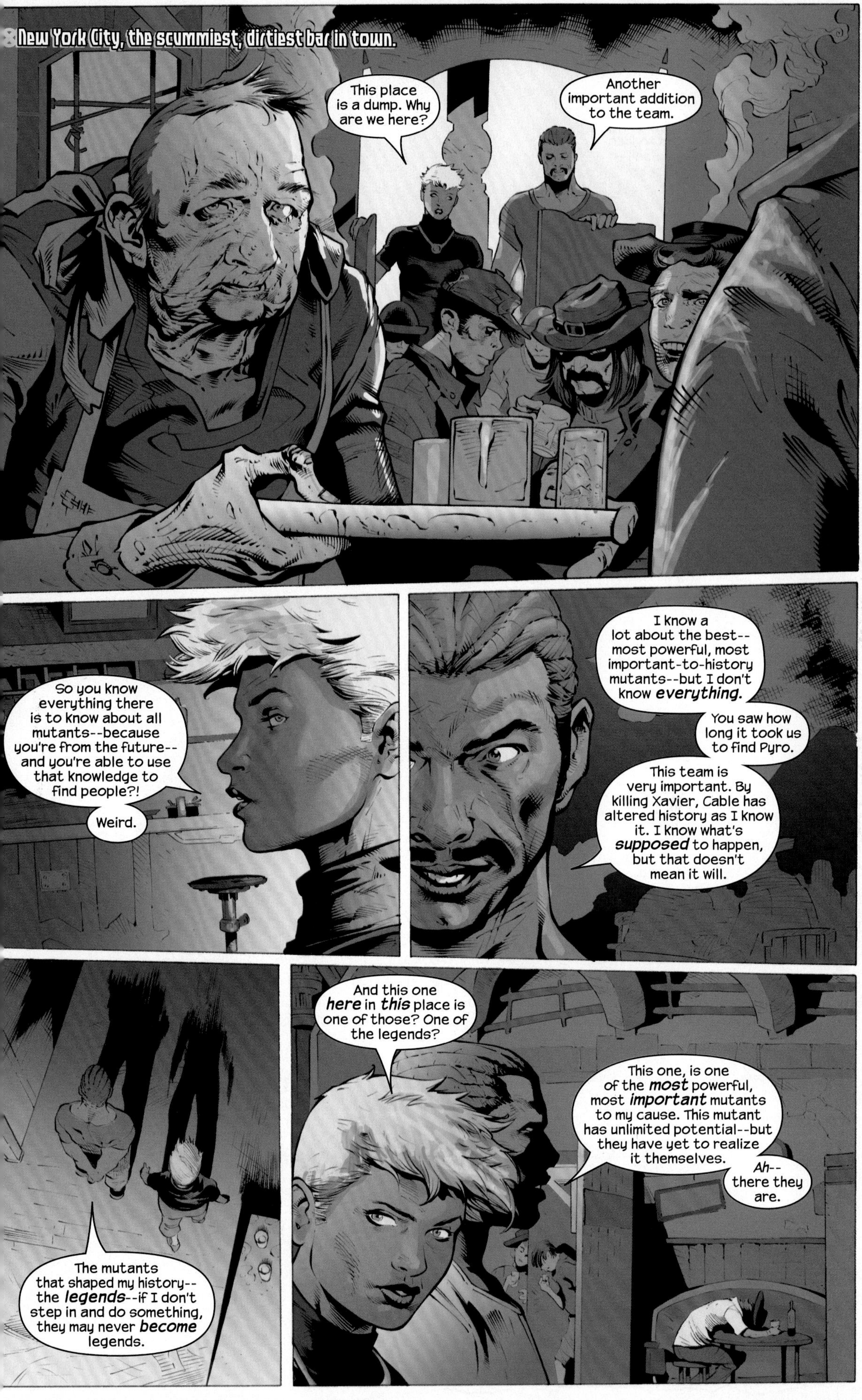
New York City, the scummiest, dirtiest bar in town.
This place is a dump. Why are we here?
Another important addition to the team.
So you know everything there is to know about all mutants--because you're from the future--and you're able to use that knowledge to find people?!
Weird.
I know a lot about the best--most powerful, most important-to-history mutants--but I don't know *everything.*
You saw how long it took us to find Pyro.
This team is very important. By killing Xavier, Cable has altered history as I know it. I know what's *supposed* to happen, but that doesn't mean it will.
The mutants that shaped my history--the *legends*--if I don't step in and do something, they may never *become* legends.
And this one *here* in *this* place is one of those? One of the legends?
This one, is one of the *most* powerful, most *important* mutants to my cause. This mutant has unlimited potential--but they have yet to realize it themselves.
Ah--there they are.

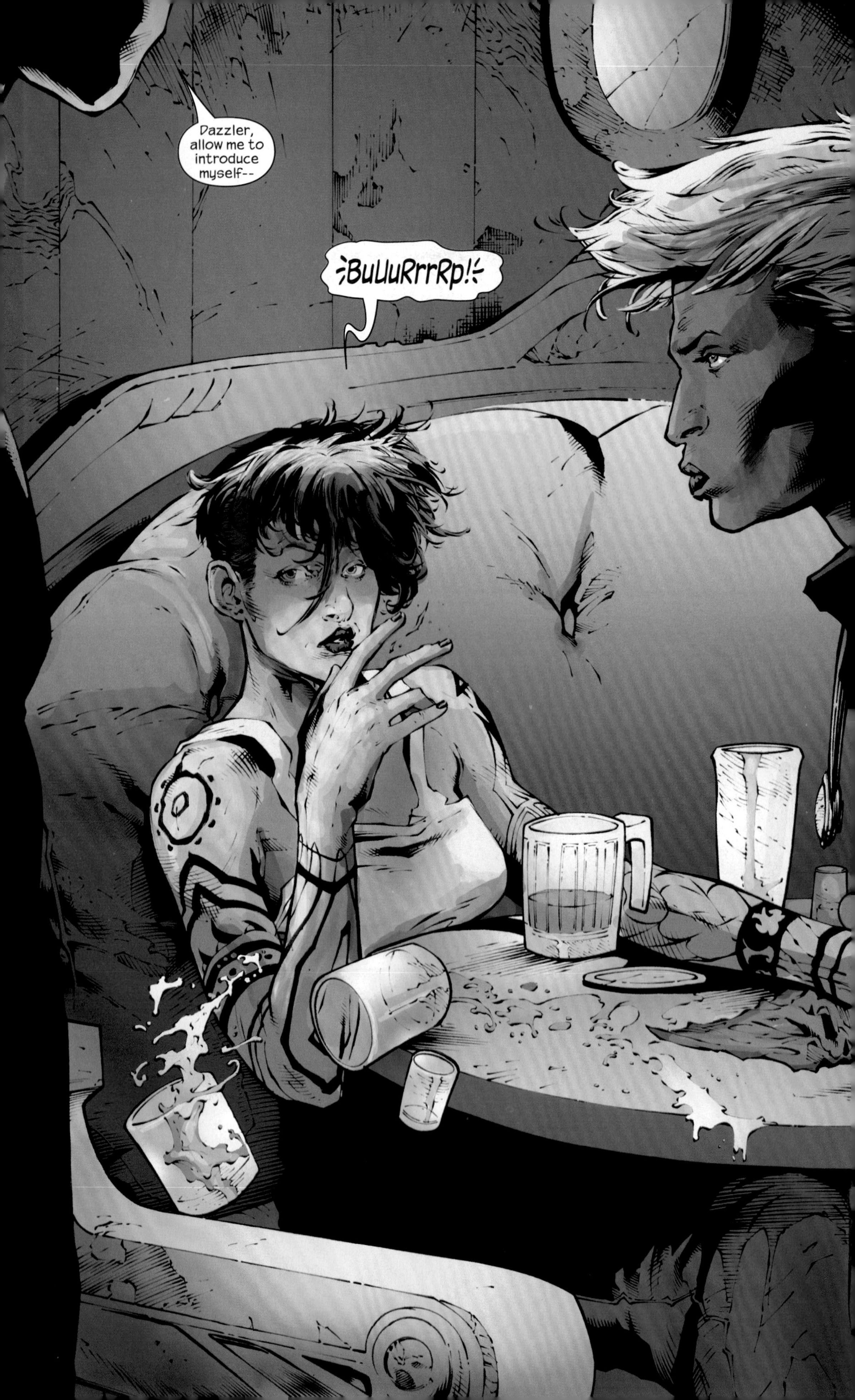
Dazzler, allow me to introduce myself--
BuUuRrrRp!

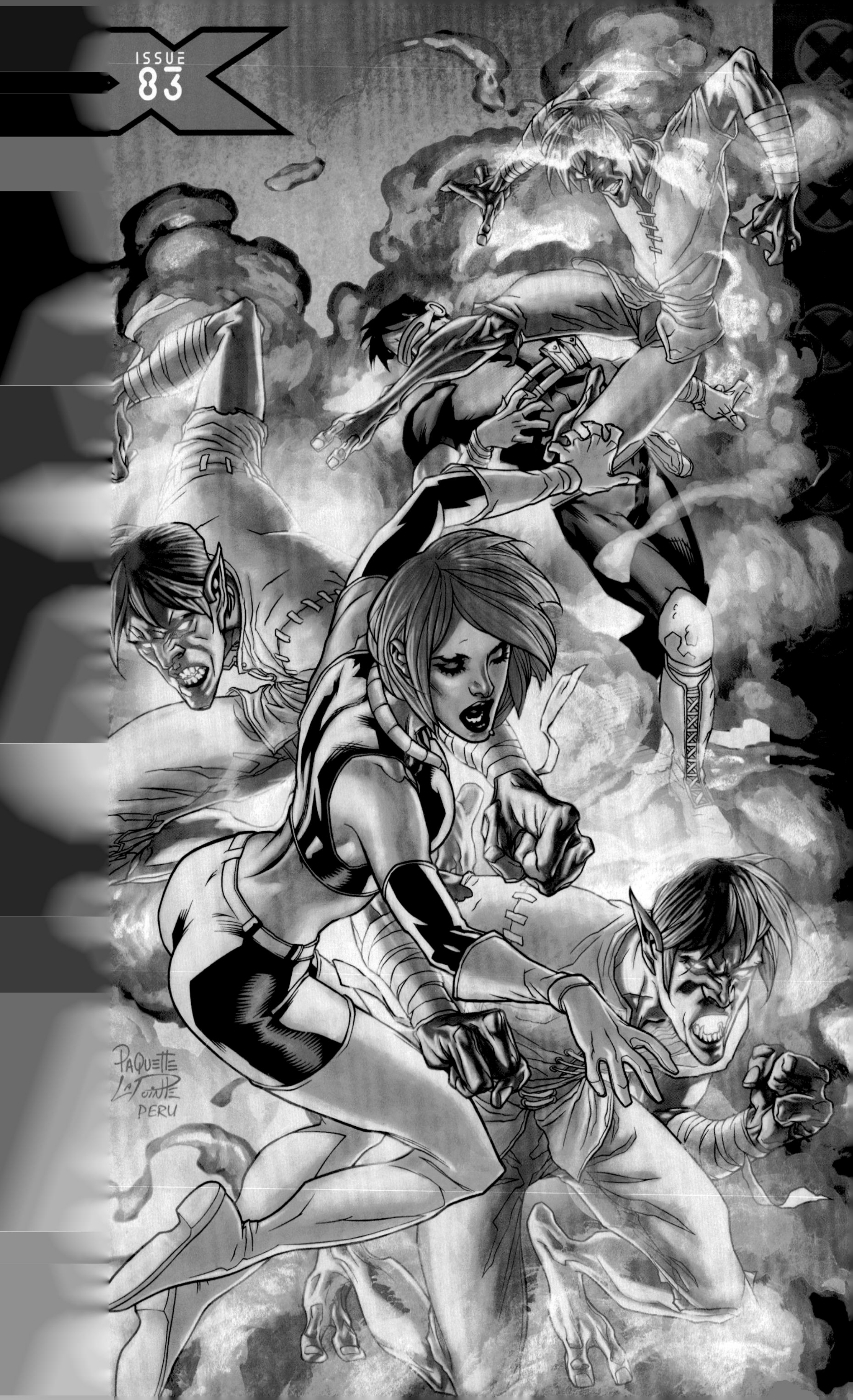
ISSUE
83
PAQUETTE
LaPOINTE
PERU

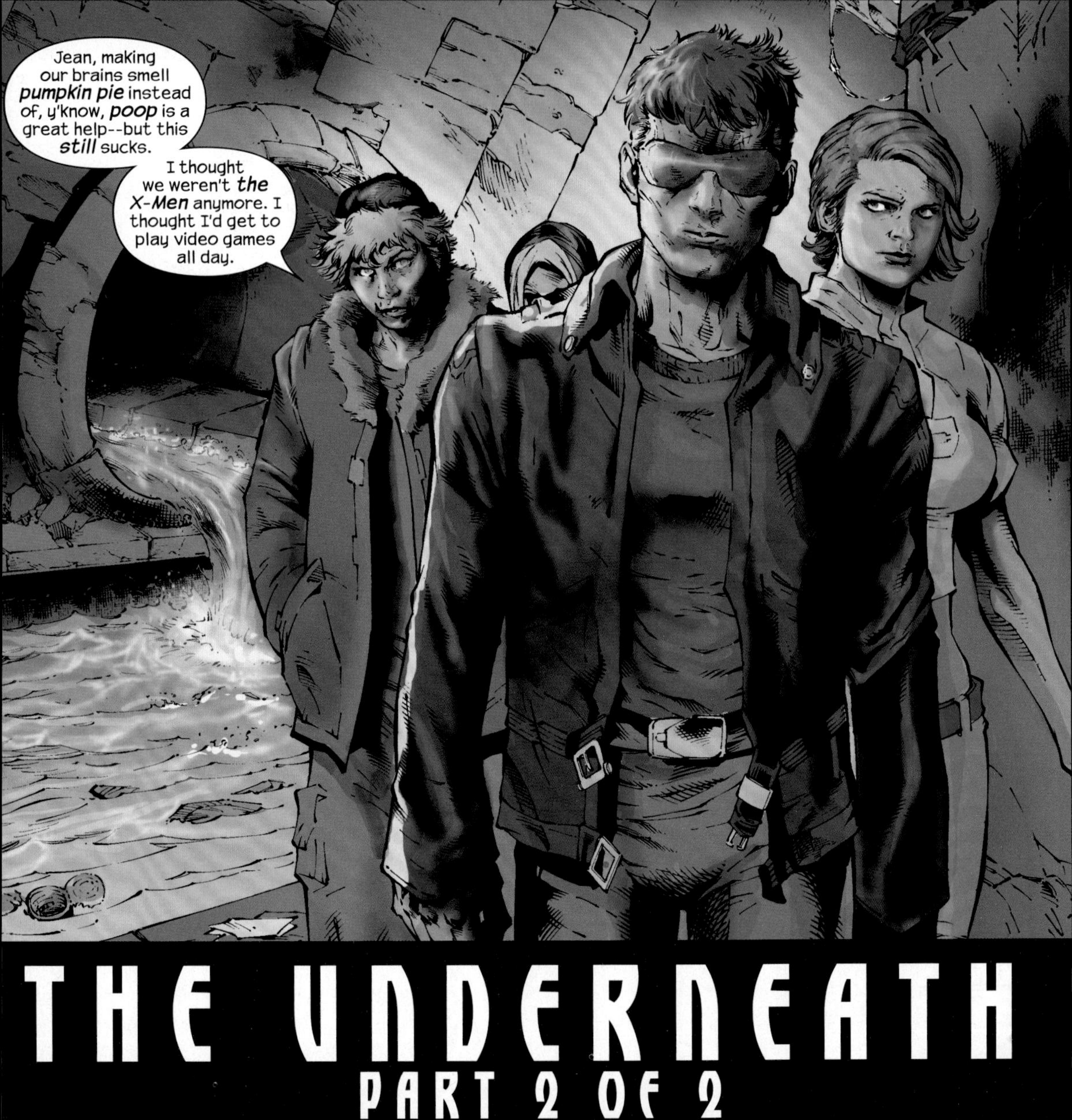
Jean, making our brains smell *pumpkin pie* instead of, y'know, *poop* is a great help--but this *still* sucks.
I thought we weren't *the X-Men* anymore. I thought I'd get to play video games all day.
THE UNDERNEATH
PART 2 OF 2

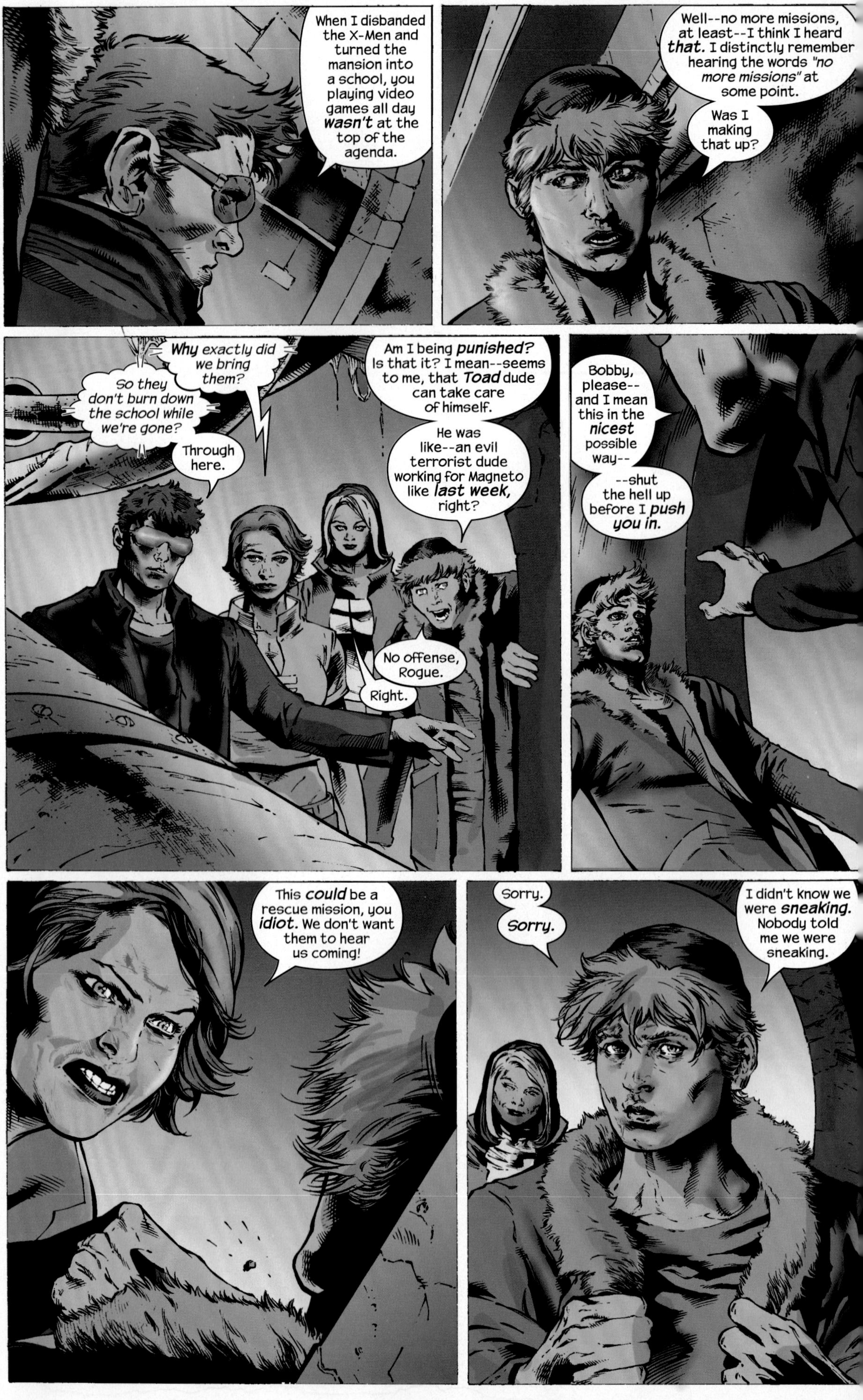
When I disbanded the X-Men and turned the mansion into a school, you playing video games all day wasn't at the top of the agenda.
Well--no more missions, at least--I think I heard that. I distinctly remember hearing the words "no more missions" at some point.
Was I making that up?
Why exactly did we bring them?
So they don't burn down the school while we're gone?
Through here.
Am I being punished? Is that it? I mean--seems to me, that Toad dude can take care of himself.
He was like--an evil terrorist dude working for Magneto like last week, right?
No offense, Rogue.
Right.
Bobby, please--and I mean this in the nicest possible way--
--shut the hell up before I push you in.
This could be a rescue mission, you idiot. We don't want them to hear us coming!
Sorry.
Sorry.
I didn't know we were sneaking. Nobody told me we were sneaking.

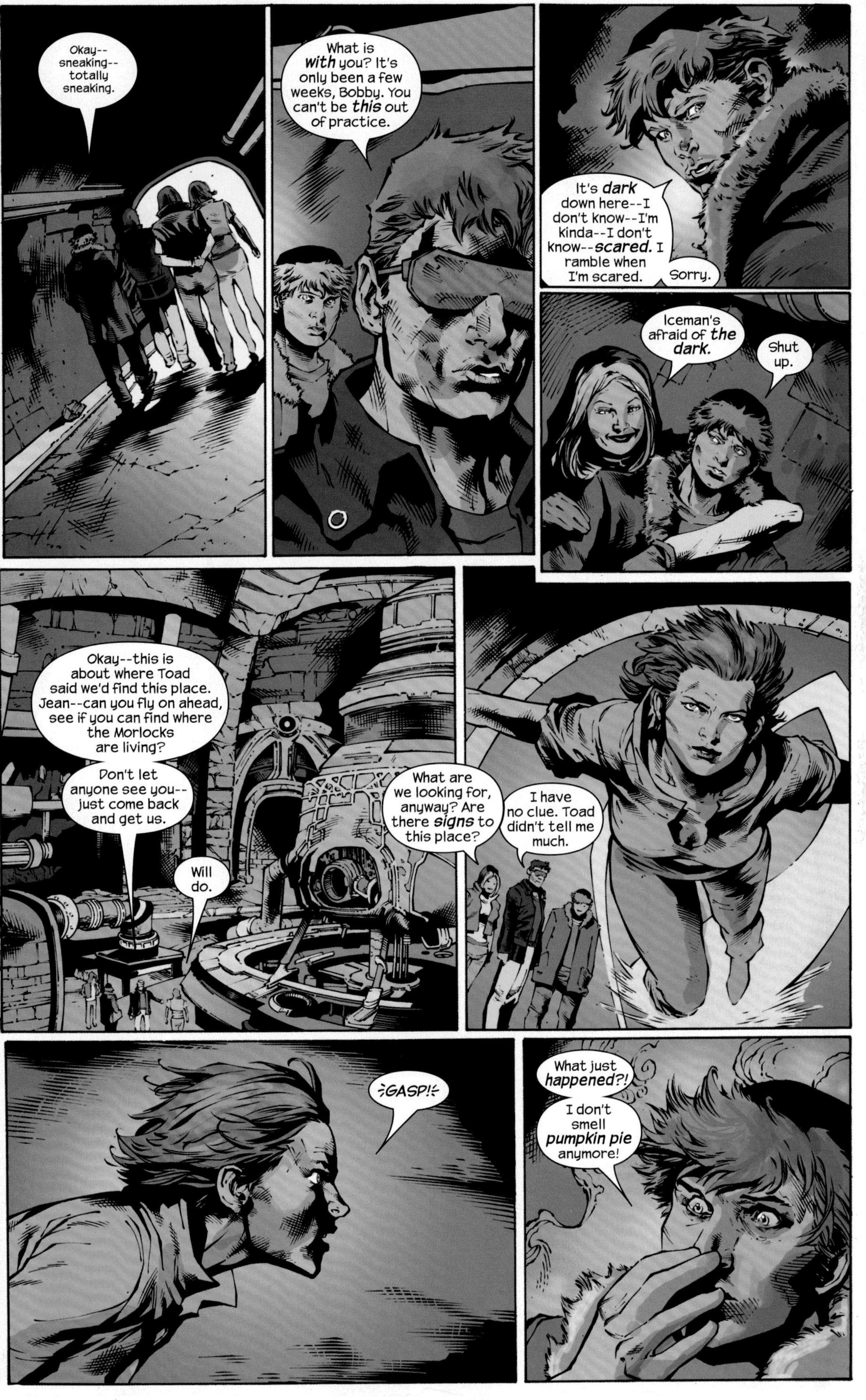
Okay--
sneaking--
totally
sneaking.
What is with you? It's only been a few weeks, Bobby. You can't be this out of practice.
It's dark down here--I don't know--I'm kinda--I don't know--scared. I ramble when I'm scared.
Sorry.
Iceman's afraid of the dark.
Shut up.
Okay--this is about where Toad said we'd find this place. Jean--can you fly on ahead, see if you can find where the Morlocks are living?
Don't let anyone see you--just come back and get us.
Will do.
What are we looking for, anyway? Are there signs to this place?
I have no clue. Toad didn't tell me much.
GASP!
What just happened?!
I don't smell pumpkin pie anymore!

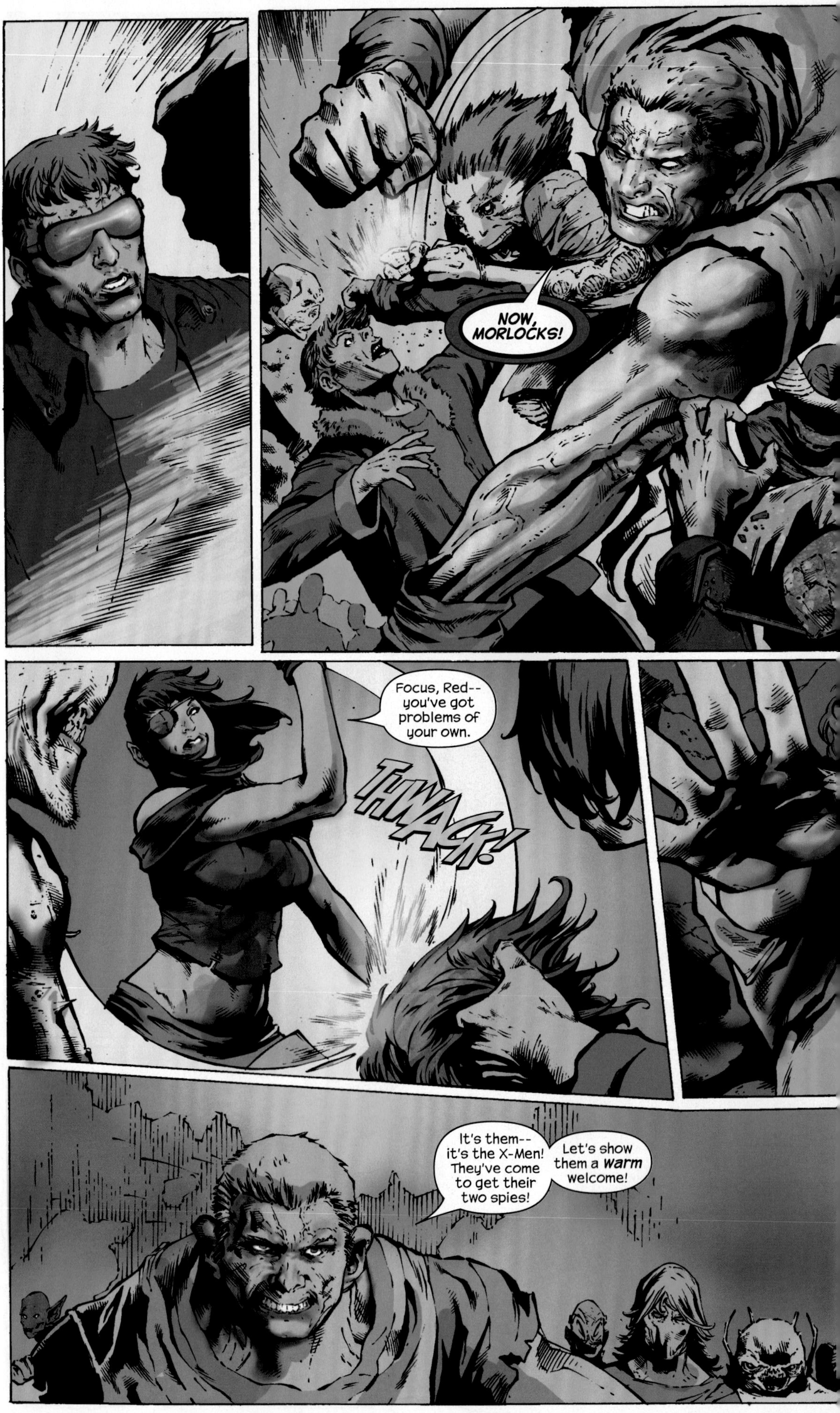
NOW, MORLOCKS!
Focus, Red-- you've got problems of your own.
THWACK!
It's them-- it's the X-Men! They've come to get their two spies!
Let's show them a *warm* welcome!

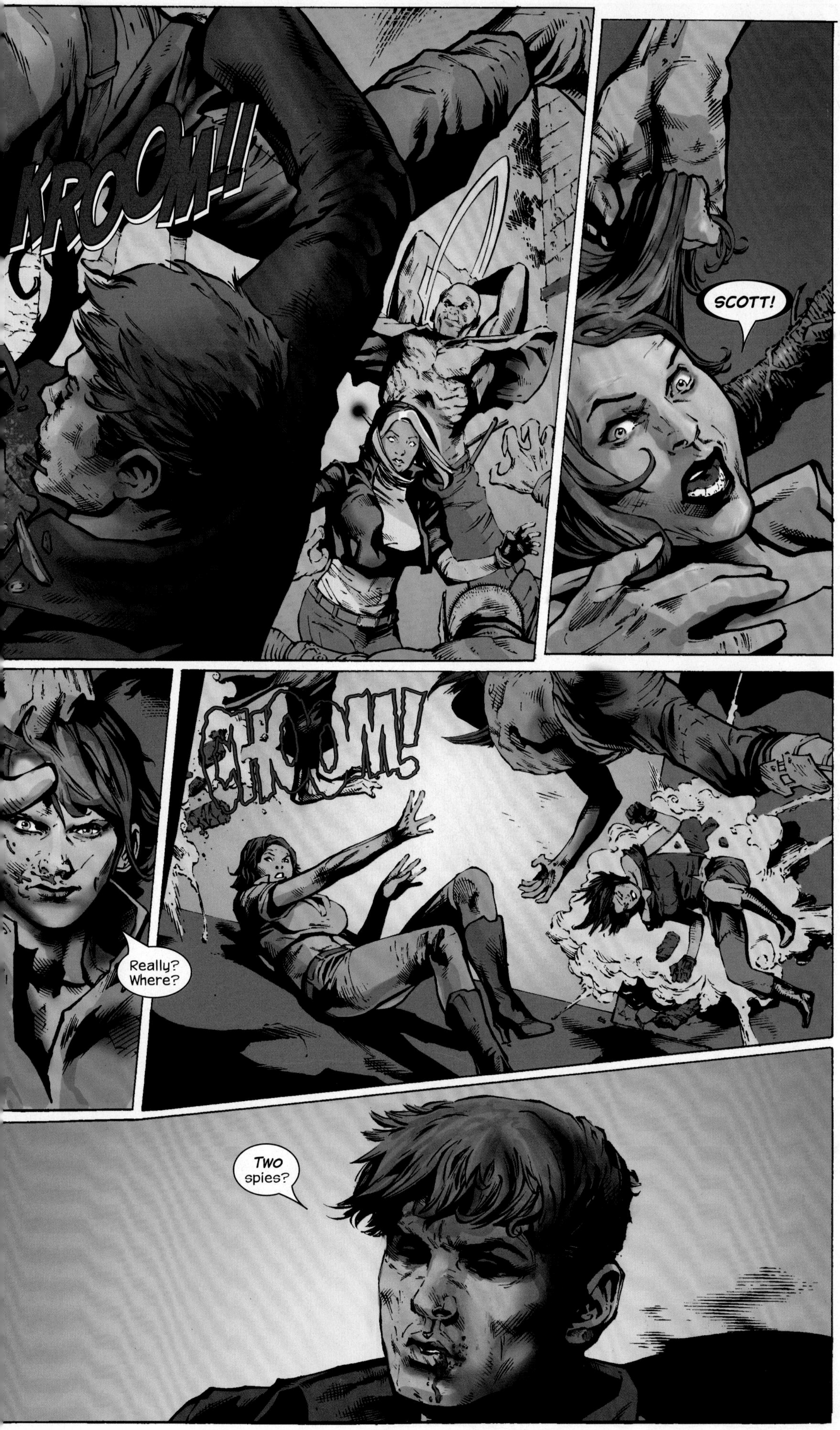
KROOM!!
SCOTT!
Really? Where?
CHOOM!
TWO spies?

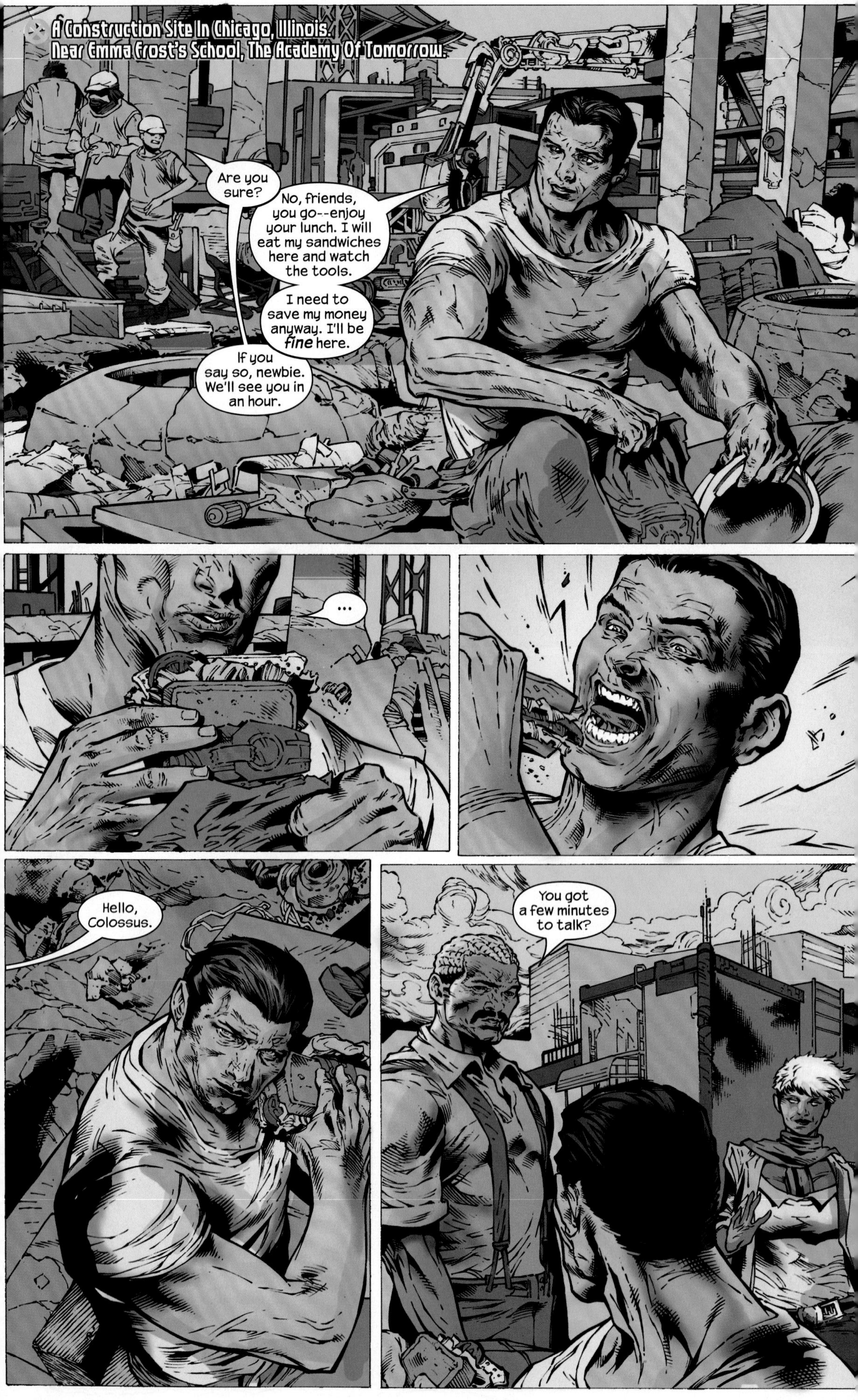
A Construction Site In Chicago, Illinois.
Near Emma Frost's School, The Academy Of Tomorrow.
Are you sure?
No, friends, you go--enjoy your lunch. I will eat my sandwiches here and watch the tools.
I need to save my money anyway. I'll be *fine* here.
If you say so, newbie. We'll see you in an hour.
...
Hello, Colossus.
You got a few minutes to talk?

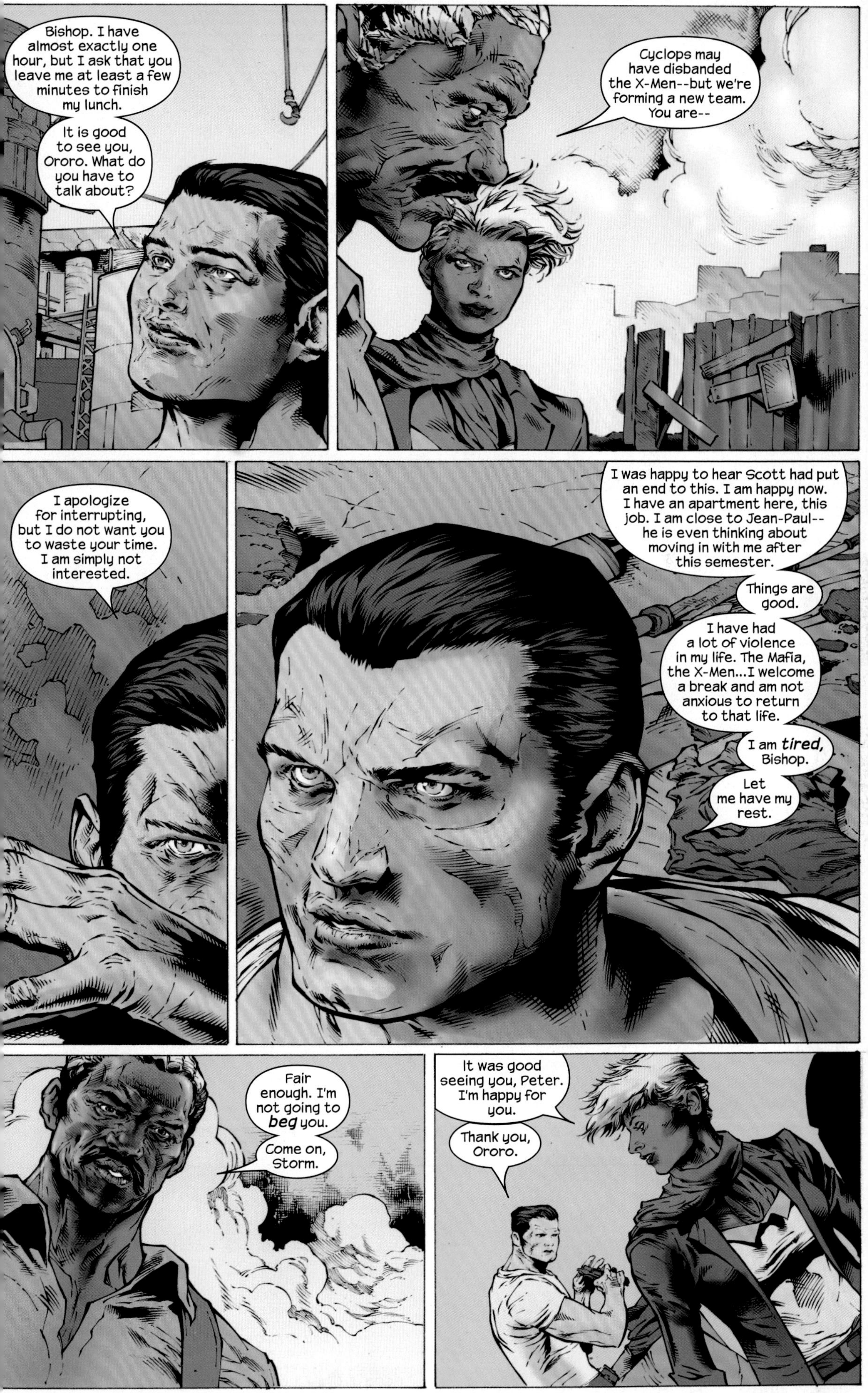
Bishop. I have almost exactly one hour, but I ask that you leave me at least a few minutes to finish my lunch.
It is good to see you, Ororo. What do you have to talk about?
Cyclops may have disbanded the X-Men--but we're forming a new team. You are--
I apologize for interrupting, but I do not want you to waste your time. I am simply not interested.
I was happy to hear Scott had put an end to this. I am happy now. I have an apartment here, this job. I am close to Jean-Paul--he is even thinking about moving in with me after this semester.
Things are good.
I have had a lot of violence in my life. The Mafia, the X-Men...I welcome a break and am not anxious to return to that life.
I am *tired,* Bishop.
Let me have my rest.
Fair enough. I'm not going to *beg* you.
Come on, Storm.
It was good seeing you, Peter. I'm happy for you.
Thank you, Ororo.

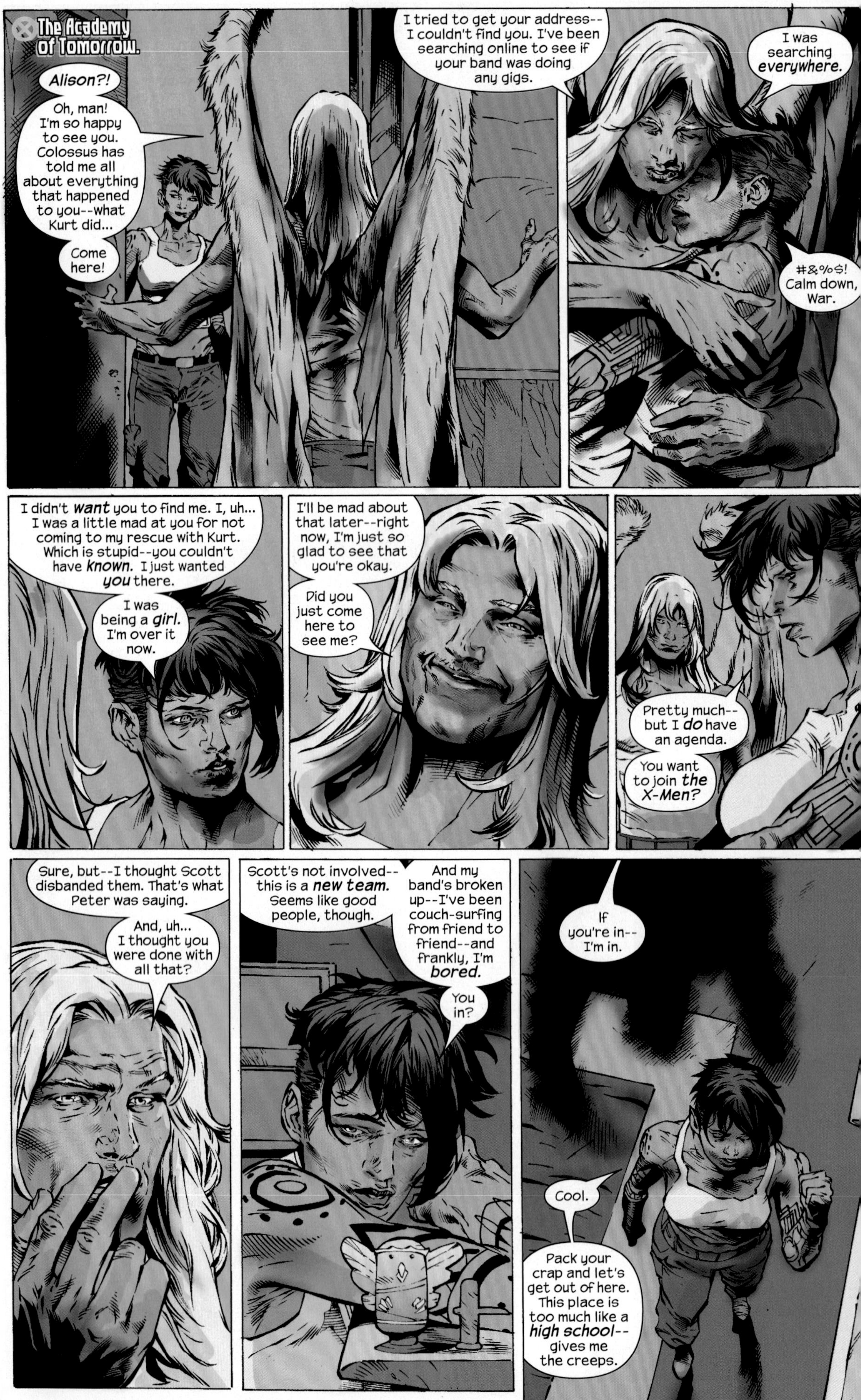
The Academy of Tomorrow.
Alison?!
Oh, man! I'm so happy to see you. Colossus has told me all about everything that happened to you--what Kurt did...
Come here!
I tried to get your address-- I couldn't find you. I've been searching online to see if your band was doing any gigs.
I was searching everywhere.
#&%$! Calm down, War.
I didn't want you to find me. I, uh... I was a little mad at you for not coming to my rescue with Kurt. Which is stupid--you couldn't have known. I just wanted you there.
I was being a girl. I'm over it now.
I'll be mad about that later--right now, I'm just so glad to see that you're okay.
Did you just come here to see me?
Pretty much-- but I do have an agenda.
You want to join the X-Men?
Sure, but--I thought Scott disbanded them. That's what Peter was saying.
And, uh... I thought you were done with all that?
Scott's not involved-- this is a new team. Seems like good people, though.
And my band's broken up--I've been couch-surfing from friend to friend--and frankly, I'm bored.
You in?
If you're in-- I'm in.
Cool.
Pack your crap and let's get out of here. This place is too much like a high school-- gives me the creeps.

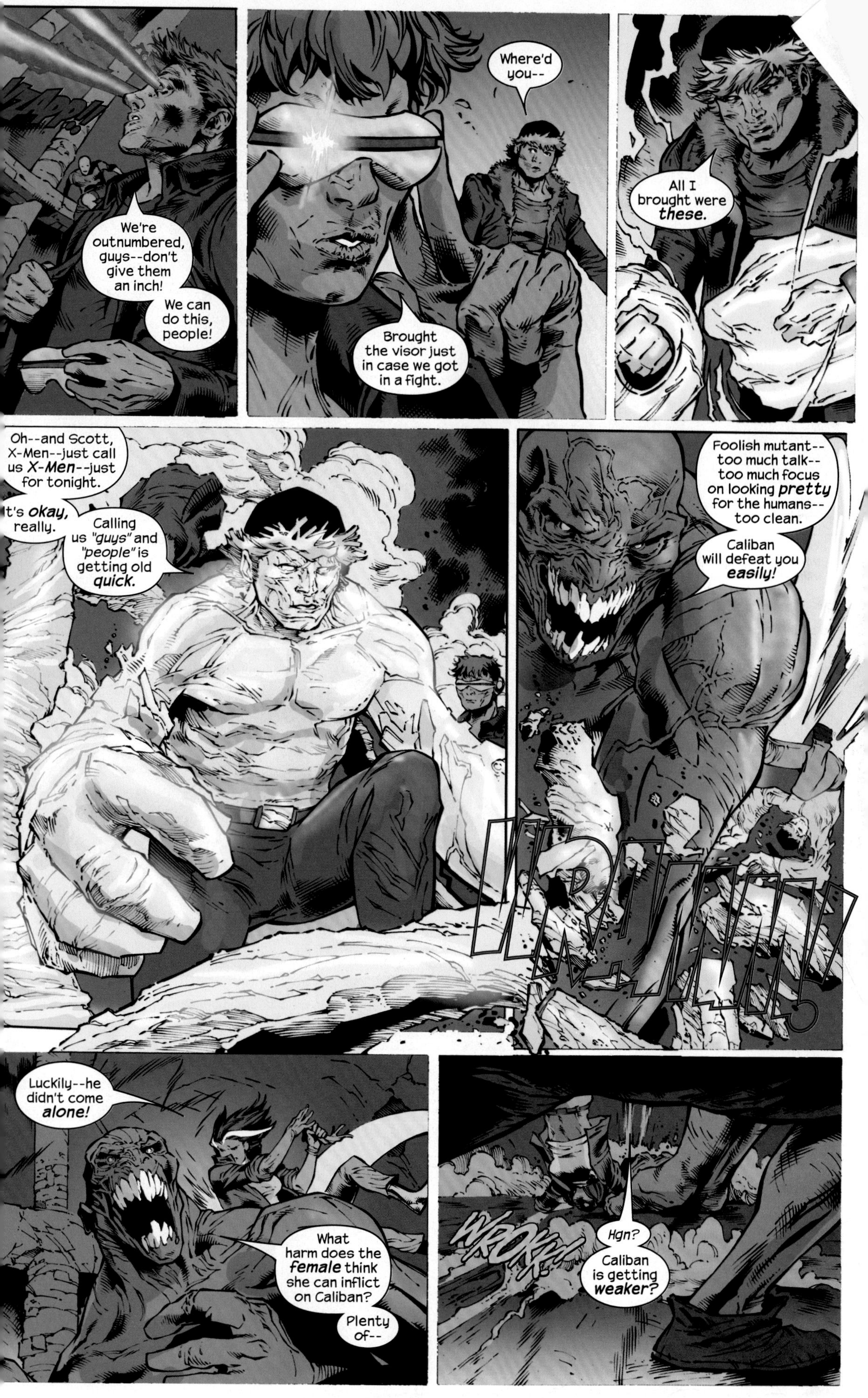

We're outnumbered, guys--don't give them an inch!
We can do this, people!
Where'd you--
Brought the visor just in case we got in a fight.
All I brought were *these.*
Oh--and Scott, X-Men--just call us *X-Men*--just for tonight.
t's *okay,* really.
Calling us *"guys"* and *"people"* is getting old *quick.*
Foolish mutant--too much talk--too much focus on looking *pretty* for the humans--too clean.
Caliban will defeat you *easily!*
Luckily--he didn't come *alone!*
What harm does the *female* think she can inflict on Caliban?
Plenty of--
Hgn?
Caliban is getting *weaker?*

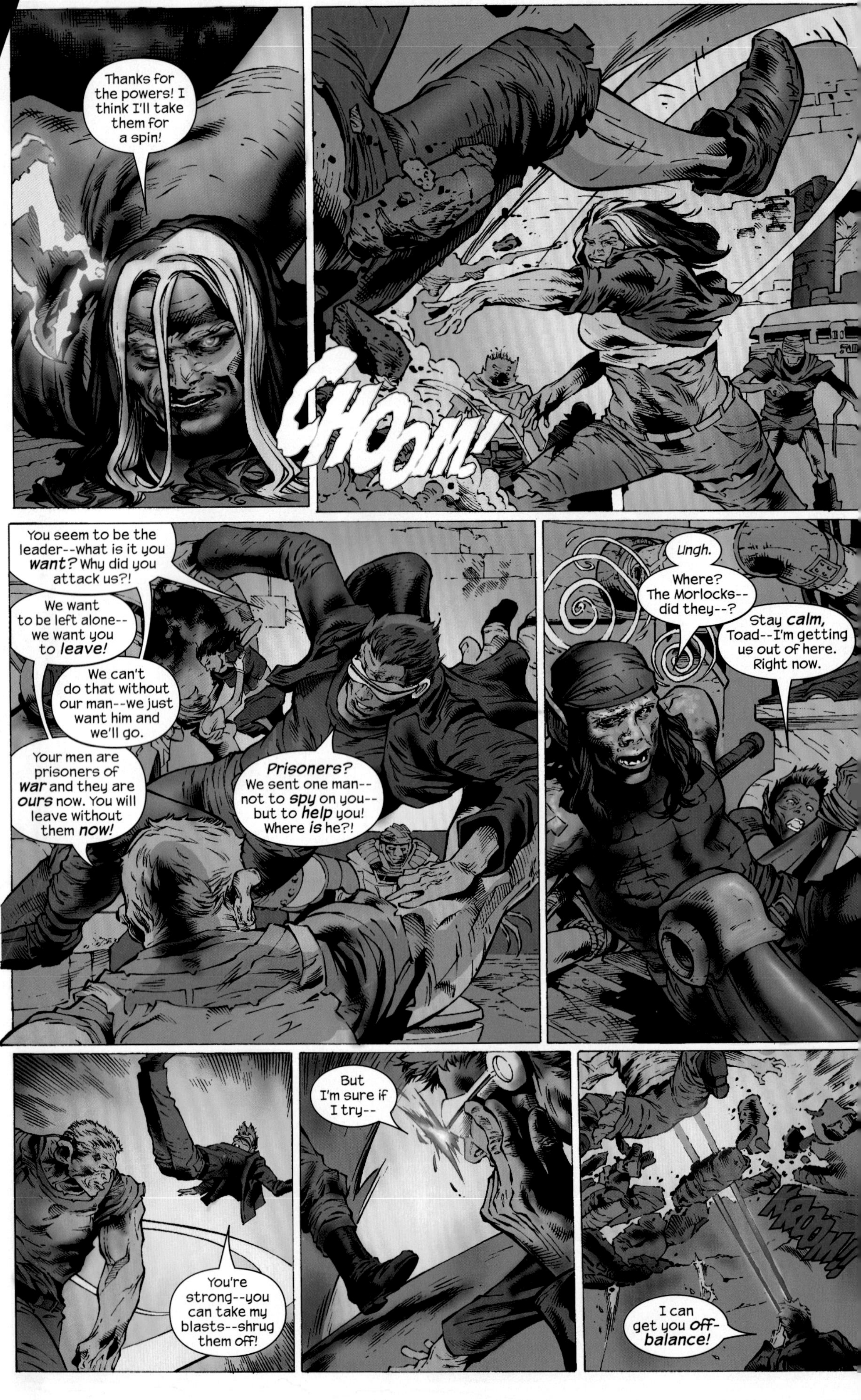

Thanks for the powers! I think I'll take them for a spin!
CHOOM!
You seem to be the leader--what is it you *want?* Why did you attack us?!
We want to be left alone--we want you to *leave!*
We can't do that without our man--we just want him and we'll go.
Your men are prisoners of *war* and they are *ours* now. You will leave without them *now!*
Prisoners? We sent one man--not to *spy* on you--but to *help* you! Where *is* he?!
Ungh.
Where? The Morlocks--did they--?
Stay *calm,* Toad--I'm getting us out of here. Right now.
You're strong--you can take my blasts--shrug them off!
But I'm sure if I try--
I can get you *off-balance!*

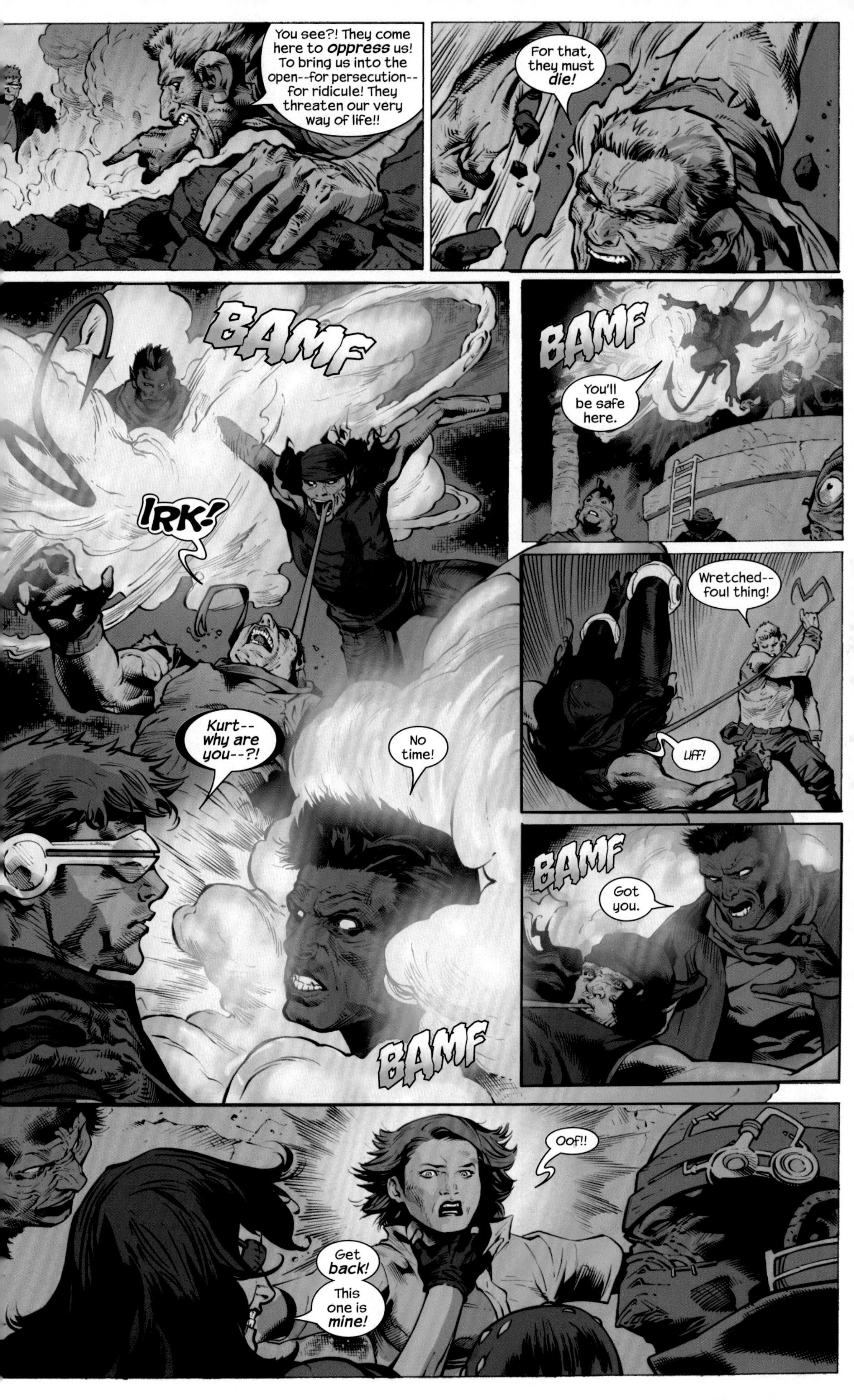
You see?! They come here to *oppress* us! To bring us into the open--for persecution--for ridicule! They threaten our very way of life!!
For that, they must *die!*
BAMF
IRK!
BAMF
You'll be safe here.
Wretched--foul thing!
Uff!
Kurt--why are you--?!
No time!
BAMF
Got you.
BAMF
Oof!!
Get *back!*
This one is *mine!*

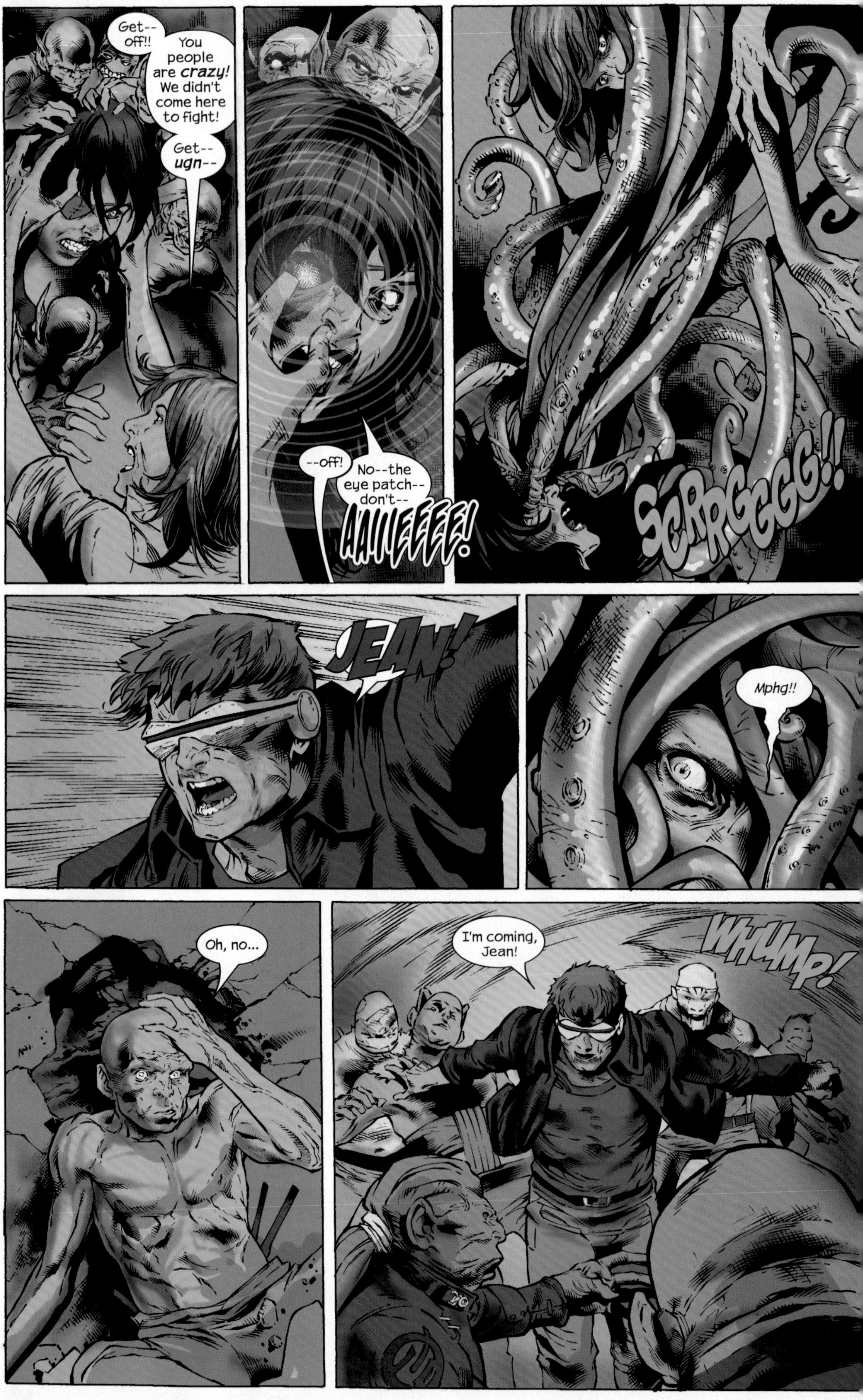
Get--
off!!
You people are crazy! We didn't come here to fight!
Get--
ugn--
--off!
No--the eye patch--don't--
AAIIIEEEE!
SCRRGGGG!!
JEAN!
Mphg!!
Oh, no...
I'm coming, Jean!
WHUMP!

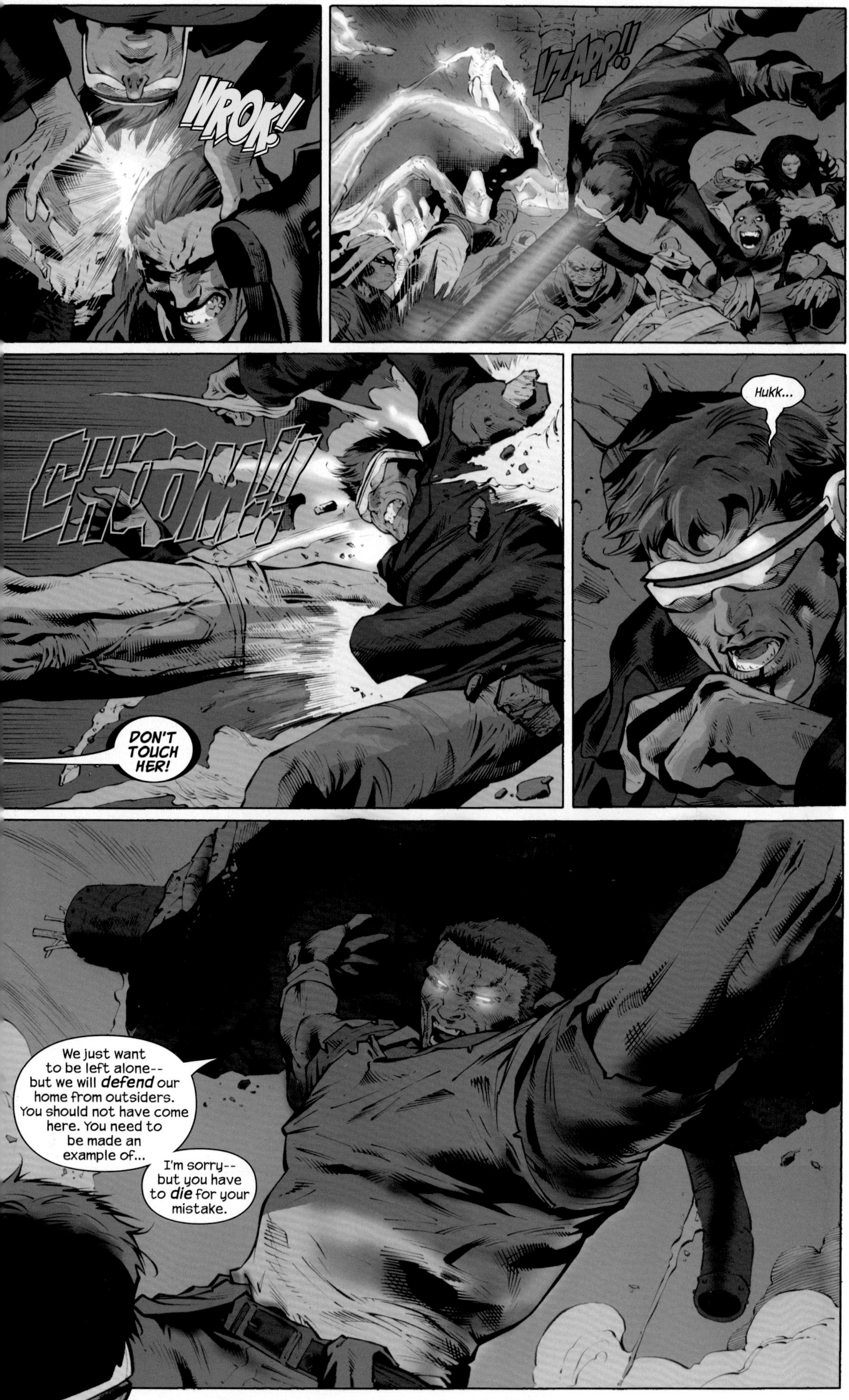
WROK!
VZAPP!!
CHOOM!!
DON'T TOUCH HER!
Hukk...
We just want to be left alone-- but we will *defend* our home from outsiders. You should not have come here. You need to be made an example of...
I'm sorry-- but you have to *die* for your mistake.

BAMF

No.

He doesn't.

RRR·RRR·RRR·KKK!

Kurt. What did you *do*?

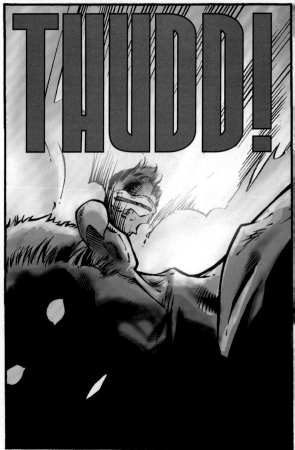

THUDD!

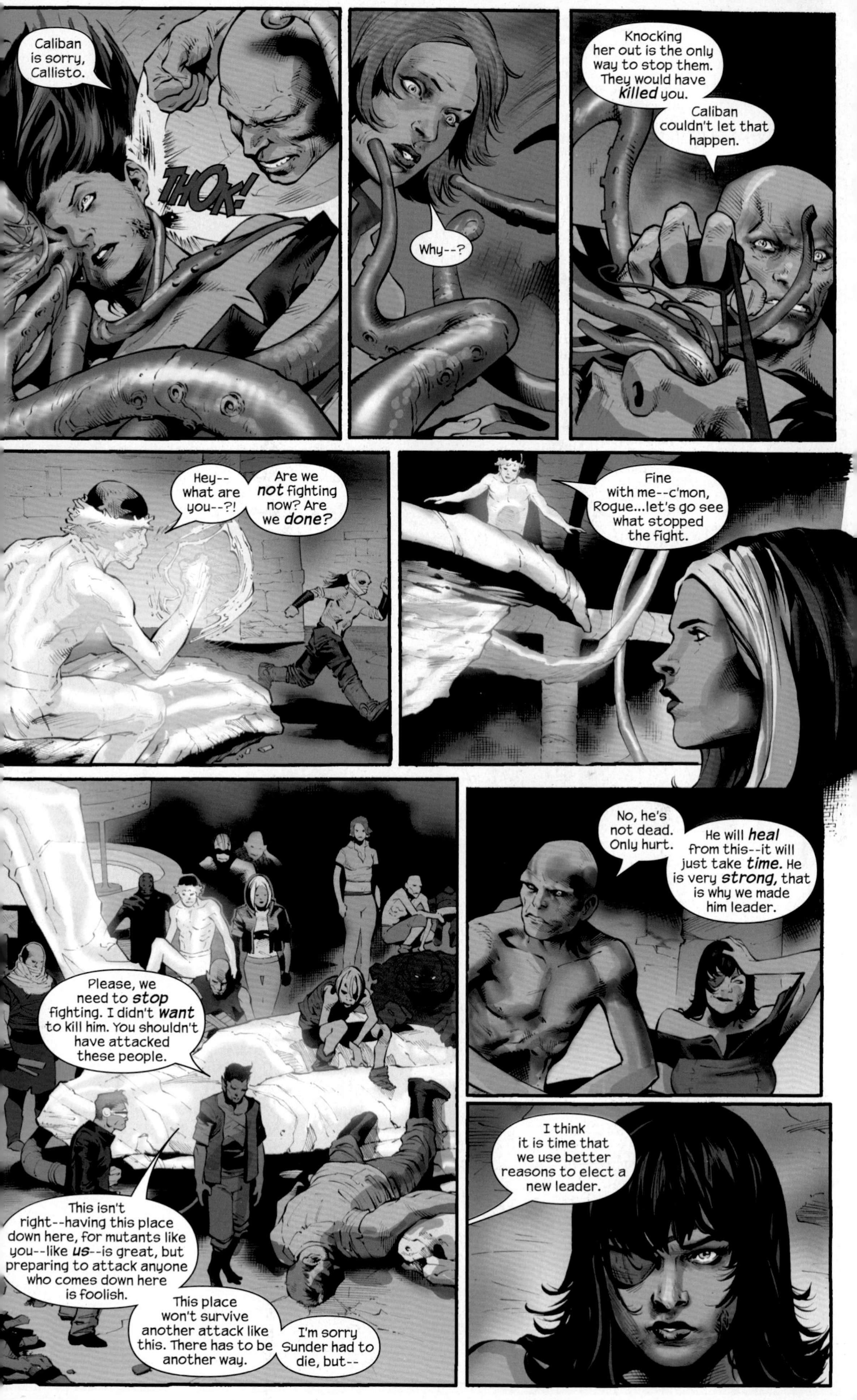
Caliban is sorry, Callisto.
THOK!
Why--?
Knocking her out is the only way to stop them. They would have *killed* you.
Caliban couldn't let that happen.
Hey--what are you--?!
Are we *not* fighting now? Are we *done?*
Fine with me--c'mon, Rogue...let's go see what stopped the fight.
Please, we need to *stop* fighting. I didn't *want* to kill him. You shouldn't have attacked these people.
This isn't right--having this place down here, for mutants like you--like *us*--is great, but preparing to attack anyone who comes down here is foolish.
This place won't survive another attack like this. There has to be another way.
I'm sorry Sunder had to die, but--
No, he's not dead. Only hurt.
He will *heal* from this--it will just take *time.* He is very *strong,* that is why we made him leader.
I think it is time that we use better reasons to elect a new leader.

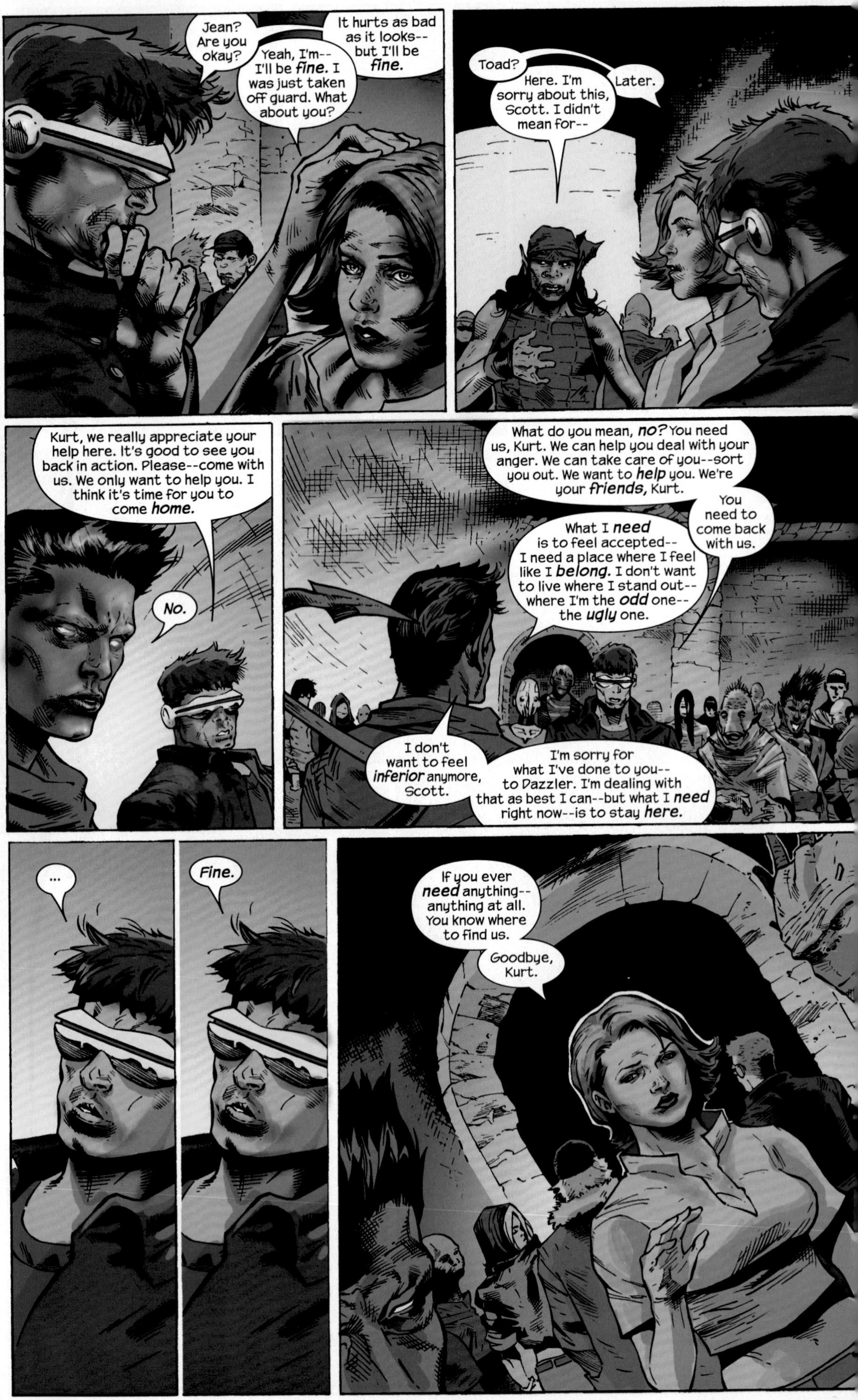
Jean? Are you okay?
Yeah, I'm-- I'll be fine. I was just taken off guard. What about you?
It hurts as bad as it looks-- but I'll be fine.
Toad?
Here. I'm sorry about this, Scott. I didn't mean for--
Later.
Kurt, we really appreciate your help here. It's good to see you back in action. Please--come with us. We only want to help you. I think it's time for you to come home.
No.
What do you mean, no? You need us, Kurt. We can help you deal with your anger. We can take care of you--sort you out. We want to help you. We're your friends, Kurt.
You need to come back with us.
What I need is to feel accepted-- I need a place where I feel like I belong. I don't want to live where I stand out-- where I'm the odd one-- the ugly one.
I don't want to feel inferior anymore, Scott.
I'm sorry for what I've done to you-- to Dazzler. I'm dealing with that as best I can--but what I need right now--is to stay here.
...
Fine.
If you ever need anything-- anything at all. You know where to find us.
Goodbye, Kurt.

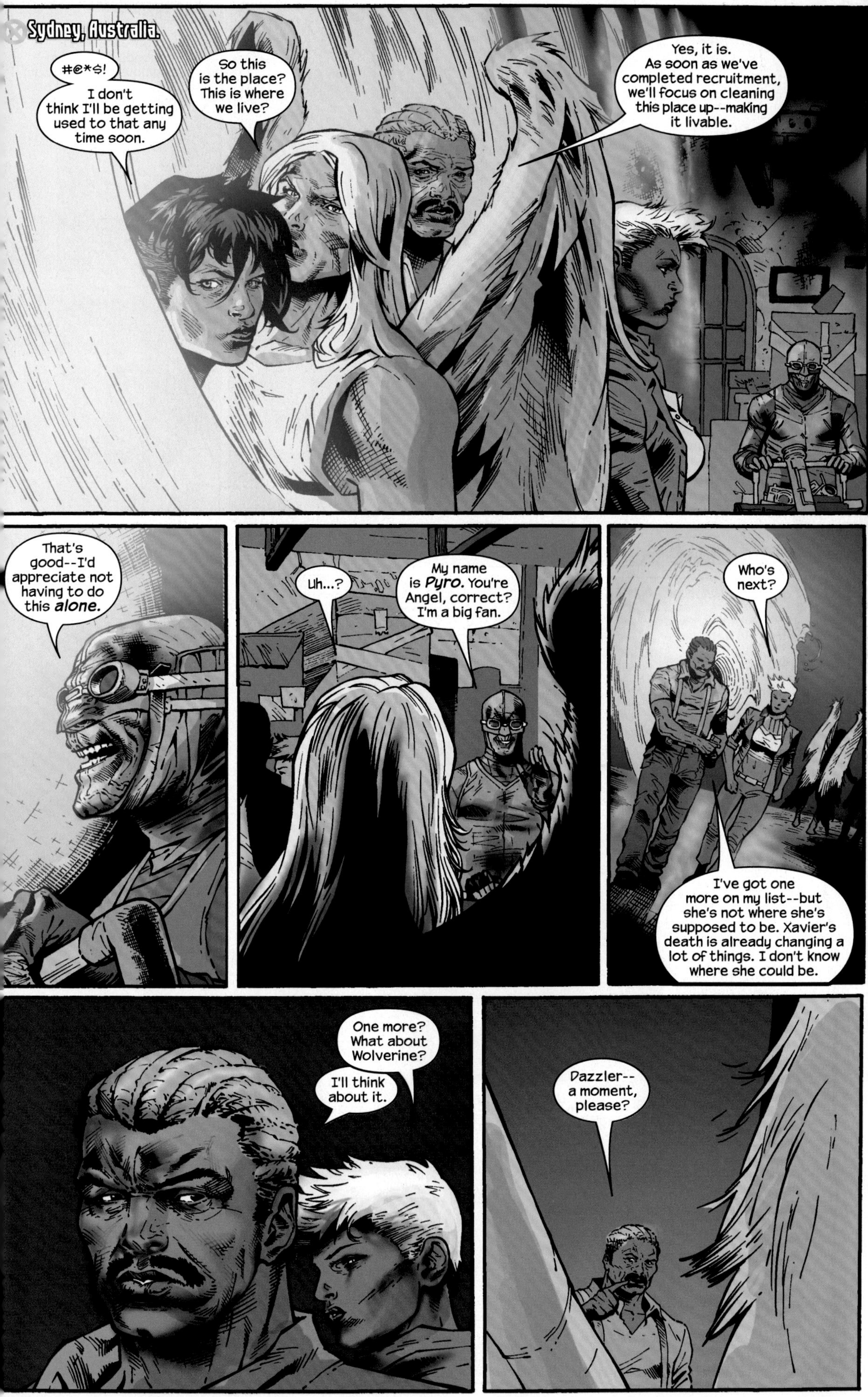
Sydney, Australia.
#@*$! I don't think I'll be getting used to that any time soon.
So this is the place? This is where we live?
Yes, it is. As soon as we've completed recruitment, we'll focus on cleaning this place up--making it livable.
That's good--I'd appreciate not having to do this *alone.*
Uh...?
My name is *Pyro.* You're Angel, correct? I'm a big fan.
Who's next?
I've got one more on my list--but she's not where she's supposed to be. Xavier's death is already changing a lot of things. I don't know where she could be.
One more? What about Wolverine?
I'll think about it.
Dazzler-- a moment, please?

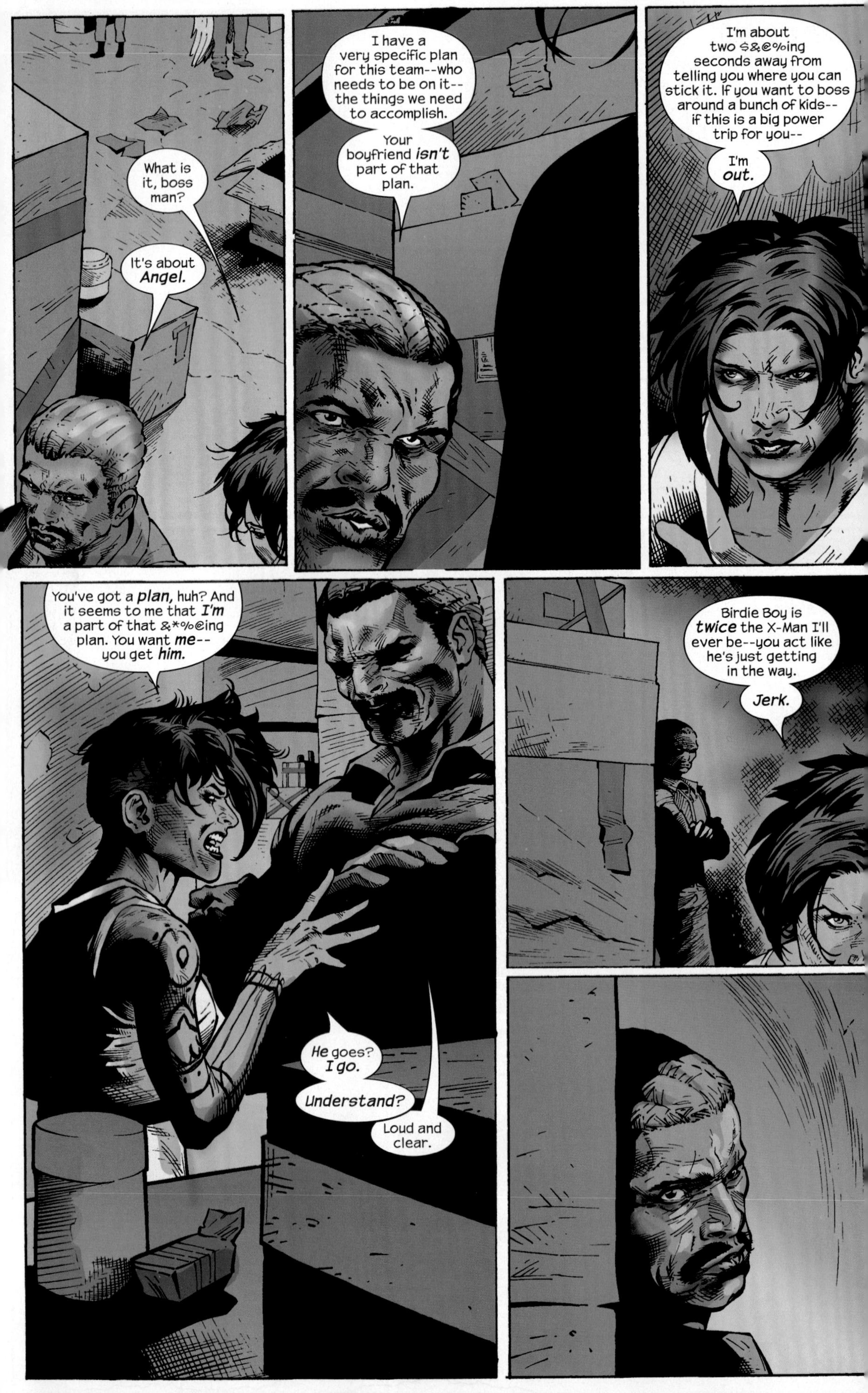
What is it, boss man?
It's about *Angel.*
I have a very specific plan for this team--who needs to be on it-- the things we need to accomplish.
Your boyfriend *isn't* part of that plan.
I'm about two $&@%ing seconds away from telling you where you can stick it. If you want to boss around a bunch of kids-- if this is a big power trip for you--
I'm *out.*
You've got a *plan,* huh? And it seems to me that *I'm* a part of that &*%@ing plan. You want *me*-- you get *him.*
He goes? *I go.*
Understand?
Loud and clear.
Birdie Boy is *twice* the X-Man I'll ever be--you act like he's just getting in the way.
Jerk.

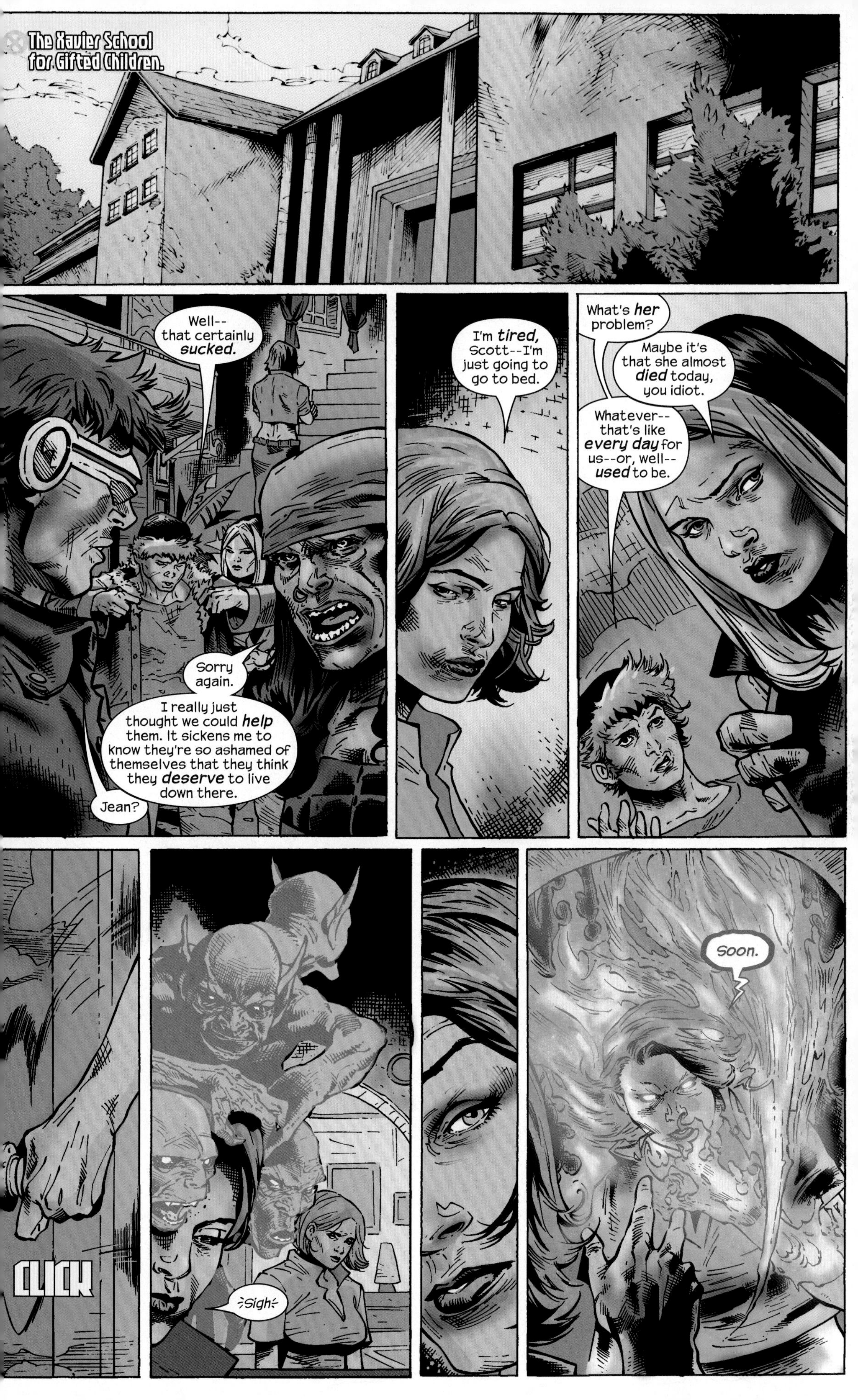
The Xavier School for Gifted Children.
Well-- that certainly *sucked.*
Sorry again.
I really just thought we could *help* them. It sickens me to know they're so ashamed of themselves that they think they *deserve* to live down there.
Jean?
I'm *tired,* Scott--I'm just going to go to bed.
What's *her* problem?
Maybe it's that she almost *died* today, you idiot.
Whatever-- that's like *every day* for us--or, well-- *used* to be.
CLICK
Sigh
Soon.

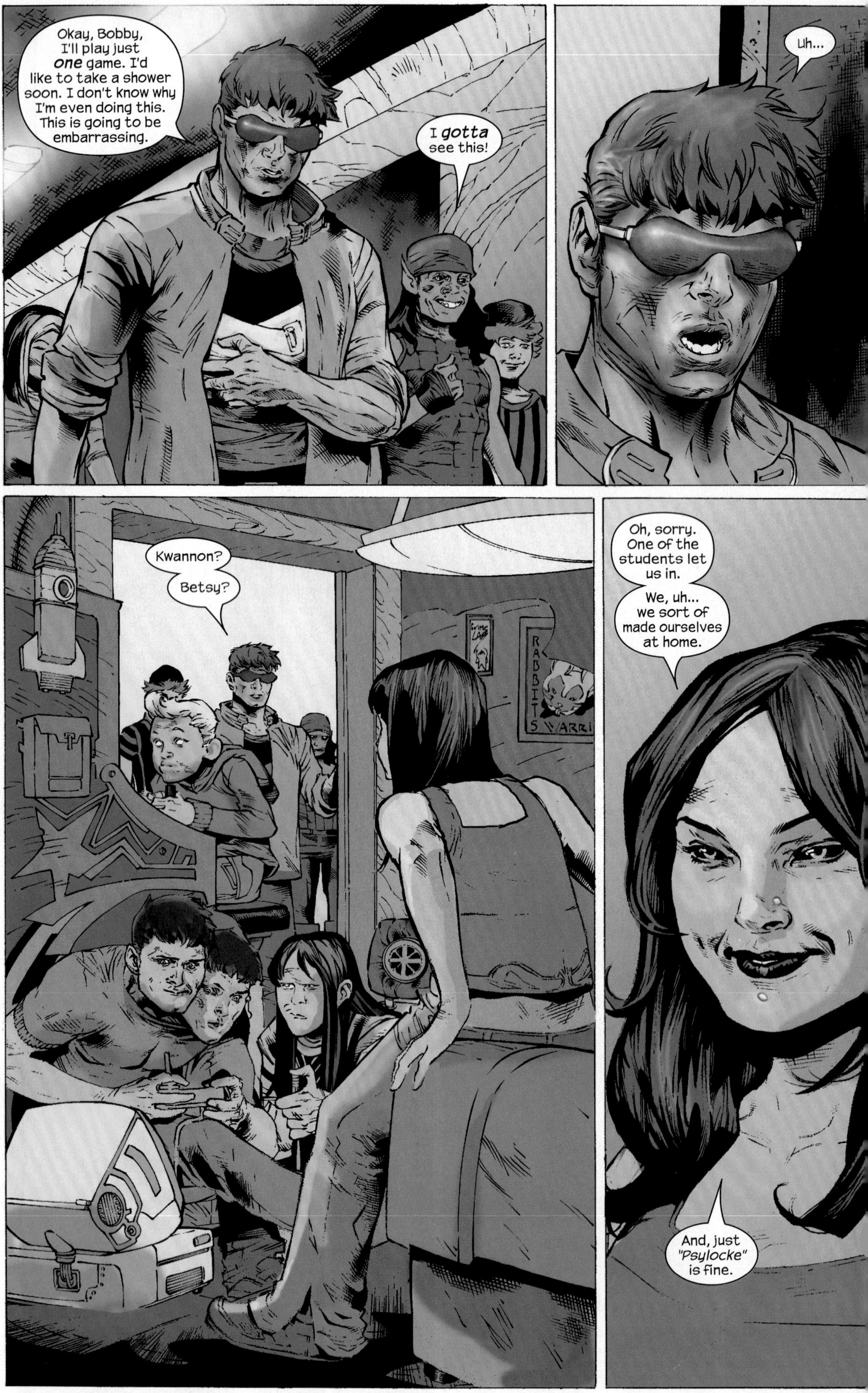

Okay, Bobby, I'll play just *one* game. I'd like to take a shower soon. I don't know why I'm even doing this. This is going to be embarrassing.
I *gotta* see this!
Uh...
Kwannon?
Betsy?
Oh, sorry. One of the students let us in.
We, uh... we sort of made ourselves at home.
And, just "*Psylocke*" is fine.

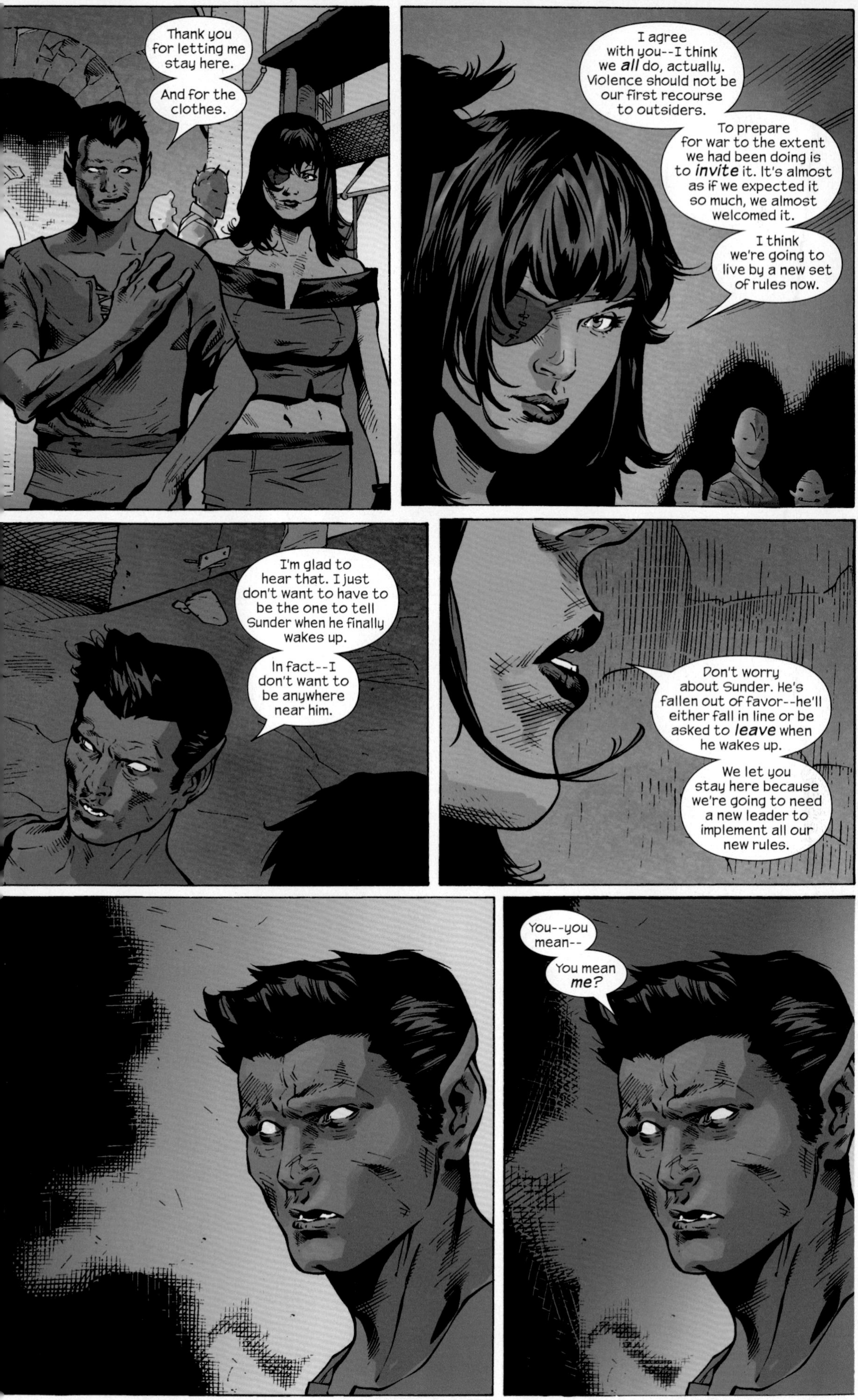
Thank you for letting me stay here.
And for the clothes.
I agree with you--I think we *all* do, actually. Violence should not be our first recourse to outsiders.
To prepare for war to the extent we had been doing is to *invite* it. It's almost as if we expected it so much, we almost welcomed it.
I think we're going to live by a new set of rules now.
I'm glad to hear that. I just don't want to have to be the one to tell Sunder when he finally wakes up.
In fact--I don't want to be anywhere near him.
Don't worry about Sunder. He's fallen out of favor--he'll either fall in line or be asked to *leave* when he wakes up.
We let you stay here because we're going to need a new leader to implement all our new rules.
You--you mean--
You mean *me?*

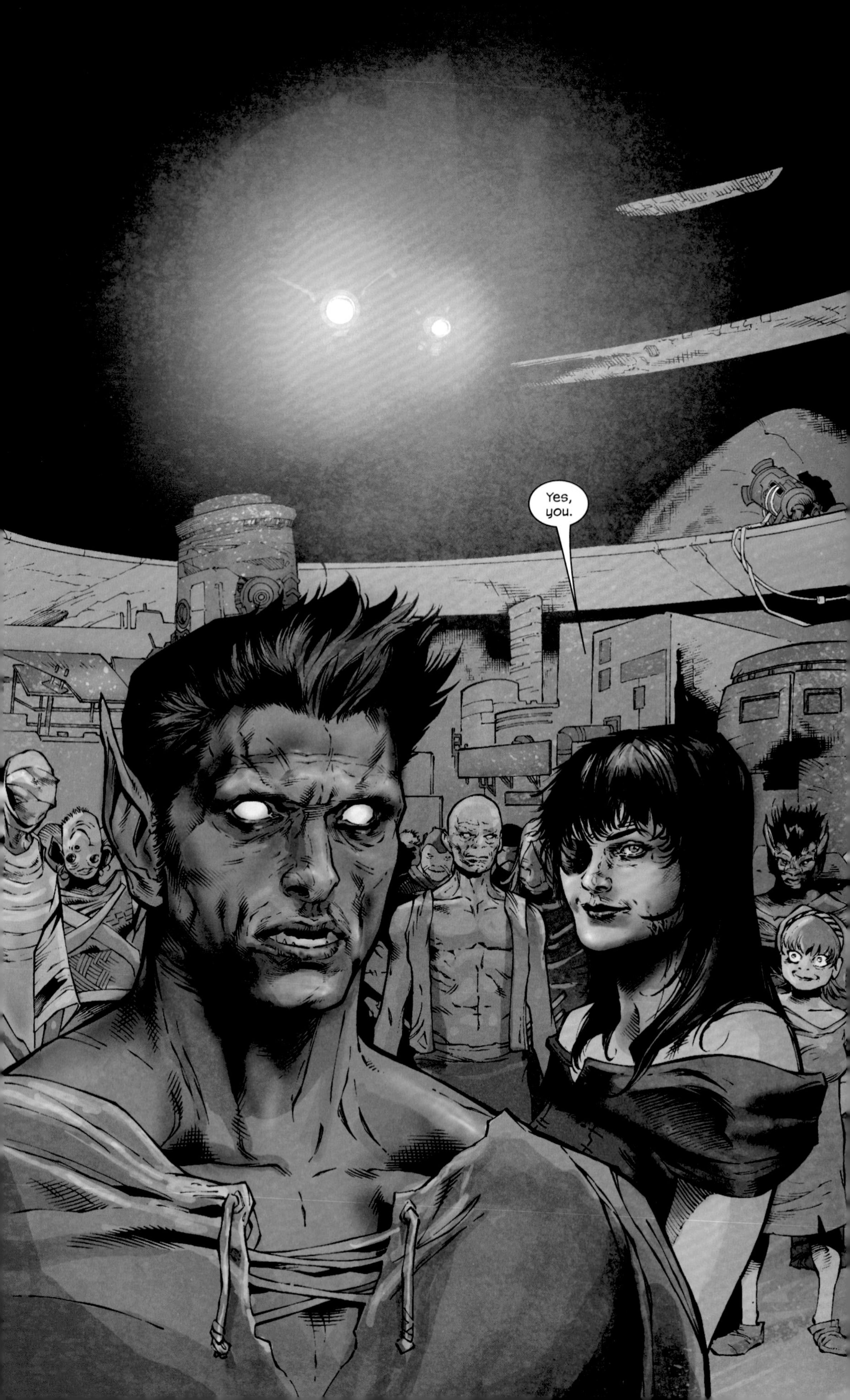
Yes, you.

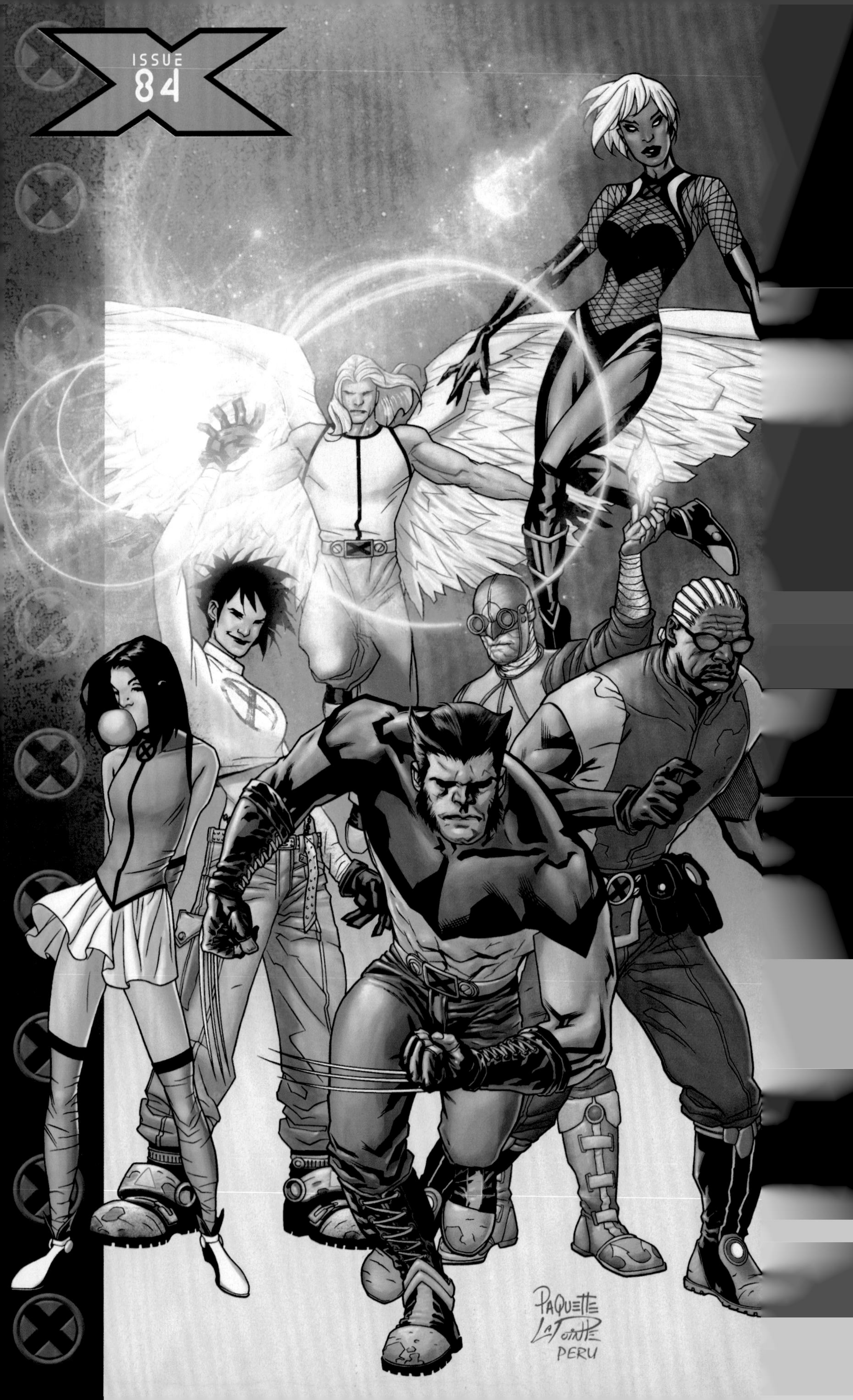
ISSUE
84
PAQUETTE
LAPOINTE
PERU

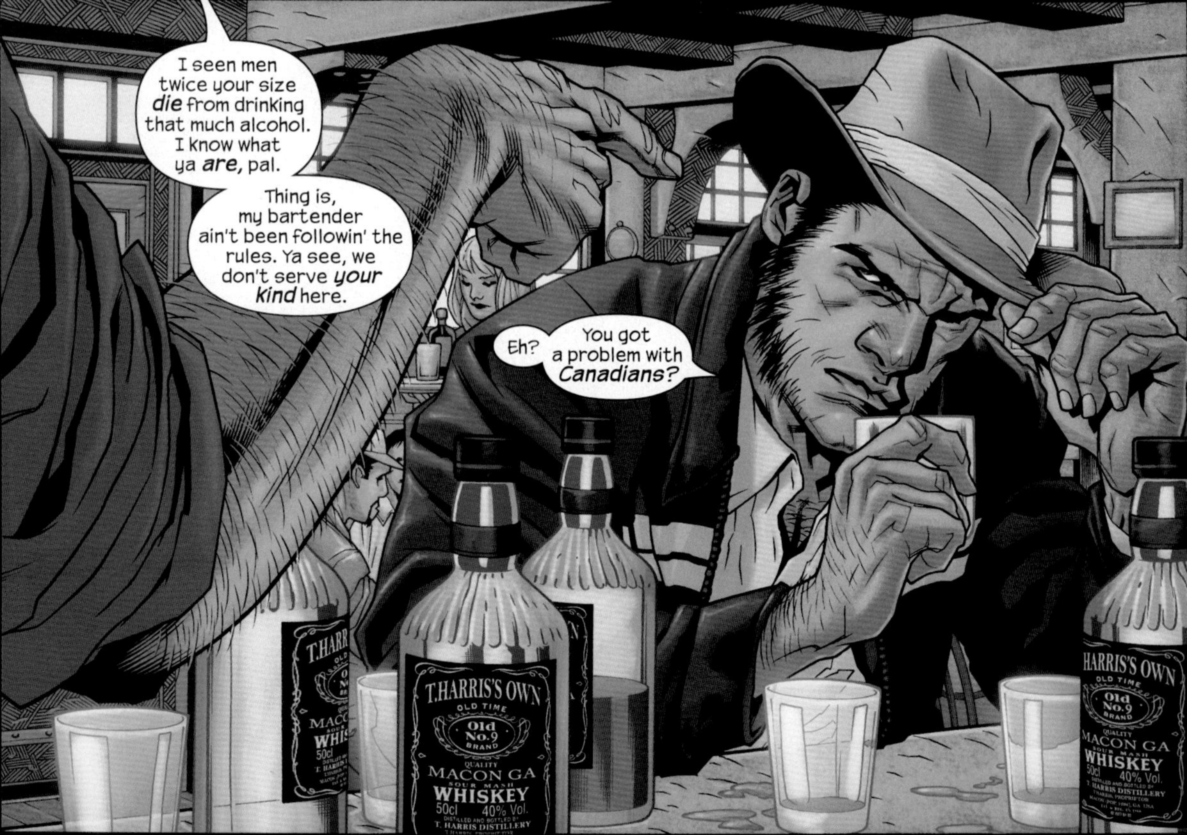
I seen men twice your size *die* from drinking that much alcohol. I know what ya *are*, pal.
Thing is, my bartender ain't been followin' the rules. Ya see, we don't serve *your kind* here.
Eh?
You got a problem with *Canadians?*
T.HARRIS'S OWN
OLD TIME
Old No.9 BRAND
QUALITY
MACON GA
SOUR MASH
WHISKEY
50cl 40% Vol.
DISTILLED AND BOTTLED BY
T. HARRIS DISTILLERY

SENTINELS

PART 1 (OF 5)

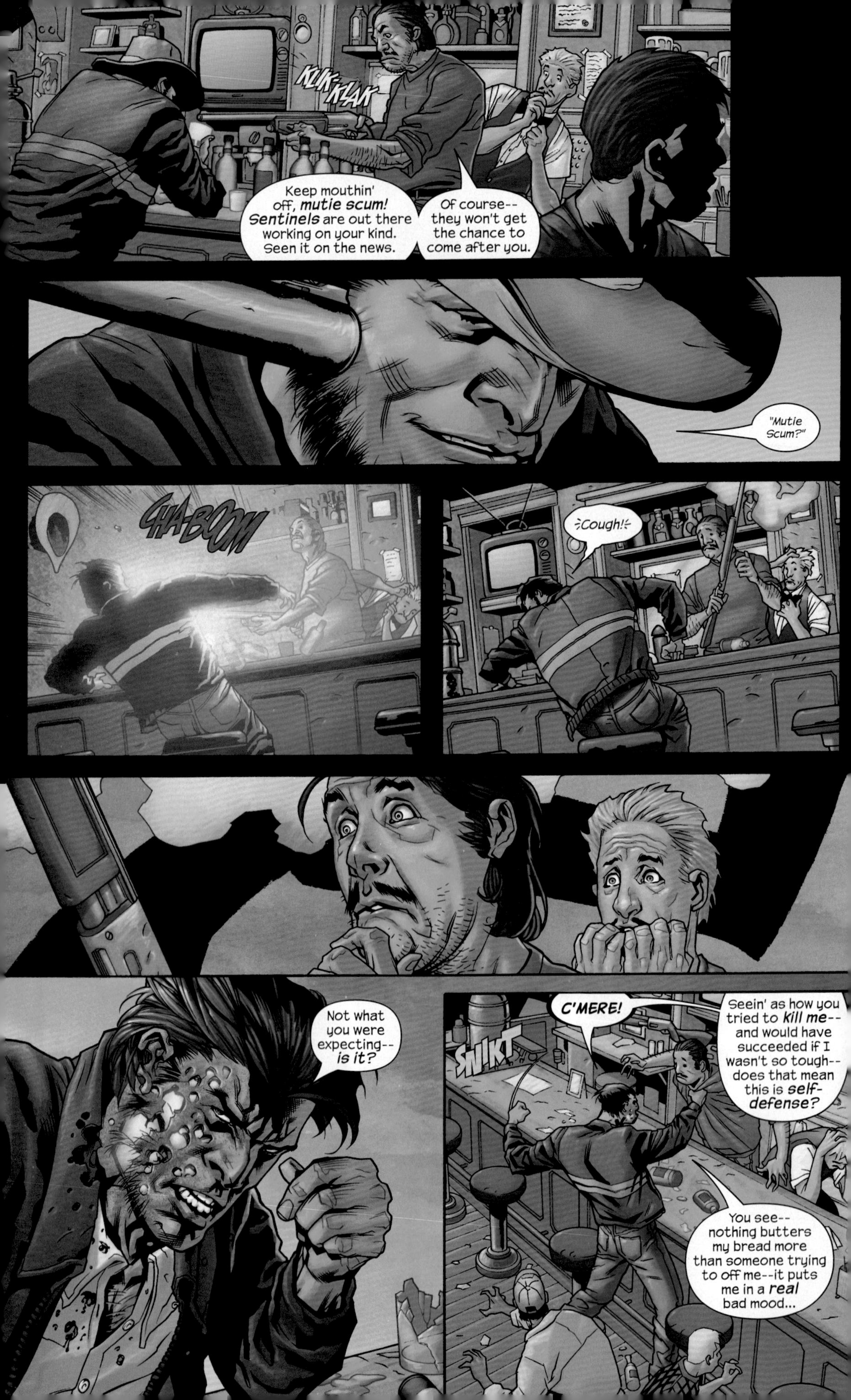
KLIK KLAK
Keep mouthin' off, *mutie scum!* *Sentinels* are out there working on your kind. Seen it on the news.
Of course-- they won't get the chance to come after you.
"Mutie Scum?"
CHA-BOOM
Cough!
Not what you were expecting-- *is it?*
SNIKT
C'MERE!
Seein' as how you tried to *kill me*-- and would have succeeded if I wasn't so tough-- does that mean this is *self-defense?*
You see-- nothing butters my bread more than someone trying to off me--it puts me in a *real* bad mood...

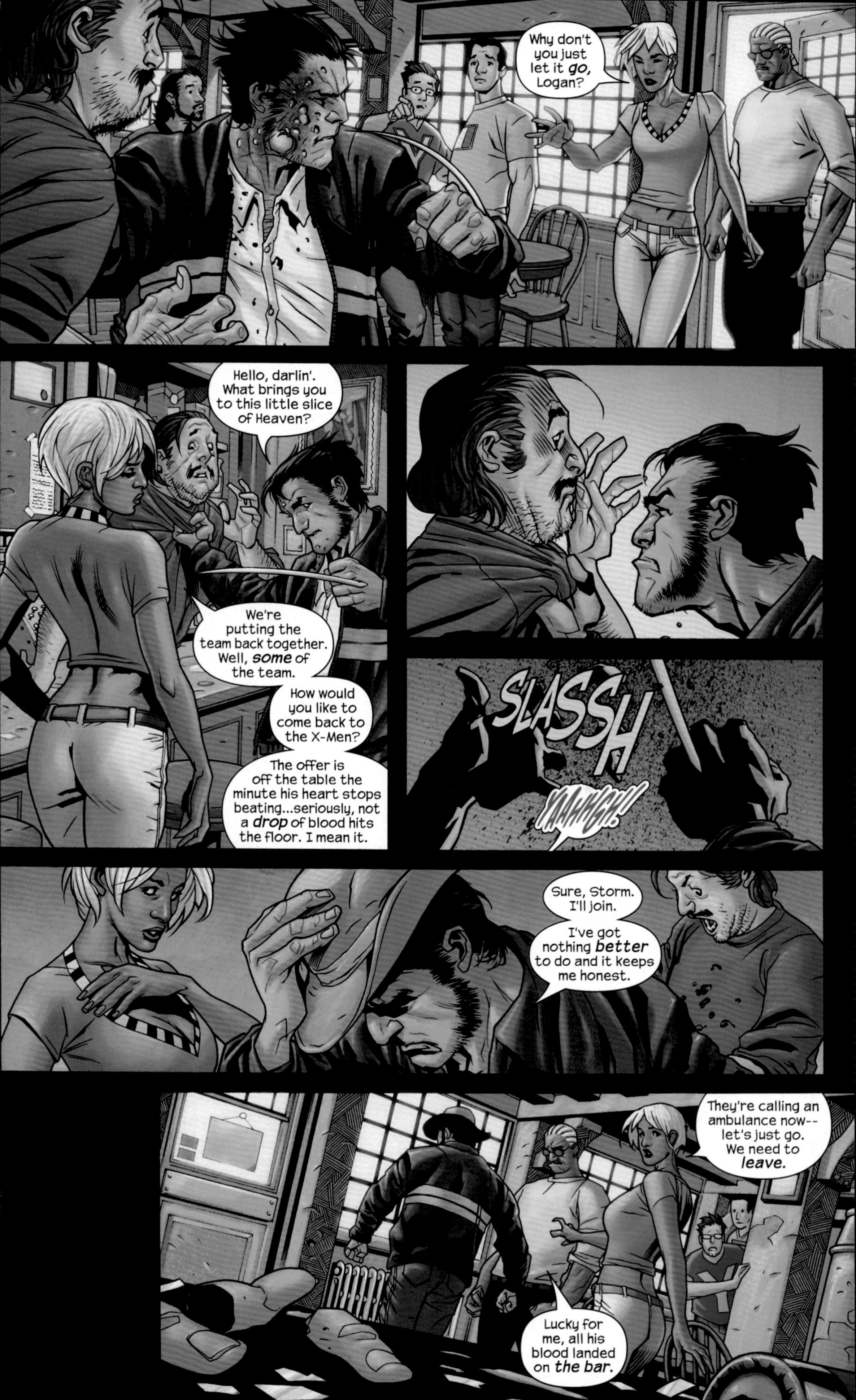
Why don't you just let it go, Logan?
Hello, darlin'. What brings you to this little slice of Heaven?
We're putting the team back together. Well, some of the team.
How would you like to come back to the X-Men?
The offer is off the table the minute his heart stops beating...seriously, not a drop of blood hits the floor. I mean it.
SLASSH
YAAHHGH!
Sure, Storm. I'll join.
I've got nothing better to do and it keeps me honest.
They're calling an ambulance now-- let's just go. We need to leave.
Lucky for me, all his blood landed on the bar.

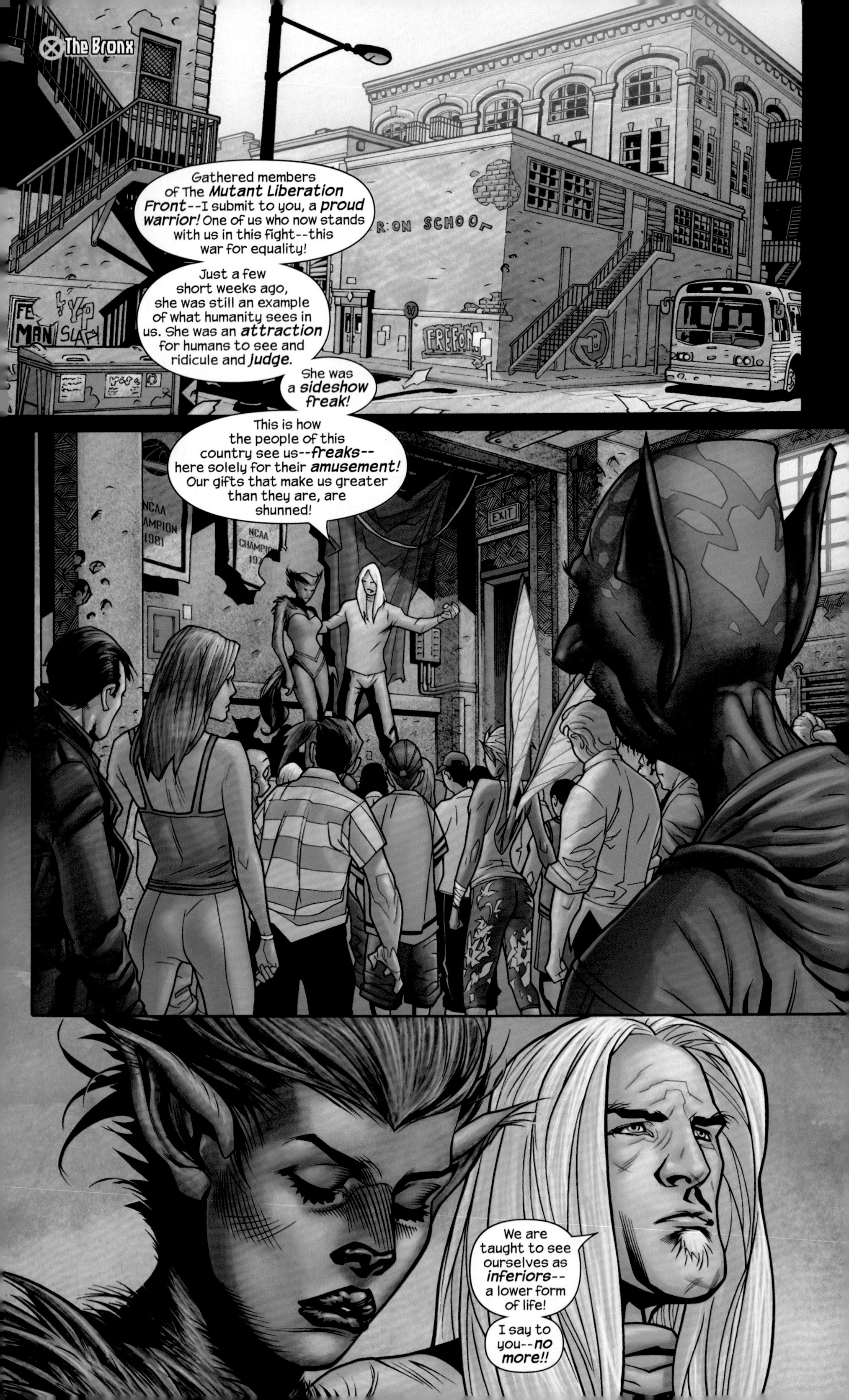
The Bronx
Gathered members of The Mutant Liberation Front--I submit to you, a proud warrior! One of us who now stands with us in this fight--this war for equality!
Just a few short weeks ago, she was still an example of what humanity sees in us. She was an attraction for humans to see and ridicule and judge.
She was a sideshow freak!
R ON SCHOO
This is how the people of this country see us--freaks--here solely for their amusement! Our gifts that make us greater than they are, are shunned!
EXIT
We are taught to see ourselves as inferiors--a lower form of life!
I say to you--no more!!

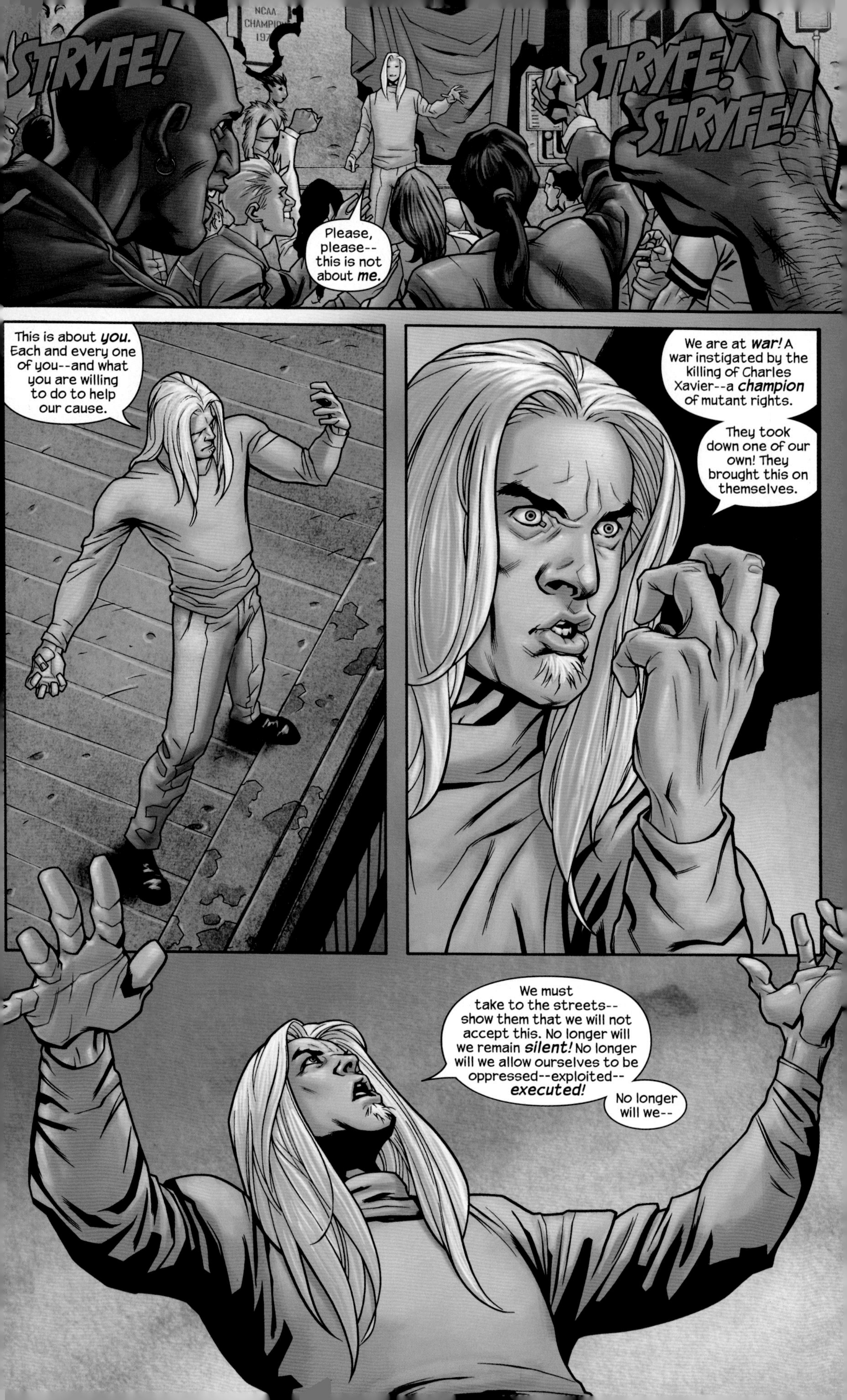
STRYFE!
STRYFE!
STRYFE!
Please, please--this is not about *me*.
This is about *you*. Each and every one of you--and what you are willing to do to help our cause.
We are at *war!* A war instigated by the killing of Charles Xavier--a *champion* of mutant rights.
They took down one of our own! They brought this on themselves.
We must take to the streets--show them that we will not accept this. No longer will we remain *silent!* No longer will we allow ourselves to be oppressed--exploited--*executed!*
No longer will we--

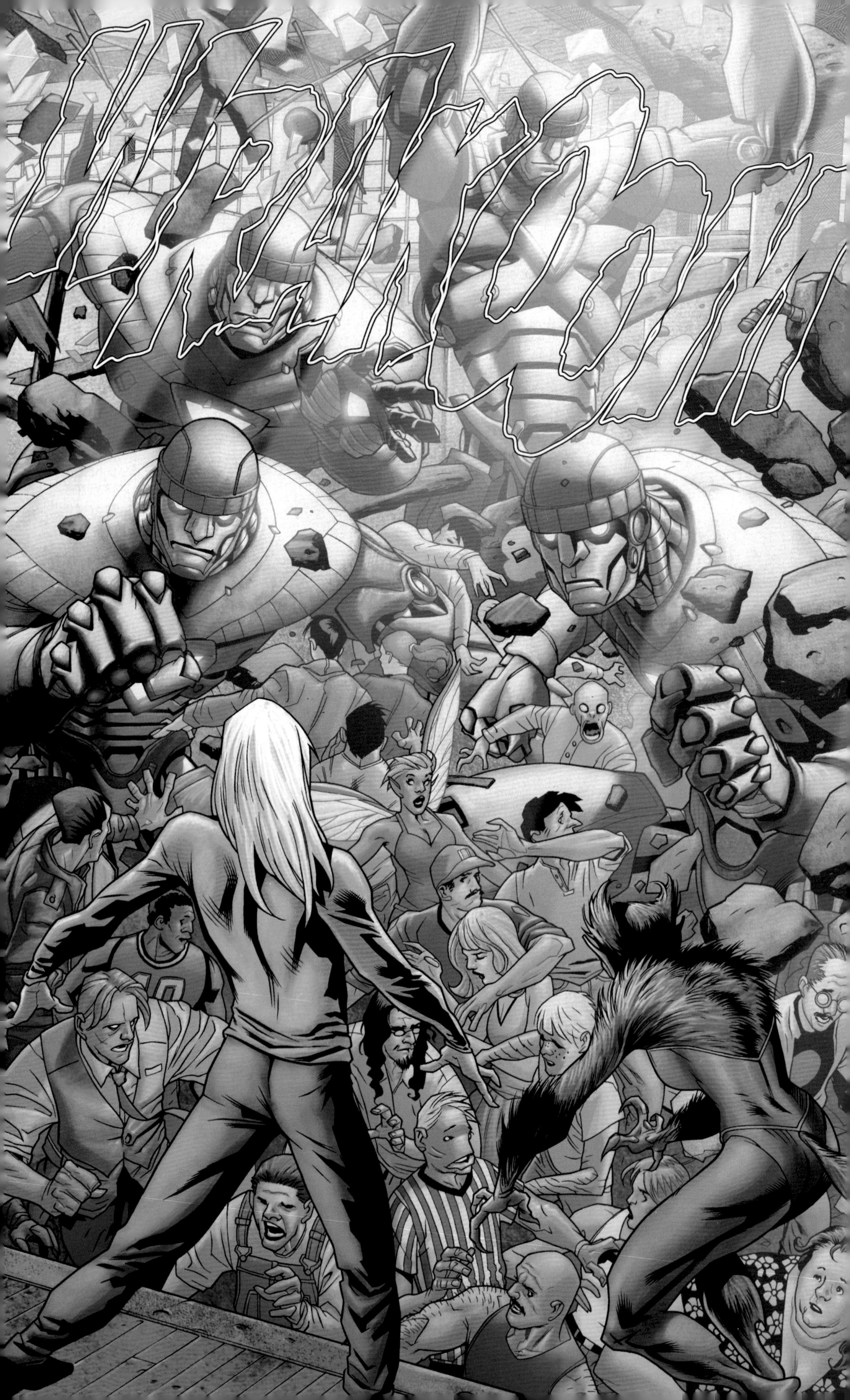

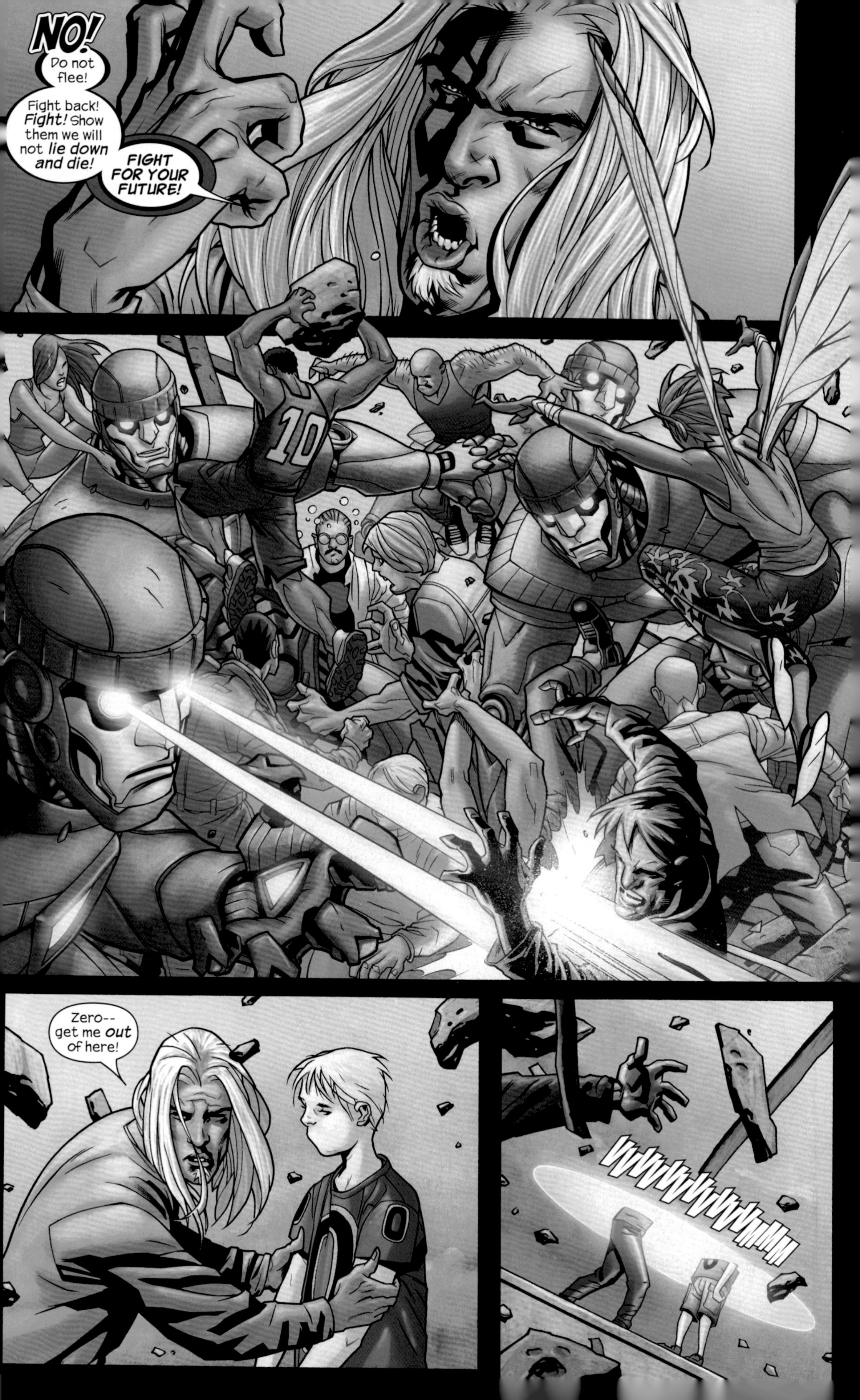
NO!
Do not flee!
Fight back! Fight! Show them we will not lie down and die!
FIGHT FOR YOUR FUTURE!
Zero-- get me out of here!
VVVVVVVVVVVVVVVMMM

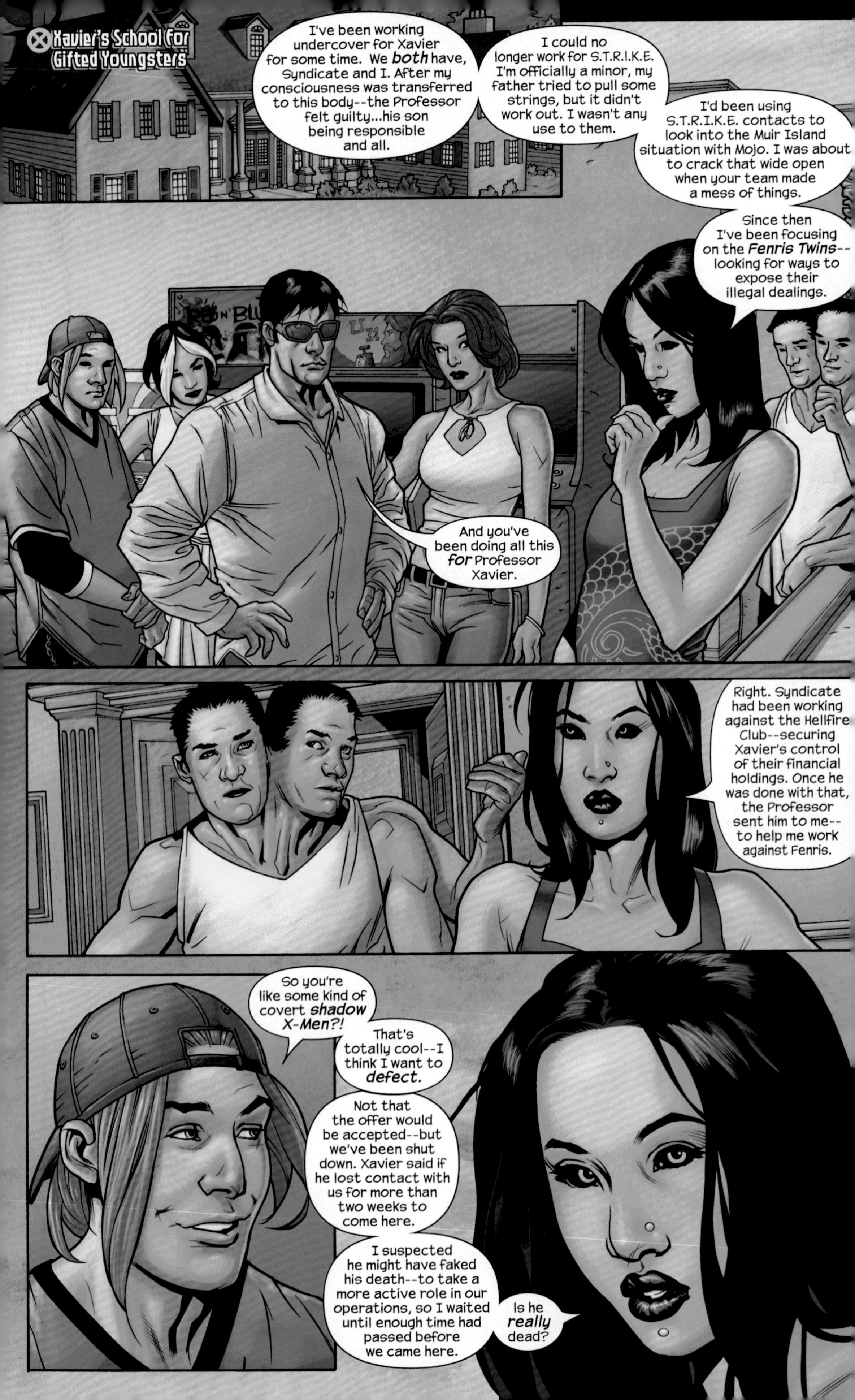
Xavier's School for Gifted Youngsters
I've been working undercover for Xavier for some time. We both have, Syndicate and I. After my consciousness was transferred to this body--the Professor felt guilty...his son being responsible and all.
I could no longer work for S.T.R.I.K.E. I'm officially a minor, my father tried to pull some strings, but it didn't work out. I wasn't any use to them.
I'd been using S.T.R.I.K.E. contacts to look into the Muir Island situation with Mojo. I was about to crack that wide open when your team made a mess of things.
Since then I've been focusing on the Fenris Twins--looking for ways to expose their illegal dealings.
And you've been doing all this for Professor Xavier.
Right. Syndicate had been working against the Hellfire Club--securing Xavier's control of their financial holdings. Once he was done with that, the Professor sent him to me--to help me work against Fenris.
So you're like some kind of covert shadow X-Men?!
That's totally cool--I think I want to defect.
Not that the offer would be accepted--but we've been shut down. Xavier said if he lost contact with us for more than two weeks to come here.
I suspected he might have faked his death--to take a more active role in our operations, so I waited until enough time had passed before we came here.
Is he really dead?

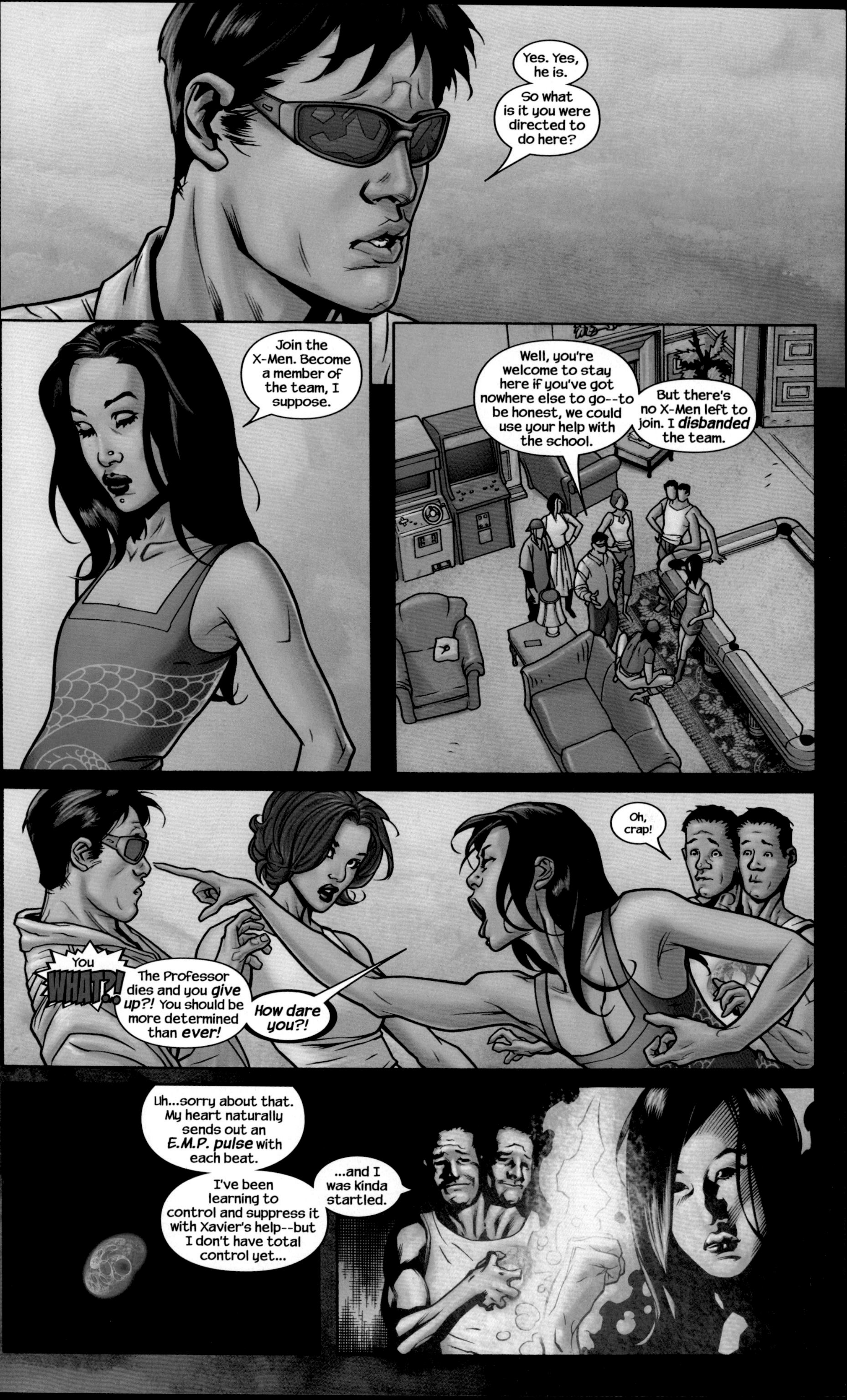
Yes. Yes, he is.
So what is it you were directed to do here?
Join the X-Men. Become a member of the team, I suppose.
Well, you're welcome to stay here if you've got nowhere else to go--to be honest, we could use your help with the school.
But there's no X-Men left to join. I *disbanded* the team.
Oh, crap!
You WHAT?!
The Professor dies and you *give up?!* You should be more determined than *ever!*
How dare you?!
Uh...sorry about that. My heart naturally sends out an *E.M.P. pulse* with each beat.
I've been learning to control and suppress it with Xavier's help--but I don't have total control yet...
...and I was kinda startled.

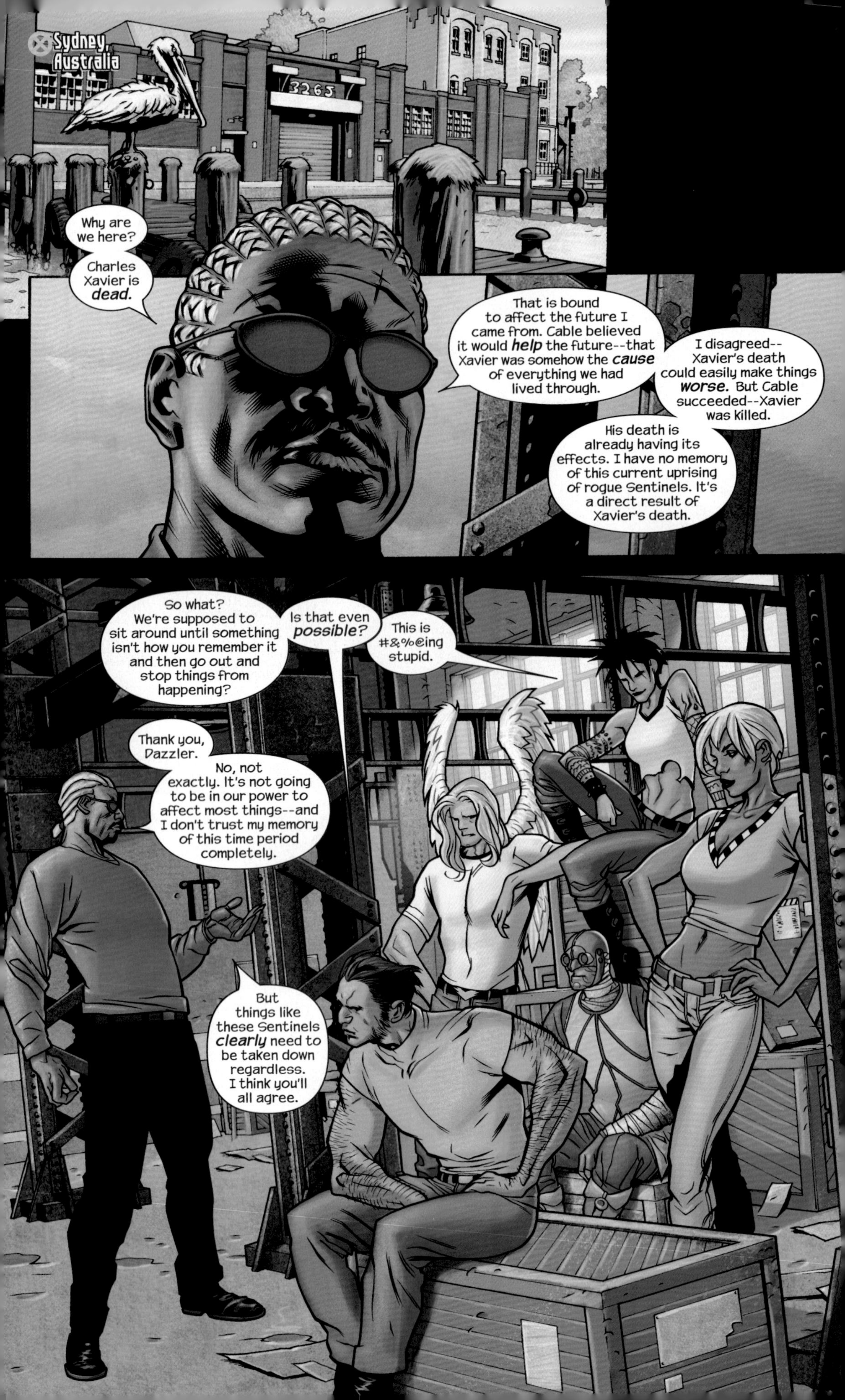

Sydney, Australia
3265
Why are we here?
Charles Xavier is **dead.**
That is bound to affect the future I came from. Cable believed it would **help** the future--that Xavier was somehow the **cause** of everything we had lived through.
I disagreed--Xavier's death could easily make things **worse.** But Cable succeeded--Xavier was killed.
His death is already having its effects. I have no memory of this current uprising of rogue Sentinels. It's a direct result of Xavier's death.
So what? We're supposed to sit around until something isn't how you remember it and then go out and stop things from happening?
Is that even **possible?**
This is #&%@ing stupid.
Thank you, Dazzler.
No, not exactly. It's not going to be in our power to affect most things--and I don't trust my memory of this time period completely.
But things like these Sentinels **clearly** need to be taken down regardless. I think you'll all agree.

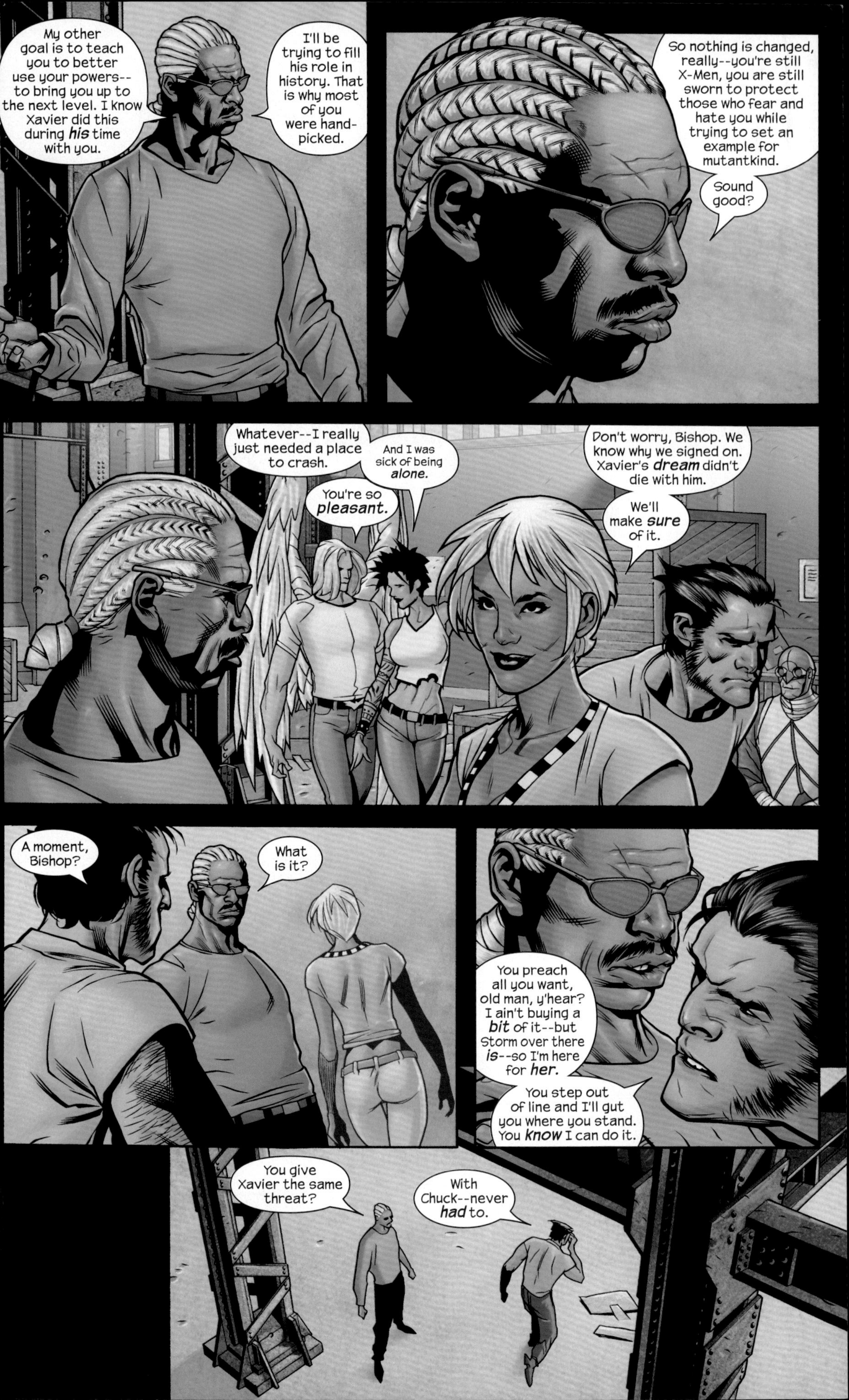

My other goal is to teach you to better use your powers--to bring you up to the next level. I know Xavier did this during *his* time with you.
I'll be trying to fill his role in history. That is why most of you were hand-picked.
So nothing is changed, really--you're still X-Men, you are still sworn to protect those who fear and hate you while trying to set an example for mutantkind.
Sound good?
Whatever--I really just needed a place to crash.
And I was sick of being *alone.*
You're so *pleasant.*
Don't worry, Bishop. We know why we signed on. Xavier's *dream* didn't die with him.
We'll make *sure* of it.
A moment, Bishop?
What is it?
You preach all you want, old man, y'hear? I ain't buying a *bit* of it--but Storm over there *is*--so I'm here for *her.*
You step out of line and I'll gut you where you stand. You *know* I can do it.
You give Xavier the same threat?
With Chuck--never *had* to.

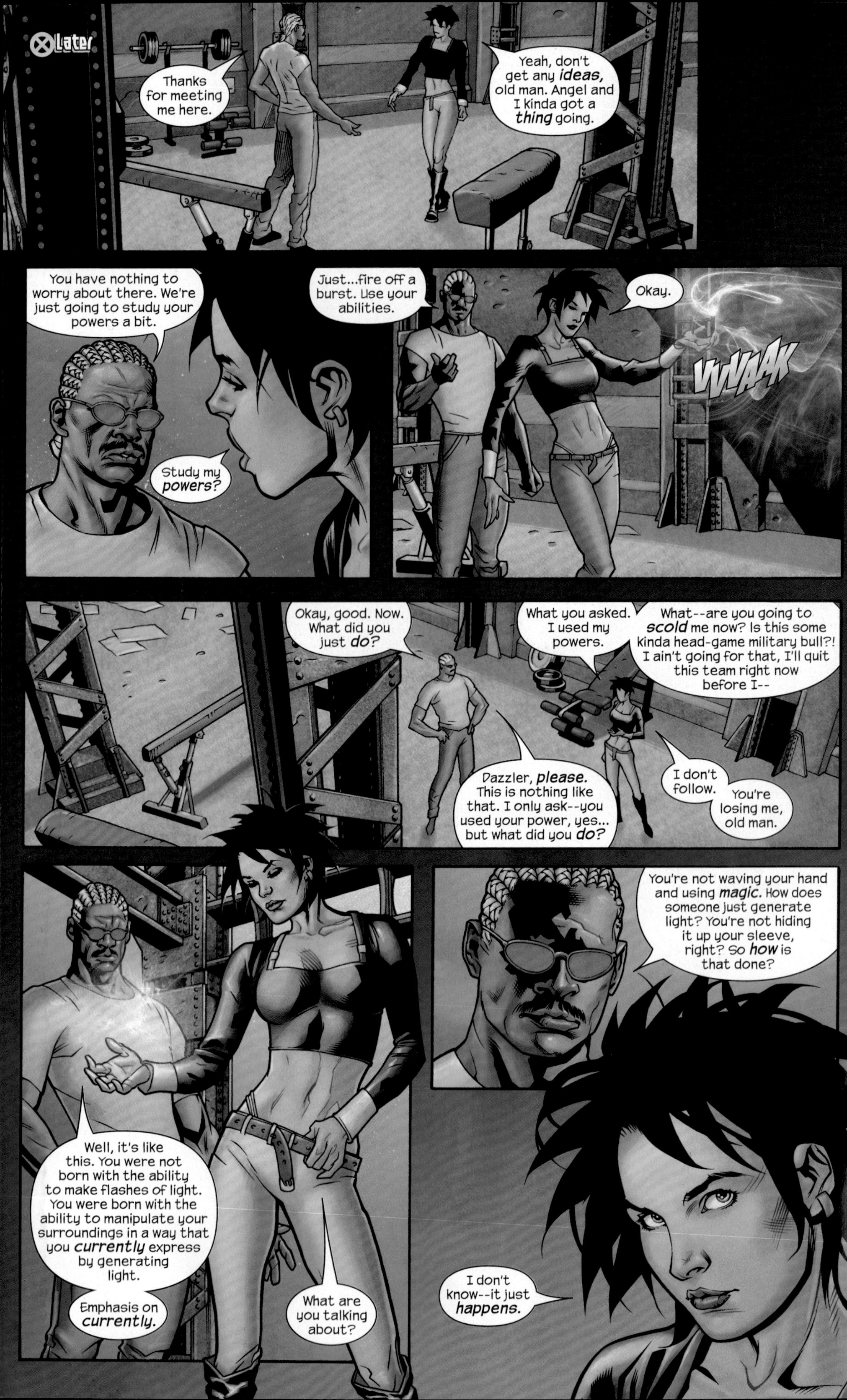
Later
Thanks for meeting me here.
Yeah, don't get any ideas, old man. Angel and I kinda got a thing going.
You have nothing to worry about there. We're just going to study your powers a bit.
Study my powers?
Just...fire off a burst. Use your abilities.
Okay.
VVVAAK
Okay, good. Now. What did you just do?
What you asked. I used my powers.
What--are you going to scold me now? Is this some kinda head-game military bull?! I ain't going for that, I'll quit this team right now before I--
Dazzler, please. This is nothing like that. I only ask--you used your power, yes... but what did you do?
I don't follow.
You're losing me, old man.
You're not waving your hand and using magic. How does someone just generate light? You're not hiding it up your sleeve, right? So how is that done?
I don't know--it just happens.
Well, it's like this. You were not born with the ability to make flashes of light. You were born with the ability to manipulate your surroundings in a way that you currently express by generating light.
Emphasis on currently.
What are you talking about?

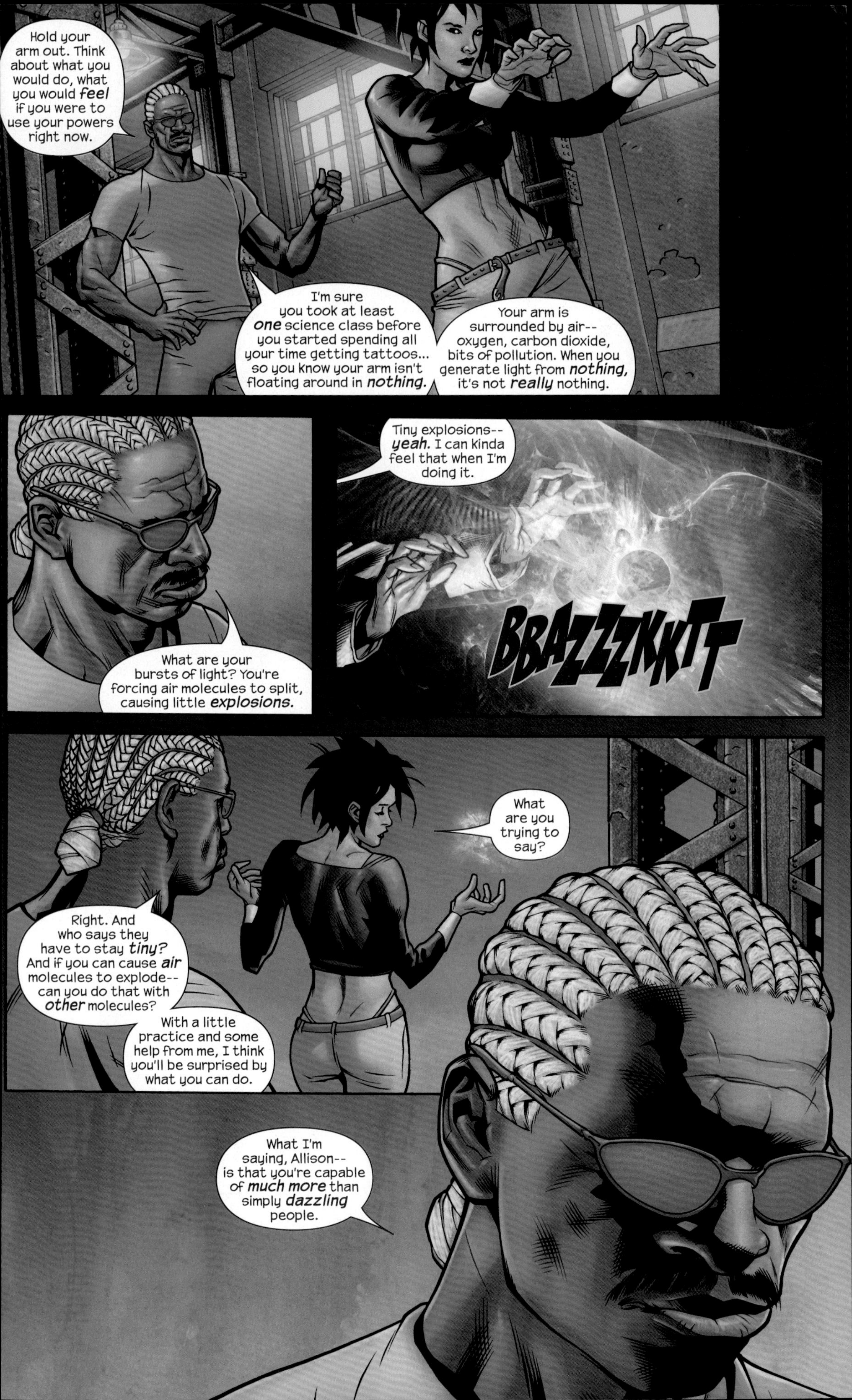

Hold your arm out. Think about what you would do, what you would *feel* if you were to use your powers right now.
I'm sure you took at least *one* science class before you started spending all your time getting tattoos... so you know your arm isn't floating around in *nothing.*
Your arm is surrounded by air-- oxygen, carbon dioxide, bits of pollution. When you generate light from *nothing,* it's not *really* nothing.
What are your bursts of light? You're forcing air molecules to split, causing little *explosions.*
Tiny explosions-- *yeah.* I can kinda feel that when I'm doing it.
BBAZZZKKITT
What are you trying to say?
Right. And who says they have to stay *tiny?* And if you can cause *air* molecules to explode-- can you do that with *other* molecules?
With a little practice and some help from me, I think you'll be surprised by what you can do.
What I'm saying, Allison-- is that you're capable of *much more* than simply *dazzling* people.

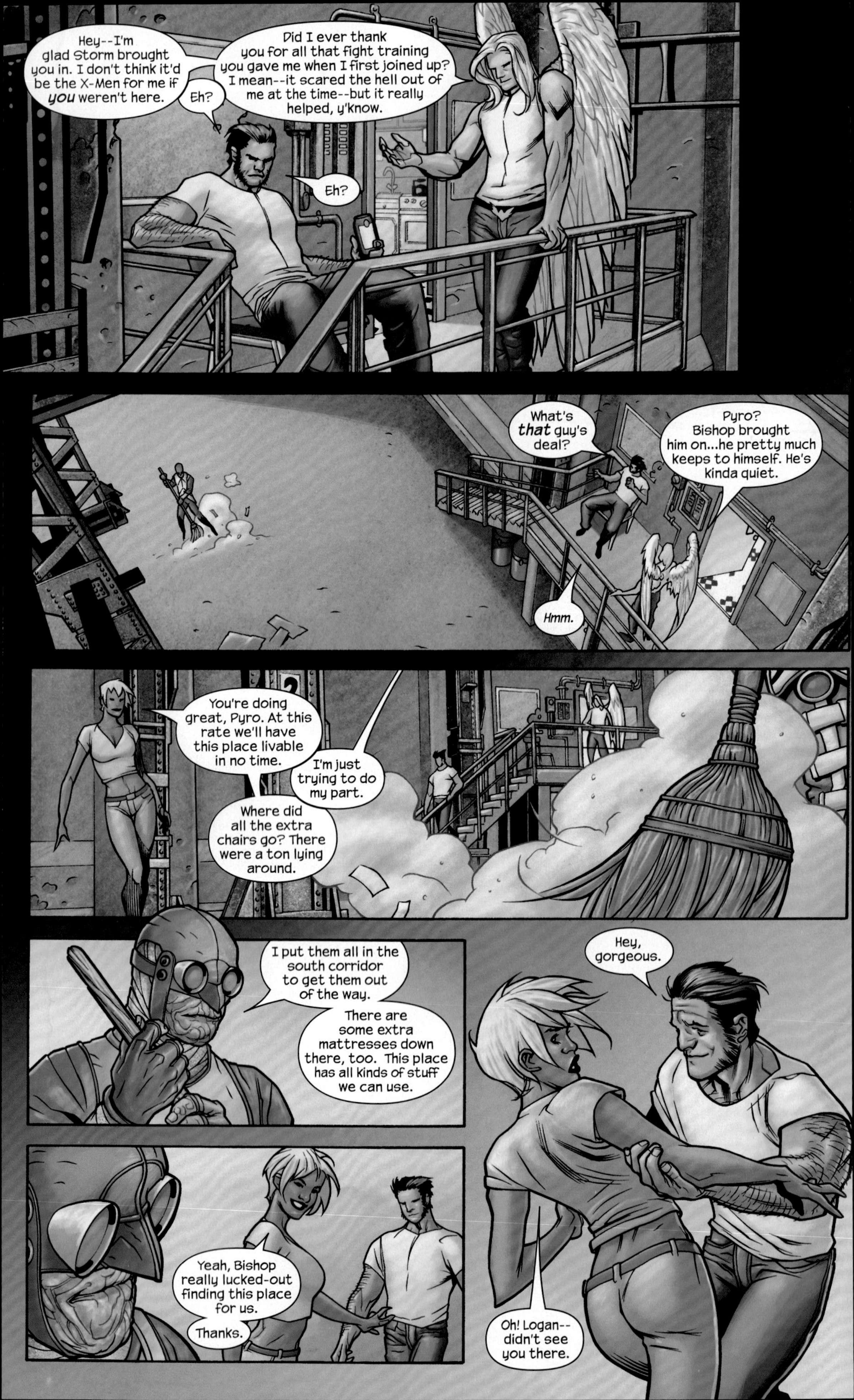
Hey--I'm glad Storm brought you in. I don't think it'd be the X-Men for me if *you* weren't here.
Eh?
Did I ever thank you for all that fight training you gave me when I first joined up? I mean--it scared the hell out of me at the time--but it really helped, y'know.
Eh?
What's *that* guy's deal?
Pyro? Bishop brought him on...he pretty much keeps to himself. He's kinda quiet.
Hmm.
You're doing great, Pyro. At this rate we'll have this place livable in no time.
I'm just trying to do my part.
Where did all the extra chairs go? There were a ton lying around.
I put them all in the south corridor to get them out of the way.
There are some extra mattresses down there, too. This place has all kinds of stuff we can use.
Yeah, Bishop really lucked-out finding this place for us.
Thanks.
Hey, gorgeous.
Oh! Logan--didn't see you there.

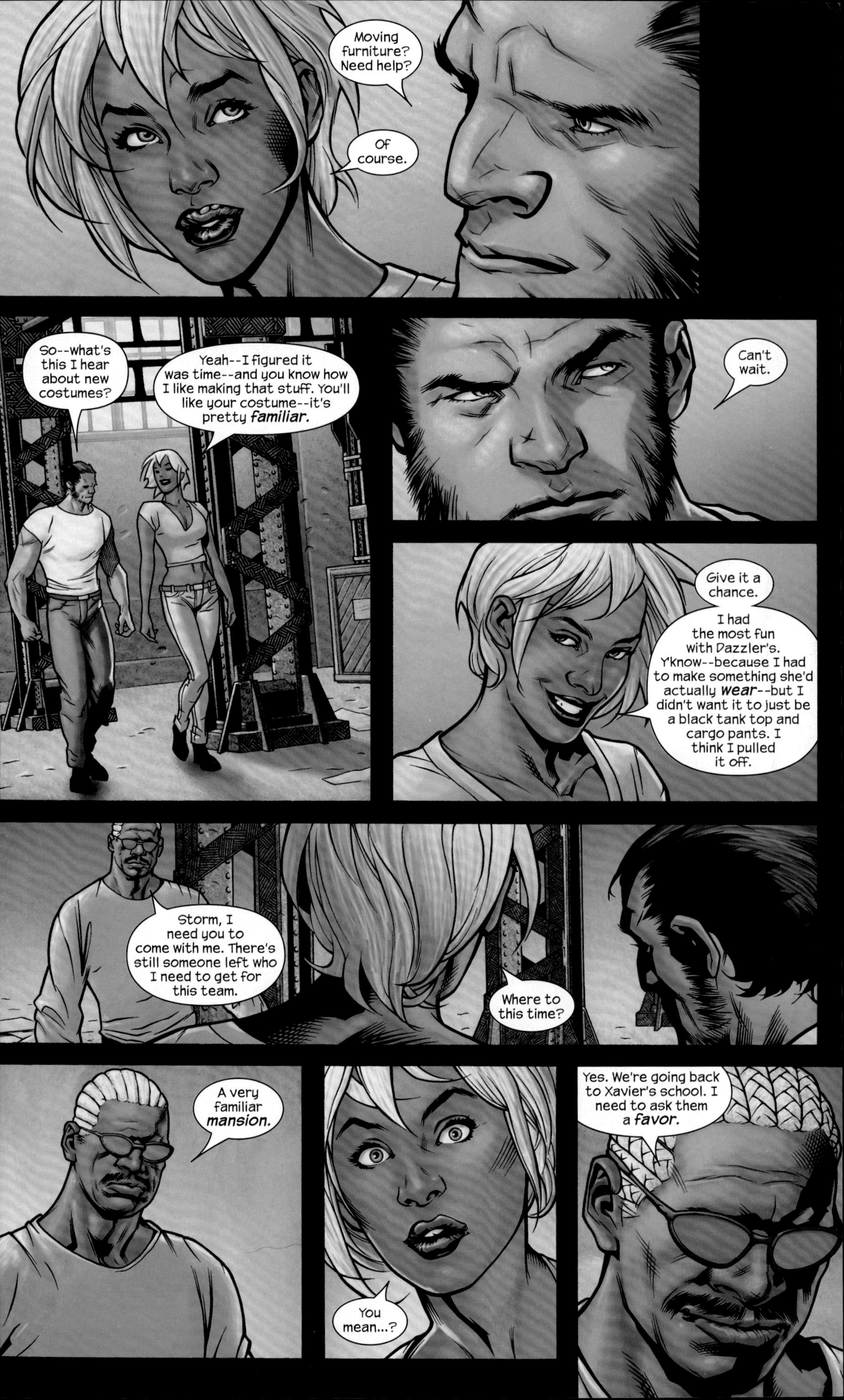
Moving furniture? Need help?
Of course.
So--what's this I hear about new costumes?
Yeah--I figured it was time--and you know how I like making that stuff. You'll like your costume--it's pretty *familiar*.
Can't wait.
Give it a chance.
I had the most fun with Dazzler's. Y'know--because I had to make something she'd actually *wear*--but I didn't want it to just be a black tank top and cargo pants. I think I pulled it off.
Storm, I need you to come with me. There's still someone left who I need to get for this team.
Where to this time?
A very familiar *mansion*.
You mean...?
Yes. We're going back to Xavier's school. I need to ask them a *favor*.

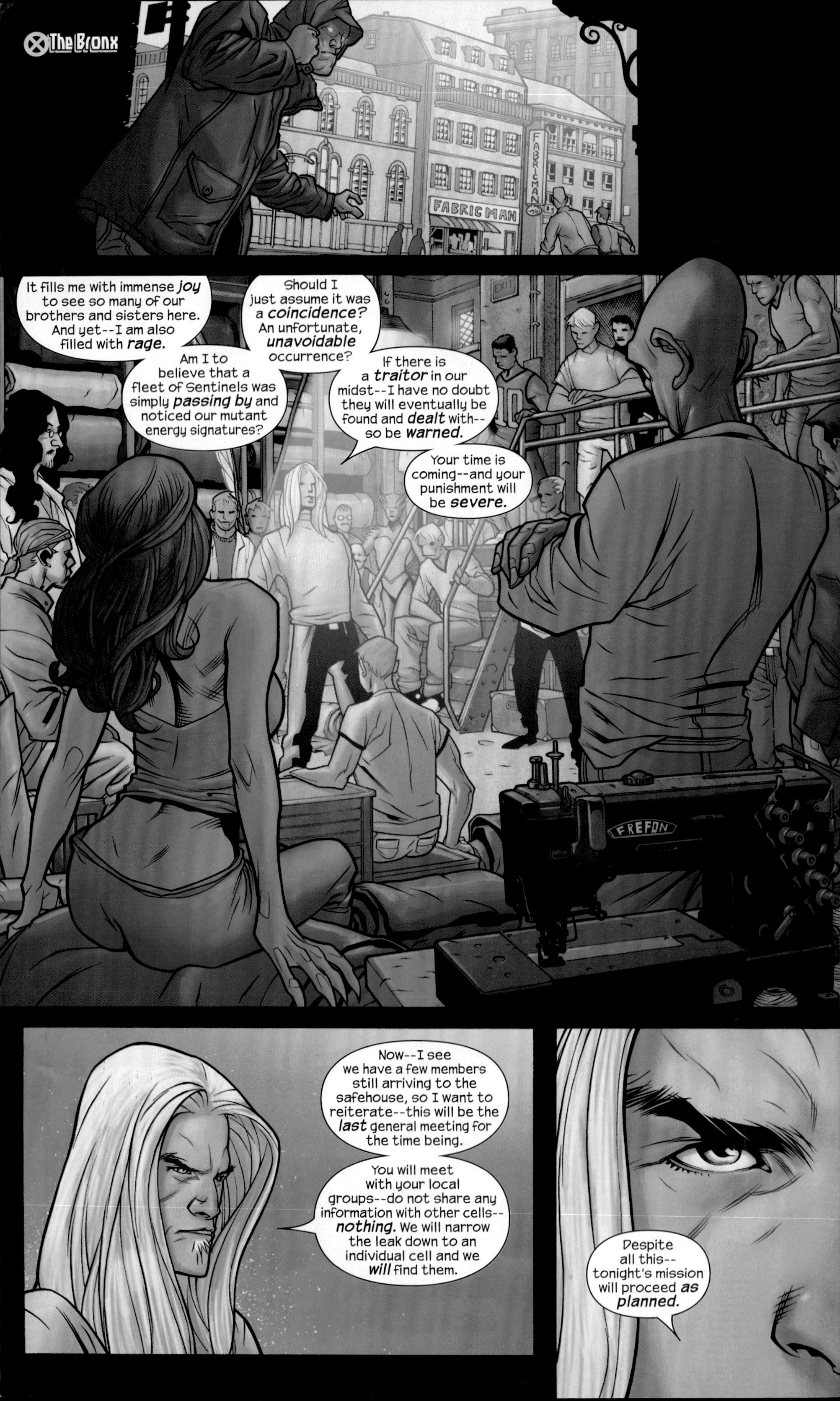

The Bronx
FABRICMAN
FABRICMAN
It fills me with immense joy to see so many of our brothers and sisters here. And yet--I am also filled with rage.
Am I to believe that a fleet of Sentinels was simply passing by and noticed our mutant energy signatures?
Should I just assume it was a coincidence? An unfortunate, unavoidable occurrence?
If there is a traitor in our midst--I have no doubt they will eventually be found and dealt with--so be warned.
Your time is coming--and your punishment will be severe.
EXIT
FREFON
Now--I see we have a few members still arriving to the safehouse, so I want to reiterate--this will be the last general meeting for the time being.
You will meet with your local groups--do not share any information with other cells--nothing. We will narrow the leak down to an individual cell and we will find them.
Despite all this--tonight's mission will proceed as planned.

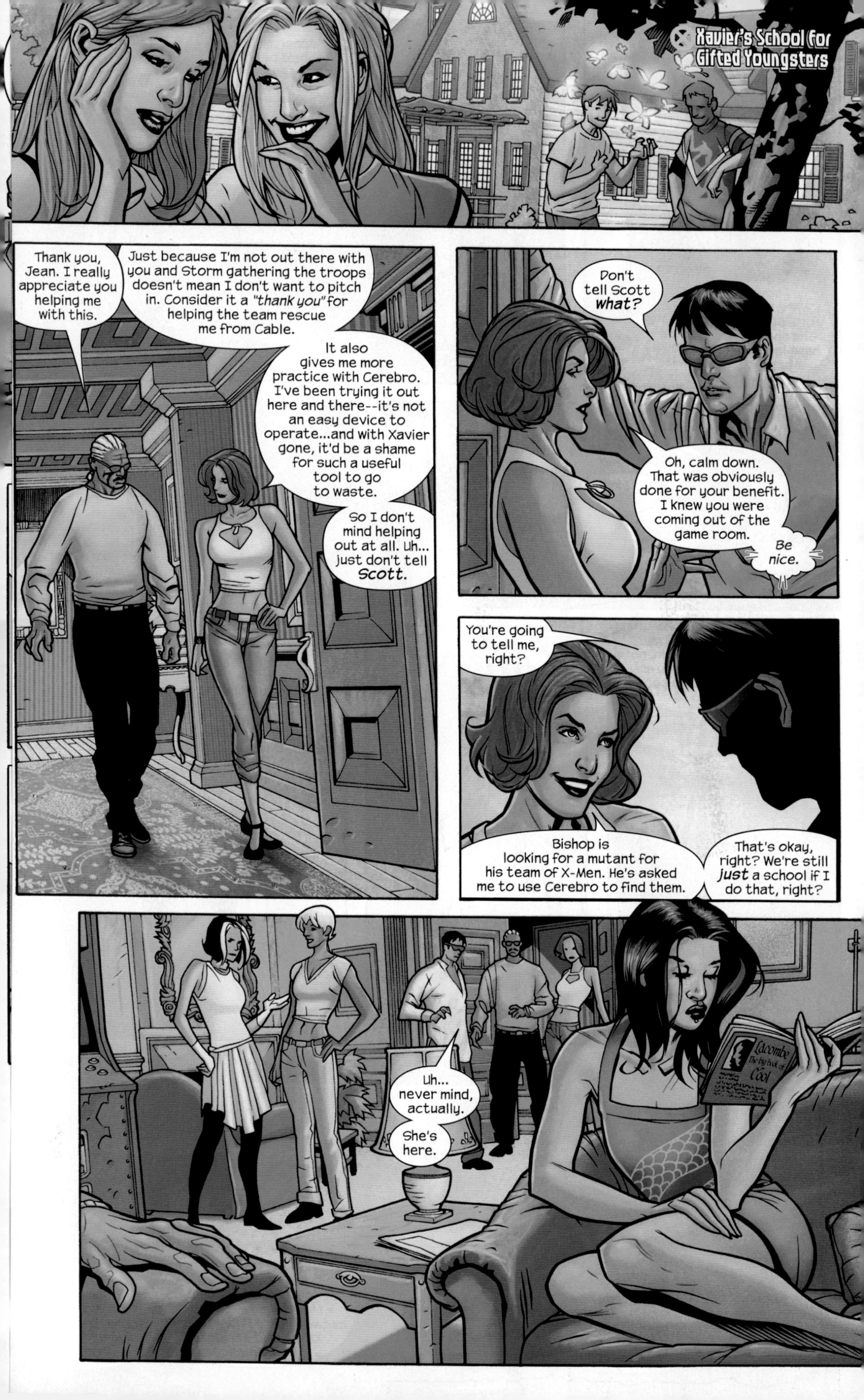
Xavier's School for Gifted Youngsters
Thank you, Jean. I really appreciate you helping me with this.
Just because I'm not out there with you and Storm gathering the troops doesn't mean I don't want to pitch in. Consider it a "thank you" for helping the team rescue me from Cable.
It also gives me more practice with Cerebro. I've been trying it out here and there--it's not an easy device to operate...and with Xavier gone, it'd be a shame for such a useful tool to go to waste.
So I don't mind helping out at all. Uh... just don't tell Scott.
Don't tell Scott what?
Oh, calm down. That was obviously done for your benefit. I knew you were coming out of the game room.
Be nice.
You're going to tell me, right?
Bishop is looking for a mutant for his team of X-Men. He's asked me to use Cerebro to find them.
That's okay, right? We're still just a school if I do that, right?
Uh... never mind, actually.
She's here.
Lacombe The Big Book of Cool

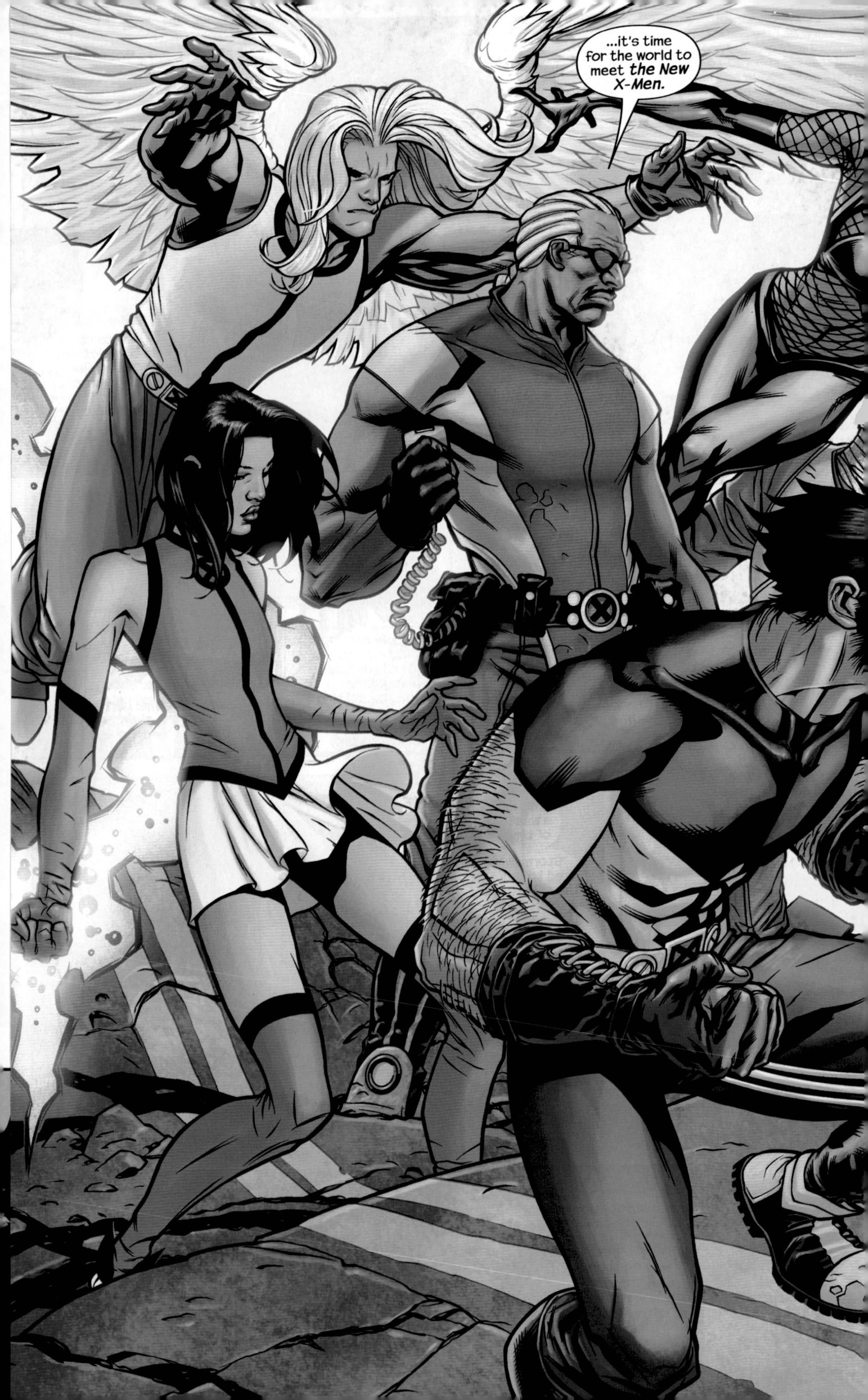
...it's time for the world to meet *the New X-Men.*

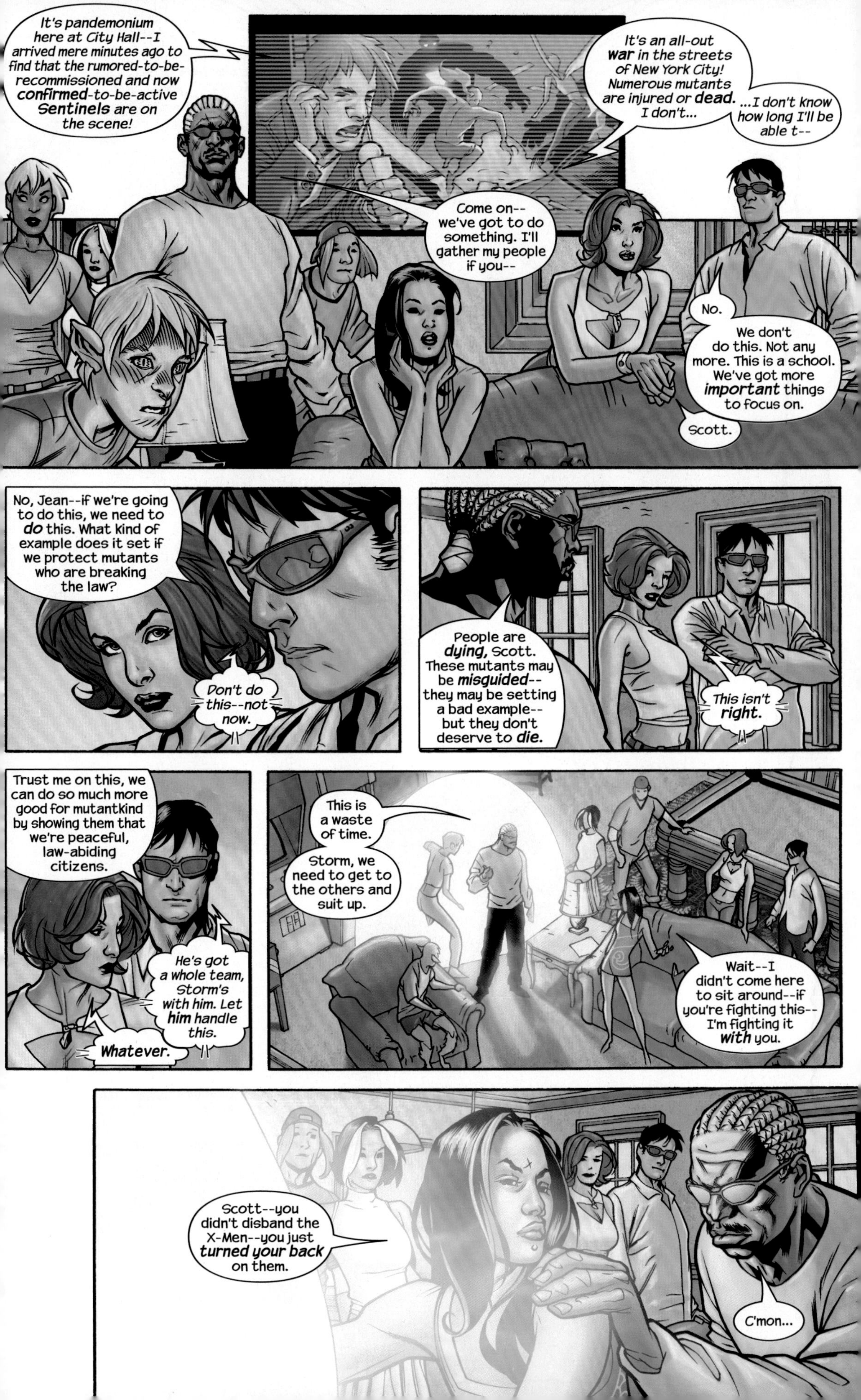
It's pandemonium here at City Hall--I arrived mere minutes ago to find that the rumored-to-be-recommissioned and now confirmed-to-be-active Sentinels are on the scene!
It's an all-out war in the streets of New York City! Numerous mutants are injured or dead. I don't...
...I don't know how long I'll be able t--
Come on-- we've got to do something. I'll gather my people if you--
No.
We don't do this. Not any more. This is a school. We've got more important things to focus on.
Scott.
No, Jean--if we're going to do this, we need to do this. What kind of example does it set if we protect mutants who are breaking the law?
Don't do this--not now.
People are dying, Scott. These mutants may be misguided-- they may be setting a bad example-- but they don't deserve to die.
This isn't right.
Trust me on this, we can do so much more good for mutantkind by showing them that we're peaceful, law-abiding citizens.
He's got a whole team, Storm's with him. Let him handle this.
Whatever.
This is a waste of time.
Storm, we need to get to the others and suit up.
Wait--I didn't come here to sit around--if you're fighting this-- I'm fighting it with you.
Scott--you didn't disband the X-Men--you just turned your back on them.
C'mon...

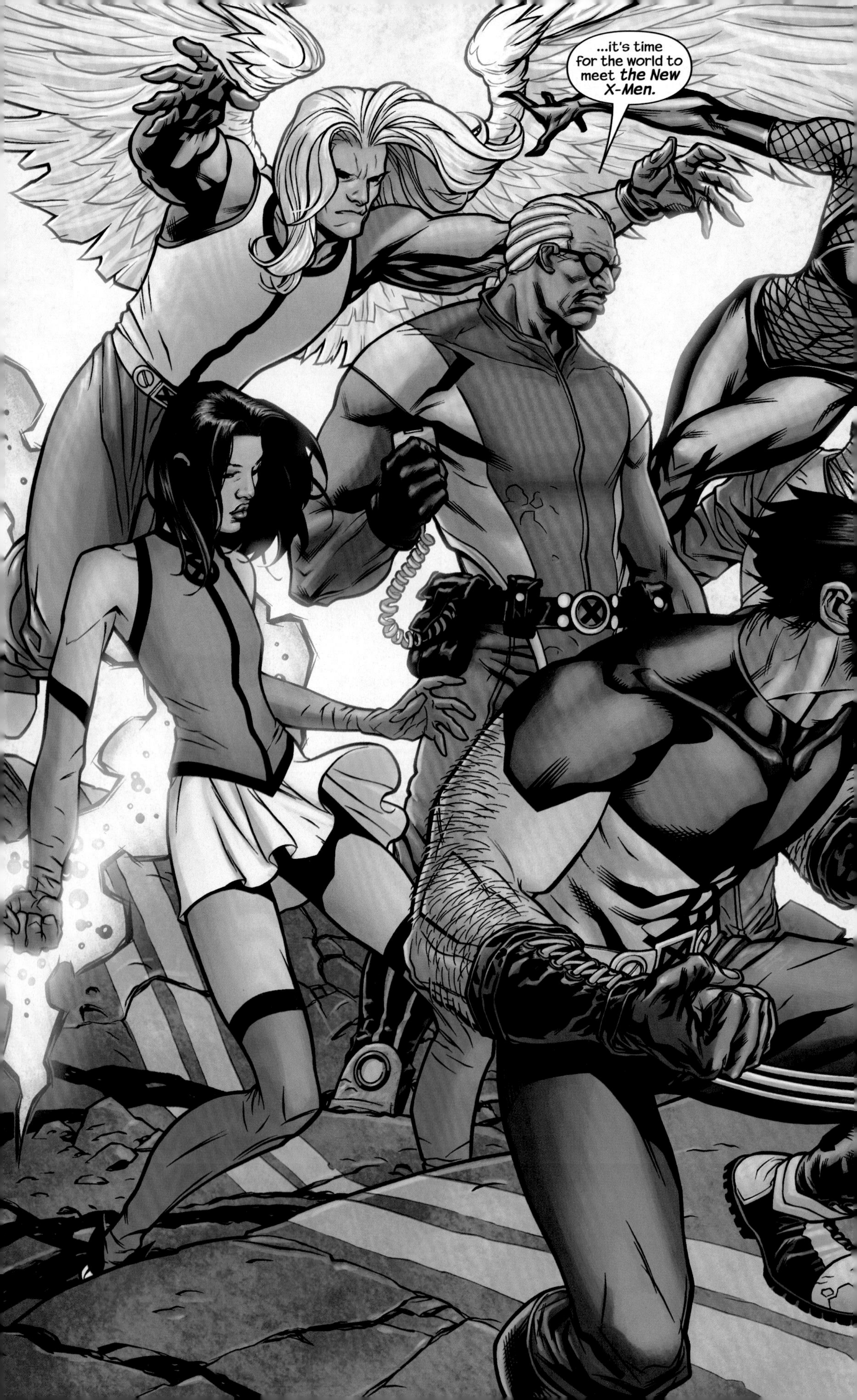
...it's time for the world to meet the New X-Men.

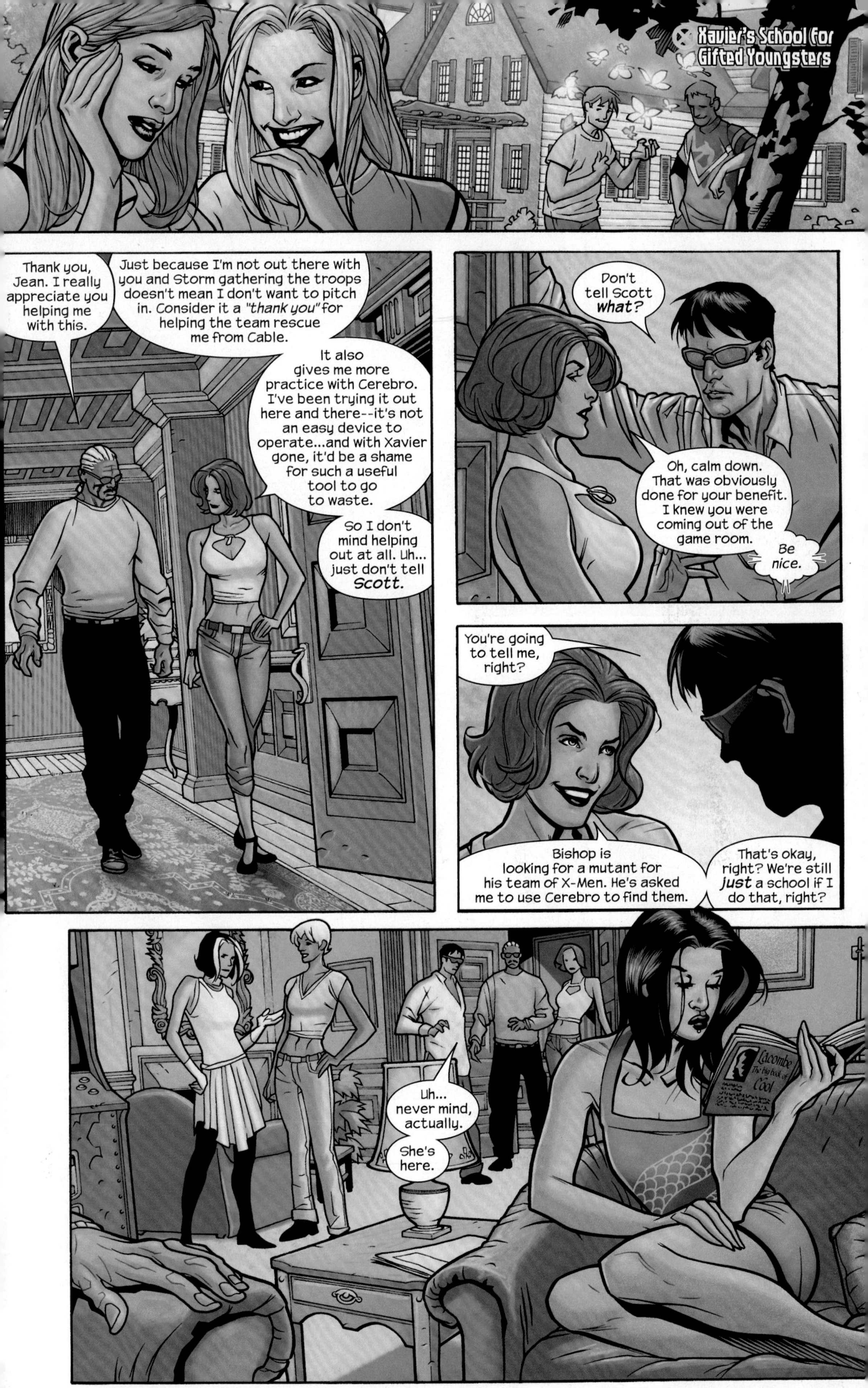
Xavier's School for Gifted Youngsters
Thank you, Jean. I really appreciate you helping me with this.
Just because I'm not out there with you and Storm gathering the troops doesn't mean I don't want to pitch in. Consider it a "thank you" for helping the team rescue me from Cable.
It also gives me more practice with Cerebro. I've been trying it out here and there--it's not an easy device to operate...and with Xavier gone, it'd be a shame for such a useful tool to go to waste.
So I don't mind helping out at all. Uh... just don't tell Scott.
Don't tell Scott what?
Oh, calm down. That was obviously done for your benefit. I knew you were coming out of the game room.
Be nice.
You're going to tell me, right?
Bishop is looking for a mutant for his team of X-Men. He's asked me to use Cerebro to find them.
That's okay, right? We're still just a school if I do that, right?
Uh... never mind, actually.
She's here.
Lacombe The big book of Cool

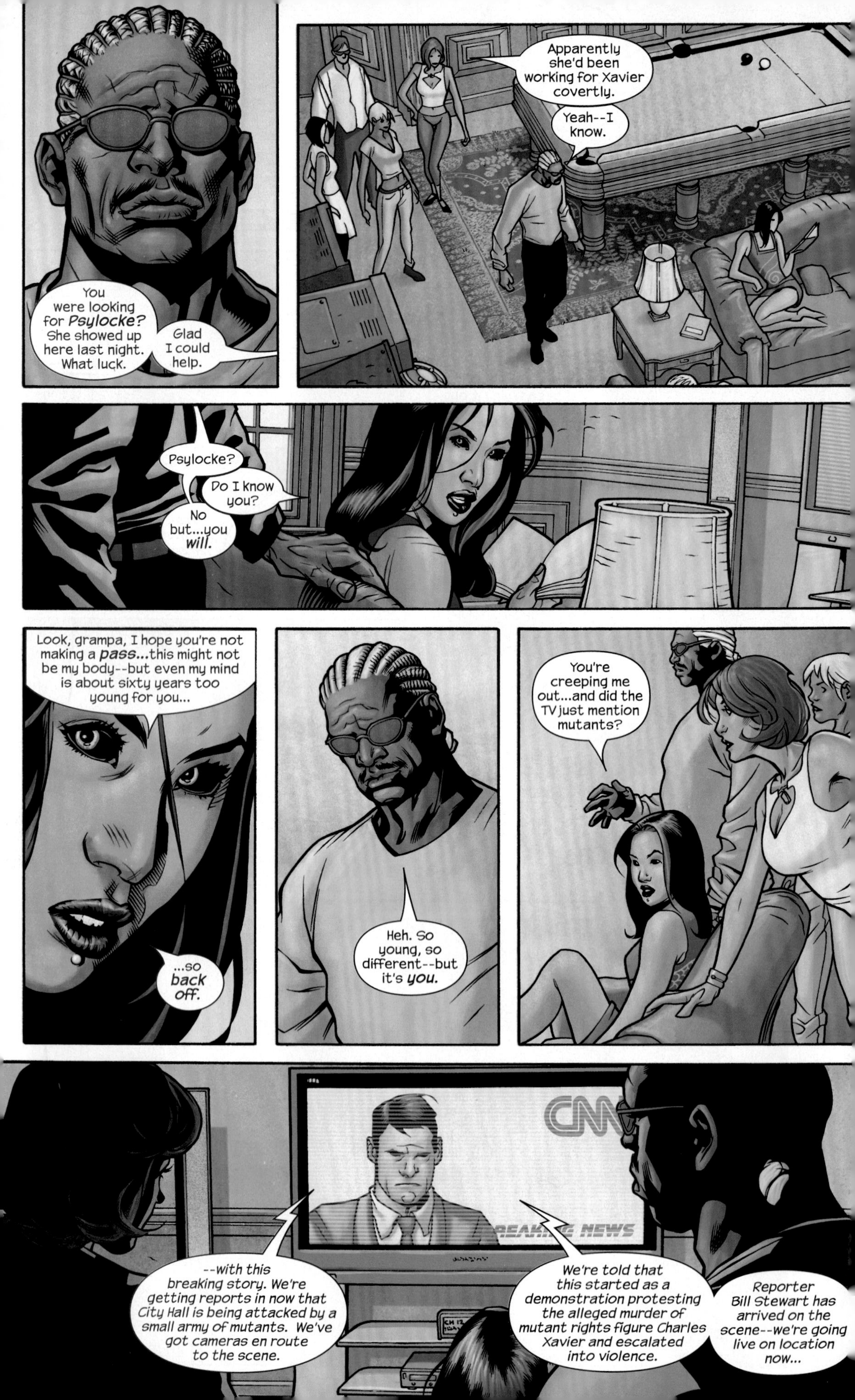
You were looking for Psylocke? She showed up here last night. What luck.
Glad I could help.
Apparently she'd been working for Xavier covertly.
Yeah--I know.
Psylocke?
Do I know you?
No but...you will.
Look, grampa, I hope you're not making a pass...this might not be my body--but even my mind is about sixty years too young for you...
...so back off.
Heh. So young, so different--but it's you.
You're creeping me out...and did the TV just mention mutants?
--with this breaking story. We're getting reports in now that City Hall is being attacked by a small army of mutants. We've got cameras en route to the scene.
We're told that this started as a demonstration protesting the alleged murder of mutant rights figure Charles Xavier and escalated into violence.
Reporter Bill Stewart has arrived on the scene--we're going live on location now...

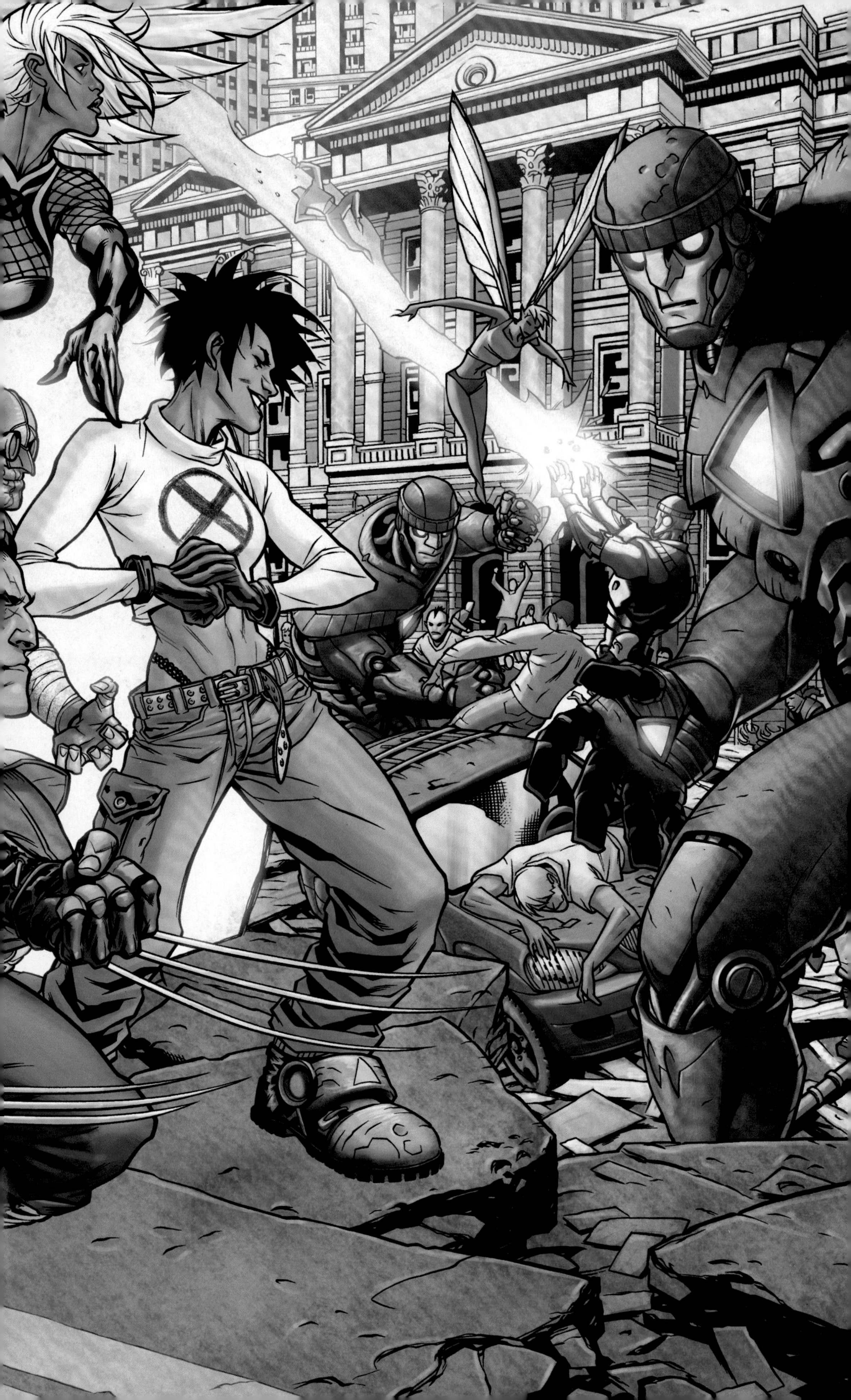

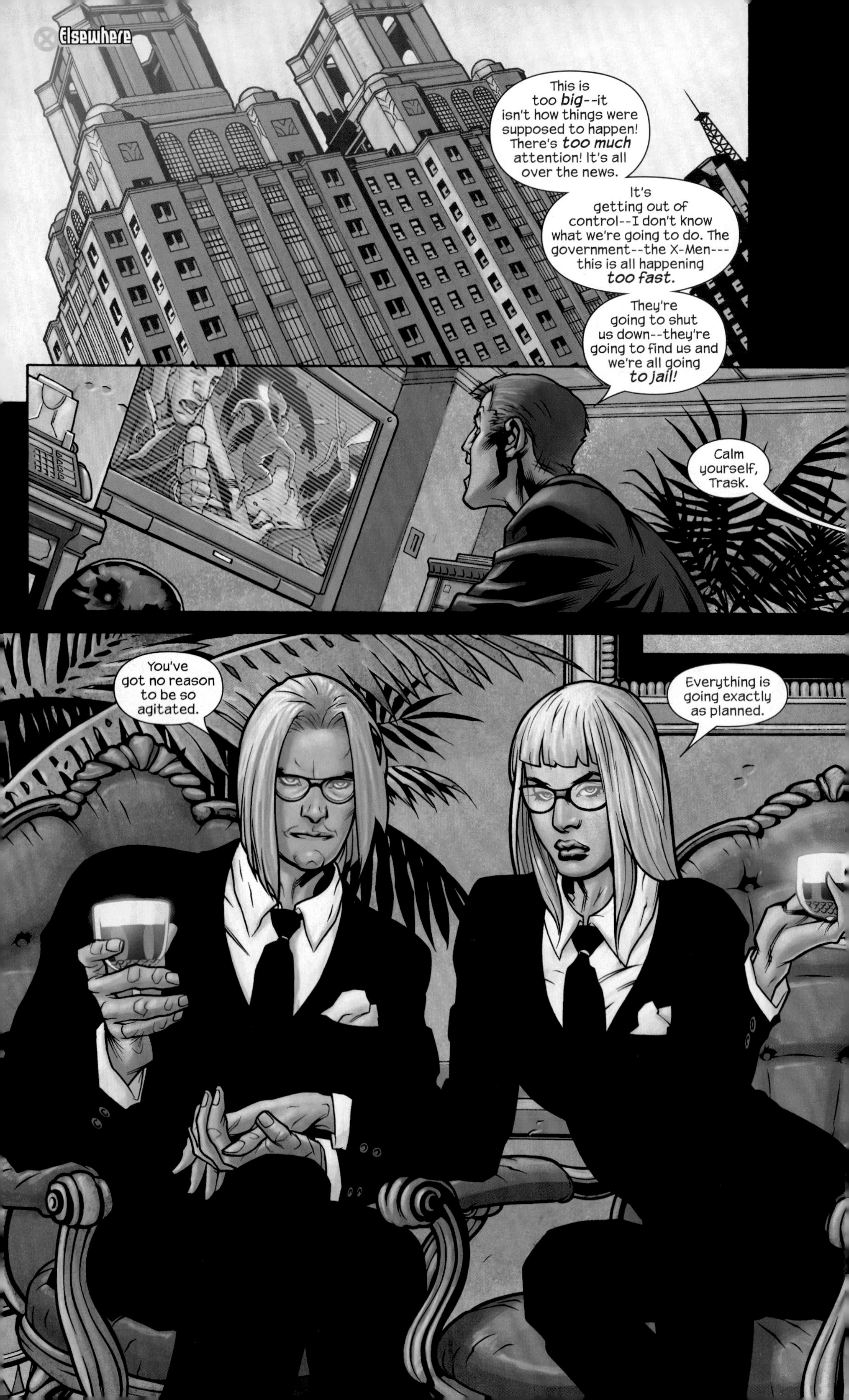
Elsewhere
This is too big--it isn't how things were supposed to happen! There's too much attention! It's all over the news.
It's getting out of control--I don't know what we're going to do. The government--the X-Men---this is all happening too fast.
They're going to shut us down--they're going to find us and we're all going to jail!
Calm yourself, Trask.
You've got no reason to be so agitated.
Everything is going exactly as planned.

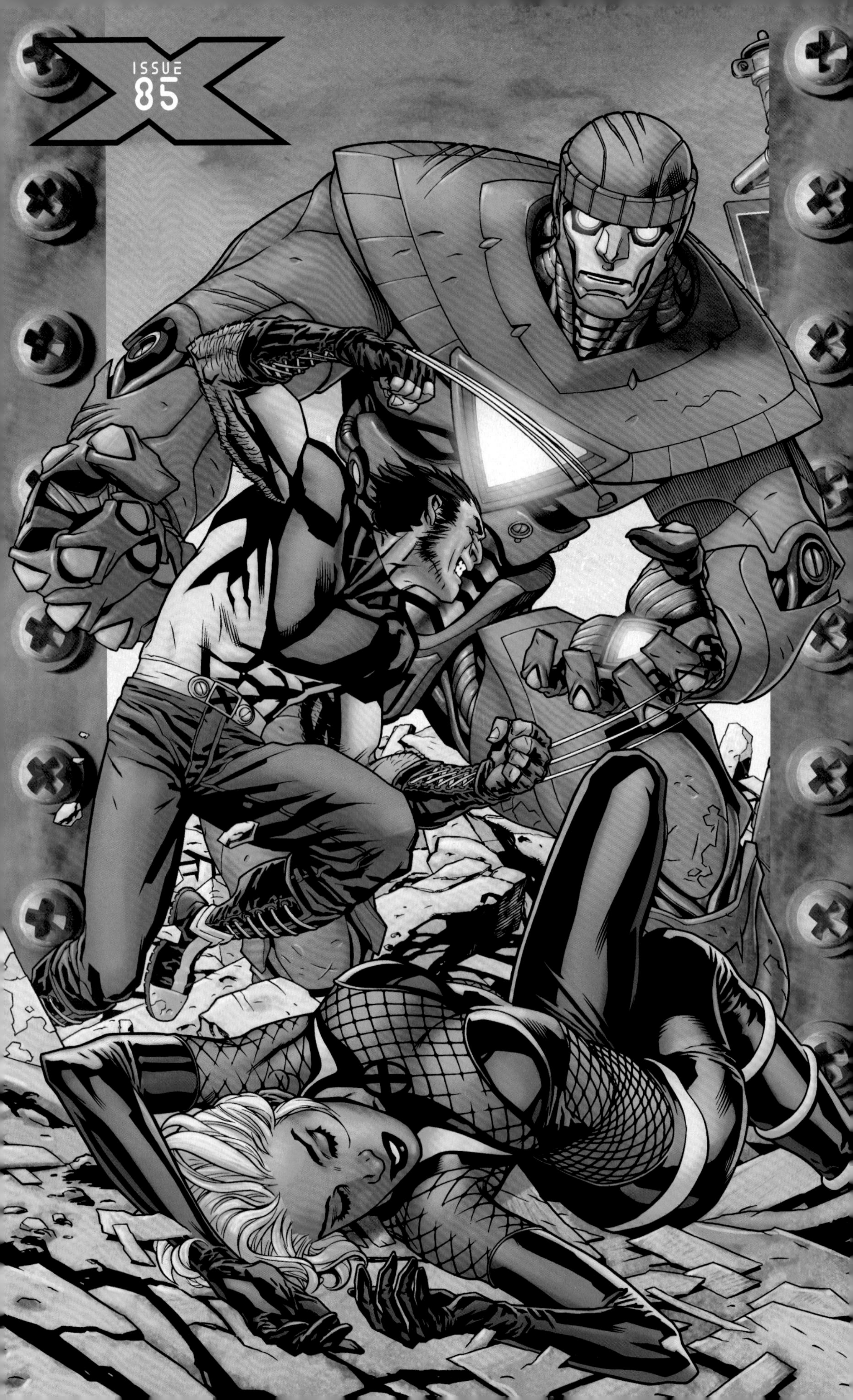
ISSUE
85

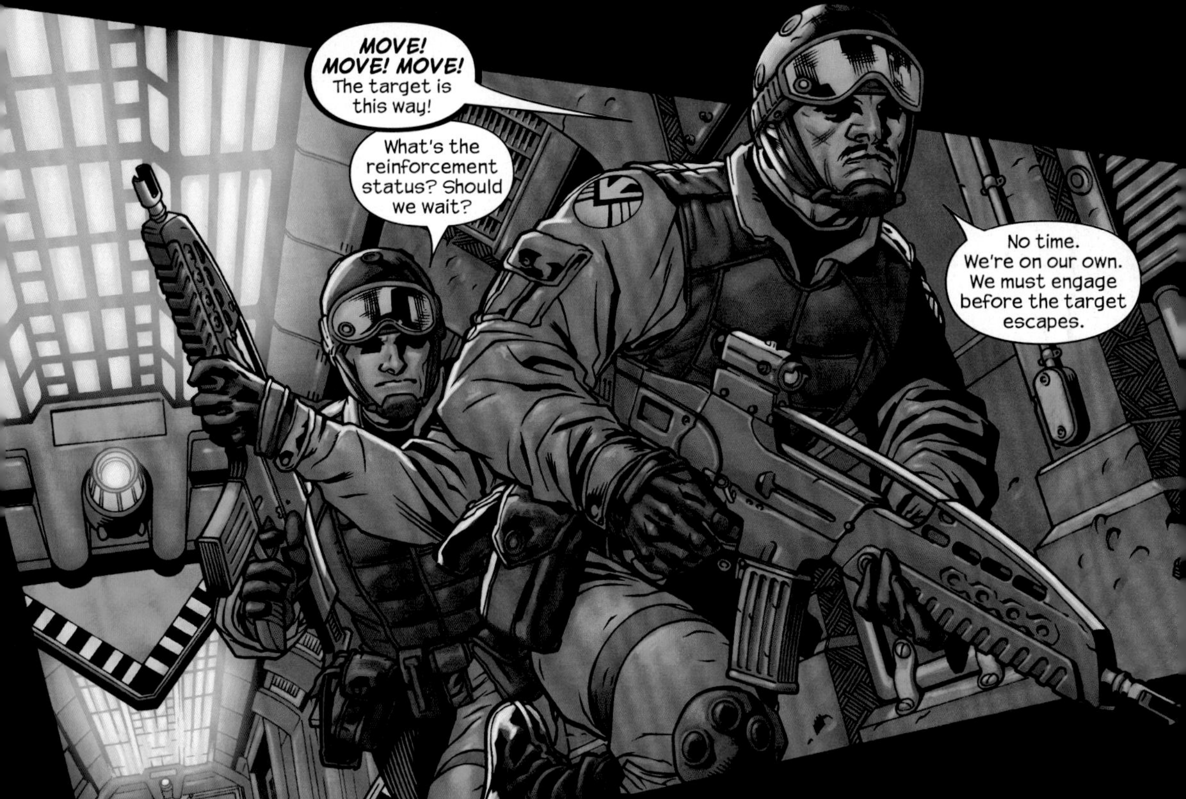
MOVE! MOVE! MOVE! The target is this way!
What's the reinforcement status? Should we wait?
No time. We're on our own. We must engage before the target escapes.

SENTINELS

PART 2 (OF 5)

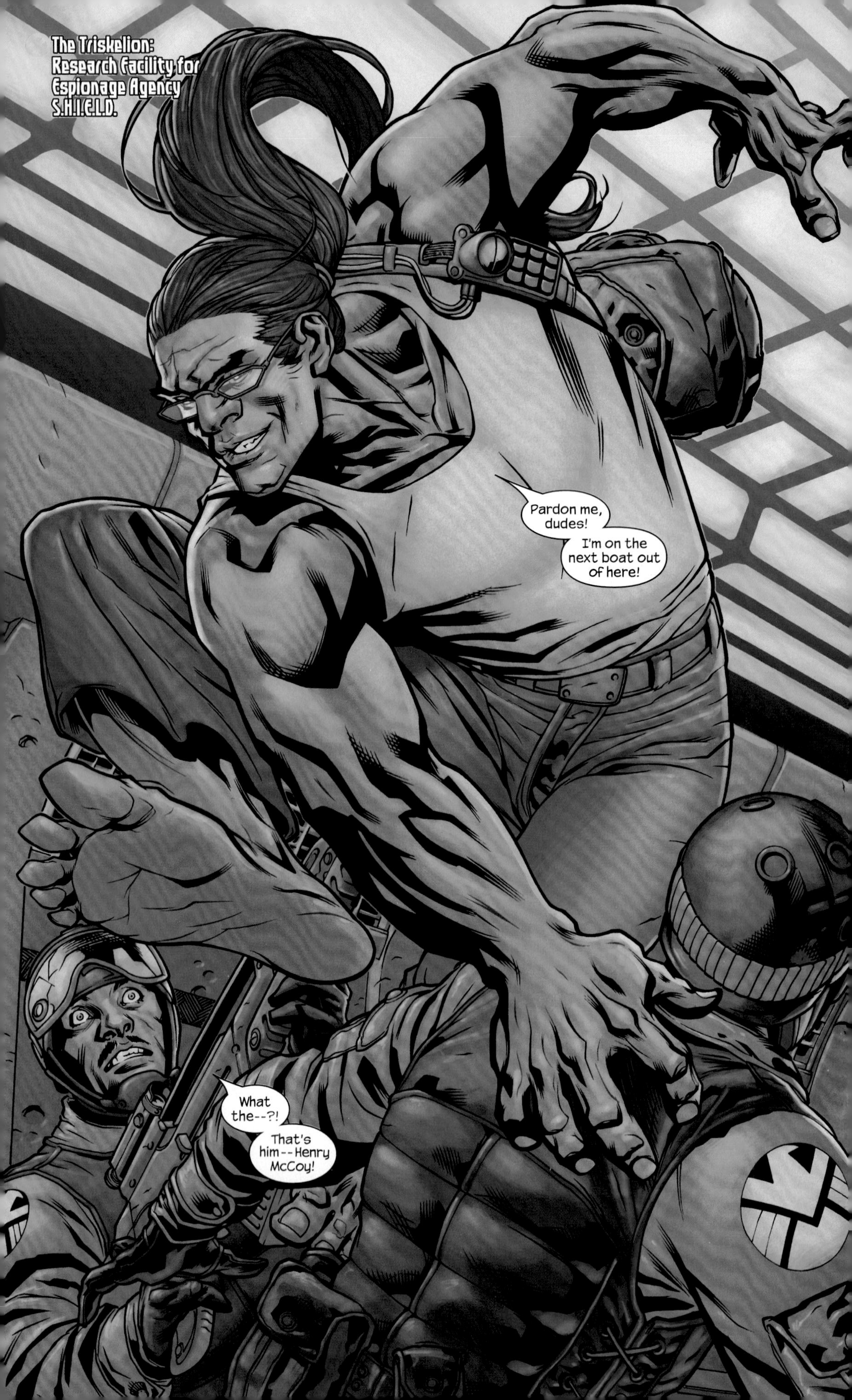
The Triskelion: Research Facility for Espionage Agency S.H.I.E.L.D.
Pardon me, dudes!
I'm on the next boat out of here!
What the--?!
That's him--Henry McCoy!

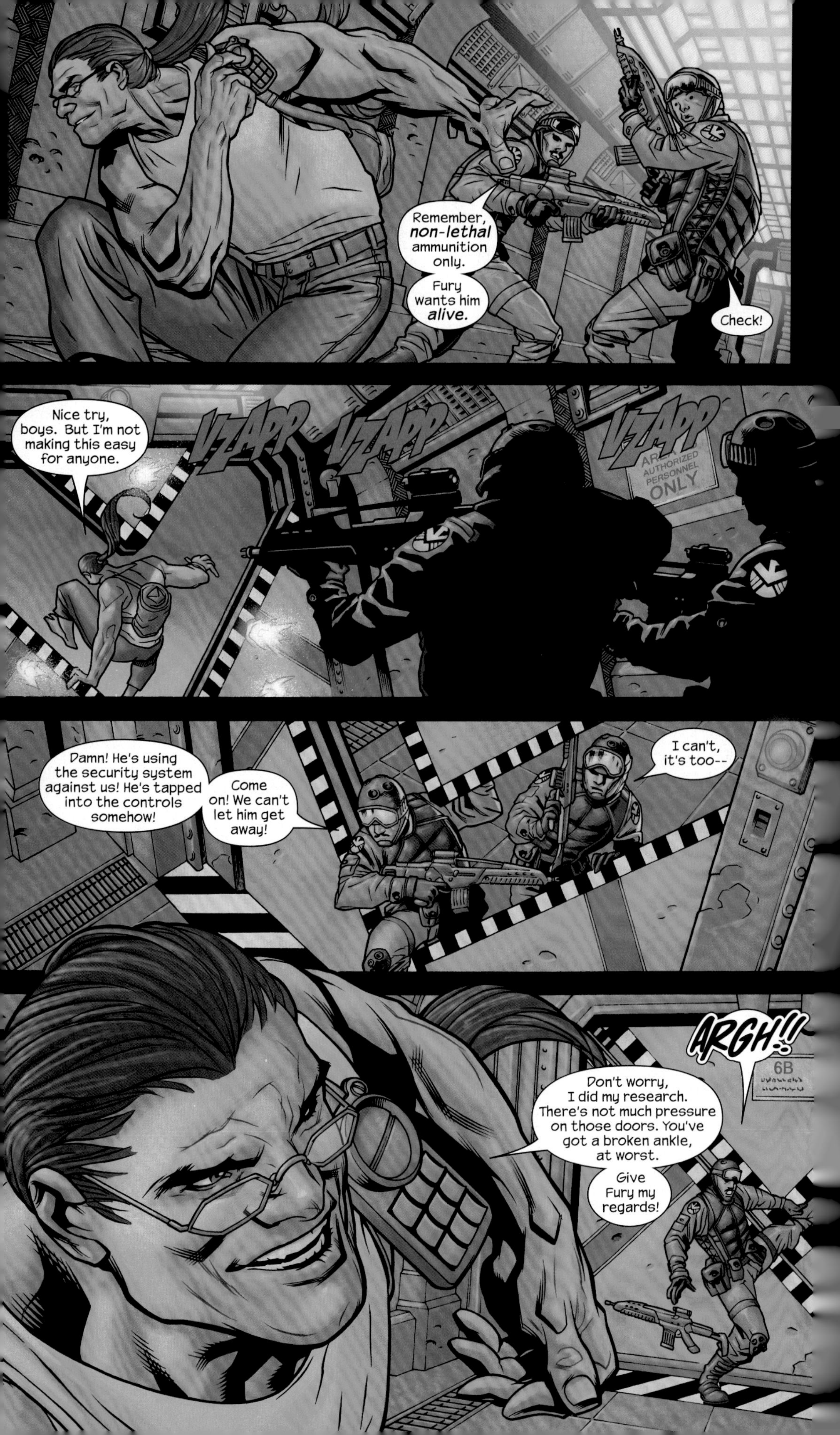
Remember, non-lethal ammunition only.
Fury wants him alive.
Check!
Nice try, boys. But I'm not making this easy for anyone.
VZAPP
VZAPP
VZAPP
AREA AUTHORIZED PERSONNEL ONLY
Damn! He's using the security system against us! He's tapped into the controls somehow!
Come on! We can't let him get away!
I can't, it's too--
ARGH!!
6B
Don't worry, I did my research. There's not much pressure on those doors. You've got a broken ankle, at worst.
Give Fury my regards!

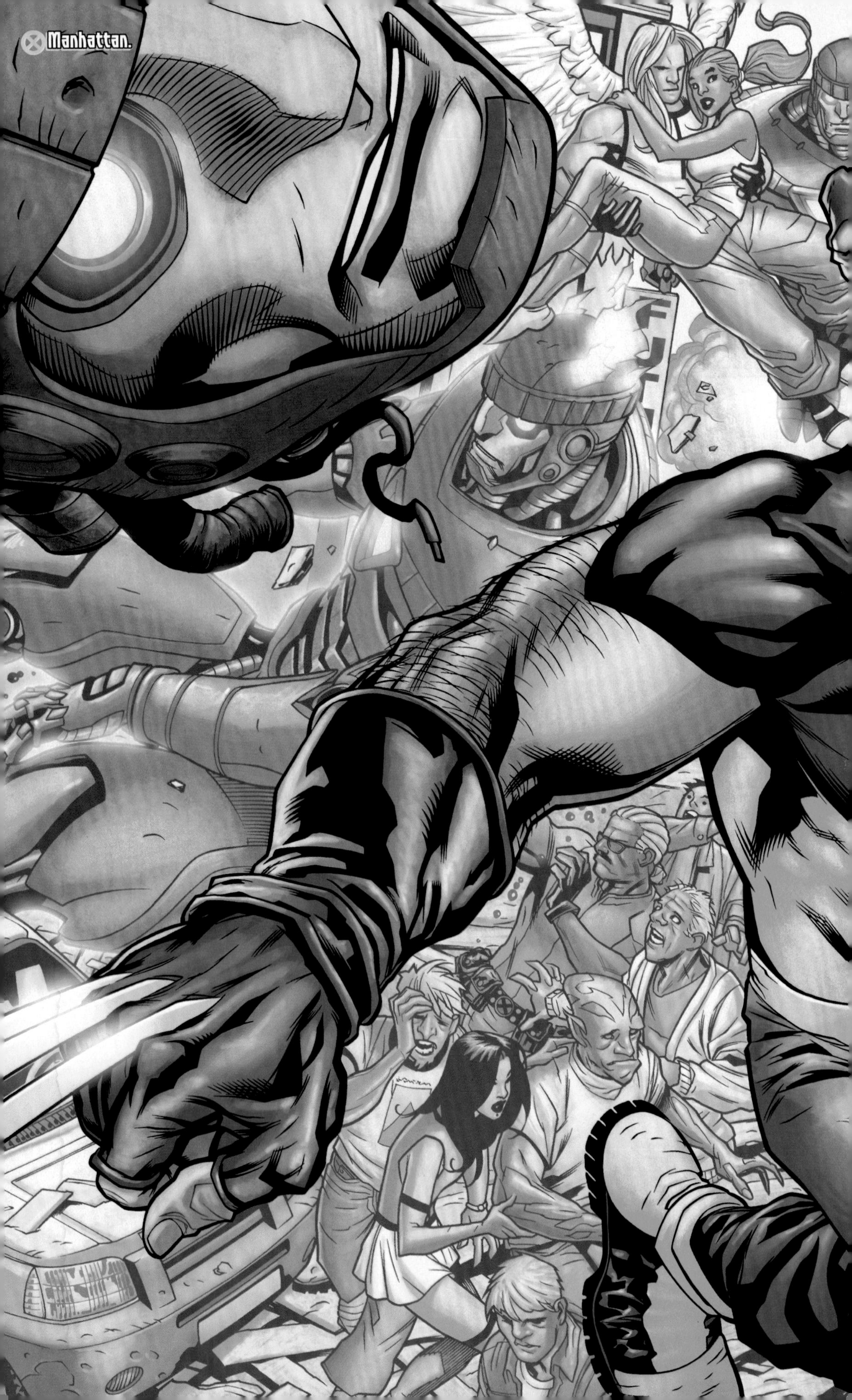
Manhattan.

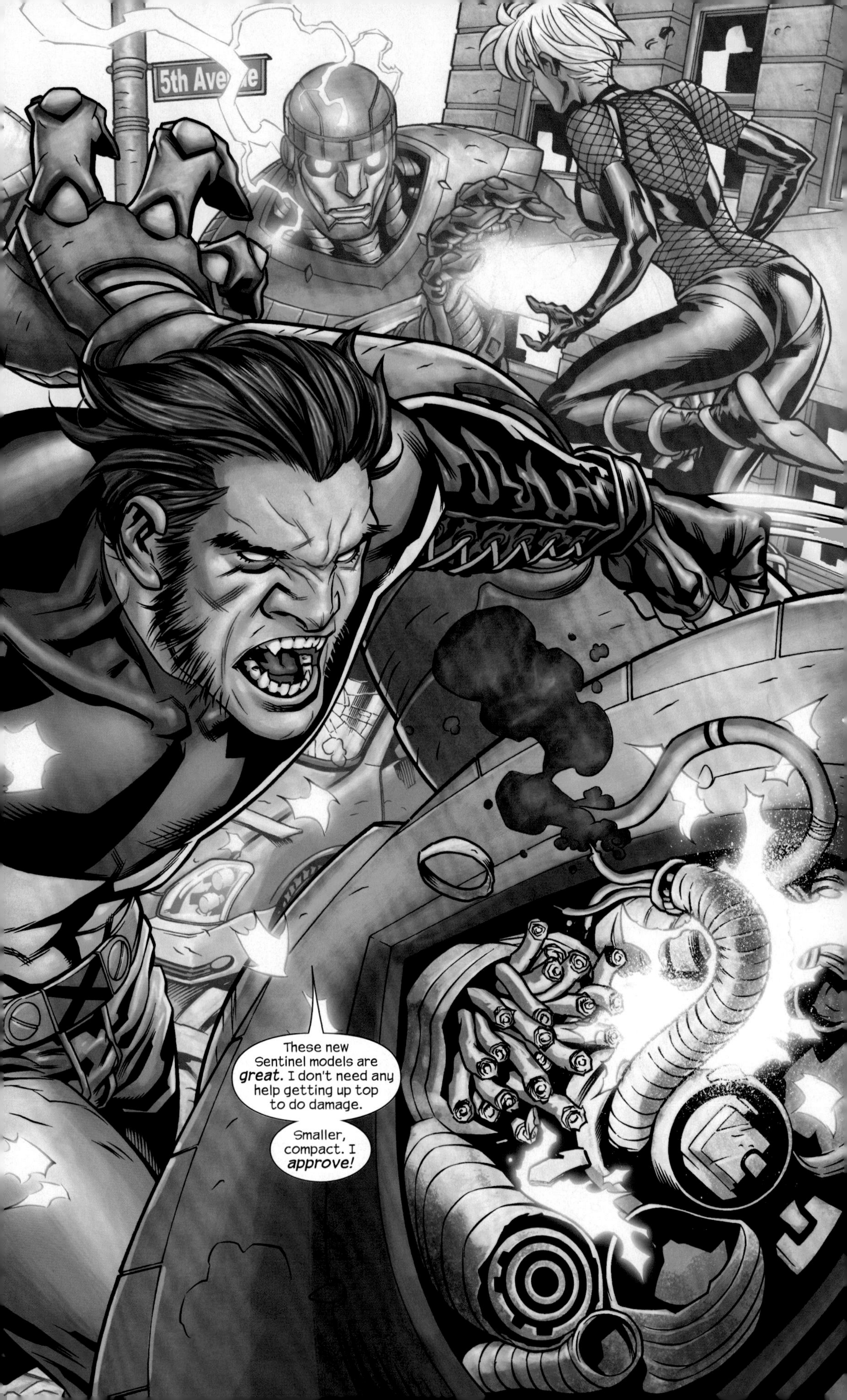
5th Ave
These new Sentinel models are *great*. I don't need any help getting up top to do damage.
Smaller, compact. I *approve!*

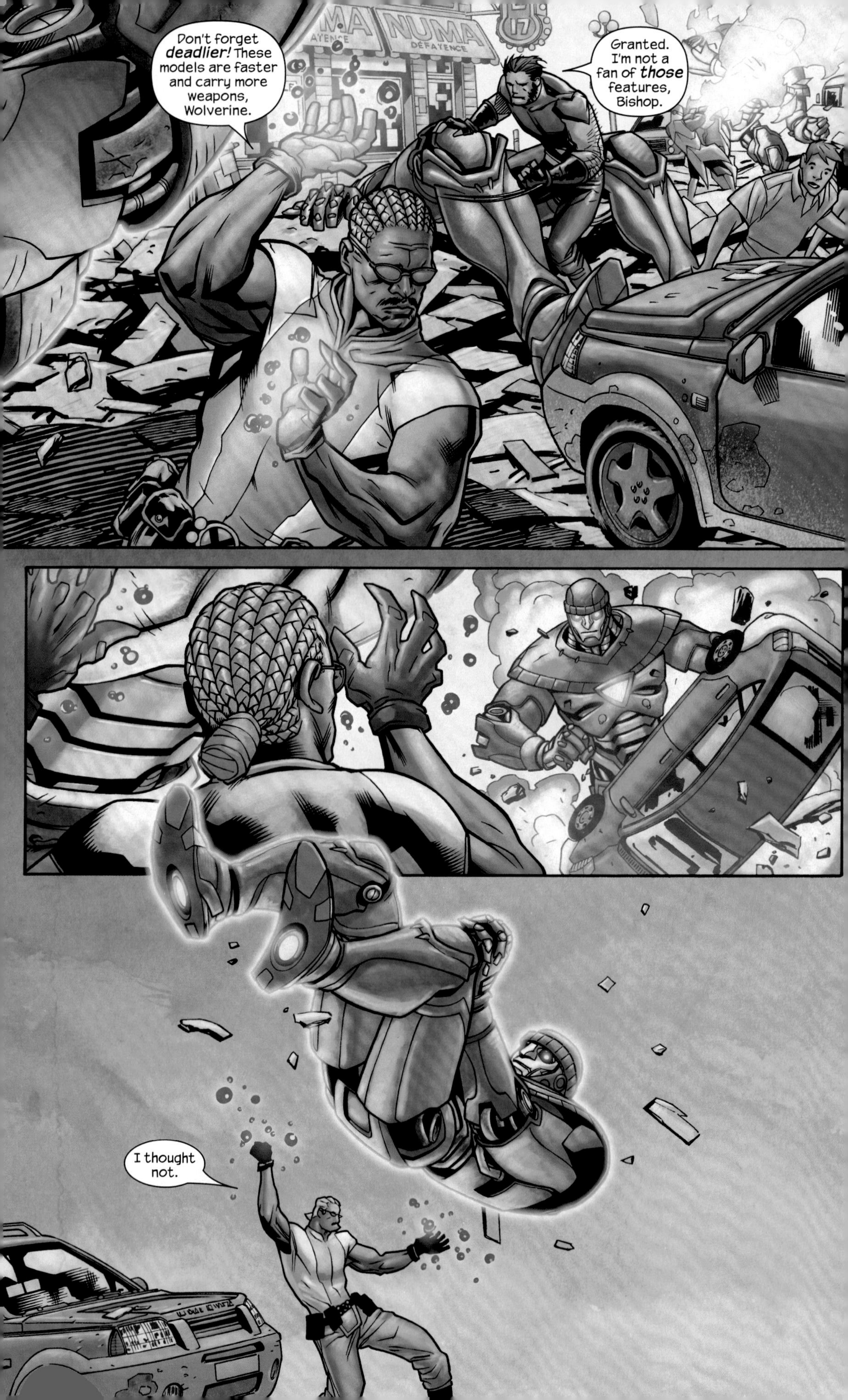
NUMA
Don't forget *deadlier!* These models are faster and carry more weapons, Wolverine.
Granted. I'm not a fan of *those* features, Bishop.
I thought not.

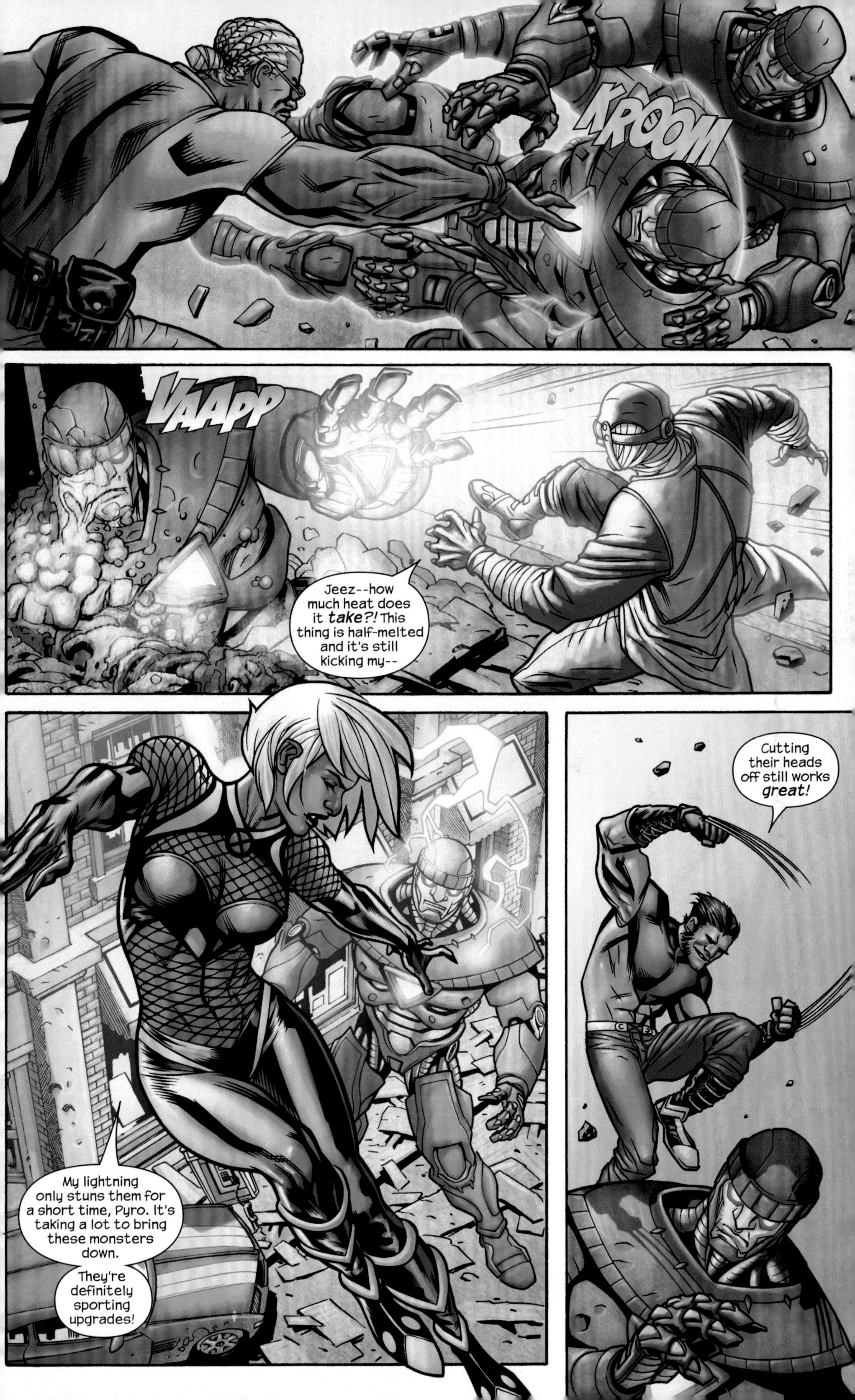
KROOM
VAAPP
Jeez--how much heat does it *take?!* This thing is half-melted and it's still kicking my--
My lightning only stuns them for a short time, Pyro. It's taking a lot to bring these monsters down.
They're definitely sporting upgrades!
Cutting their heads off still works *great!*

WHOOSH

KROOM

If it's brute force that'll bring them down, I can do that, too!

It's taking time but we're weeding them out. We could--

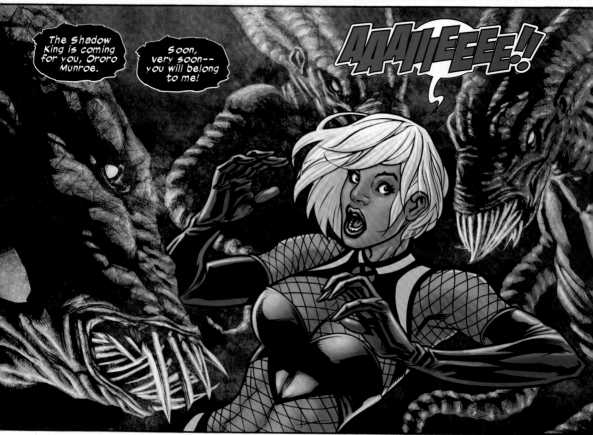

The Shadow King is coming for you, Ororo Munroe.

Soon, very soon-- you will belong to me!

AAAIIEEEE!!

Storm!

Just dreams... they're just dreams...

Never happened-- when I was-- awake.

C'mon, girl--pull it together.

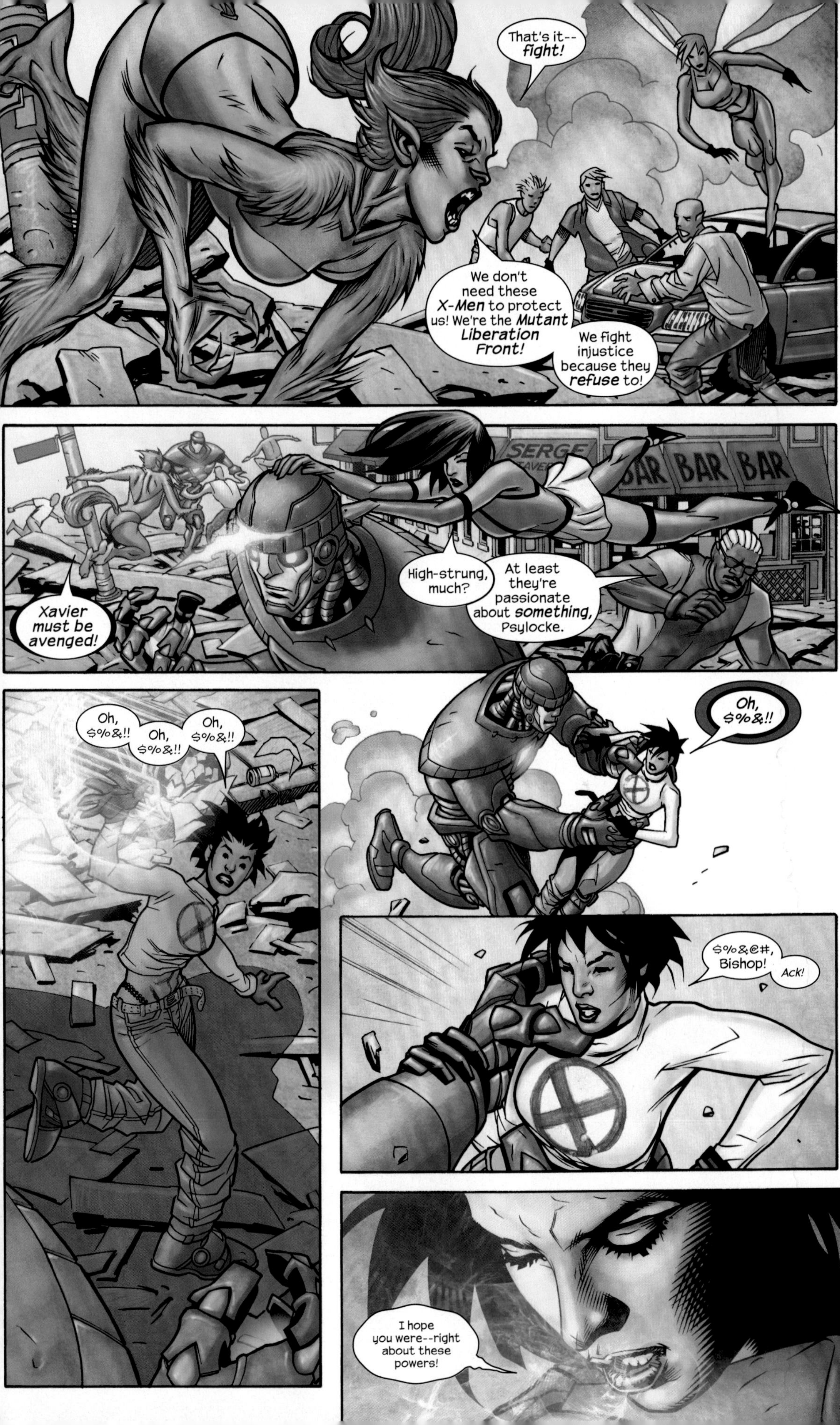
That's it--
fight!
We don't need these X-Men to protect us! We're the Mutant Liberation Front!
We fight injustice because they refuse to!
SERGE
BAR BAR BAR
Xavier must be avenged!
High-strung, much?
At least they're passionate about something, Psylocke.
Oh, $%&!!
Oh, $%&!!
Oh, $%&!!
Oh, $%&!!
$%&@#, Bishop!
Ack!
I hope you were--right about these powers!

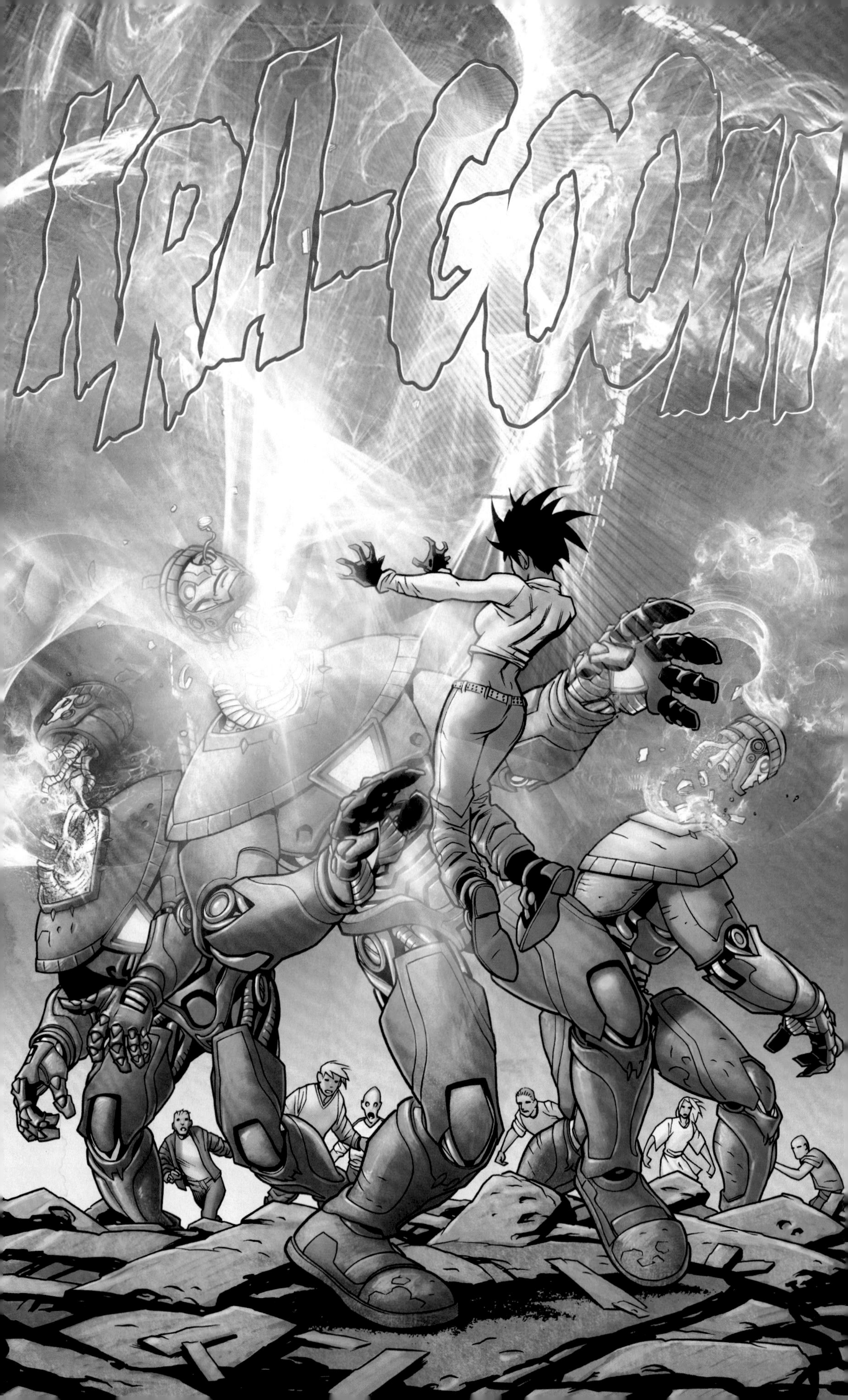
KRA-GOOM

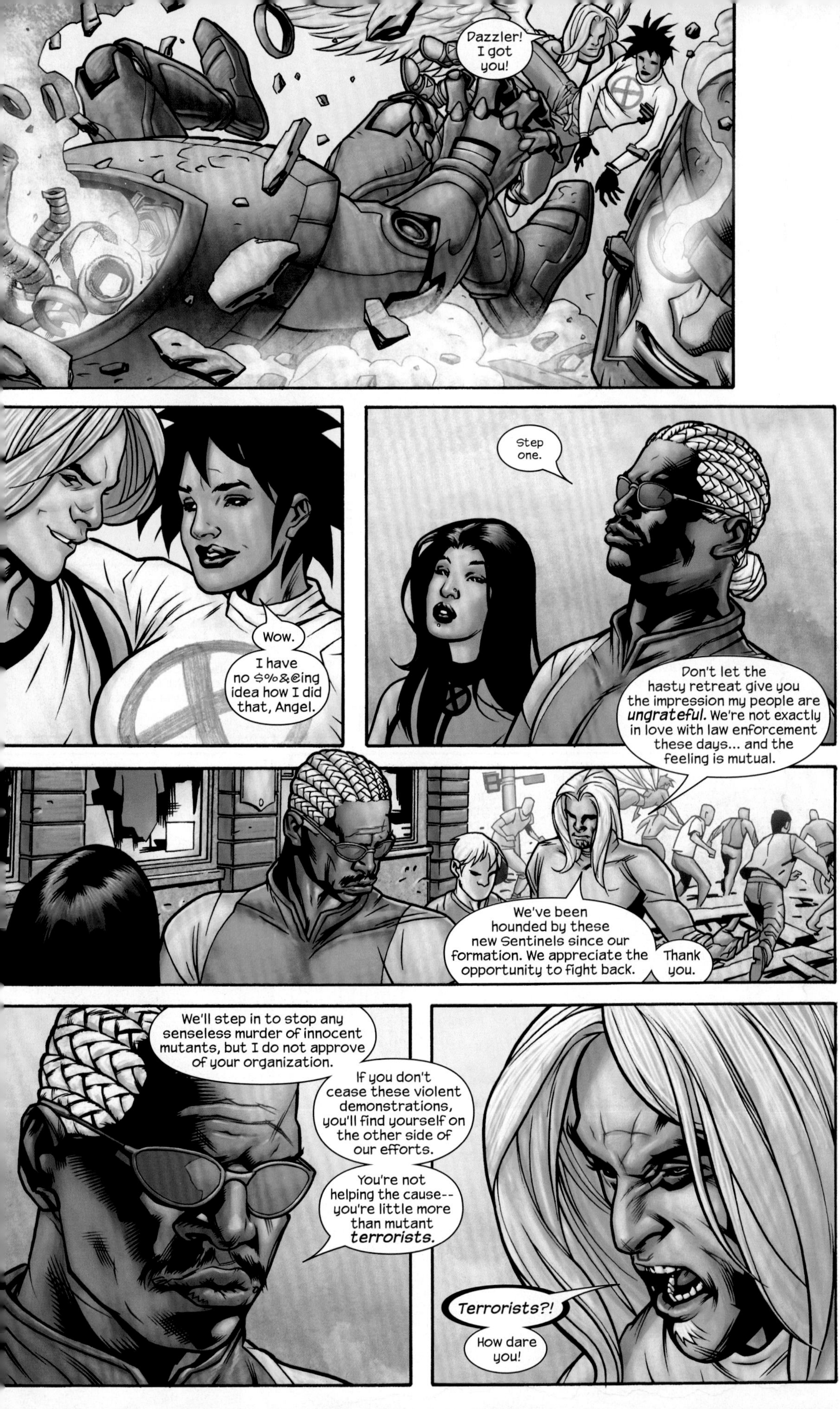
Dazzler! I got you!
Wow.
I have no $%&@ing idea how I did that, Angel.
Step one.
Don't let the hasty retreat give you the impression my people are *ungrateful.* We're not exactly in love with law enforcement these days... and the feeling is mutual.
We've been hounded by these new Sentinels since our formation. We appreciate the opportunity to fight back.
Thank you.
We'll step in to stop any senseless murder of innocent mutants, but I do not approve of your organization.
If you don't cease these violent demonstrations, you'll find yourself on the other side of our efforts.
You're not helping the cause--you're little more than mutant *terrorists.*
Terrorists?!
How dare you!

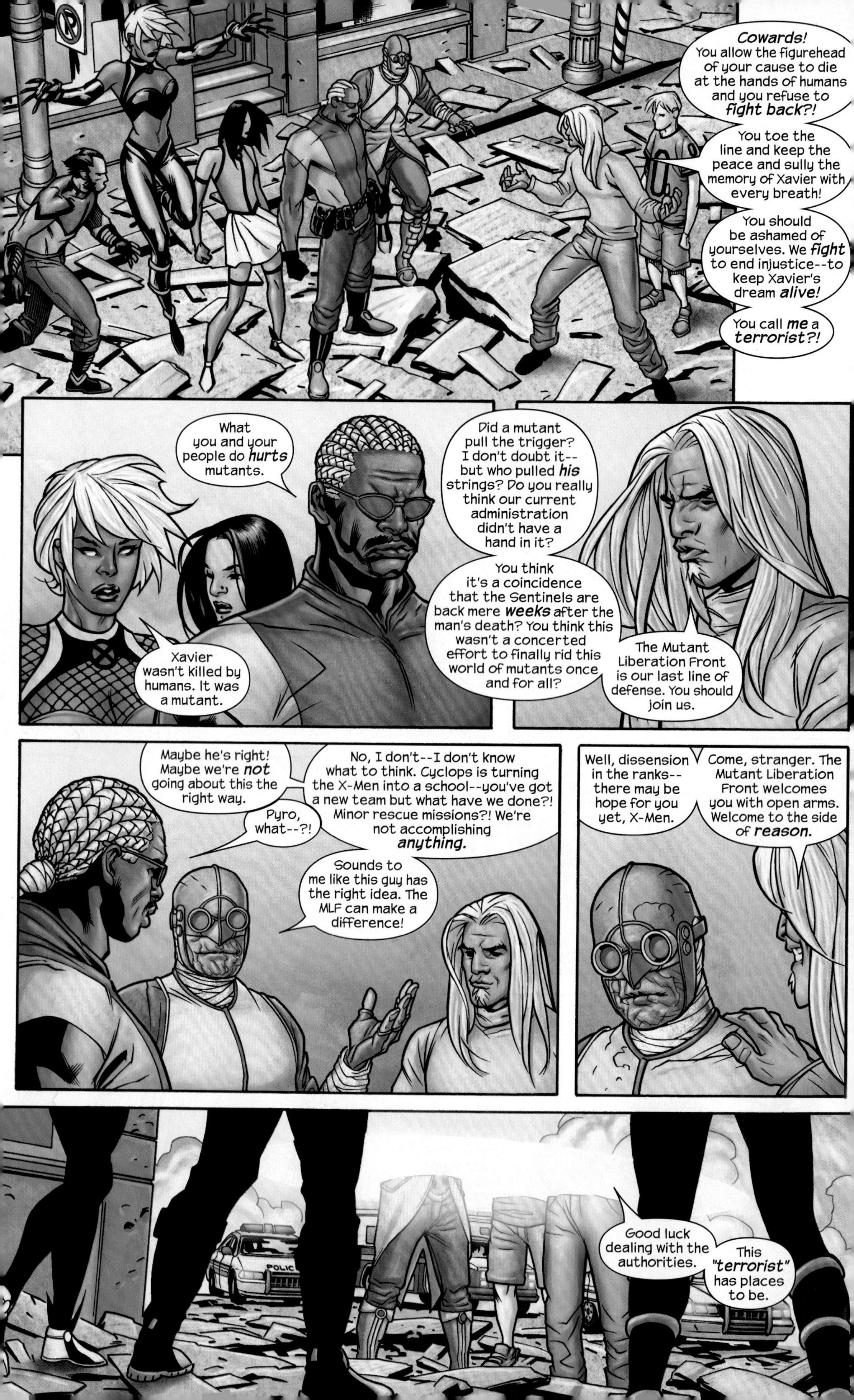
Cowards! You allow the figurehead of your cause to die at the hands of humans and you refuse to fight back?!
You toe the line and keep the peace and sully the memory of Xavier with every breath!
You should be ashamed of yourselves. We fight to end injustice--to keep Xavier's dream alive!
You call me a terrorist?!
What you and your people do hurts mutants.
Xavier wasn't killed by humans. It was a mutant.
Did a mutant pull the trigger? I don't doubt it--but who pulled his strings? Do you really think our current administration didn't have a hand in it?
You think it's a coincidence that the Sentinels are back mere weeks after the man's death? You think this wasn't a concerted effort to finally rid this world of mutants once and for all?
The Mutant Liberation Front is our last line of defense. You should join us.
Maybe he's right! Maybe we're not going about this the right way.
Pyro, what--?!
No, I don't--I don't know what to think. Cyclops is turning the X-Men into a school--you've got a new team but what have we done?! Minor rescue missions?! We're not accomplishing anything.
Sounds to me like this guy has the right idea. The MLF can make a difference!
Well, dissension in the ranks--there may be hope for you yet, X-Men.
Come, stranger. The Mutant Liberation Front welcomes you with open arms. Welcome to the side of reason.
POLIC
Good luck dealing with the authorities.
This "terrorist" has places to be.

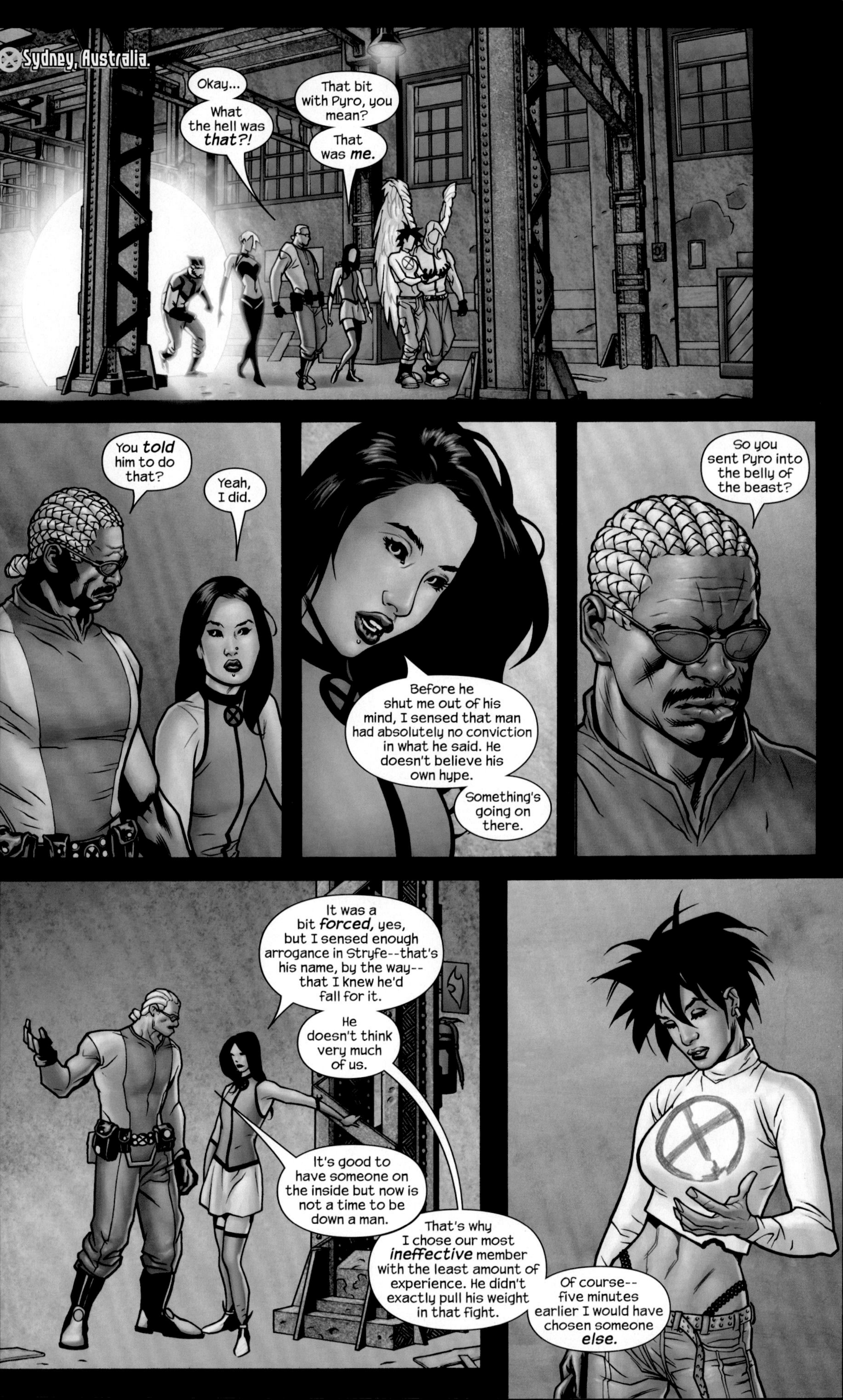

Sydney, Australia.
Okay... What the hell was *that?!*
That bit with Pyro, you mean?
That was **me.**
You **told** him to do that?
Yeah, I did.
Before he shut me out of his mind, I sensed that man had absolutely no conviction in what he said. He doesn't believe his own hype.
Something's going on there.
So you sent Pyro into the belly of the beast?
It was a bit *forced,* yes, but I sensed enough arrogance in Stryfe--that's his name, by the way--that I knew he'd fall for it.
He doesn't think very much of us.
It's good to have someone on the inside but now is not a time to be down a man.
That's why I chose our most ***ineffective*** member with the least amount of experience. He didn't exactly pull his weight in that fight.
Of course-- five minutes earlier I would have chosen someone ***else.***

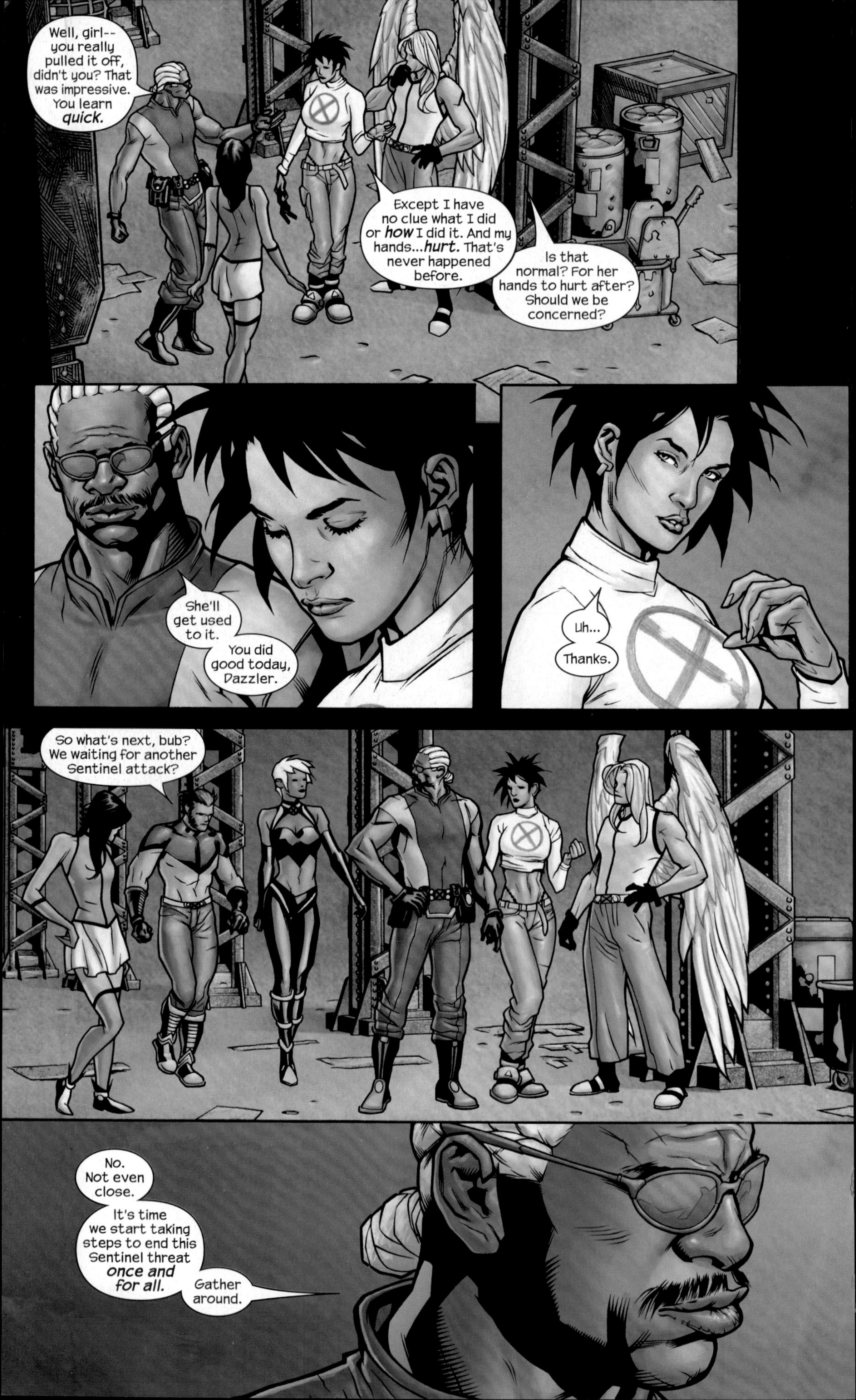
Well, girl-- you really pulled it off, didn't you? That was impressive. You learn *quick.*
Except I have no clue what I did or *how* I did it. And my hands...*hurt.* That's never happened before.
Is that normal? For her hands to hurt after? Should we be concerned?
She'll get used to it.
You did good today, Dazzler.
Uh...
Thanks.
So what's next, bub? We waiting for another Sentinel attack?
No. Not even close.
It's time we start taking steps to end this Sentinel threat *once and for all.*
Gather around.

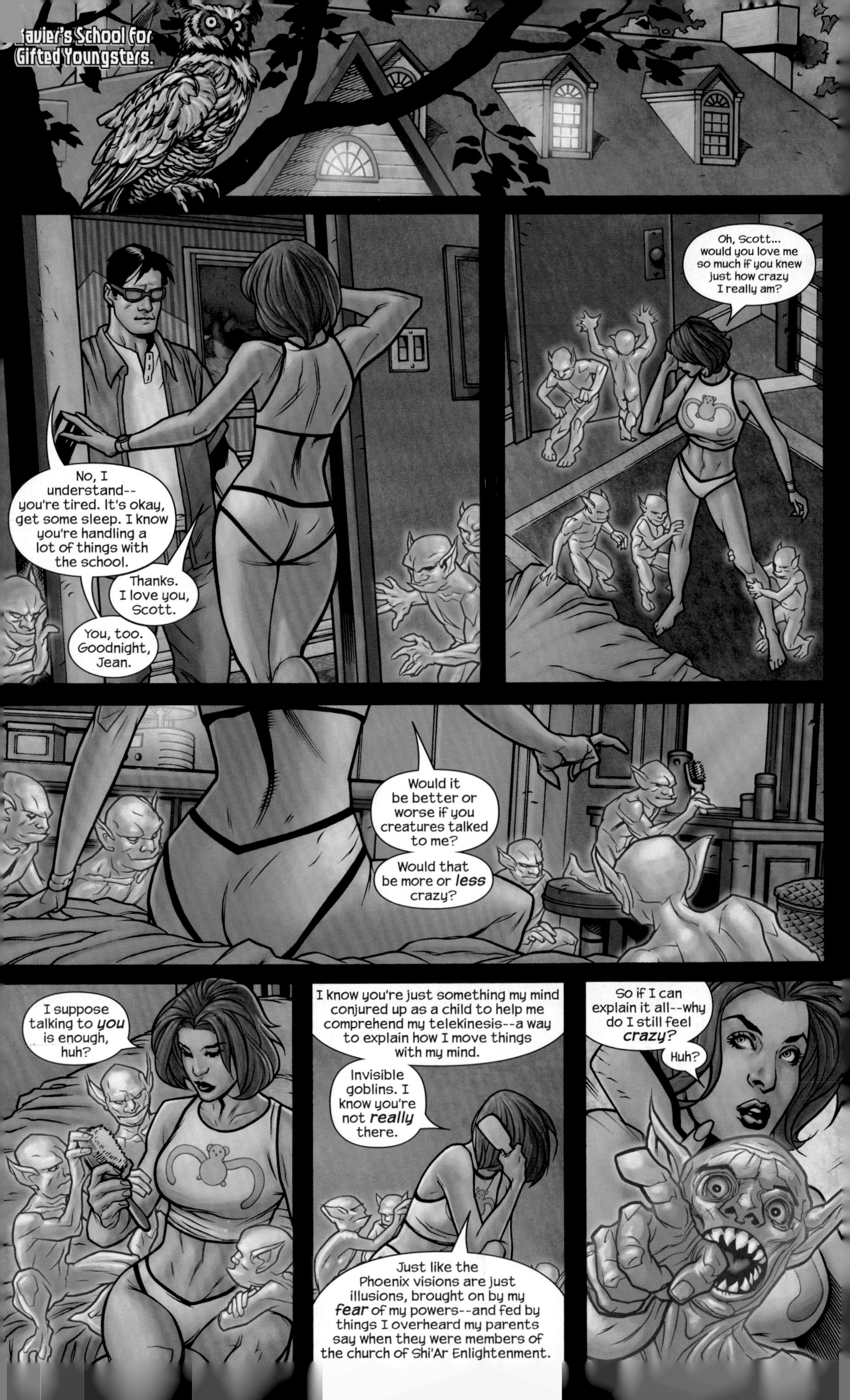
Xavier's School for Gifted Youngsters.
No, I understand--you're tired. It's okay, get some sleep. I know you're handling a lot of things with the school.
Thanks. I love you, Scott.
You, too. Goodnight, Jean.
Oh, Scott... would you love me so much if you knew just how crazy I really am?
Would it be better or worse if you creatures talked to me?
Would that be more or less crazy?
I suppose talking to you is enough, huh?
I know you're just something my mind conjured up as a child to help me comprehend my telekinesis--a way to explain how I move things with my mind.
Invisible goblins. I know you're not really there.
Just like the Phoenix visions are just illusions, brought on by my fear of my powers--and fed by things I overheard my parents say when they were members of the church of Shi'Ar Enlightenment.
So if I can explain it all--why do I still feel crazy?
Huh?

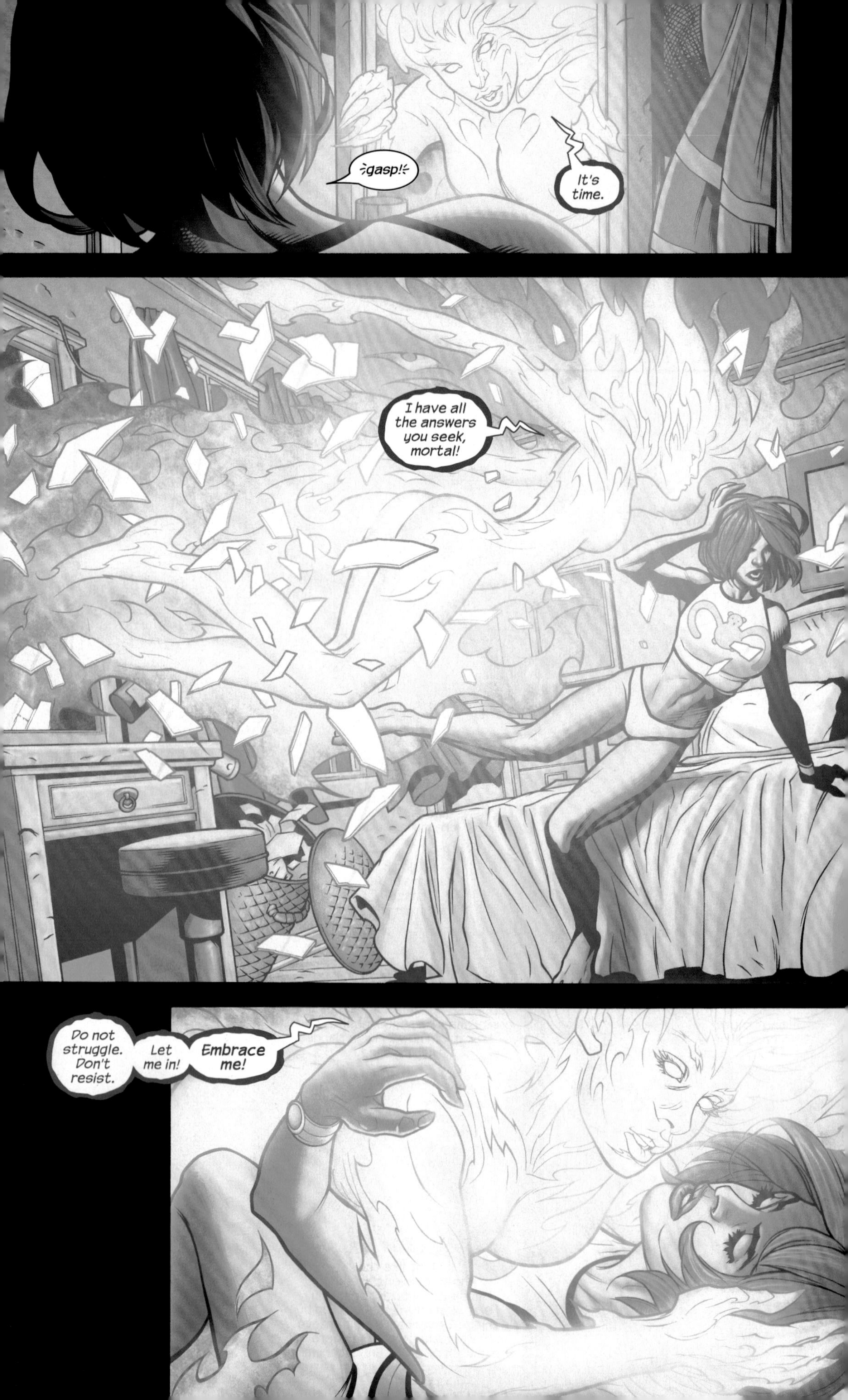

gasp!
It's time.
I have all the answers you seek, mortal!
Do not struggle. Don't resist.
Let me in!
Embrace me!

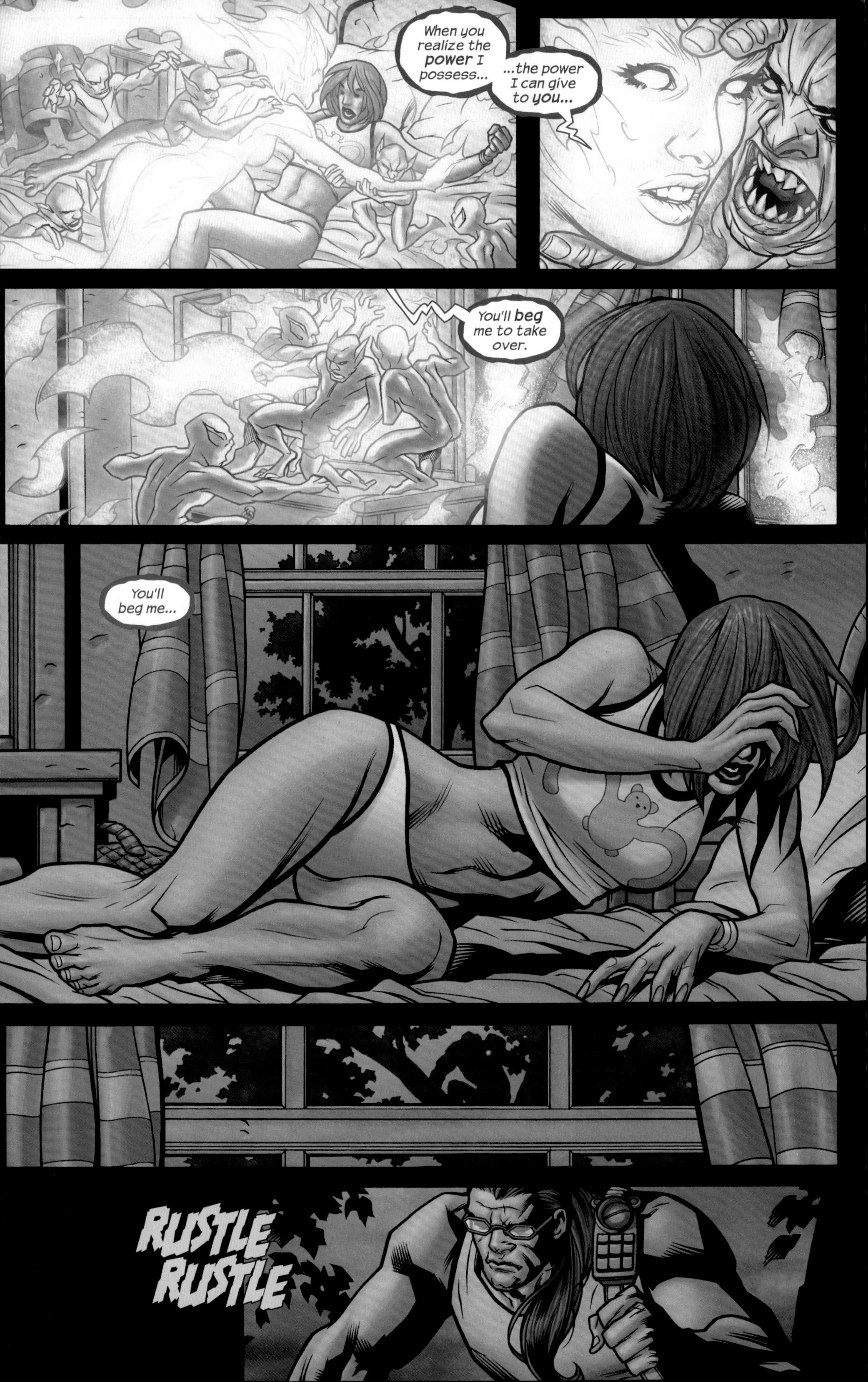
When you realize the power I possess...
...the power I can give to you...
You'll beg me to take over.
You'll beg me...
RUSTLE RUSTLE

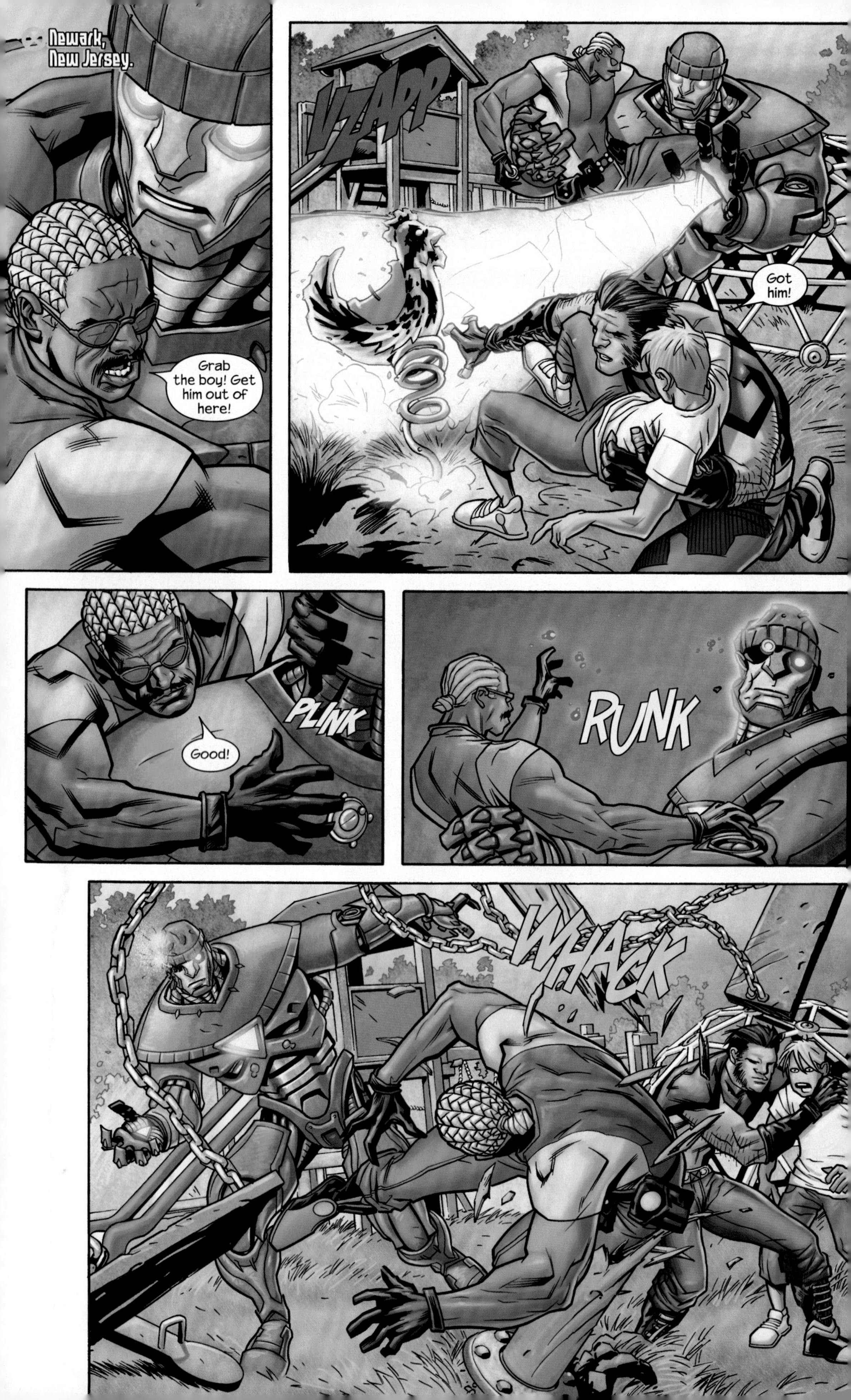
Newark, New Jersey.
Grab the boy! Get him out of here!
VZAPP
Got him!
PLINK
Good!
RUNK
WHACK

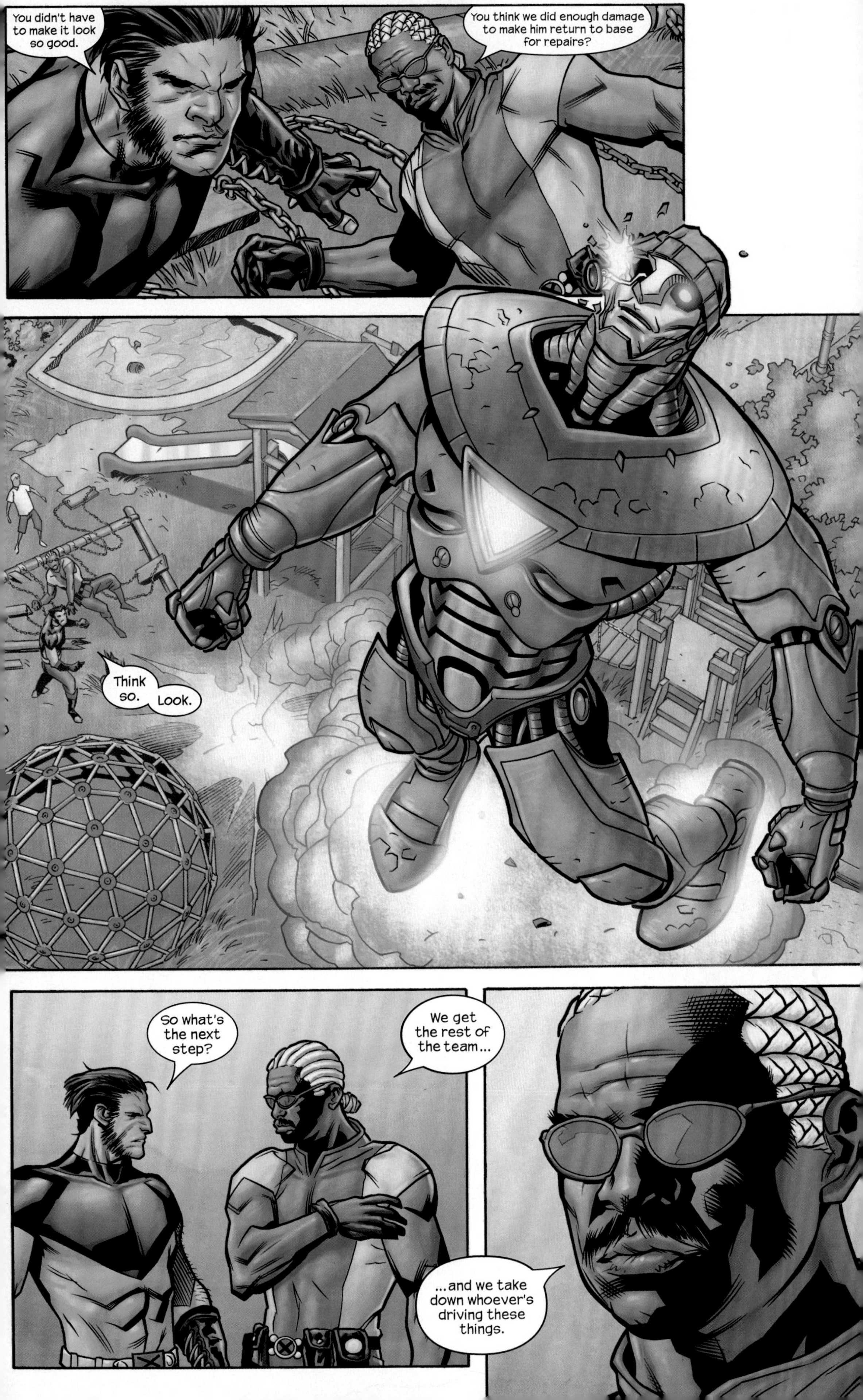
You didn't have to make it look so good.
You think we did enough damage to make him return to base for repairs?
Think so.
Look.
So what's the next step?
We get the rest of the team...
...and we take down whoever's driving these things.

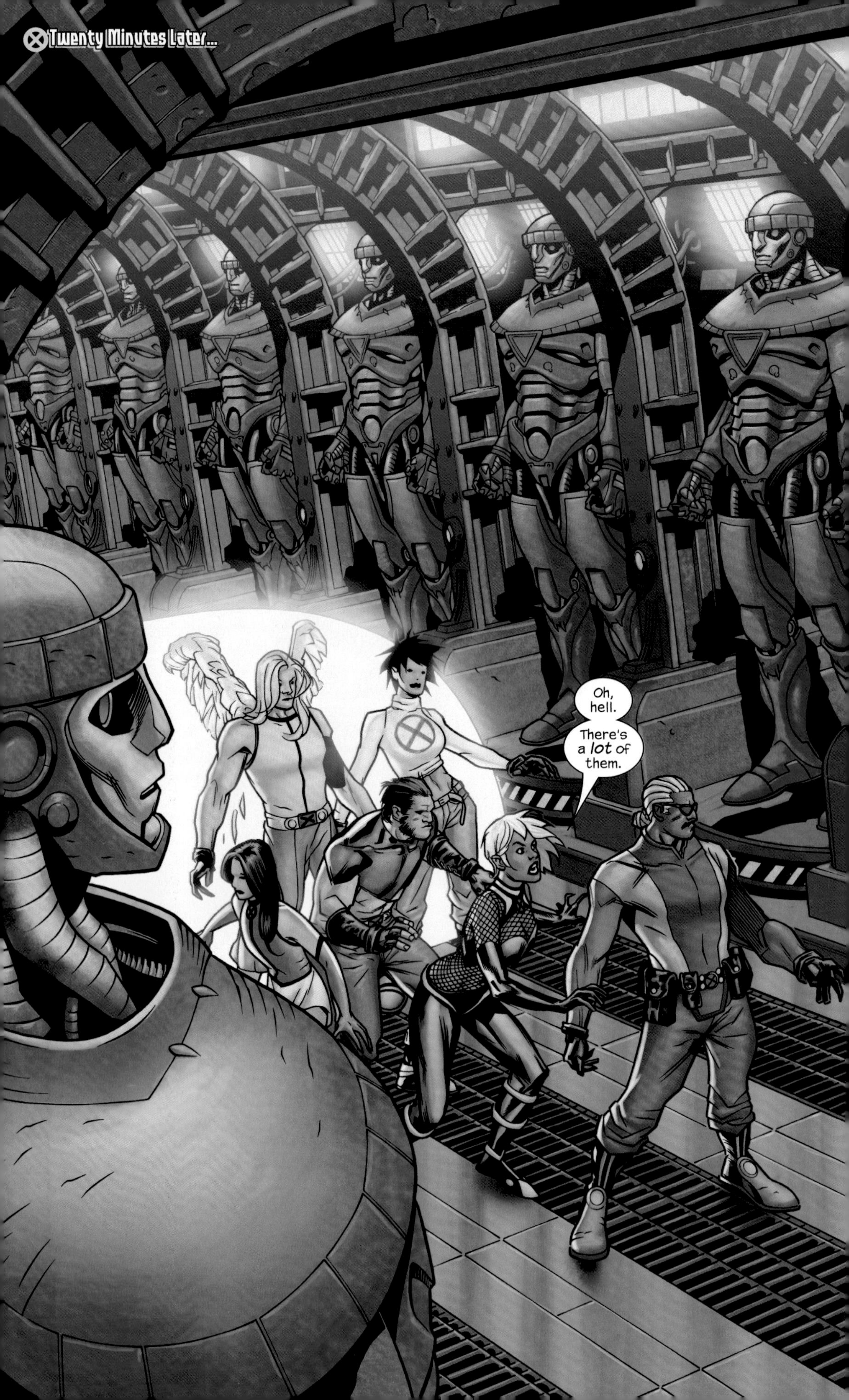
Twenty Minutes Later...
Oh, hell.
There's a *lot* of them.

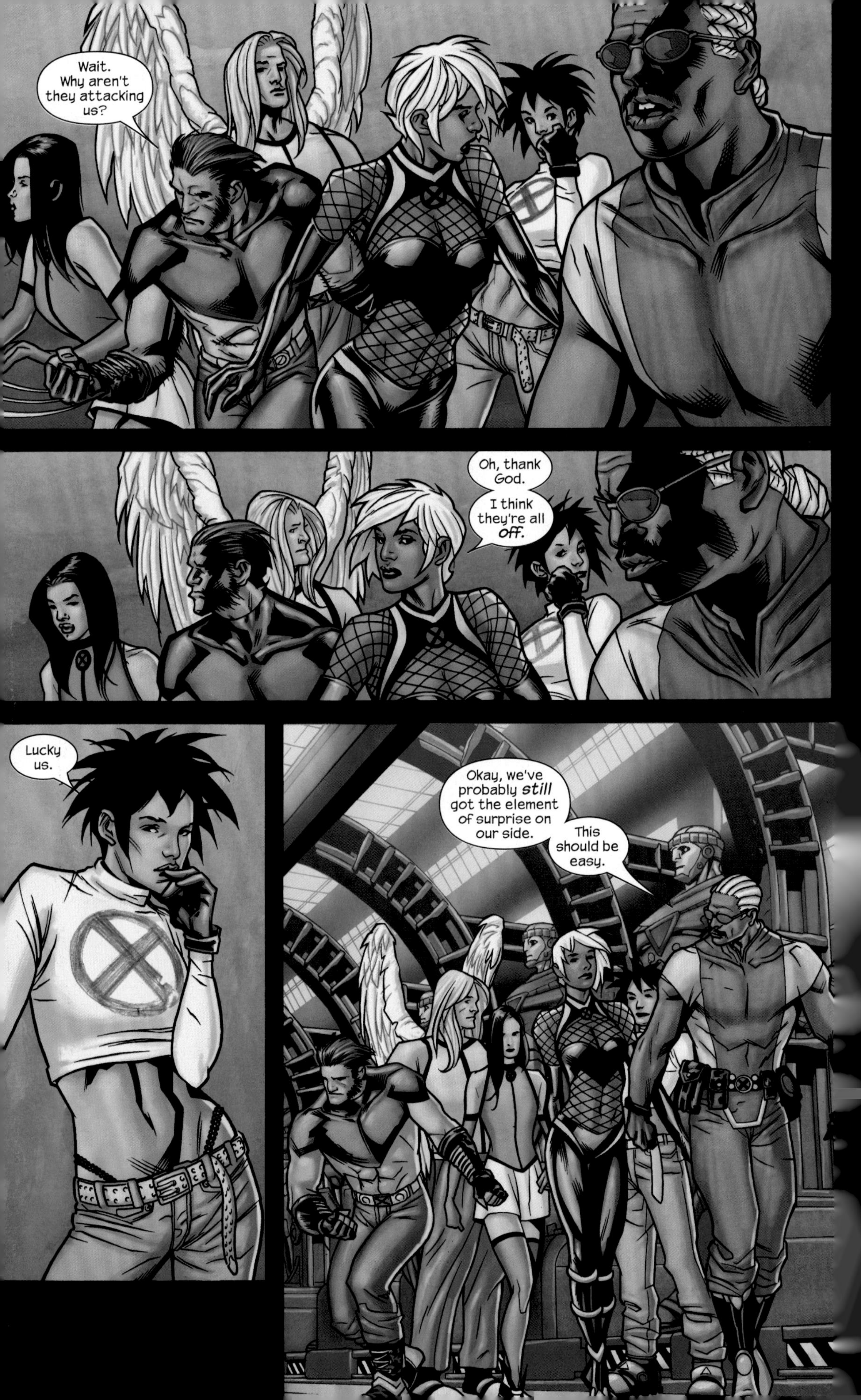
Wait. Why aren't they attacking us?
Oh, thank God.
I think they're all ***off.***
Lucky us.
Okay, we've probably ***still*** got the element of surprise on our side.
This should be easy.

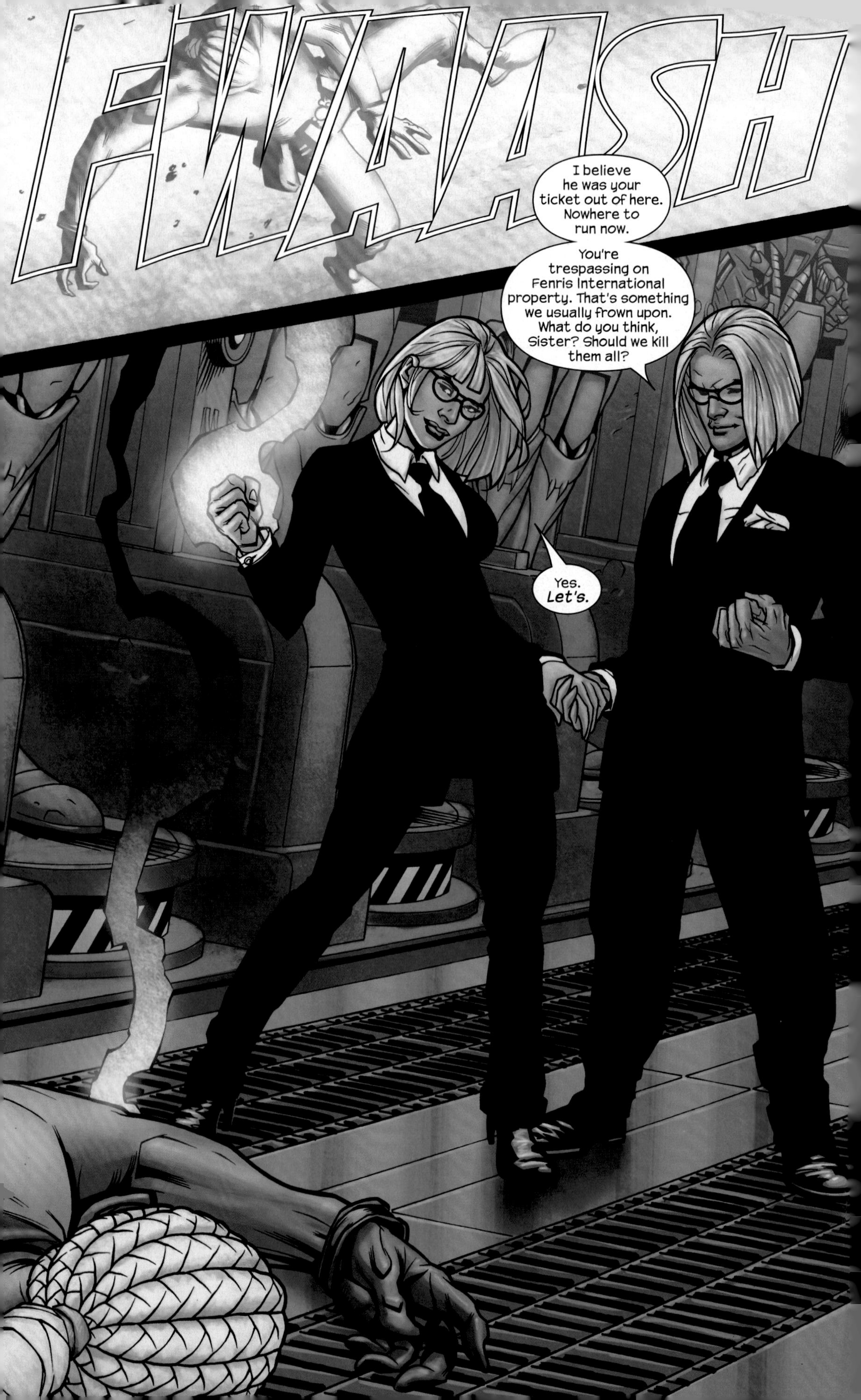
FWASH
I believe he was your ticket out of here. Nowhere to run now.
You're trespassing on Fenris International property. That's something we usually frown upon. What do you think, Sister? Should we kill them all?
Yes. **Let's.**

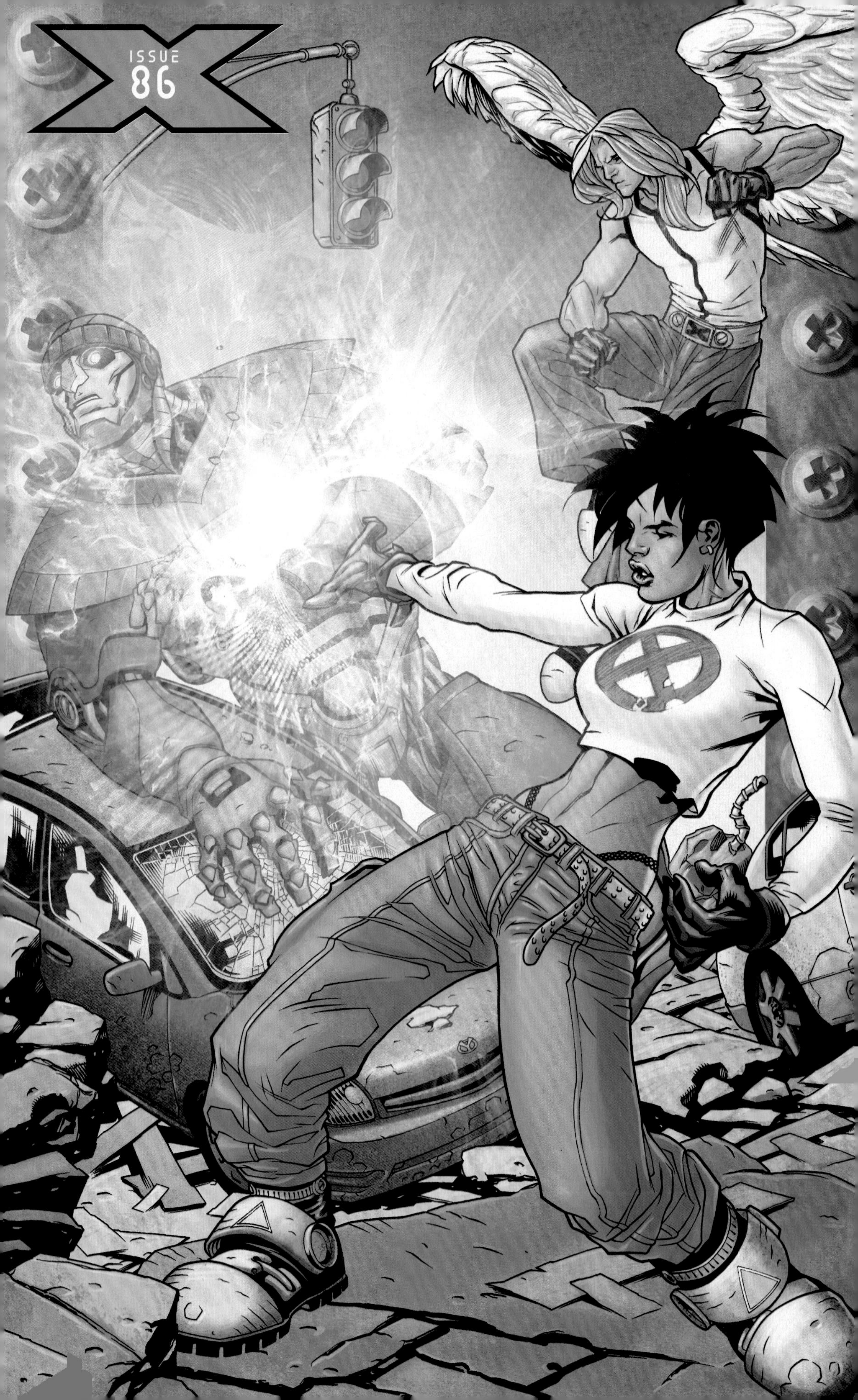
ISSUE
86

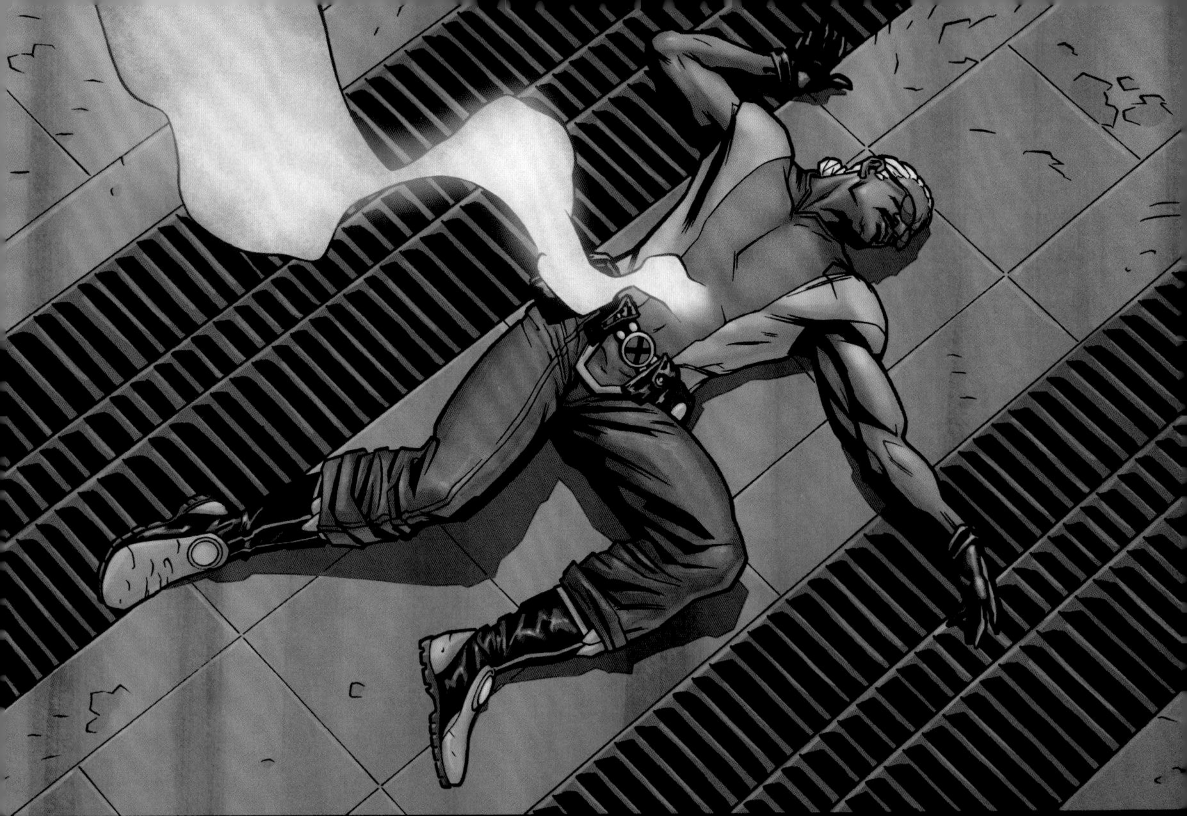

SENTINELS

PART 3 (OF 5)

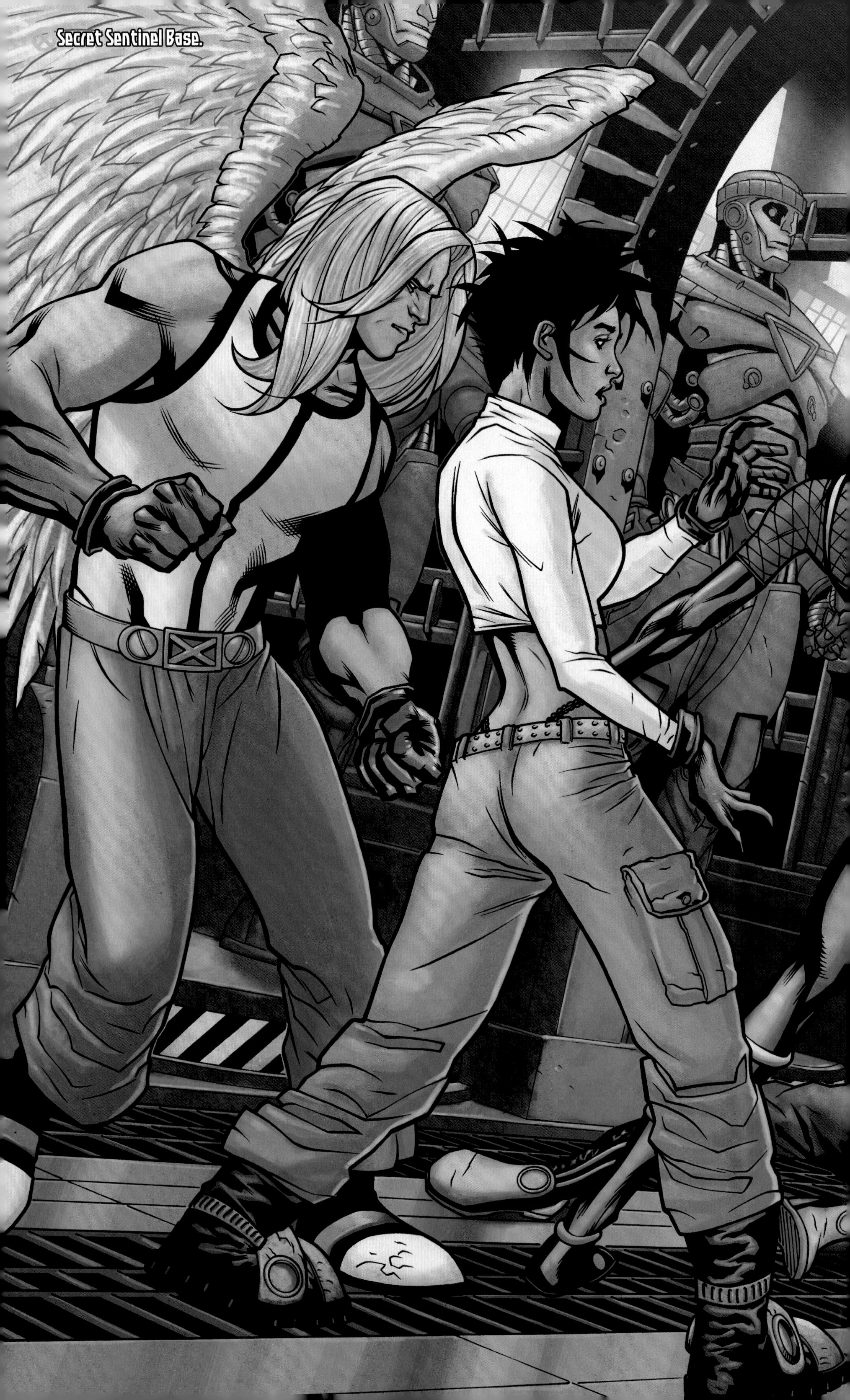
Secret Sentinel Base.

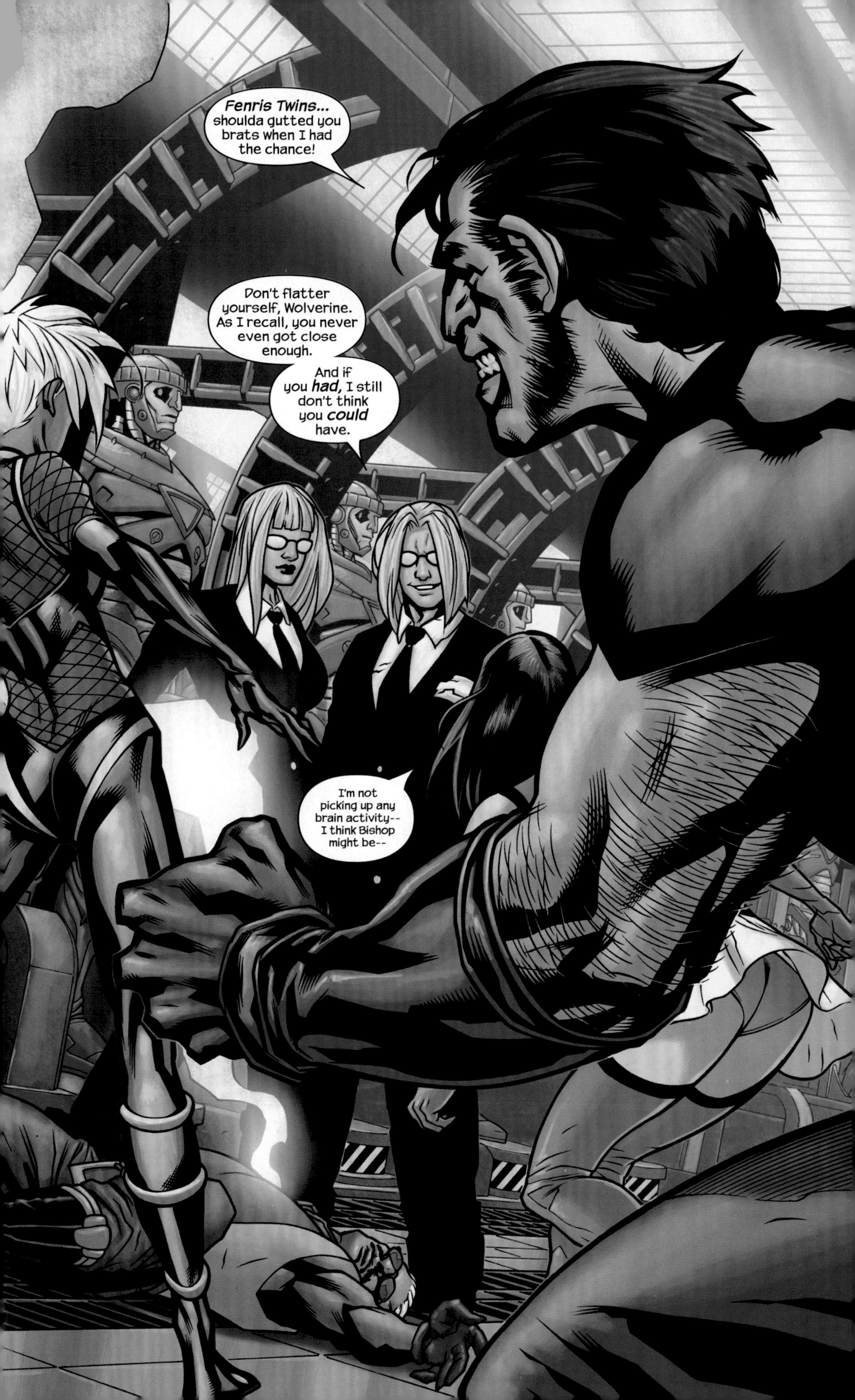
Fenris Twins... shoulda gutted you brats when I had the chance!
Don't flatter yourself, Wolverine. As I recall, you never even got close enough.
And if you had, I still don't think you could have.
I'm not picking up any brain activity-- I think Bishop might be--

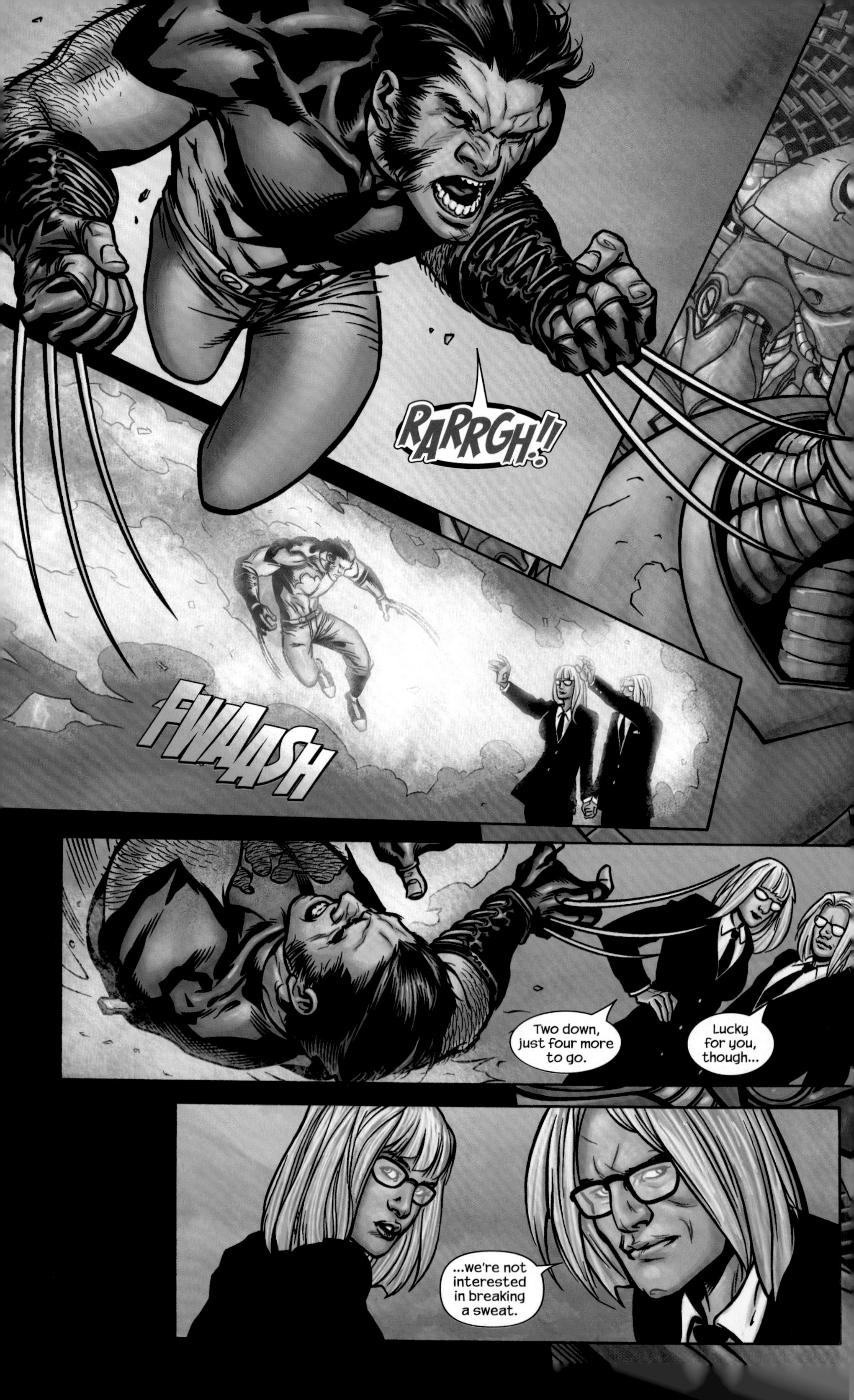
RARRGH!!
FWAASH
Two down, just four more to go.
Lucky for you, though...
...we're not interested in breaking a sweat.

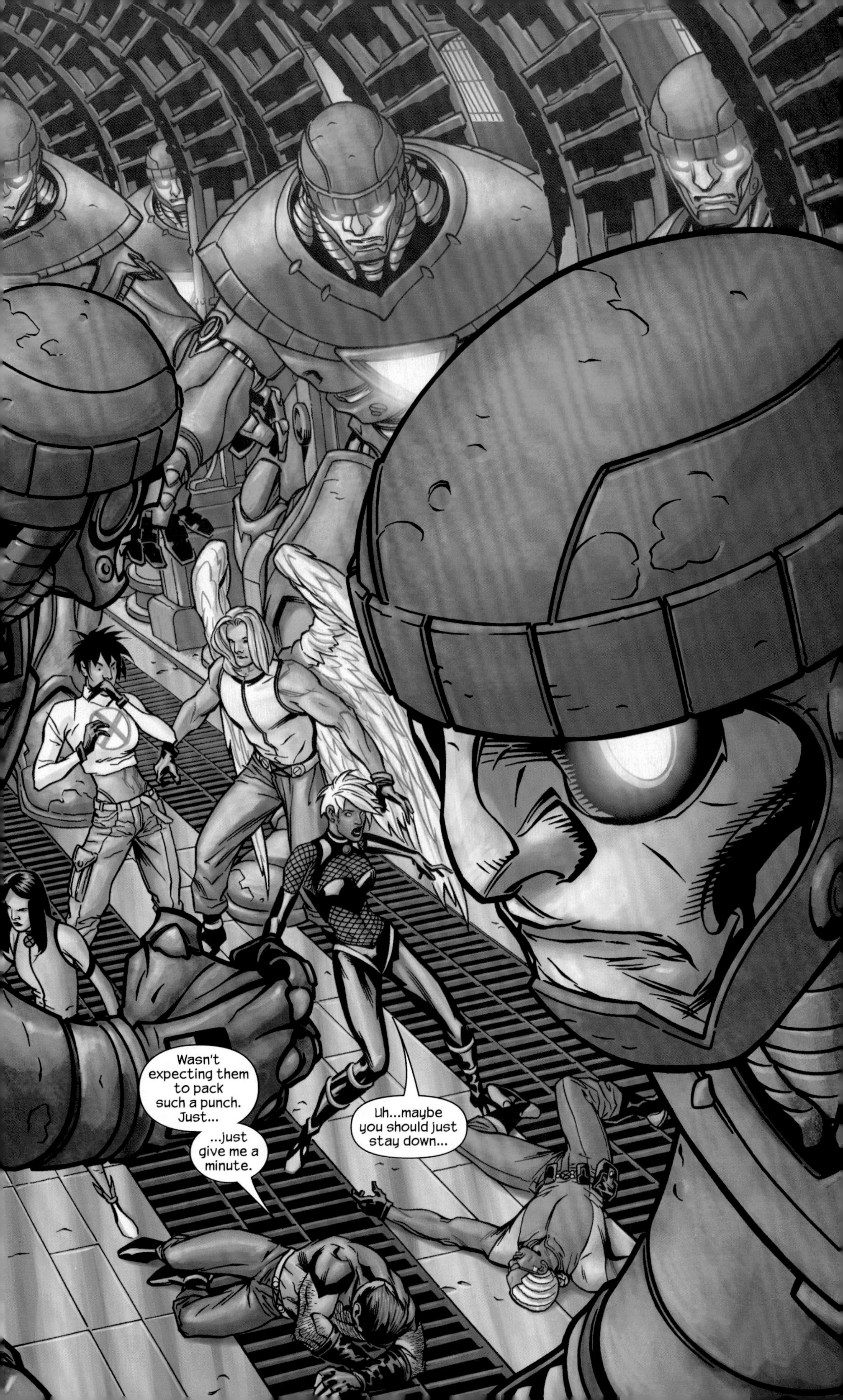
Wasn't expecting them to pack such a punch. Just...
...just give me a minute.
Uh...maybe you should just stay down...

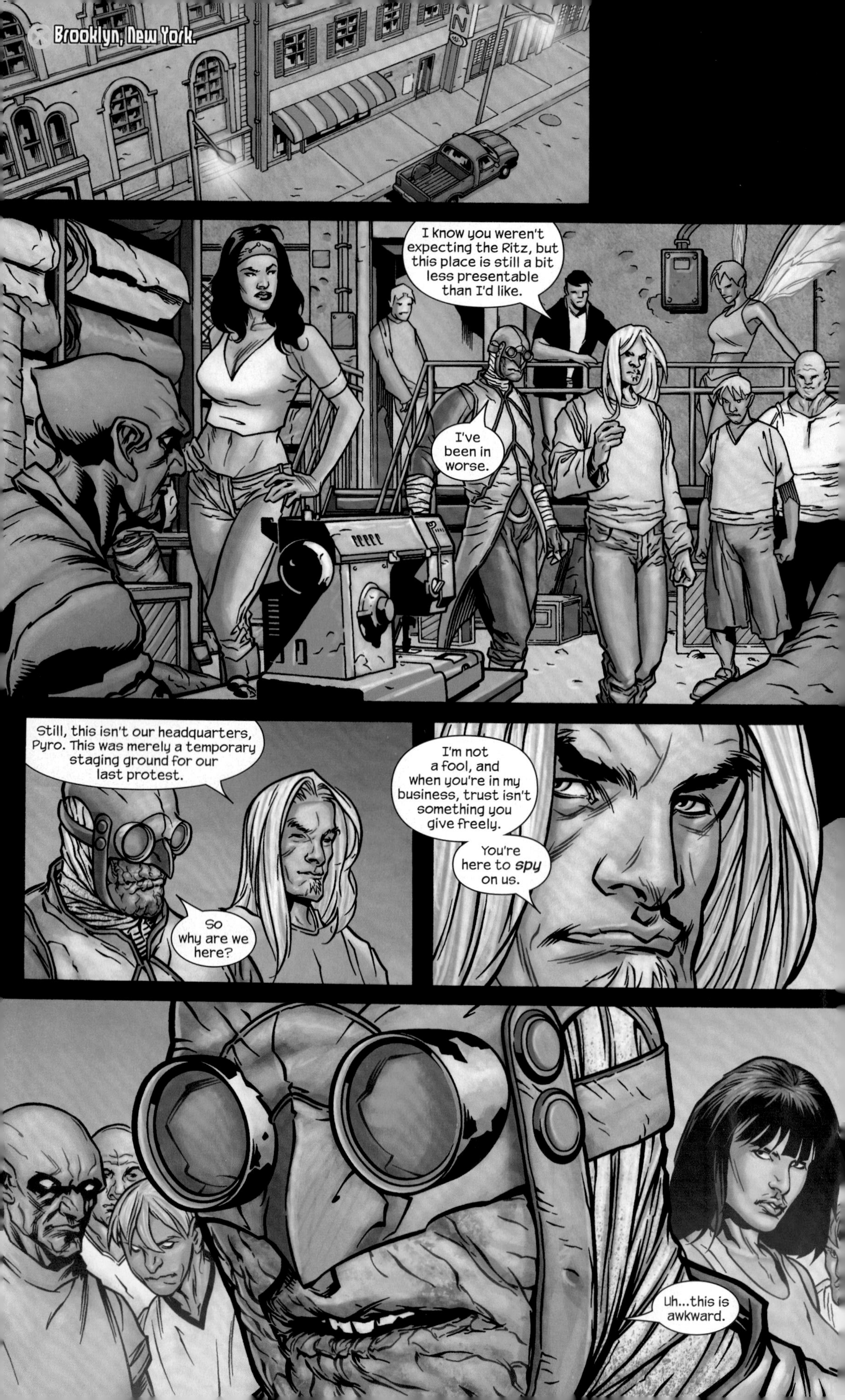
Brooklyn, New York.
I know you weren't expecting the Ritz, but this place is still a bit less presentable than I'd like.
I've been in worse.
Still, this isn't our headquarters, Pyro. This was merely a temporary staging ground for our last protest.
So why are we here?
I'm not a fool, and when you're in my business, trust isn't something you give freely.
You're here to spy on us.
Uh...this is awkward.

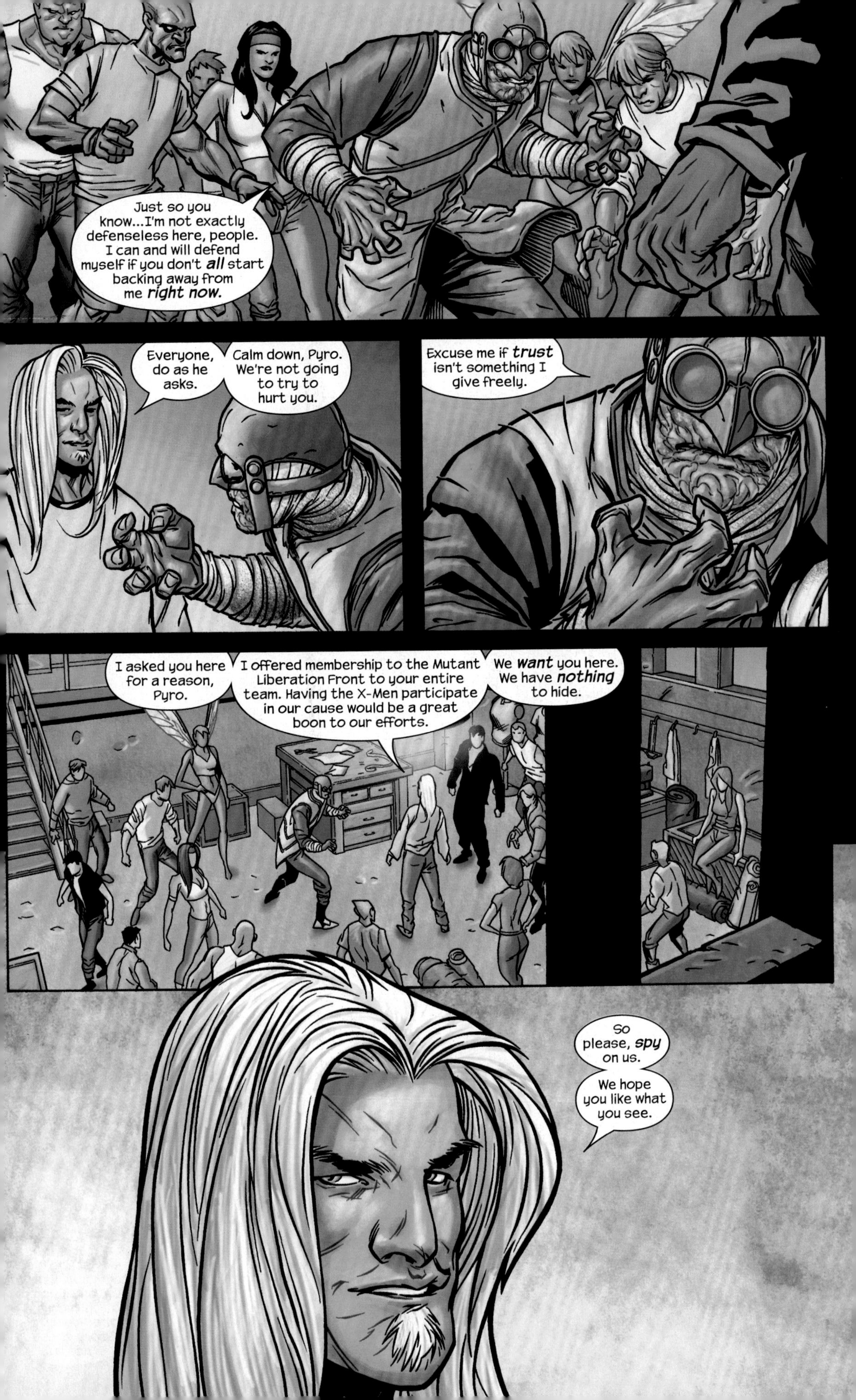
Just so you know...I'm not exactly defenseless here, people. I can and will defend myself if you don't *all* start backing away from me *right now.*
Everyone, do as he asks.
Calm down, Pyro. We're not going to try to hurt you.
Excuse me if *trust* isn't something I give freely.
I asked you here for a reason, Pyro.
I offered membership to the Mutant Liberation Front to your entire team. Having the X-Men participate in our cause would be a great boon to our efforts.
We *want* you here. We have *nothing* to hide.
So please, *spy* on us.
We hope you like what you see.

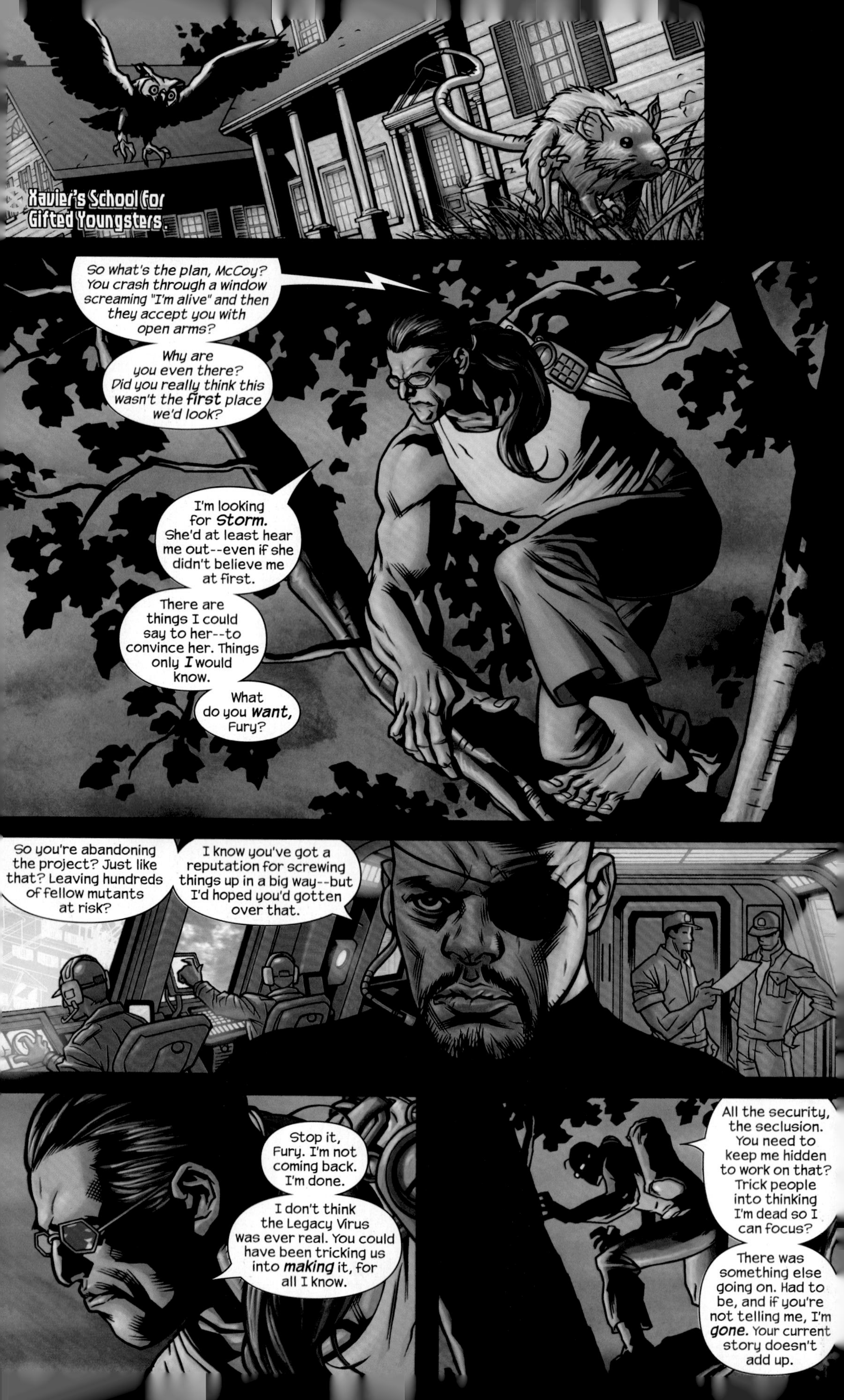
Xavier's School for Gifted Youngsters.
So what's the plan, McCoy? You crash through a window screaming "I'm alive" and then they accept you with open arms?
Why are you even there? Did you really think this wasn't the first place we'd look?
I'm looking for Storm. She'd at least hear me out--even if she didn't believe me at first.
There are things I could say to her--to convince her. Things only I would know.
What do you want, Fury?
So you're abandoning the project? Just like that? Leaving hundreds of fellow mutants at risk?
I know you've got a reputation for screwing things up in a big way--but I'd hoped you'd gotten over that.
Stop it, Fury. I'm not coming back. I'm done.
I don't think the Legacy Virus was ever real. You could have been tricking us into making it, for all I know.
All the security, the seclusion. You need to keep me hidden to work on that? Trick people into thinking I'm dead so I can focus?
There was something else going on. Had to be, and if you're not telling me, I'm gone. Your current story doesn't add up.

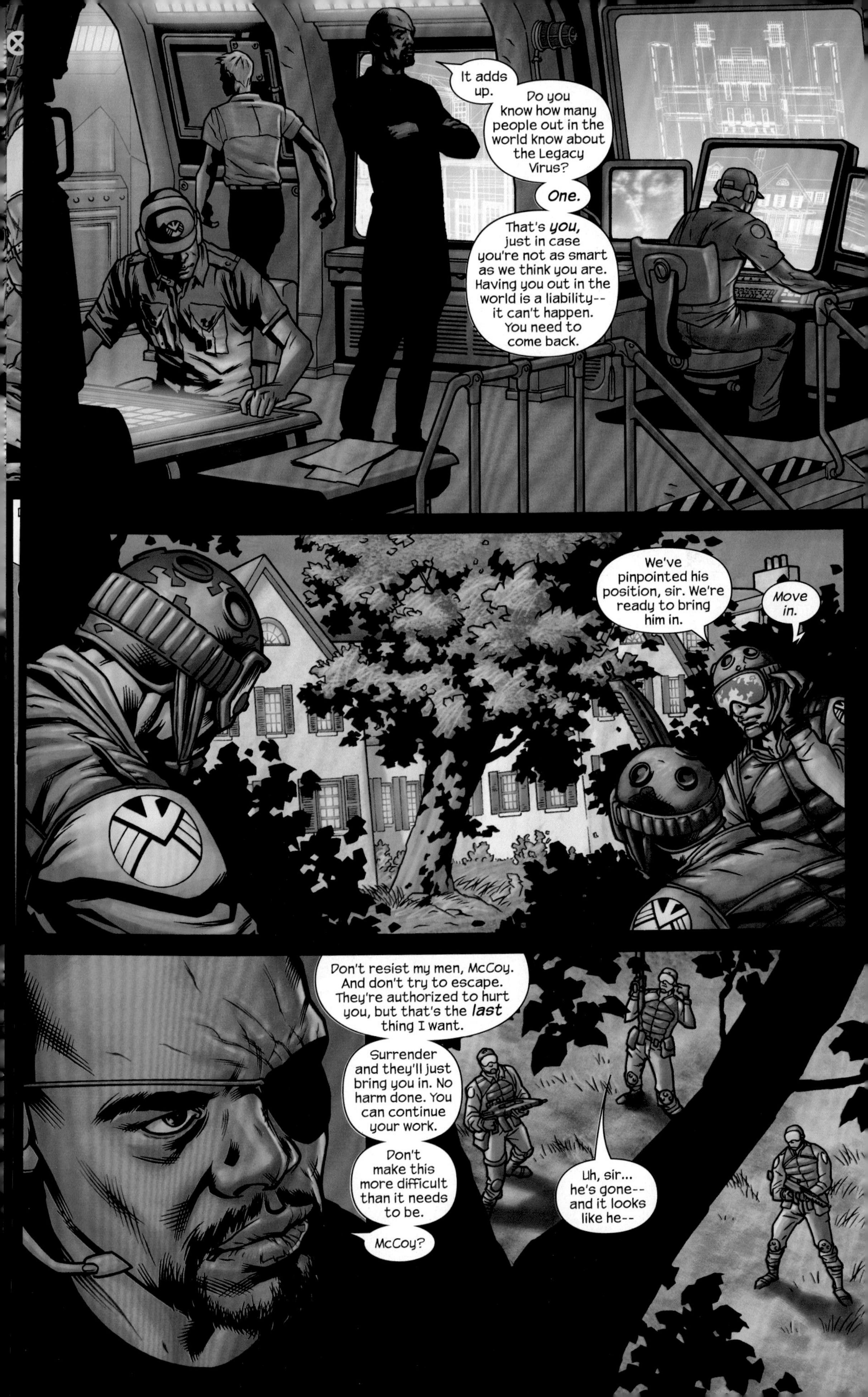
It adds up.
Do you know how many people out in the world know about the Legacy Virus?
One.
That's *you,* just in case you're not as smart as we think you are. Having you out in the world is a liability-- it can't happen. You need to come back.
We've pinpointed his position, sir. We're ready to bring him in.
Move in.
Don't resist my men, McCoy. And don't try to escape. They're authorized to hurt you, but that's the *last* thing I want.
Surrender and they'll just bring you in. No harm done. You can continue your work.
Don't make this more difficult than it needs to be.
McCoy?
Uh, sir... he's gone-- and it looks like he--

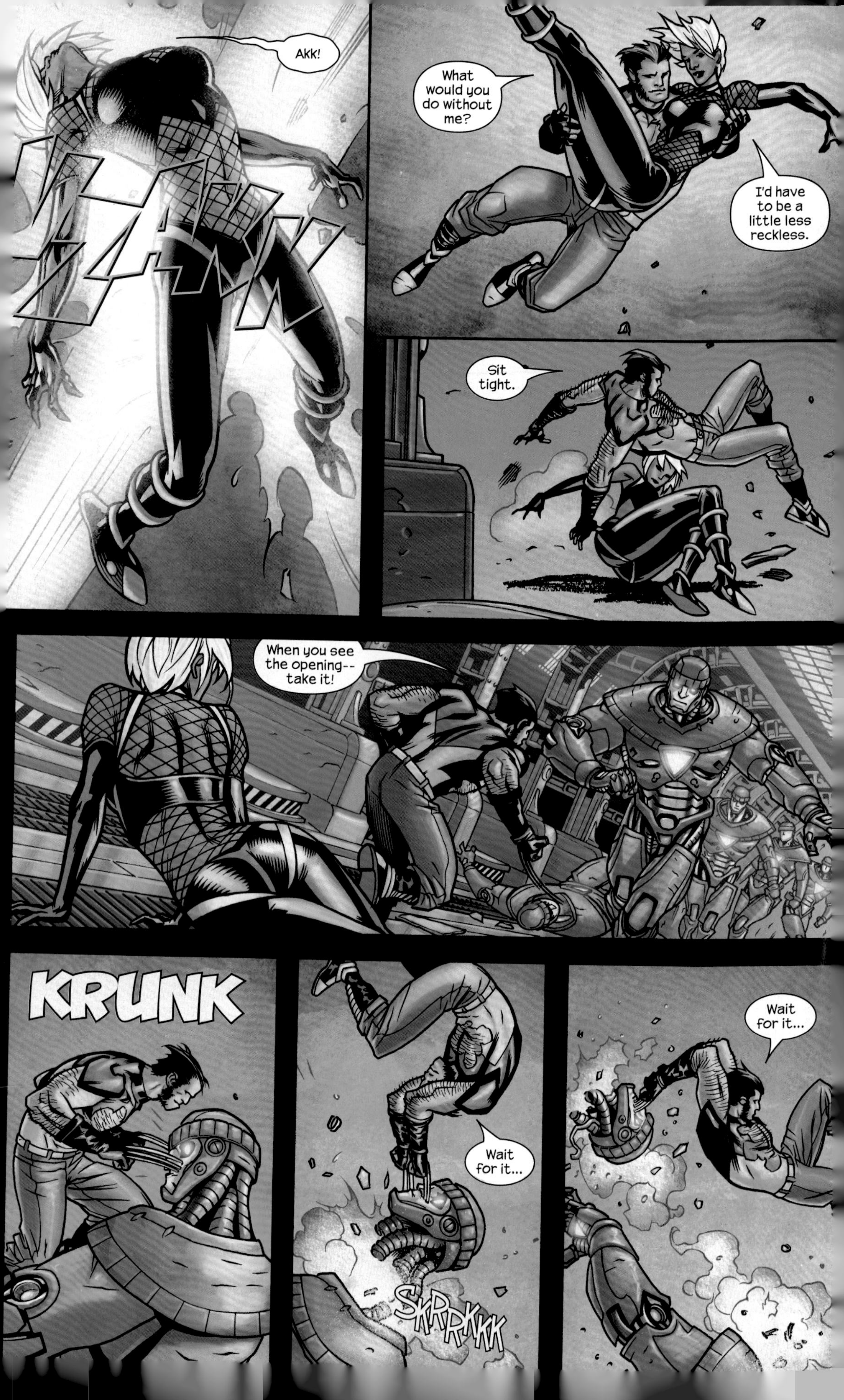
Akk!
What would you do without me?
I'd have to be a little less reckless.
Sit tight.
When you see the opening-- take it!
KRUNK
Wait for it...
SKRRKKK
Wait for it...

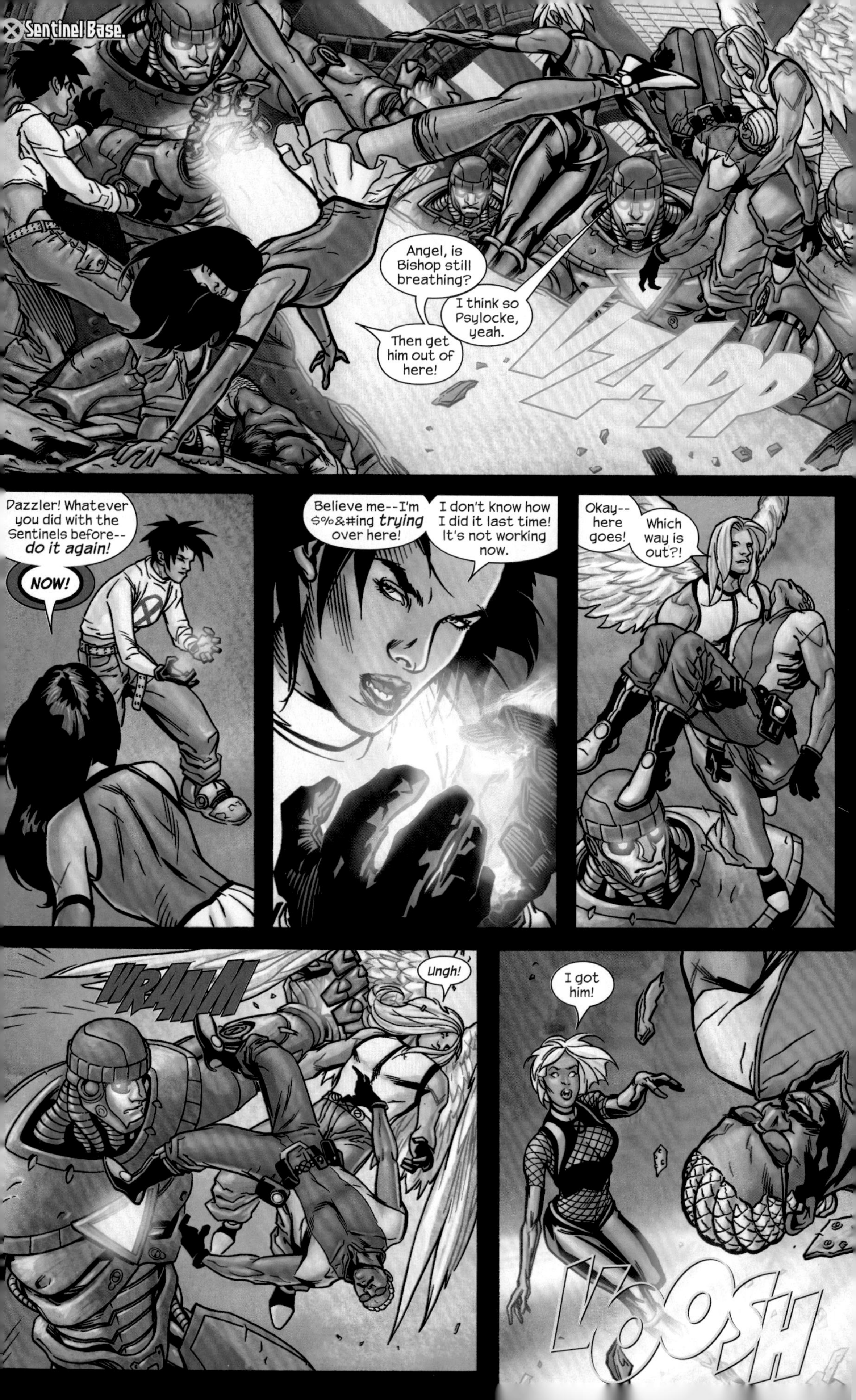
Sentinel Base.
Angel, is Bishop still breathing?
I think so Psylocke, yeah.
Then get him out of here!
VZAPP
Dazzler! Whatever you did with the Sentinels before-- *do it again!*
NOW!
Believe me--I'm $%&#ing *trying* over here!
I don't know how I did it last time! It's not working now.
Okay-- here goes!
Which way is out?!
WRAMM
Ungh!
I got him!
WOOSH

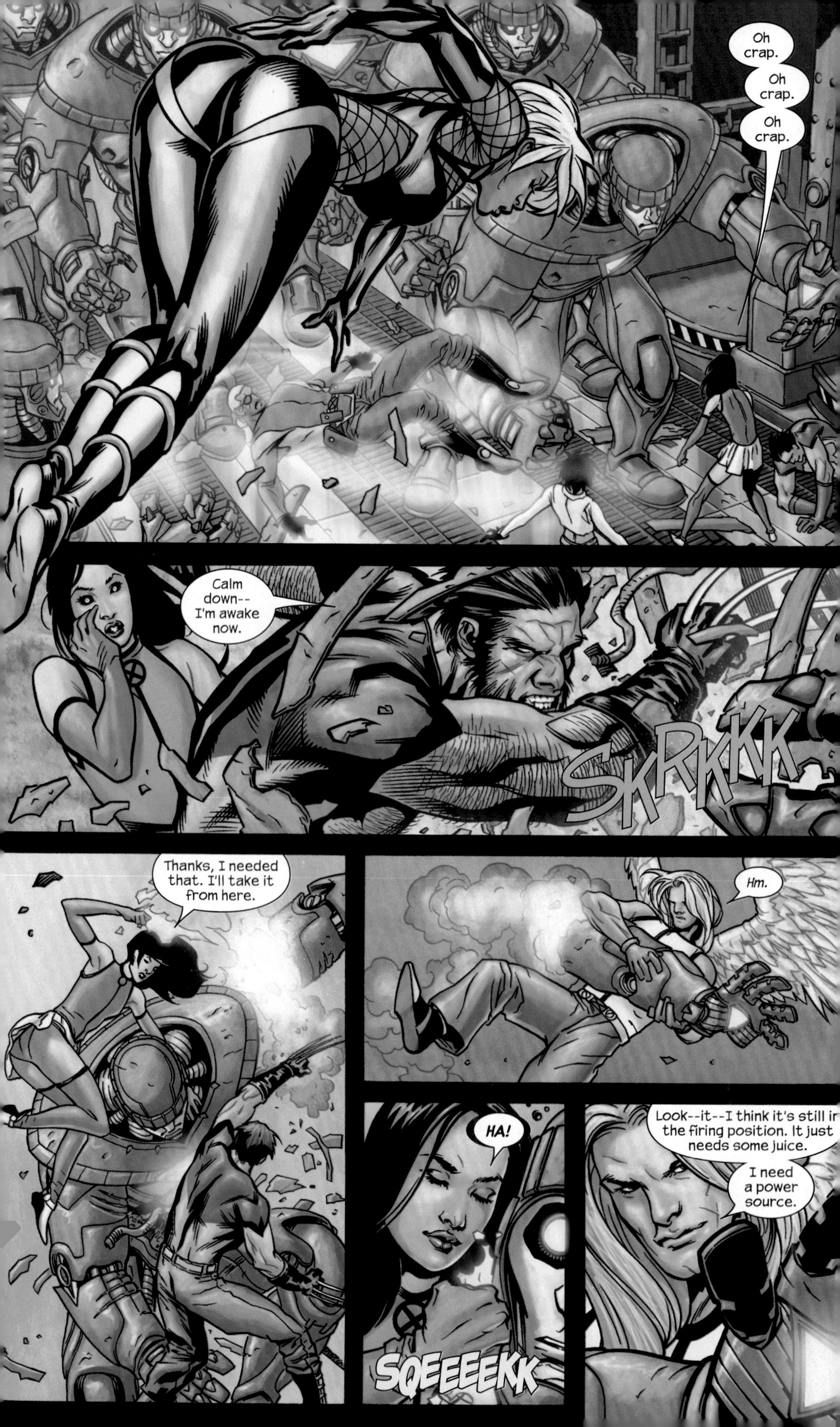
Oh crap.
Oh crap.
Oh crap.
Calm down-- I'm awake now.
SKRKKK
Thanks, I needed that. I'll take it from here.
Hm.
HA!
SQEEEEKK
Look--it--I think it's still in the firing position. It just needs some juice.
I need a power source.

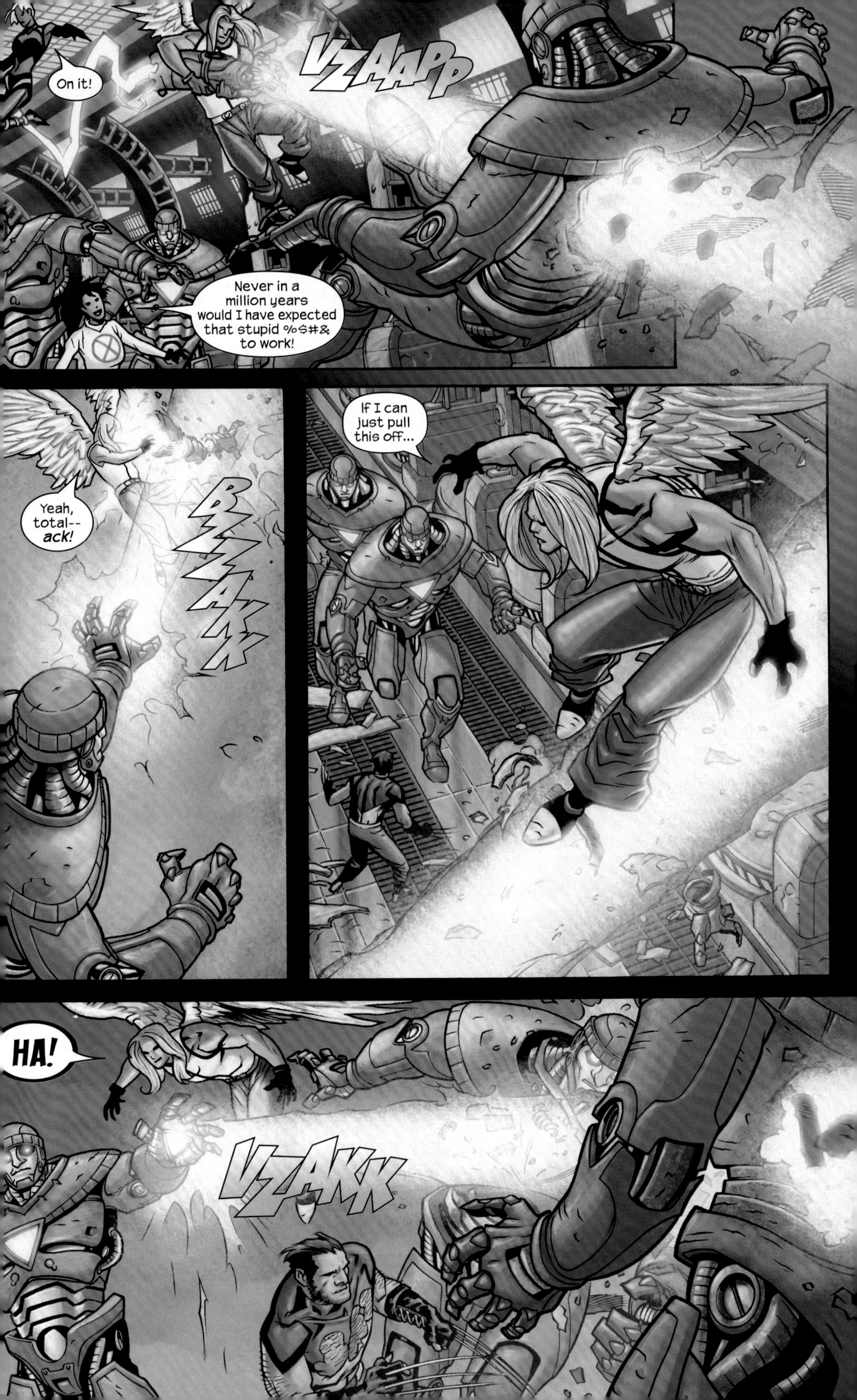
On it!
VZAAPP
Never in a million years would I have expected that stupid %$#& to work!
Yeah, total-- *ack!*
BWAKK
If I can just pull this off...
HA!
VZAKK

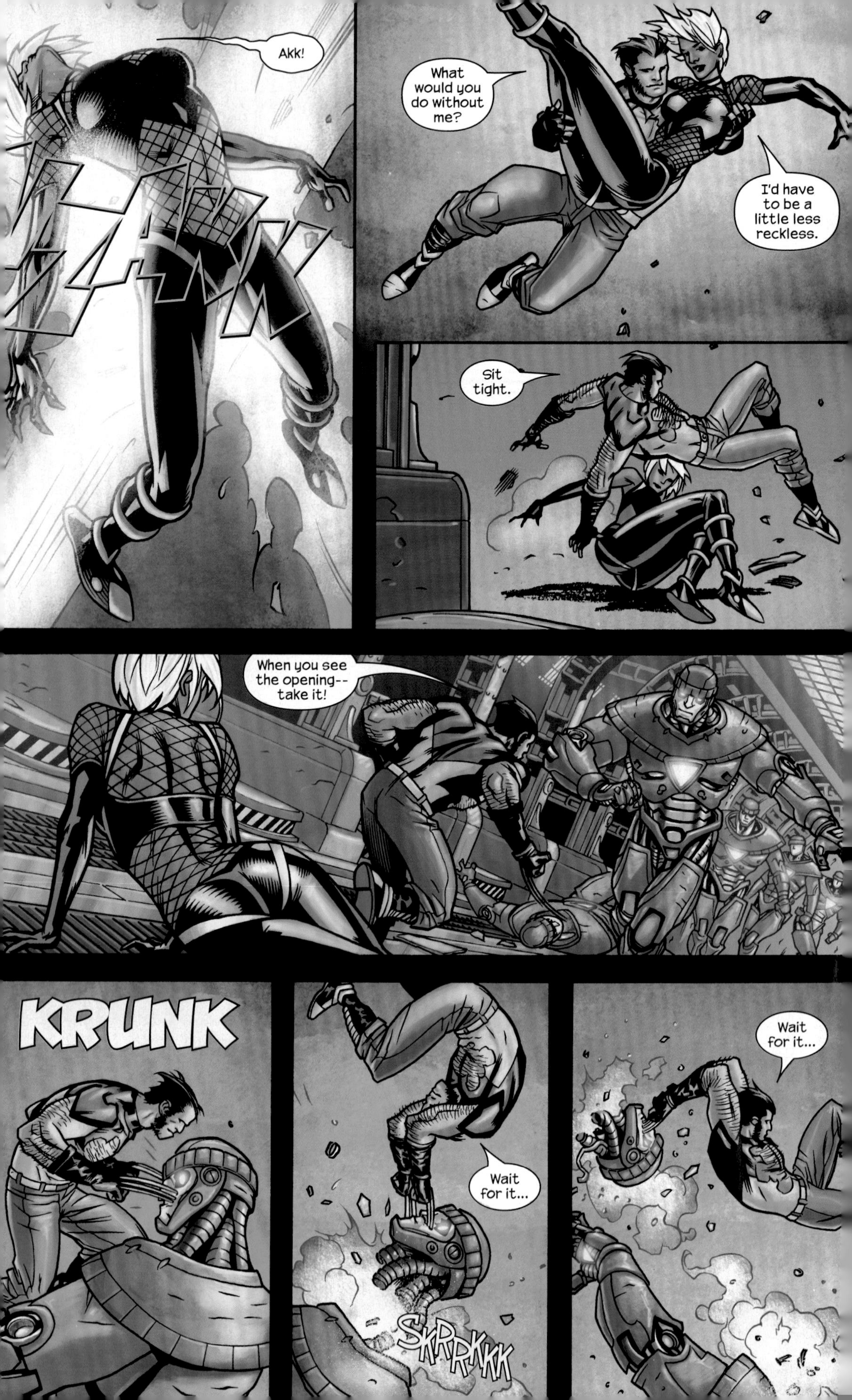
Akk!
What would you do without me?
I'd have to be a little less reckless.
Sit tight.
When you see the opening--take it!
KRUNK
Wait for it...
SKRRKKK
Wait for it...

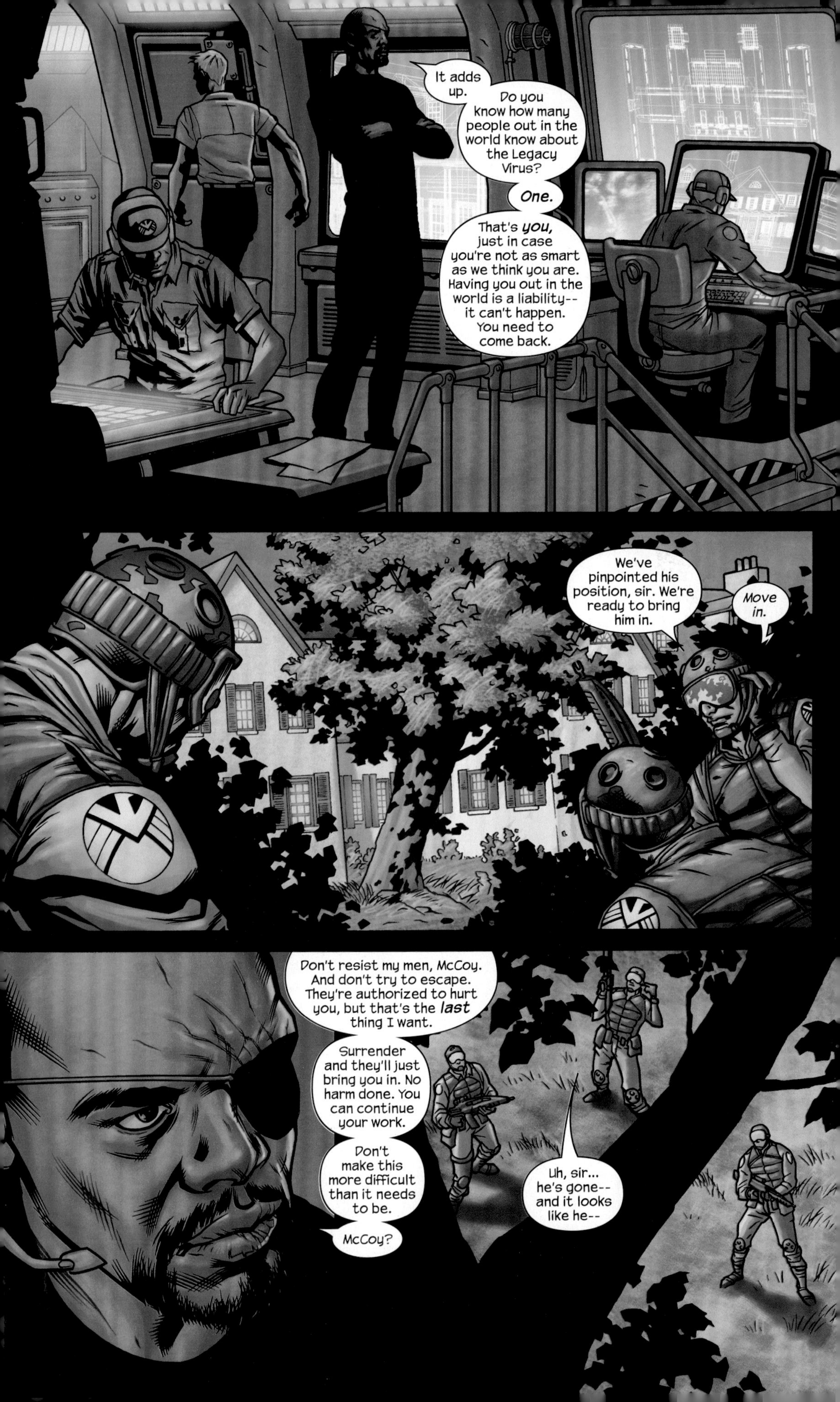
It adds up.
Do you know how many people out in the world know about the Legacy Virus?
One.
That's you, just in case you're not as smart as we think you are. Having you out in the world is a liability-- it can't happen. You need to come back.
We've pinpointed his position, sir. We're ready to bring him in.
Move in.
Don't resist my men, McCoy. And don't try to escape. They're authorized to hurt you, but that's the last thing I want.
Surrender and they'll just bring you in. No harm done. You can continue your work.
Don't make this more difficult than it needs to be.
McCoy?
Uh, sir... he's gone-- and it looks like he--

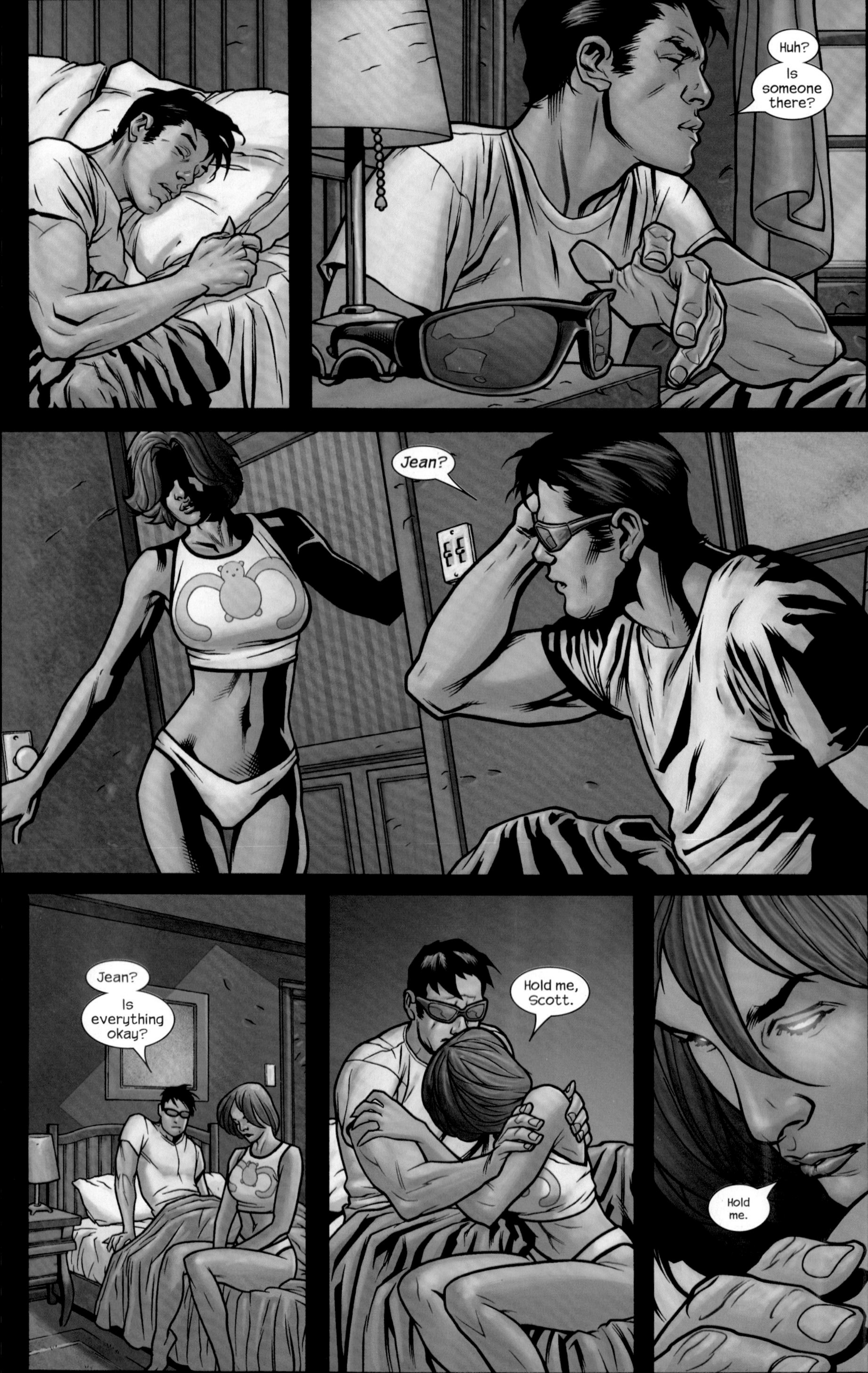
Huh?
Is someone there?
Jean?
Jean?
Is everything okay?
Hold me, Scott.
Hold me.

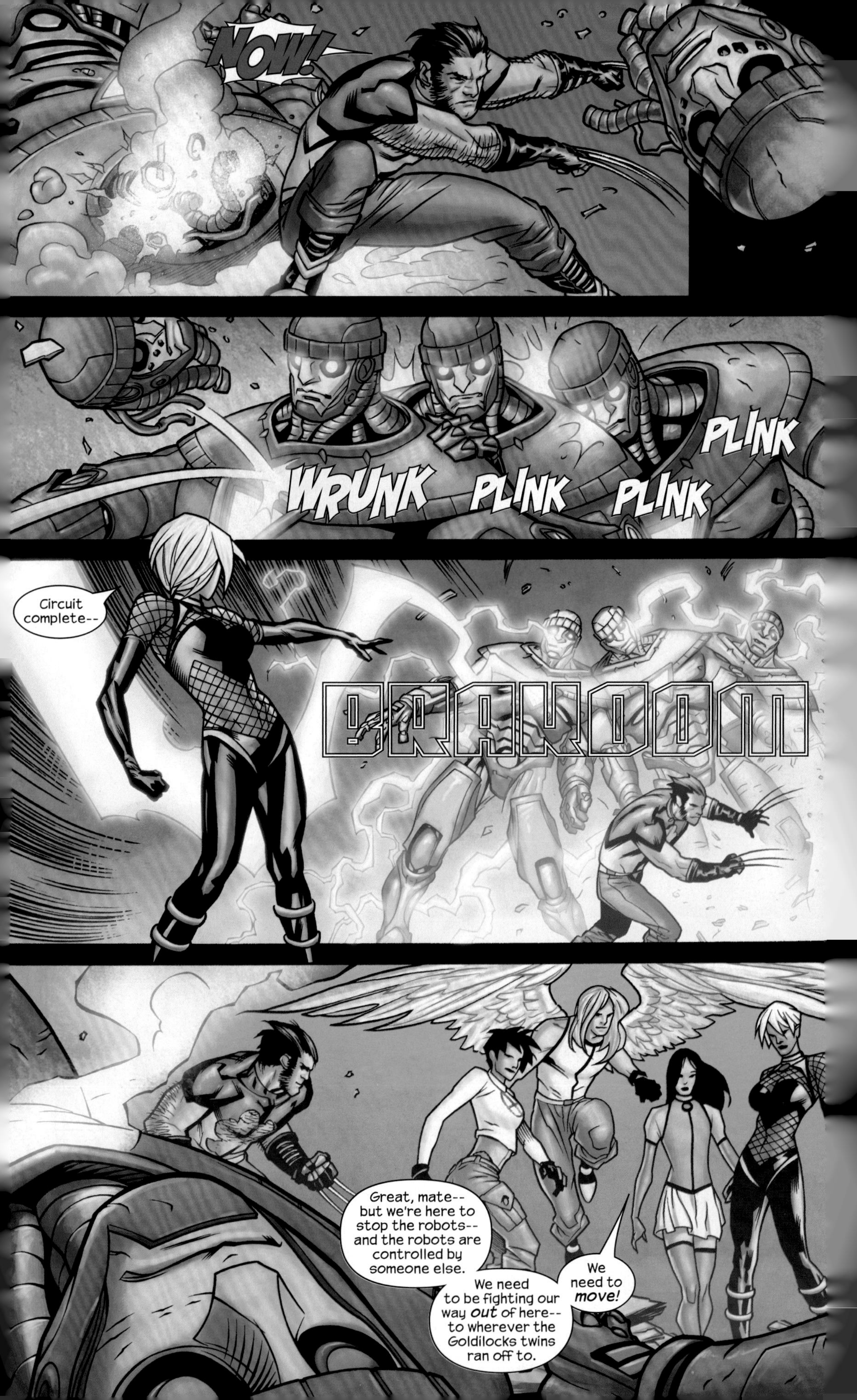
NOW!
WRUNK
PLINK
PLINK
PLINK
Circuit complete--
BRAKOOM
Great, mate-- but we're here to stop the robots-- and the robots are controlled by someone else.
We need to be fighting our way *out* of here-- to wherever the Goldilocks twins ran off to.
We need to *move!*

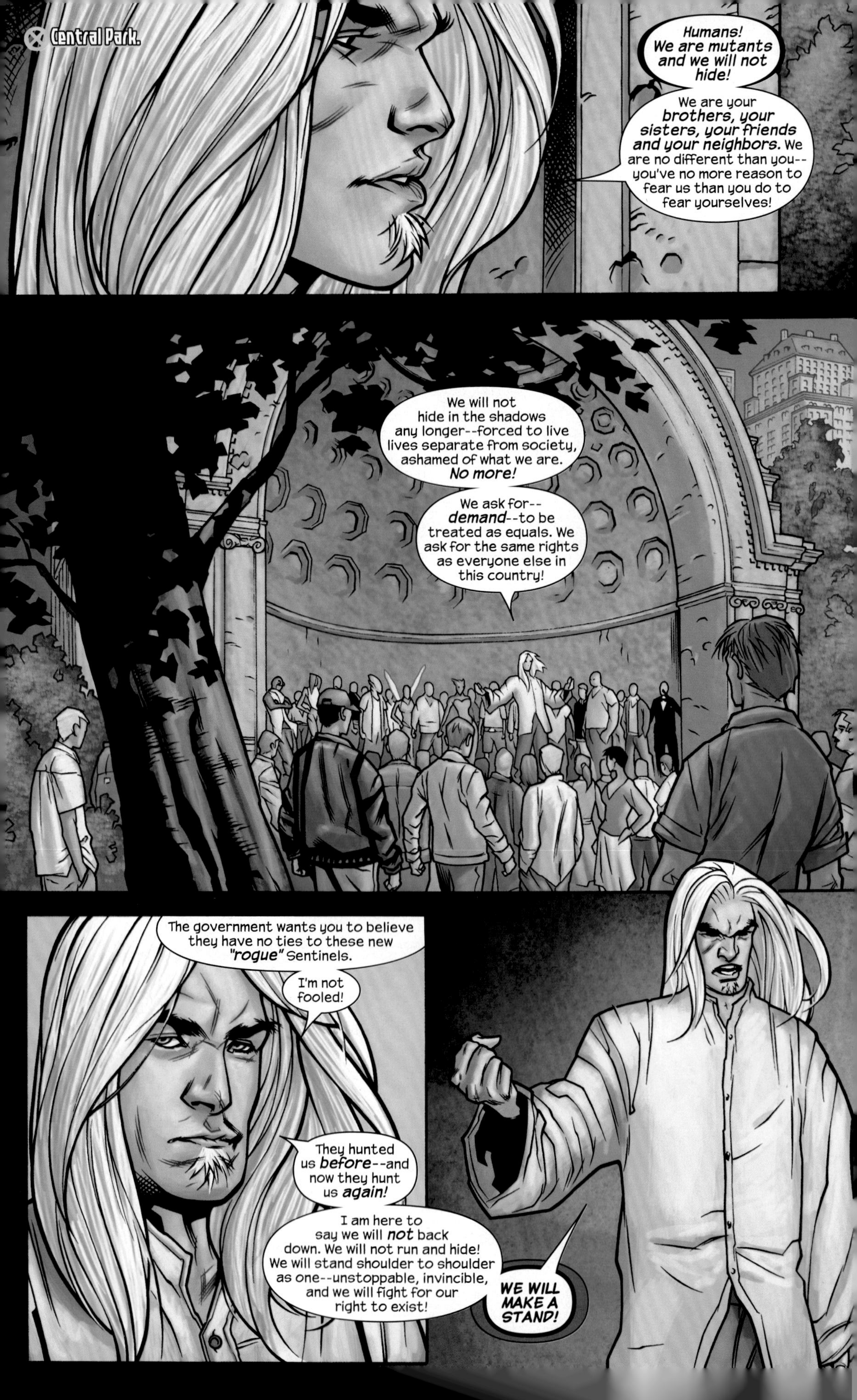
Central Park.
Humans! We are mutants and we will not hide!
We are your brothers, your sisters, your friends and your neighbors. We are no different than you--you've no more reason to fear us than you do to fear yourselves!
We will not hide in the shadows any longer--forced to live lives separate from society, ashamed of what we are. No more!
We ask for--demand--to be treated as equals. We ask for the same rights as everyone else in this country!
The government wants you to believe they have no ties to these new "rogue" Sentinels.
I'm not fooled!
They hunted us before--and now they hunt us again!
I am here to say we will not back down. We will not run and hide! We will stand shoulder to shoulder as one--unstoppable, invincible, and we will fight for our right to exist!
WE WILL MAKE A STAND!

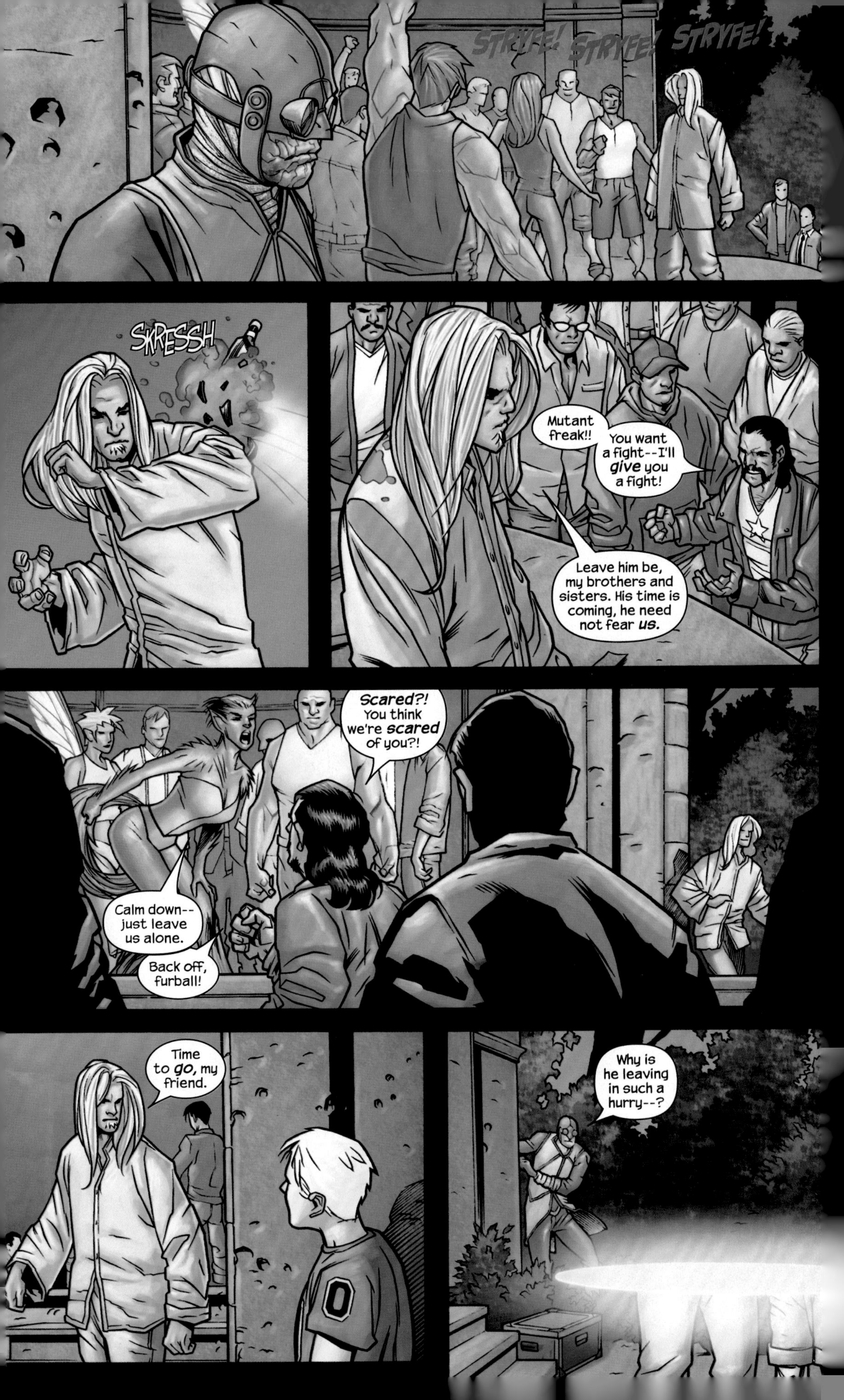
STRYFE! STRYFE! STRYFE!
SKRESSH
Mutant freak!!
You want a fight--I'll give you a fight!
Leave him be, my brothers and sisters. His time is coming, he need not fear us.
Scared?! You think we're scared of you?!
Calm down--just leave us alone.
Back off, furball!
Time to go, my friend.
Why is he leaving in such a hurry--?

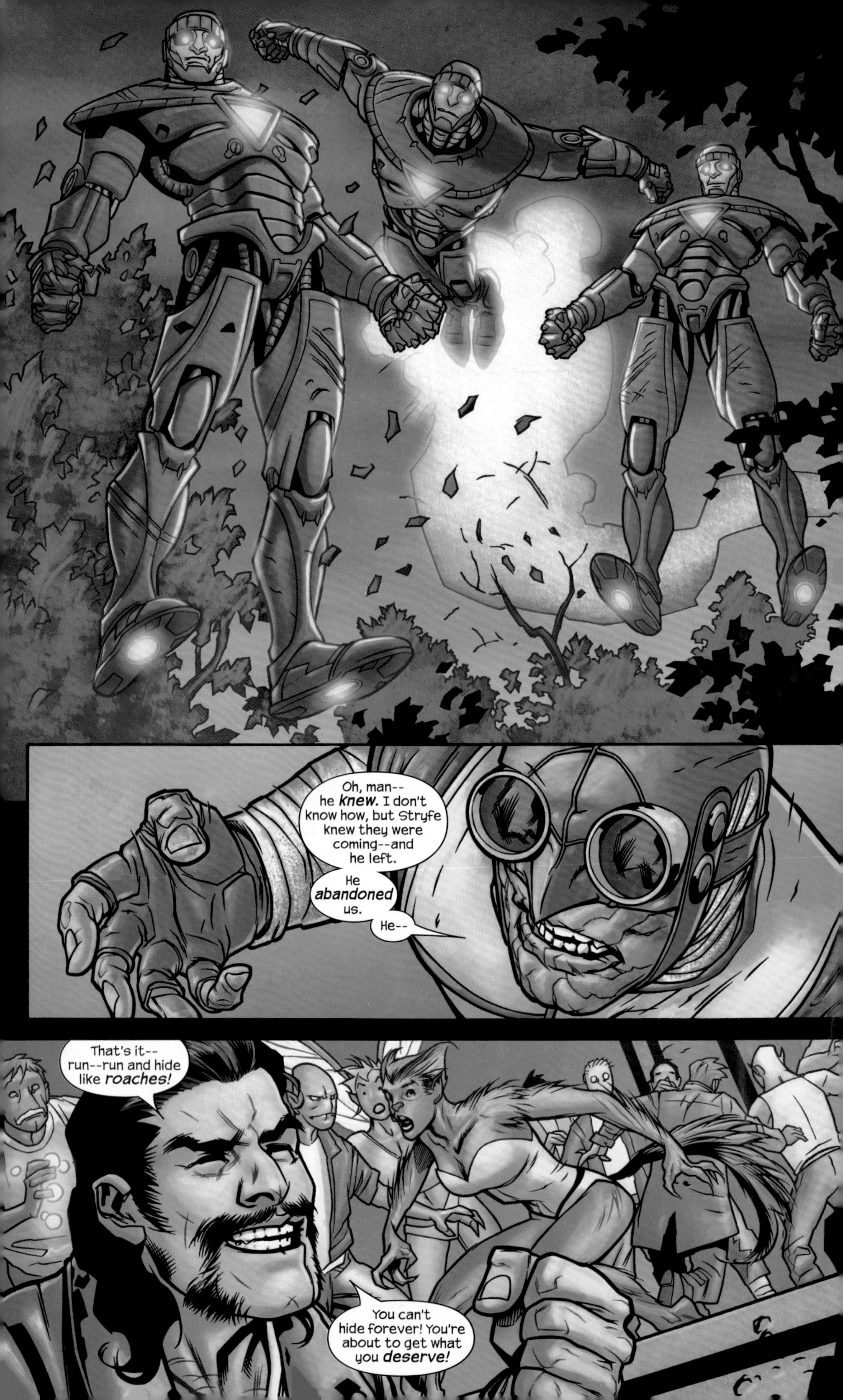
Oh, man--
he *knew.* I don't know how, but Stryfe knew they were coming--and he left.
He *abandoned* us.
He--
That's it--run--run and hide like *roaches!*
You can't hide forever! You're about to get what you *deserve!*

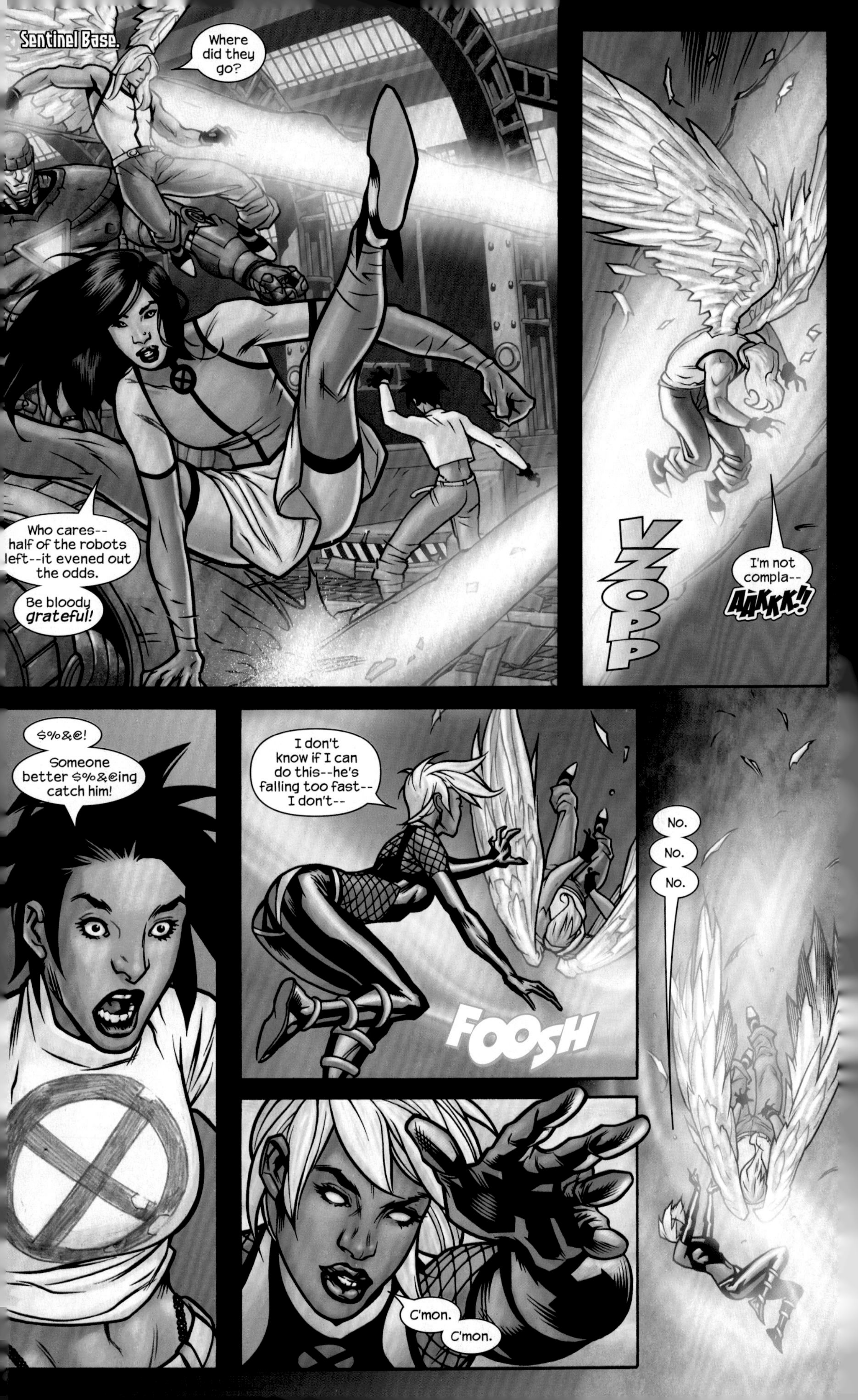
Sentinel Base.
Where did they go?
Who cares--half of the robots left--it evened out the odds.
Be bloody *grateful!*
VZOPP
I'm not compla--
AAKKK!!
$%&@!
Someone better $%&@ing catch him!
I don't know if I can do this--he's falling too fast--I don't--
FOOSH
No.
No.
No.
C'mon.
C'mon.

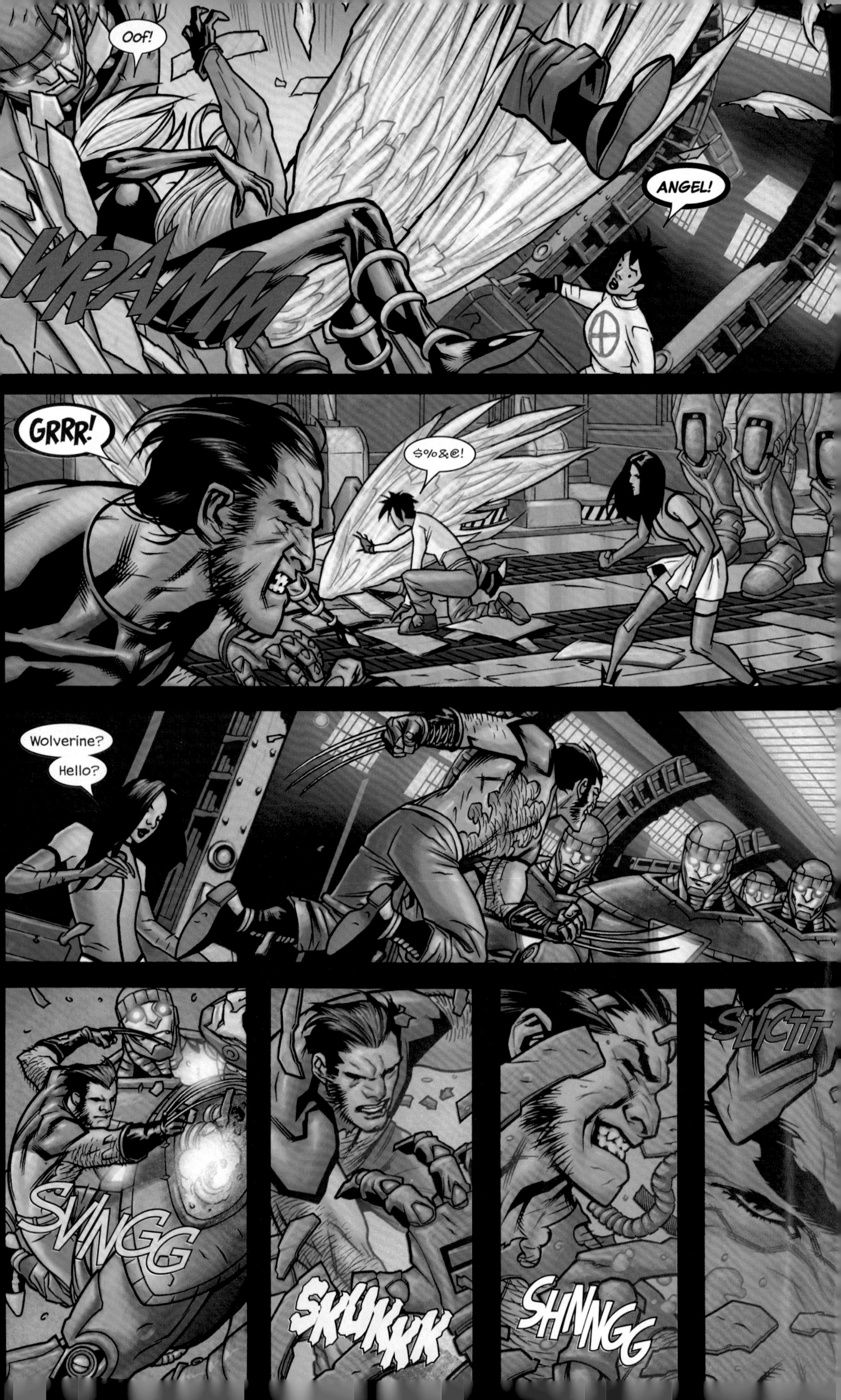
Oof!
WRAMM
ANGEL!
GRRR!
$%&@!
Wolverine?
Hello?
SVNGG
SKUKKK
SHNNGG
SLICTTT

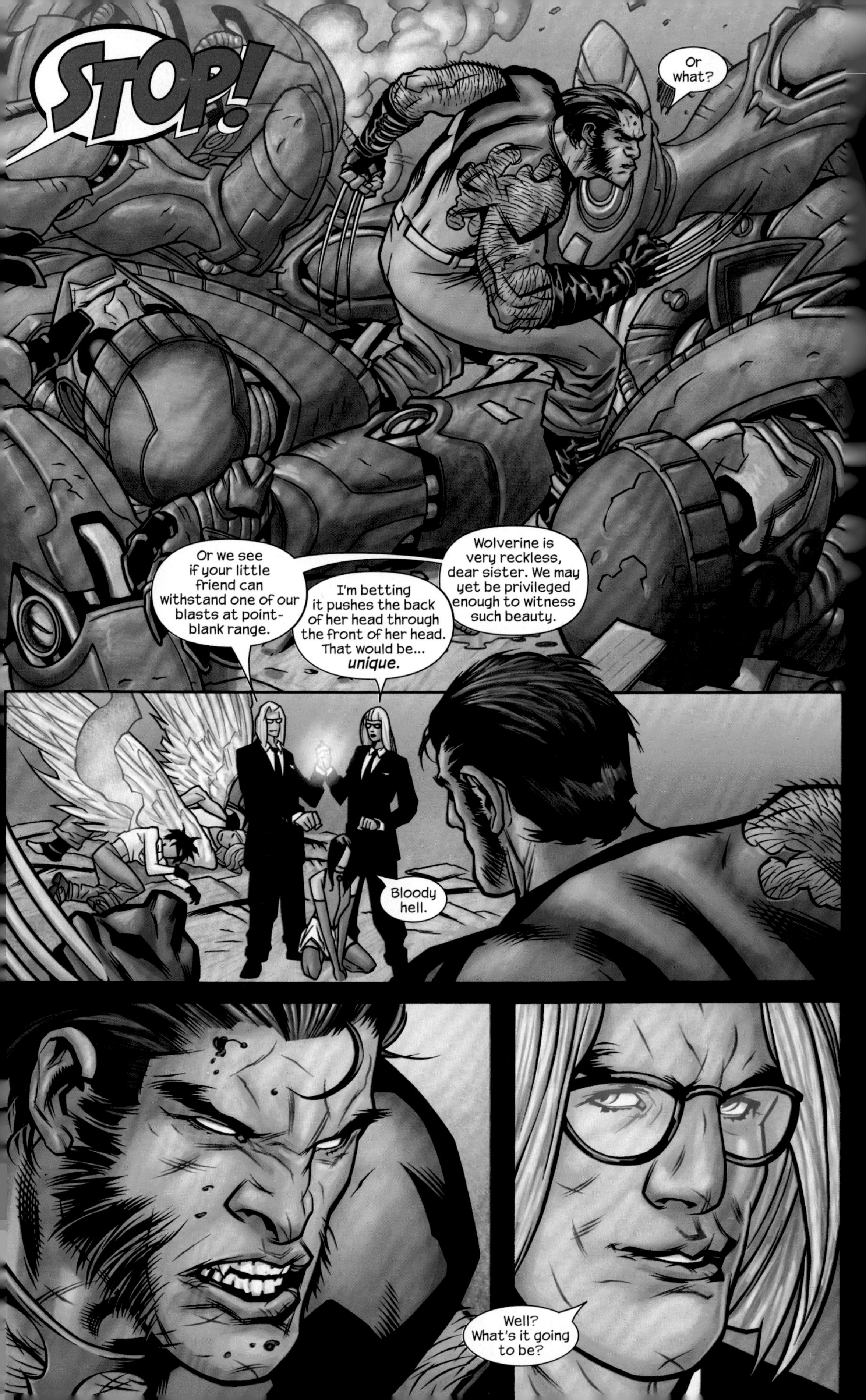
STOP!
Or what?
Or we see if your little friend can withstand one of our blasts at point-blank range.
I'm betting it pushes the back of her head through the front of her head. That would be... *unique.*
Wolverine is very reckless, dear sister. We may yet be privileged enough to witness such beauty.
Bloody hell.
Well? What's it going to be?

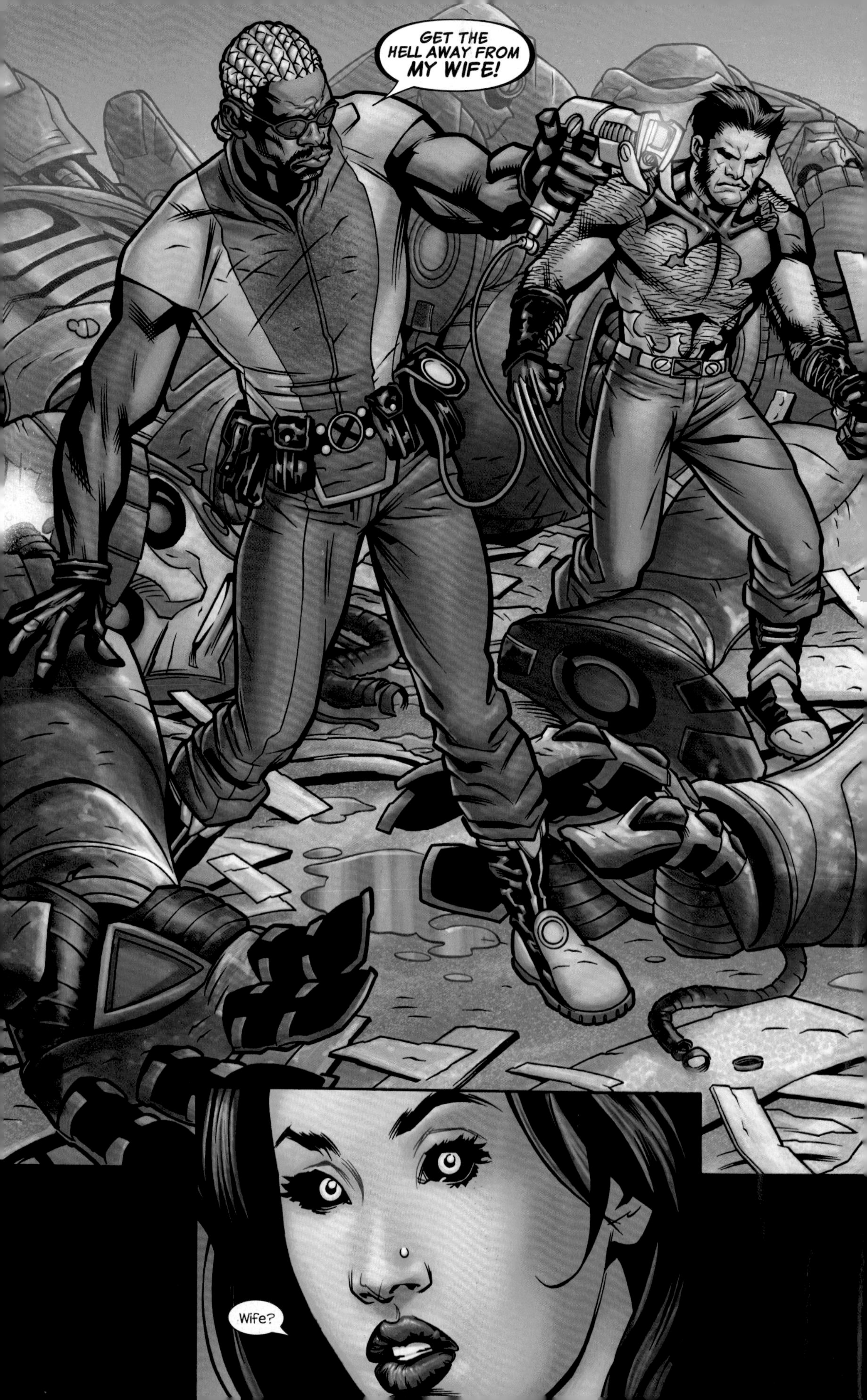
GET THE HELL AWAY FROM MY WIFE!
Wife?

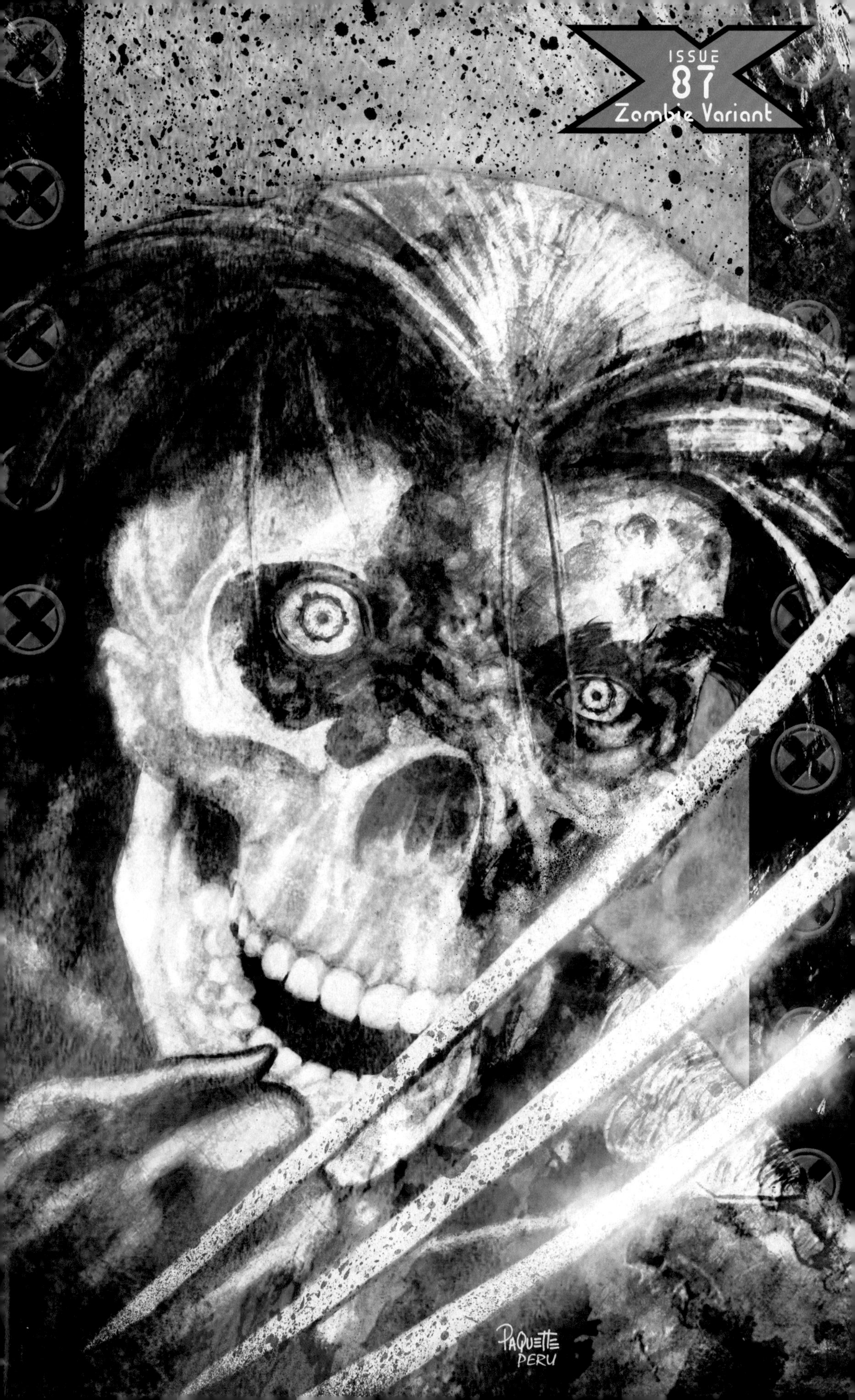
ISSUE
87
Zombie Variant
PAQUETTE
PERU

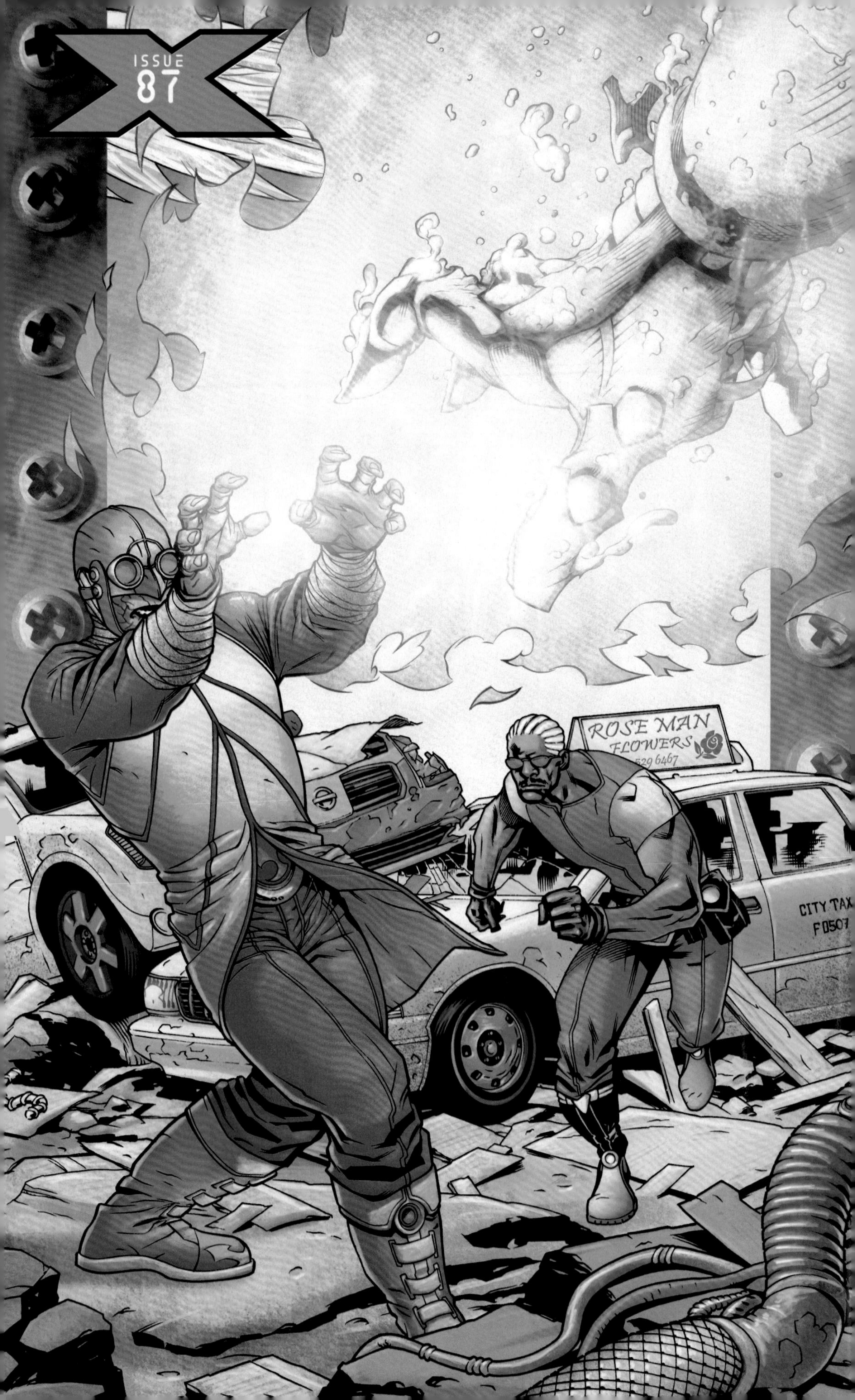
ISSUE
87
ROSE MAN
FLOWERS
CITY TAX
F0507

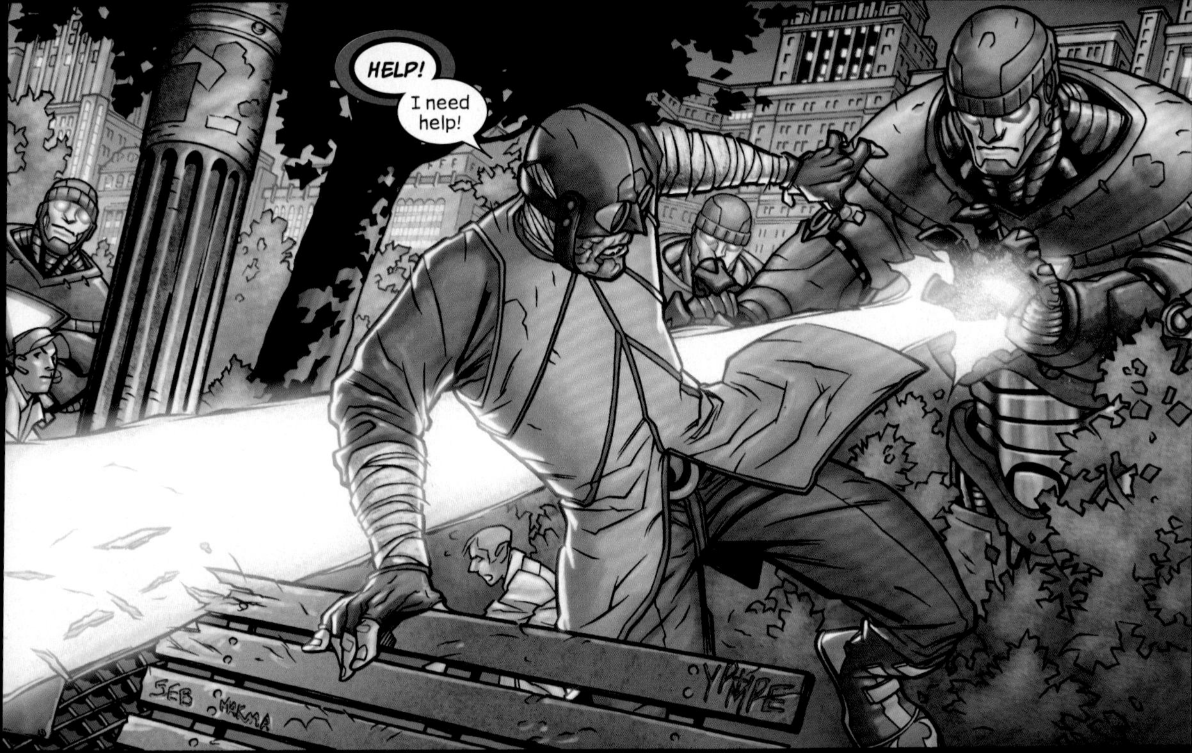
HELP!
I need help!
SEB

SENTINELS

PART 4 (OF 5)

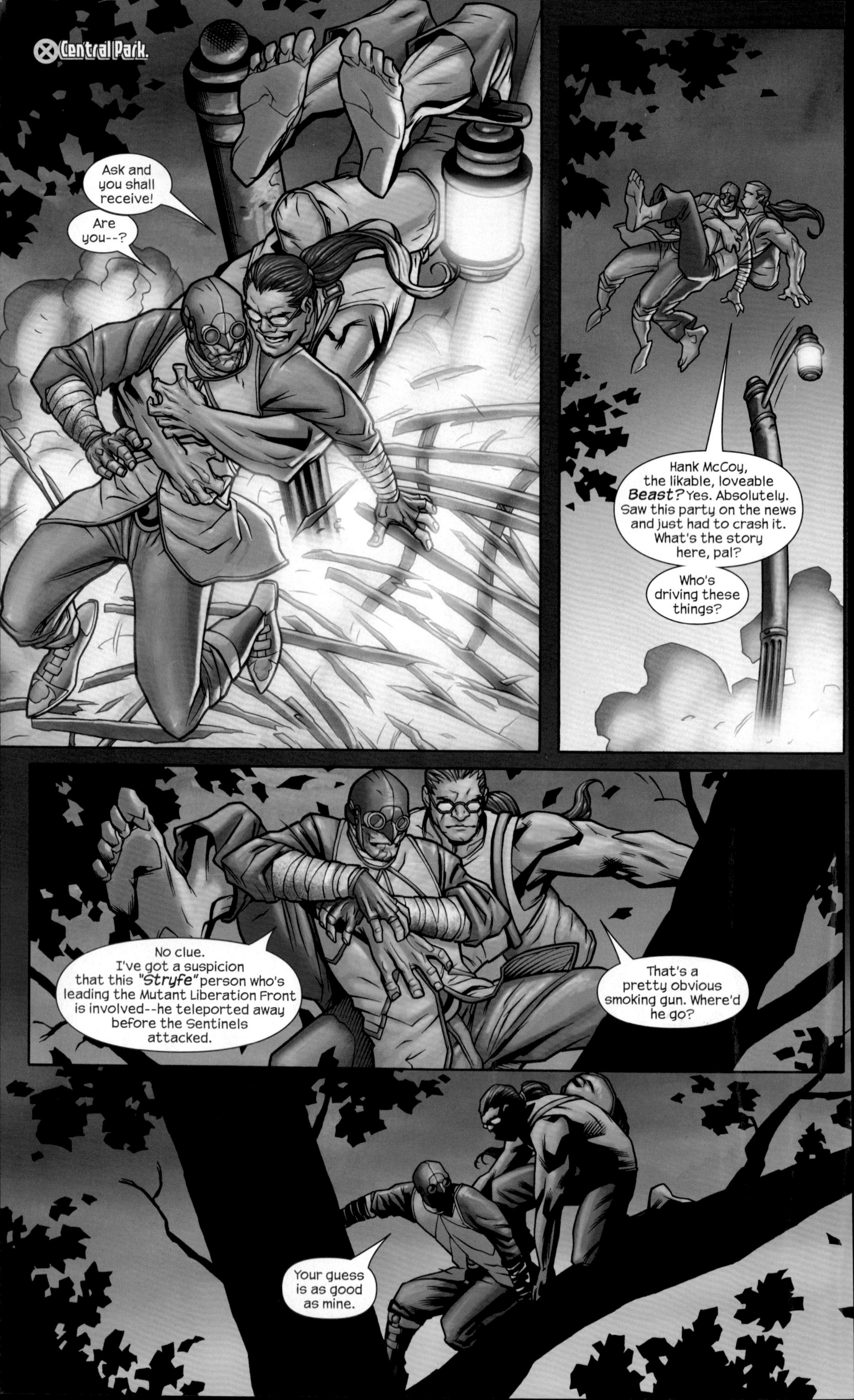
Central Park.
Ask and you shall receive!
Are you--?
Hank McCoy, the likable, loveable Beast? Yes. Absolutely. Saw this party on the news and just had to crash it. What's the story here, pal?
Who's driving these things?
No clue. I've got a suspicion that this "Stryfe" person who's leading the Mutant Liberation Front is involved--he teleported away before the Sentinels attacked.
That's a pretty obvious smoking gun. Where'd he go?
Your guess is as good as mine.

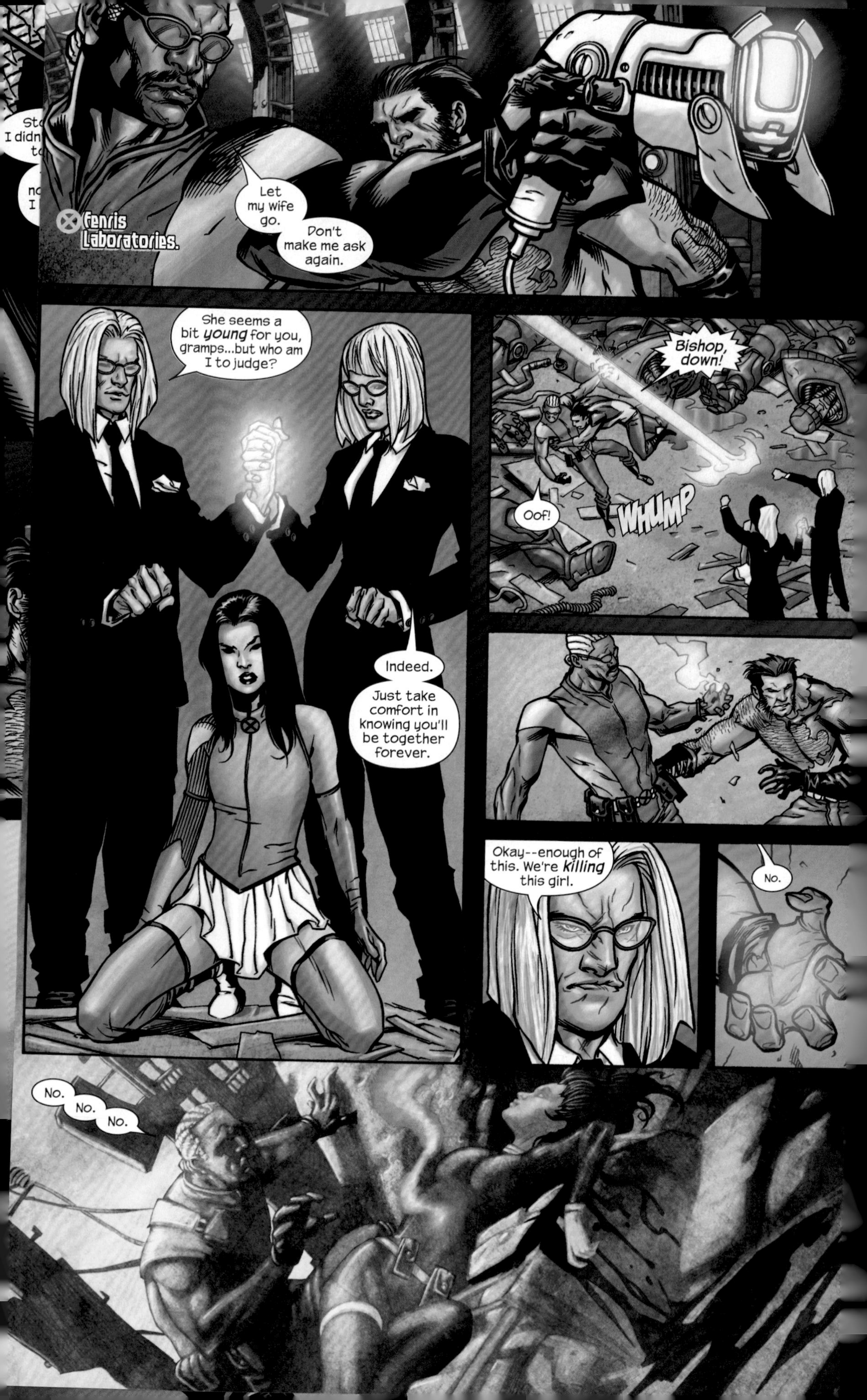
Fenris Laboratories.
Let my wife go.
Don't make me ask again.
She seems a bit *young* for you, gramps...but who am I to judge?
Indeed.
Just take comfort in knowing you'll be together forever.
Bishop, down!
Oof!
WHUMP
Okay--enough of this. We're *killing* this girl.
No.
No.
No.
No.

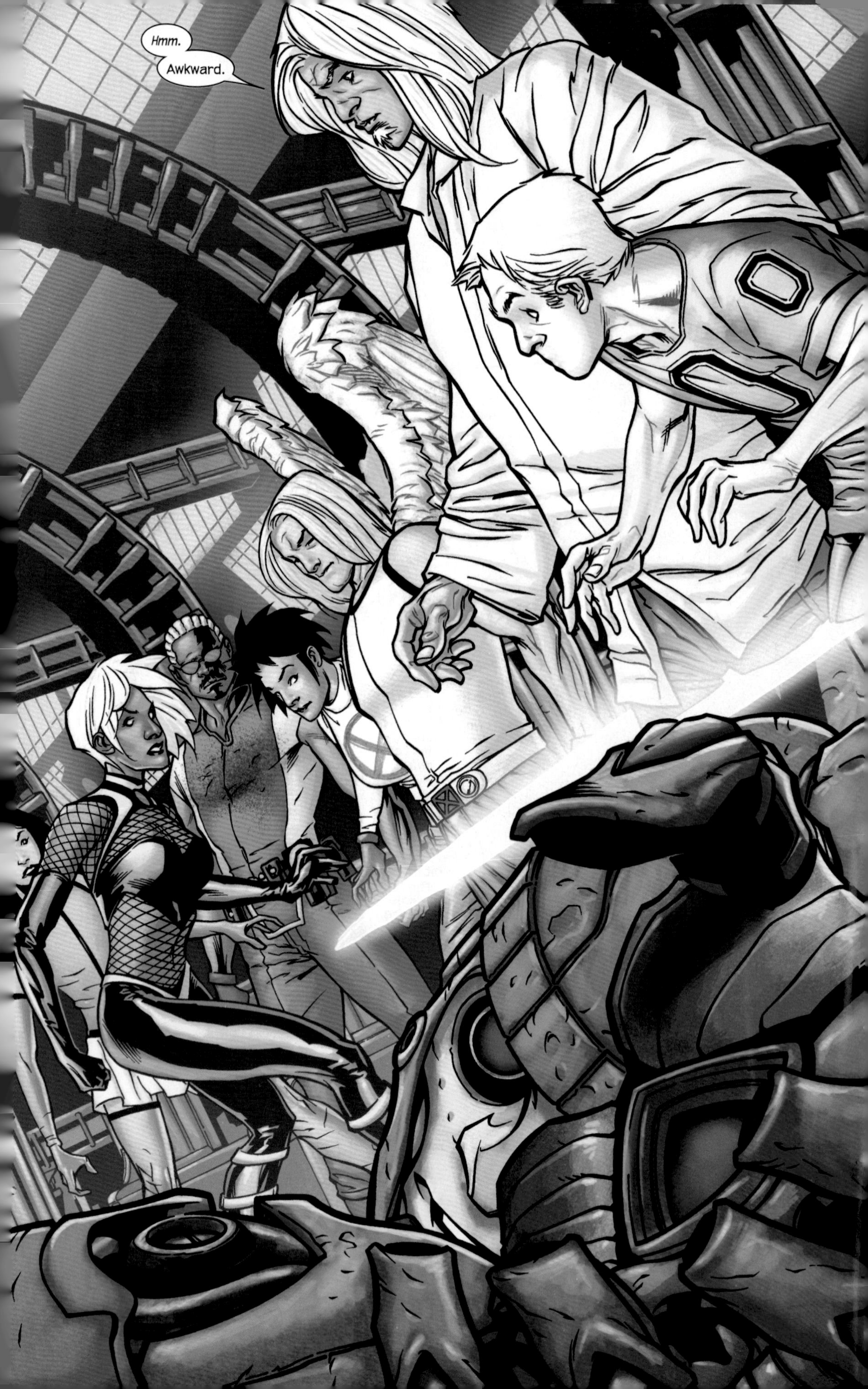
Hmm.
Awkward.

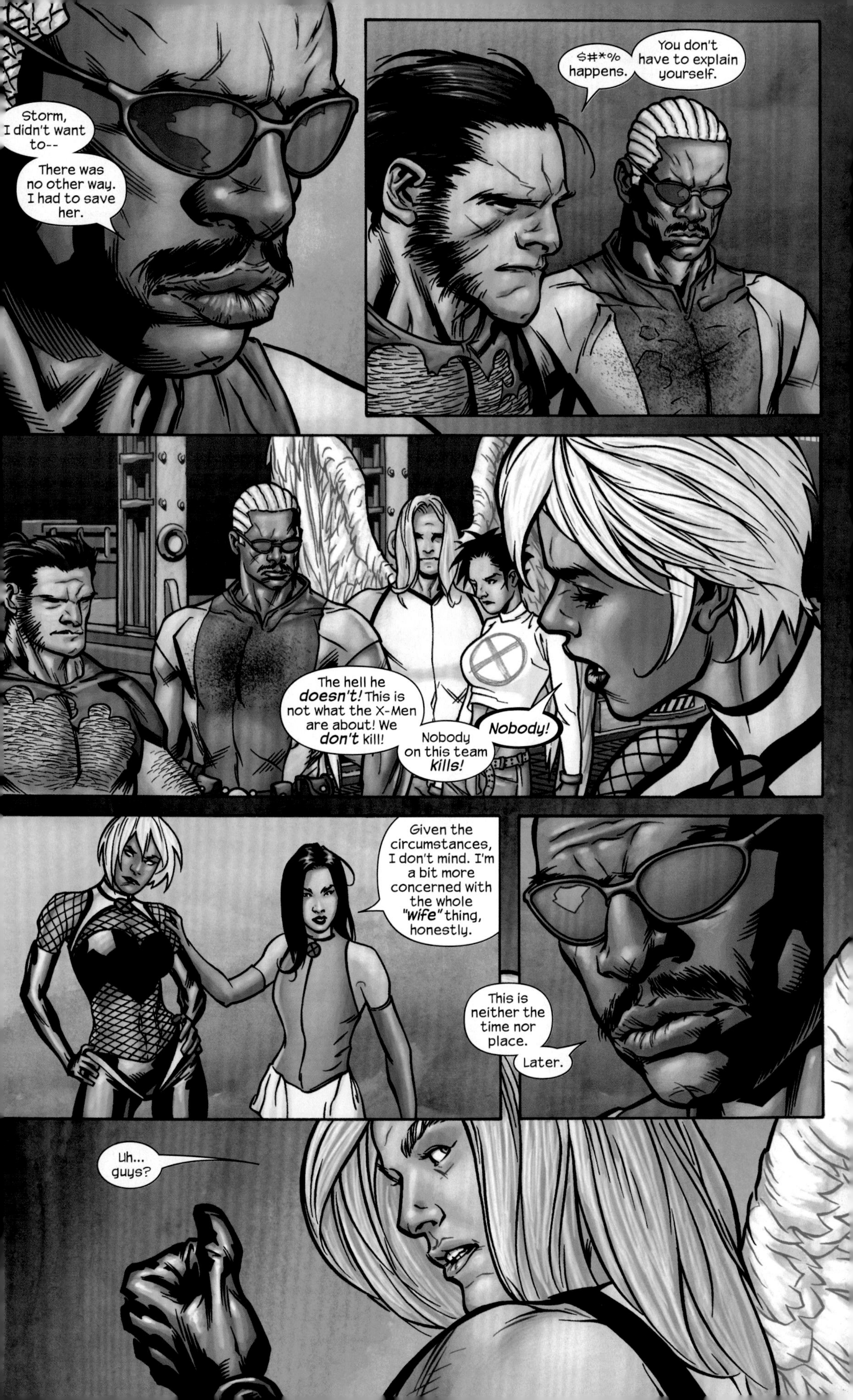
Storm, I didn't want to--
There was no other way. I had to save her.
$#*% happens.
You don't have to explain yourself.
The hell he *doesn't!* This is not what the X-Men are about! We *don't* kill!
Nobody on this team *kills!*
Nobody!
Given the circumstances, I don't mind. I'm a bit more concerned with the whole *"wife"* thing, honestly.
This is neither the time nor place.
Later.
Uh... guys?

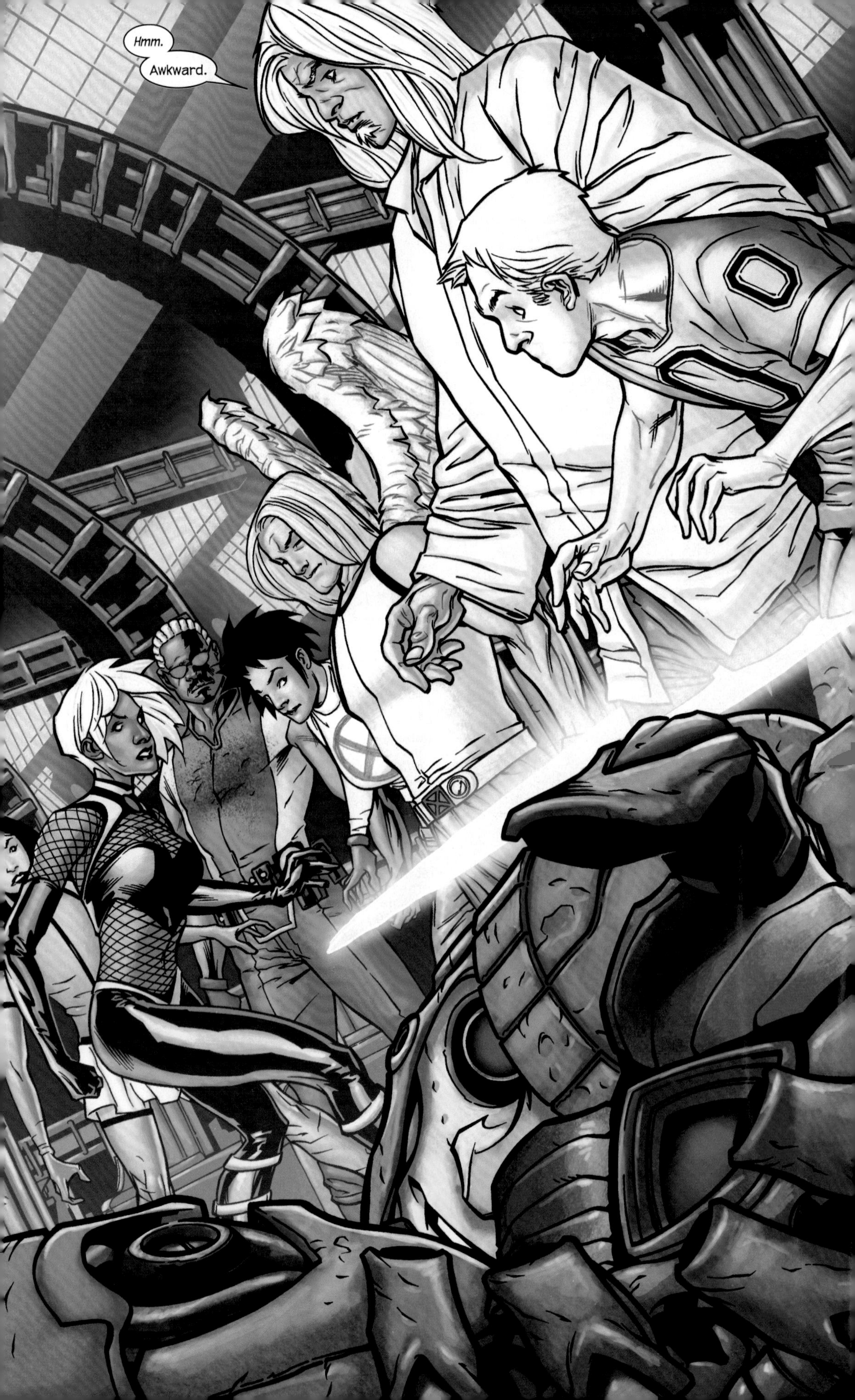
Hmm.
Awkward.

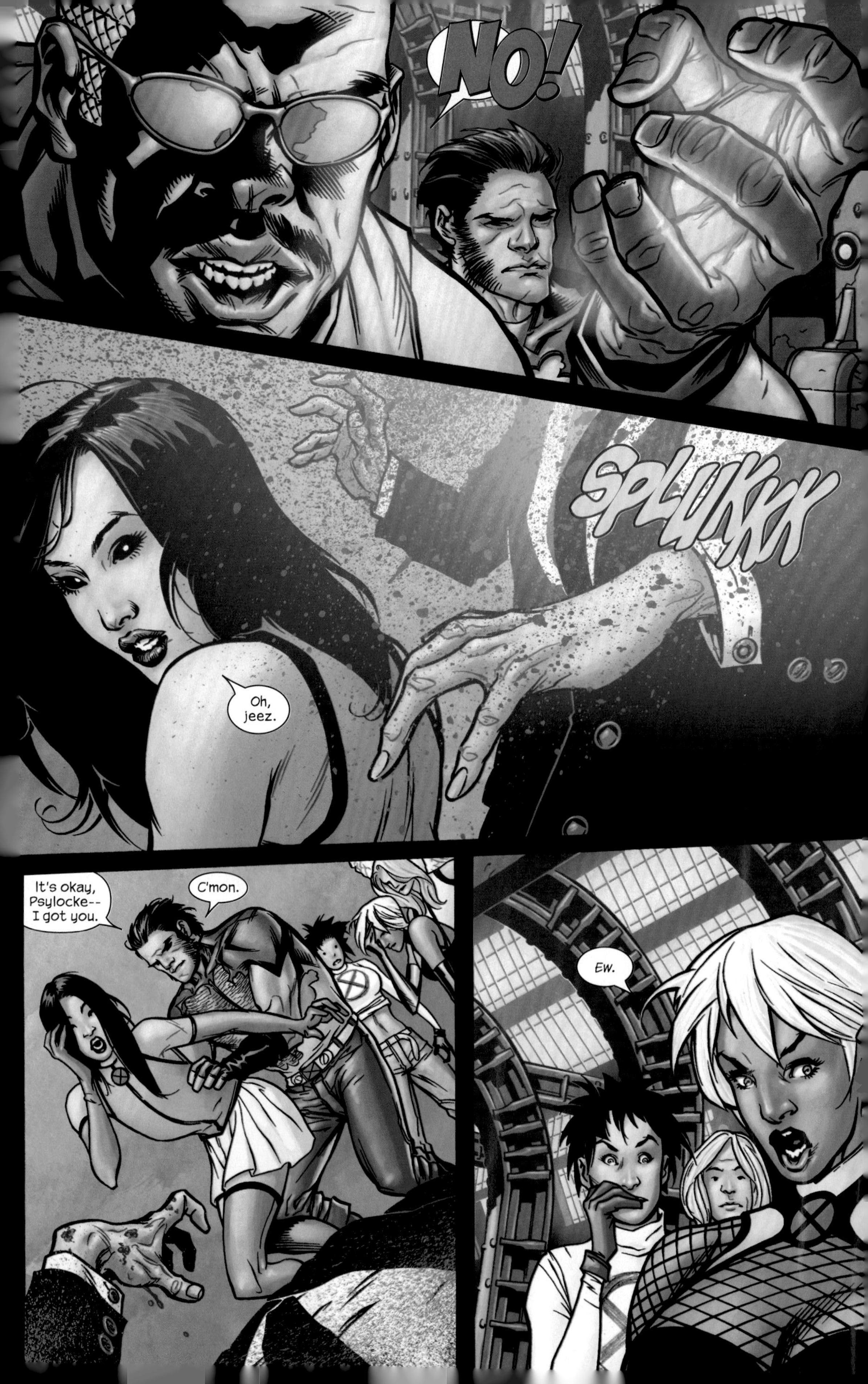
NO!
SPLUKKK
Oh, jeez.
It's okay, Psylocke-- I got you.
C'mon.
Ew.

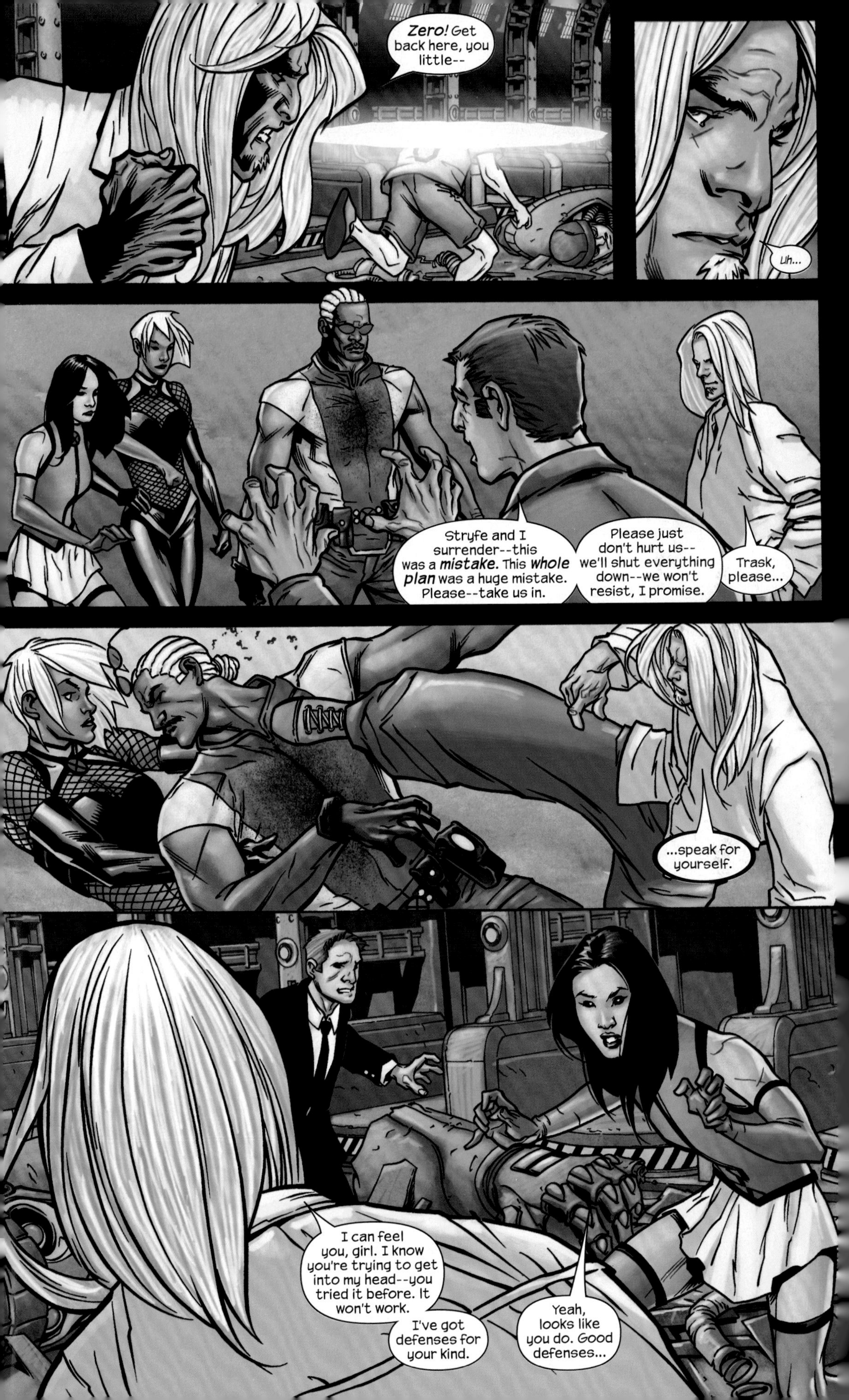
Zero! Get back here, you little--
Uh...
Stryfe and I surrender--this was a mistake. This whole plan was a huge mistake. Please--take us in.
Please just don't hurt us--we'll shut everything down--we won't resist, I promise.
Trask, please...
...speak for yourself.
I can feel you, girl. I know you're trying to get into my head--you tried it before. It won't work.
I've got defenses for your kind.
Yeah, looks like you do. Good defenses...

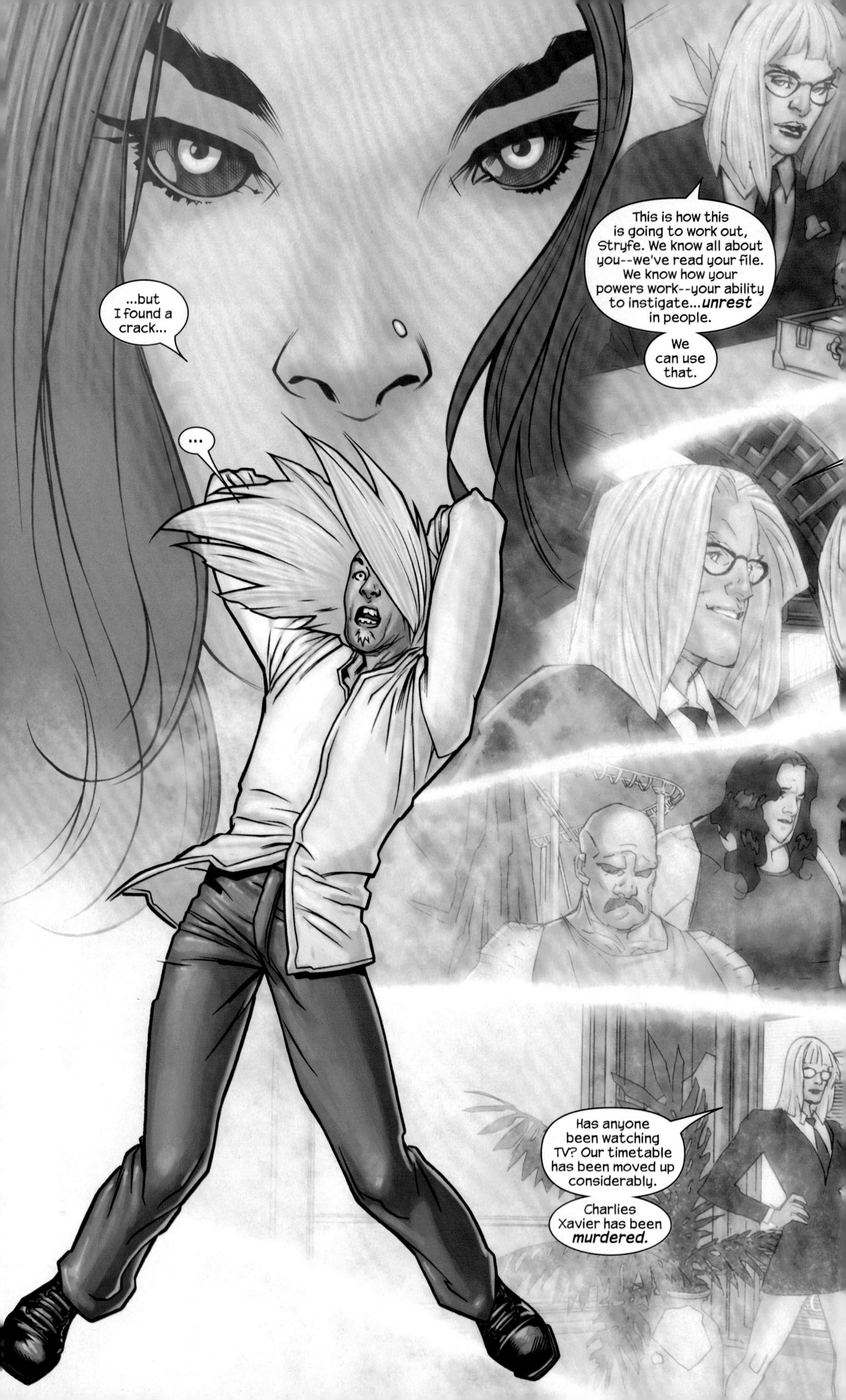
...but I found a crack...
...
This is how this is going to work out, Stryfe. We know all about you--we've read your file. We know how your powers work--your ability to instigate...*unrest* in people.
We can use that.
Has anyone been watching TV? Our timetable has been moved up considerably.
Charlies Xavier has been *murdered.*

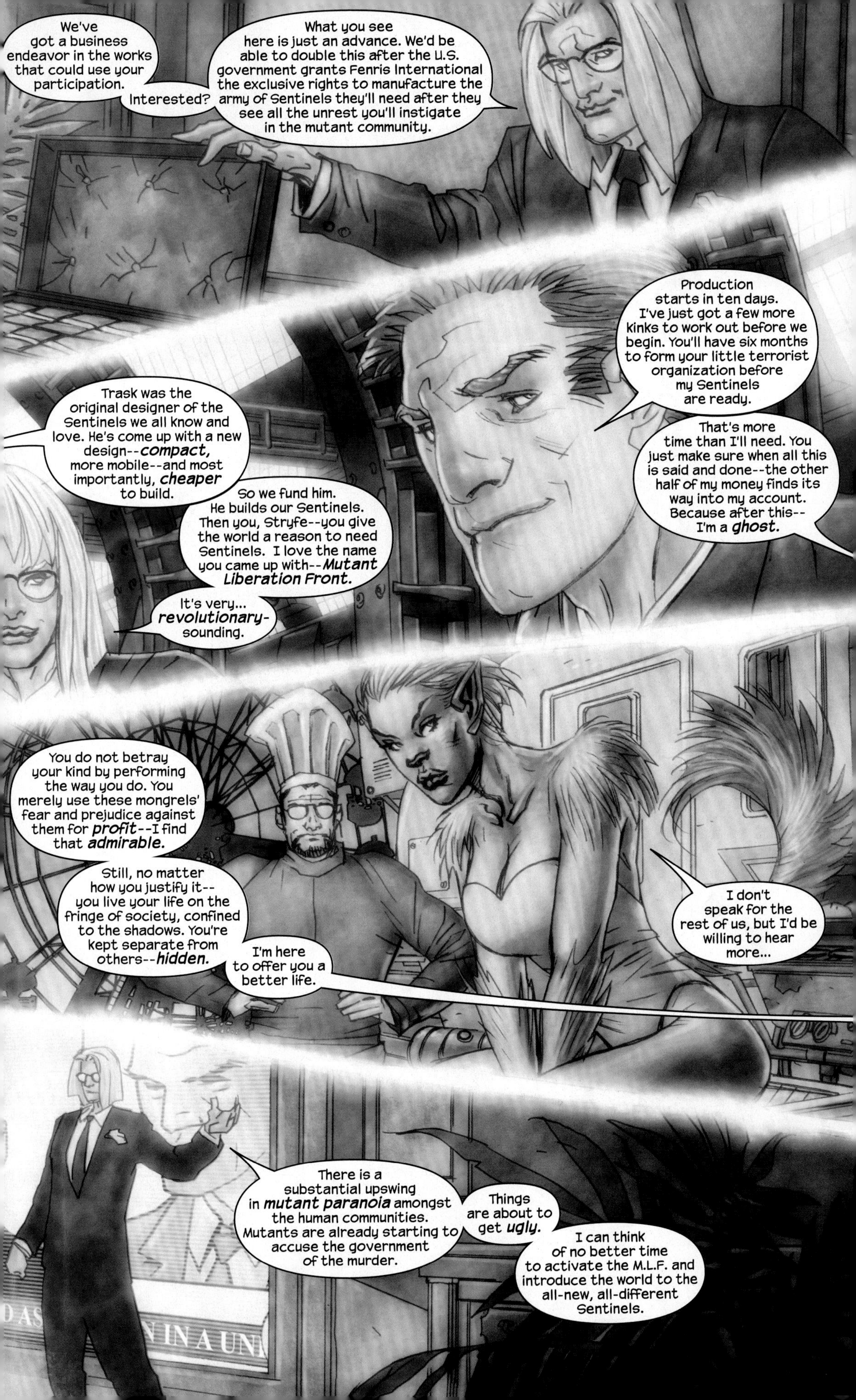
We've got a business endeavor in the works that could use your participation.
Interested?
What you see here is just an advance. We'd be able to double this after the U.S. government grants Fenris International the exclusive rights to manufacture the army of Sentinels they'll need after they see all the unrest you'll instigate in the mutant community.
Production starts in ten days. I've just got a few more kinks to work out before we begin. You'll have six months to form your little terrorist organization before my Sentinels are ready.
Trask was the original designer of the Sentinels we all know and love. He's come up with a new design--compact, more mobile--and most importantly, cheaper to build.
So we fund him. He builds our Sentinels. Then you, Stryfe--you give the world a reason to need Sentinels. I love the name you came up with--Mutant Liberation Front.
It's very... revolutionary-sounding.
That's more time than I'll need. You just make sure when all this is said and done--the other half of my money finds its way into my account. Because after this--I'm a ghost.
You do not betray your kind by performing the way you do. You merely use these mongrels' fear and prejudice against them for profit--I find that admirable.
Still, no matter how you justify it--you live your life on the fringe of society, confined to the shadows. You're kept separate from others--hidden.
I'm here to offer you a better life.
I don't speak for the rest of us, but I'd be willing to hear more...
There is a substantial upswing in mutant paranoia amongst the human communities. Mutants are already starting to accuse the government of the murder.
Things are about to get ugly.
I can think of no better time to activate the M.L.F. and introduce the world to the all-new, all-different Sentinels.

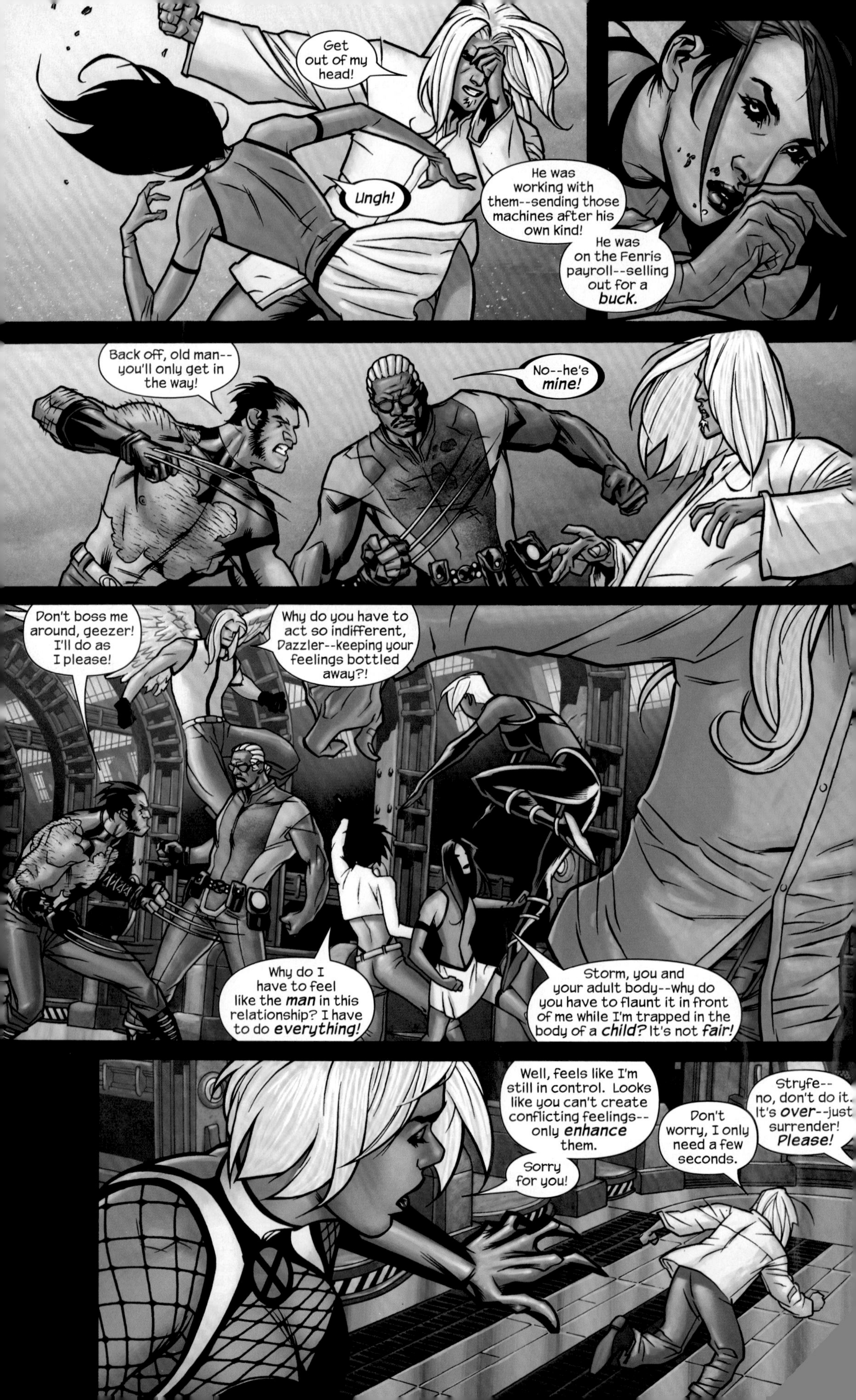
Get out of my head!
Ungh!
He was working with them--sending those machines after his own kind!
He was on the Fenris payroll--selling out for a **buck.**
Back off, old man--you'll only get in the way!
No--he's ***mine!***
Don't boss me around, geezer! I'll do as I please!
Why do you have to act so indifferent, Dazzler--keeping your feelings bottled away?!
Why do I have to feel like the ***man*** in this relationship? I have to do ***everything!***
Storm, you and your adult body--why do you have to flaunt it in front of me while I'm trapped in the body of a ***child?*** It's not ***fair!***
Well, feels like I'm still in control. Looks like you can't create conflicting feelings--only ***enhance*** them.
Sorry for you!
Don't worry, I only need a few seconds.
Stryfe--no, don't do it. It's ***over***--just surrender! ***Please!***

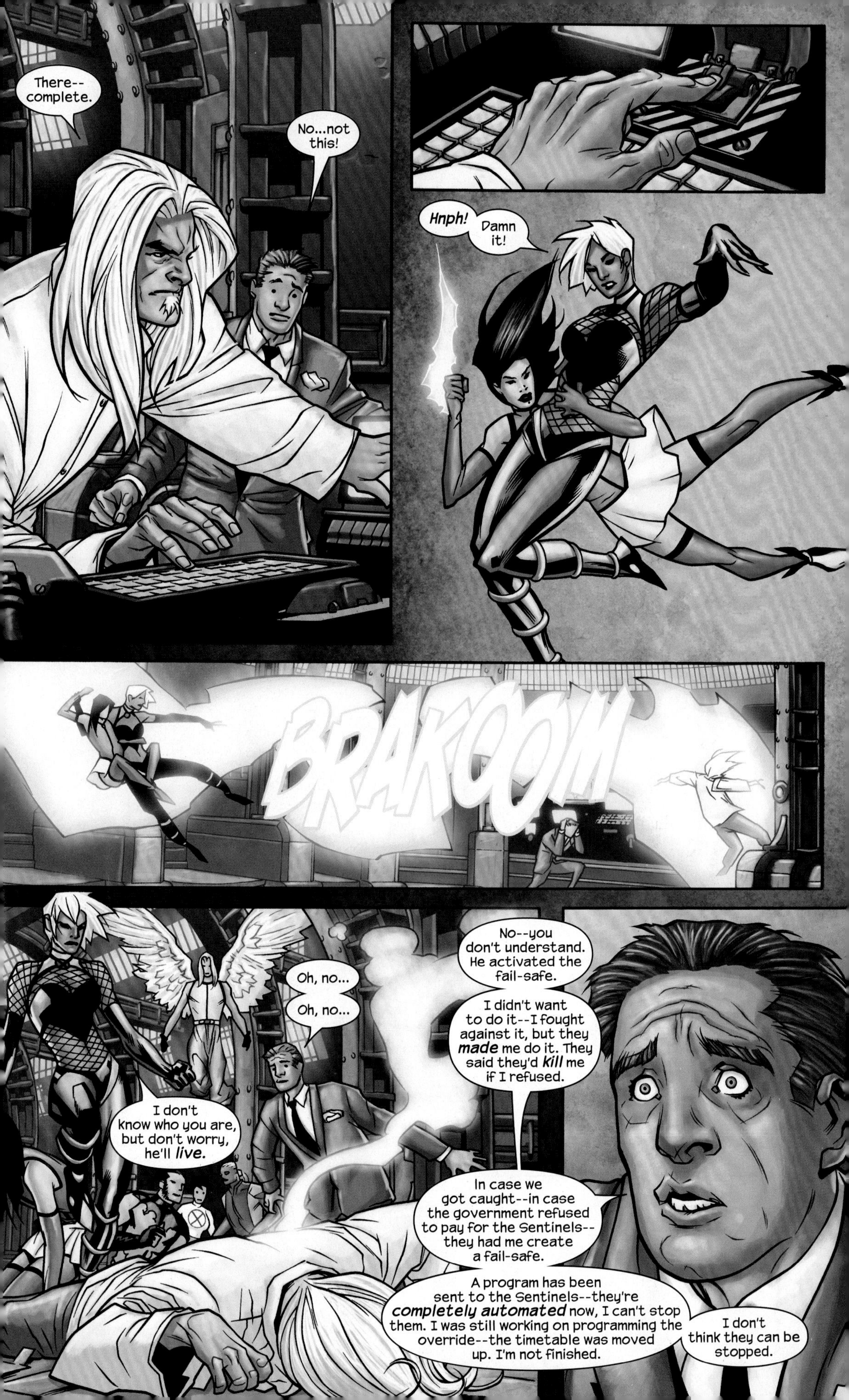
There--
complete.
No...not
this!
Hnph!
Damn
it!
BRAKOOM
Oh, no...
Oh, no...
I don't
know who you are,
but don't worry,
he'll *live.*
No--you
don't understand.
He activated the
fail-safe.
I didn't want
to do it--I fought
against it, but they
made me do it. They
said they'd *kill* me
if I refused.
In case we
got caught--in case
the government refused
to pay for the Sentinels--
they had me create
a fail-safe.
A program has been
sent to the Sentinels--they're
completely automated now, I can't stop
them. I was still working on programming the
override--the timetable was moved
up. I'm not finished.
I don't
think they can be
stopped.

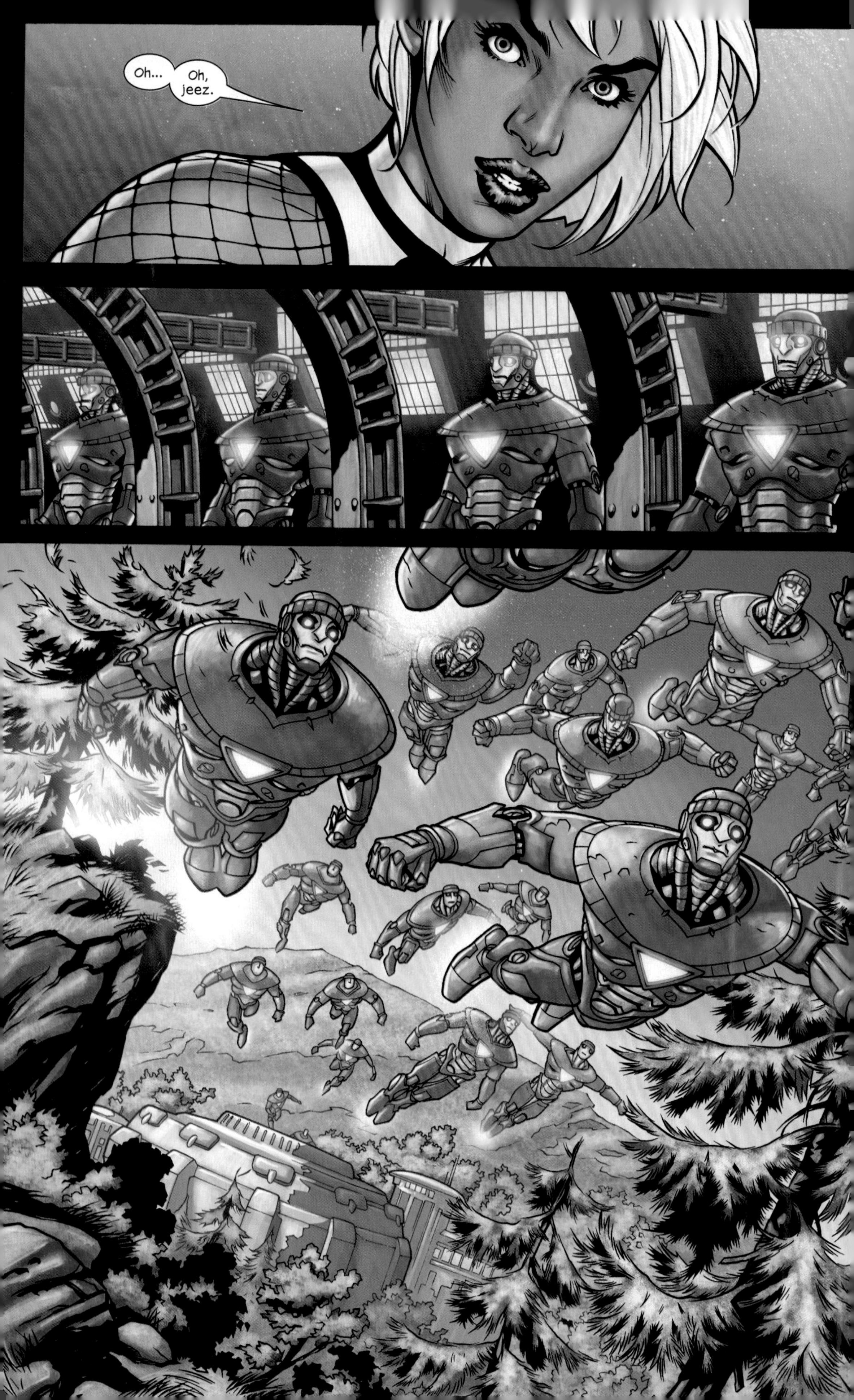
Oh...
Oh, jeez.

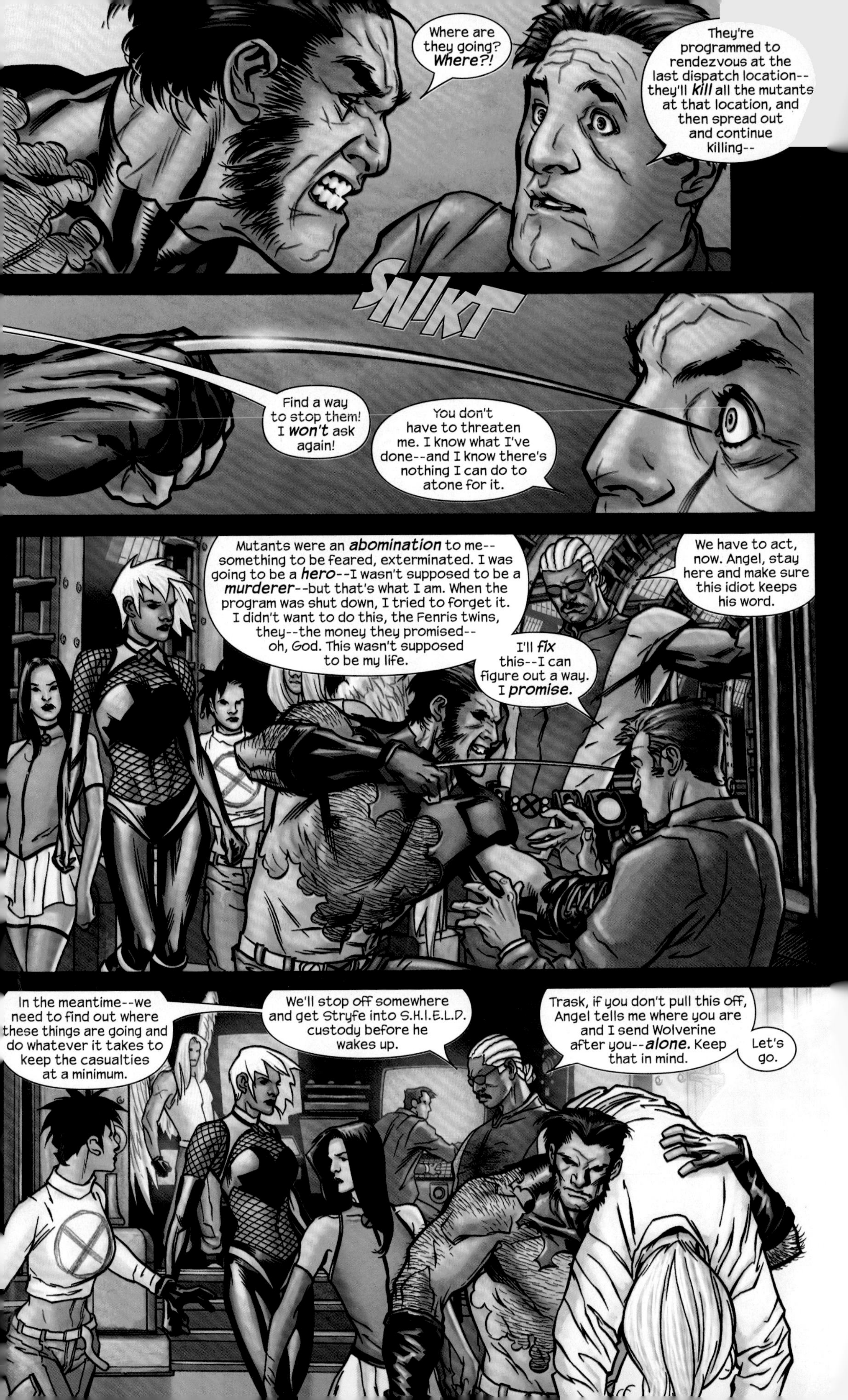
Where are they going? *Where?!*
They're programmed to rendezvous at the last dispatch location--they'll *kill* all the mutants at that location, and then spread out and continue killing--
SNIKT
Find a way to stop them! I *won't* ask again!
You don't have to threaten me. I know what I've done--and I know there's nothing I can do to atone for it.
Mutants were an *abomination* to me--something to be feared, exterminated. I was going to be a *hero*--I wasn't supposed to be a *murderer*--but that's what I am. When the program was shut down, I tried to forget it. I didn't want to do this, the Fenris twins, they--the money they promised--oh, God. This wasn't supposed to be my life.
We have to act, now. Angel, stay here and make sure this idiot keeps his word.
I'll *fix* this--I can figure out a way. I *promise.*
In the meantime--we need to find out where these things are going and do whatever it takes to keep the casualties at a minimum.
We'll stop off somewhere and get Stryfe into S.H.I.E.L.D. custody before he wakes up.
Trask, if you don't pull this off, Angel tells me where you are and I send Wolverine after you--*alone.* Keep that in mind.
Let's go.

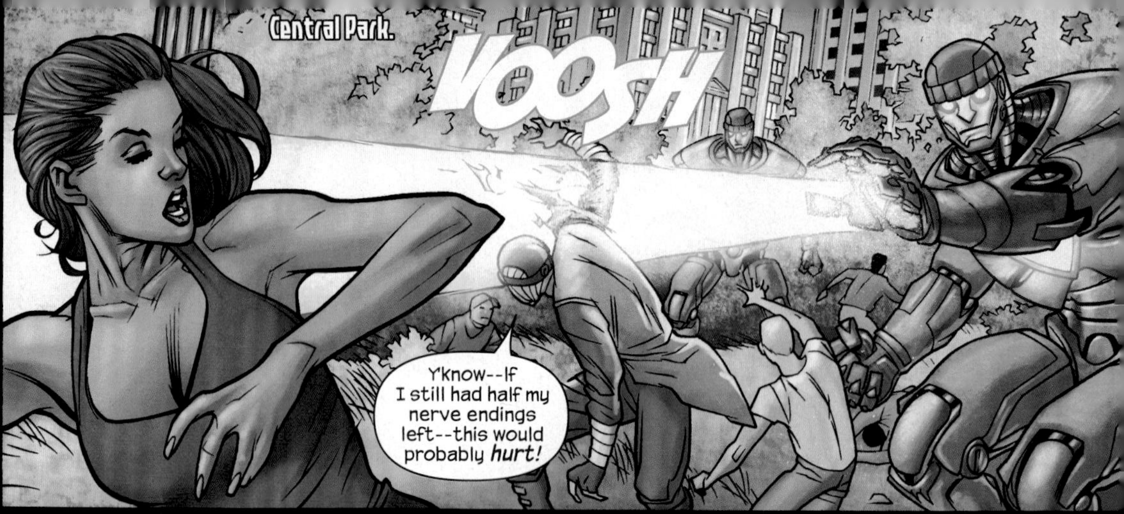
Central Park.
VOOSH
Y'know--If I still had half my nerve endings left--this would probably *hurt!*

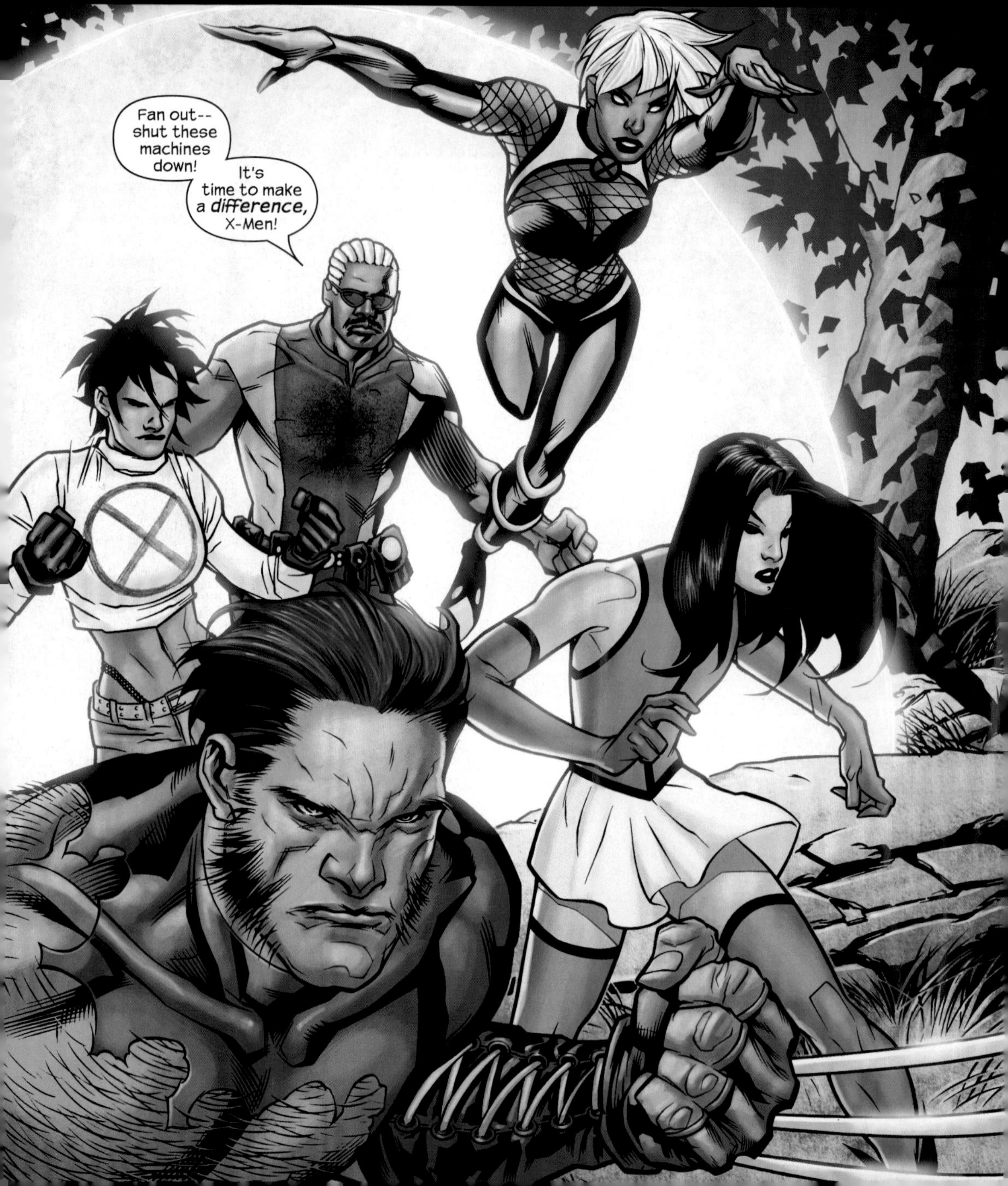
Fan out--shut these machines down!
It's time to make a *difference,* X-Men!

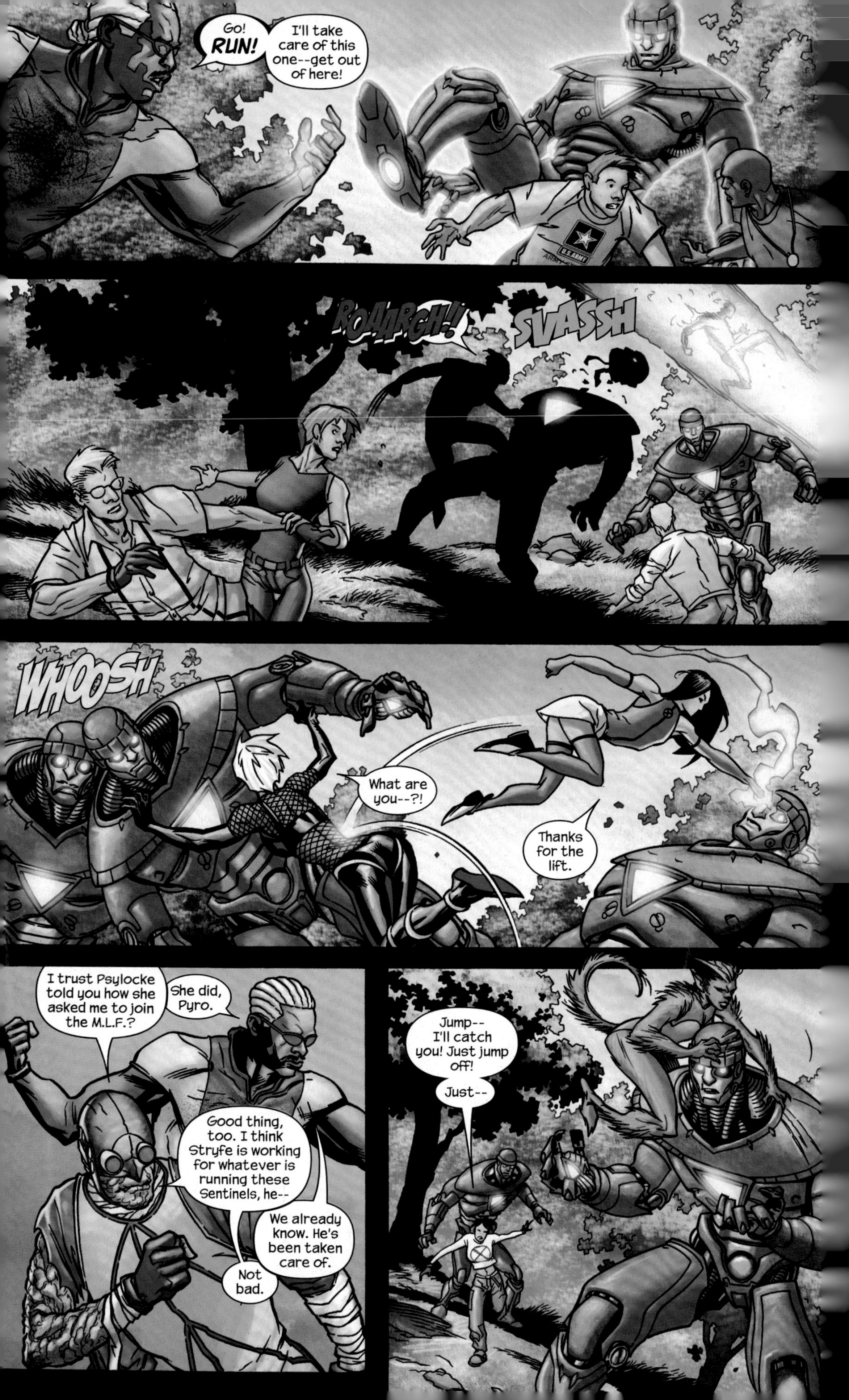

Go! RUN!
I'll take care of this one--get out of here!
U.S. ARMY
ROAAARGH!!
SVASSH
WHOOSH
What are you--?!
Thanks for the lift.
I trust Psylocke told you how she asked me to join the M.L.F.?
She did, Pyro.
Good thing, too. I think Stryfe is working for whatever is running these Sentinels, he--
We already know. He's been taken care of.
Not bad.
Jump-- I'll catch you! Just jump off!
Just--

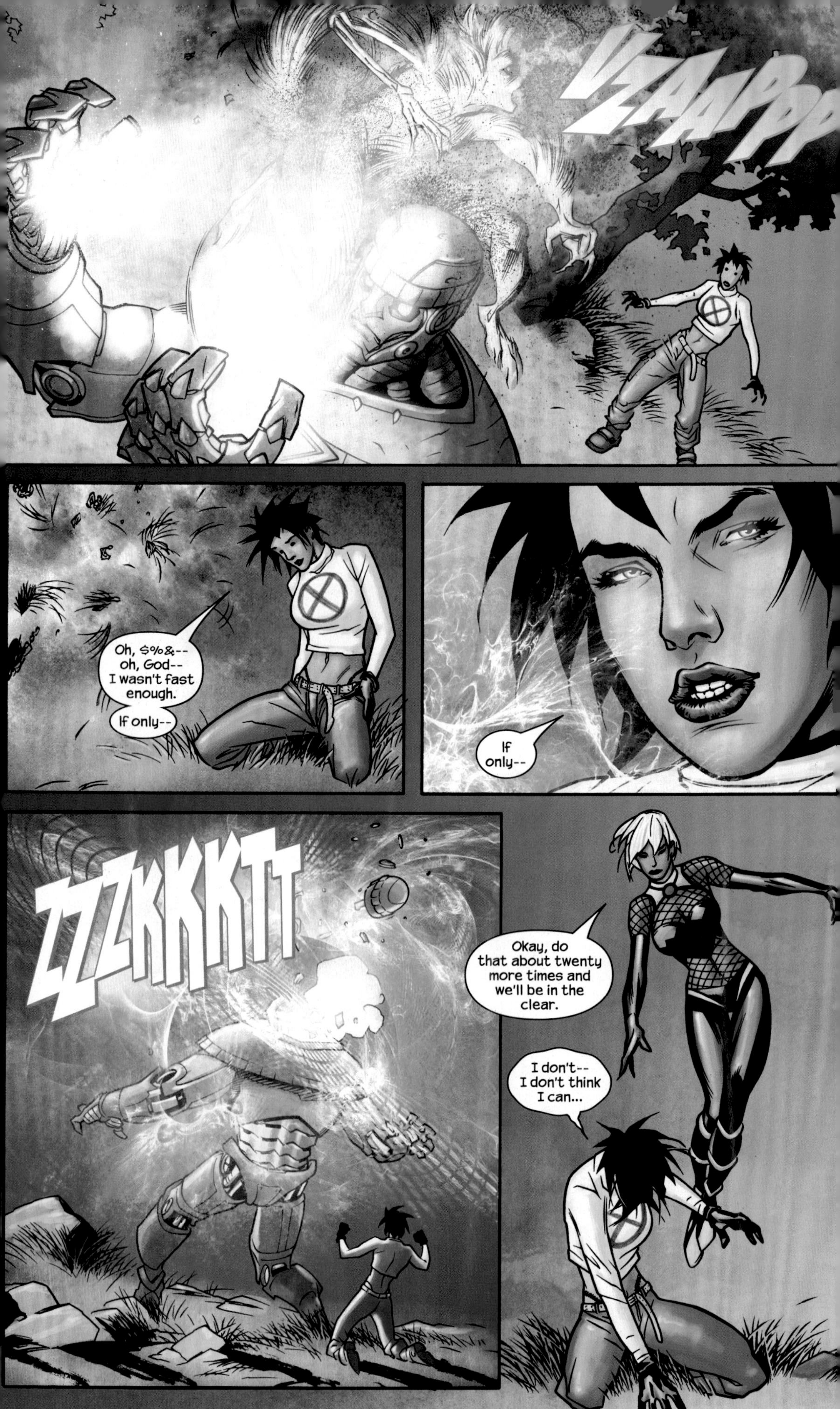
VZAAPPP
Oh, $%&--
oh, God--
I wasn't fast
enough.
If only--
If
only--
ZZZKKKTT
Okay, do
that about twenty
more times and
we'll be in the
clear.
I don't--
I don't think
I can...

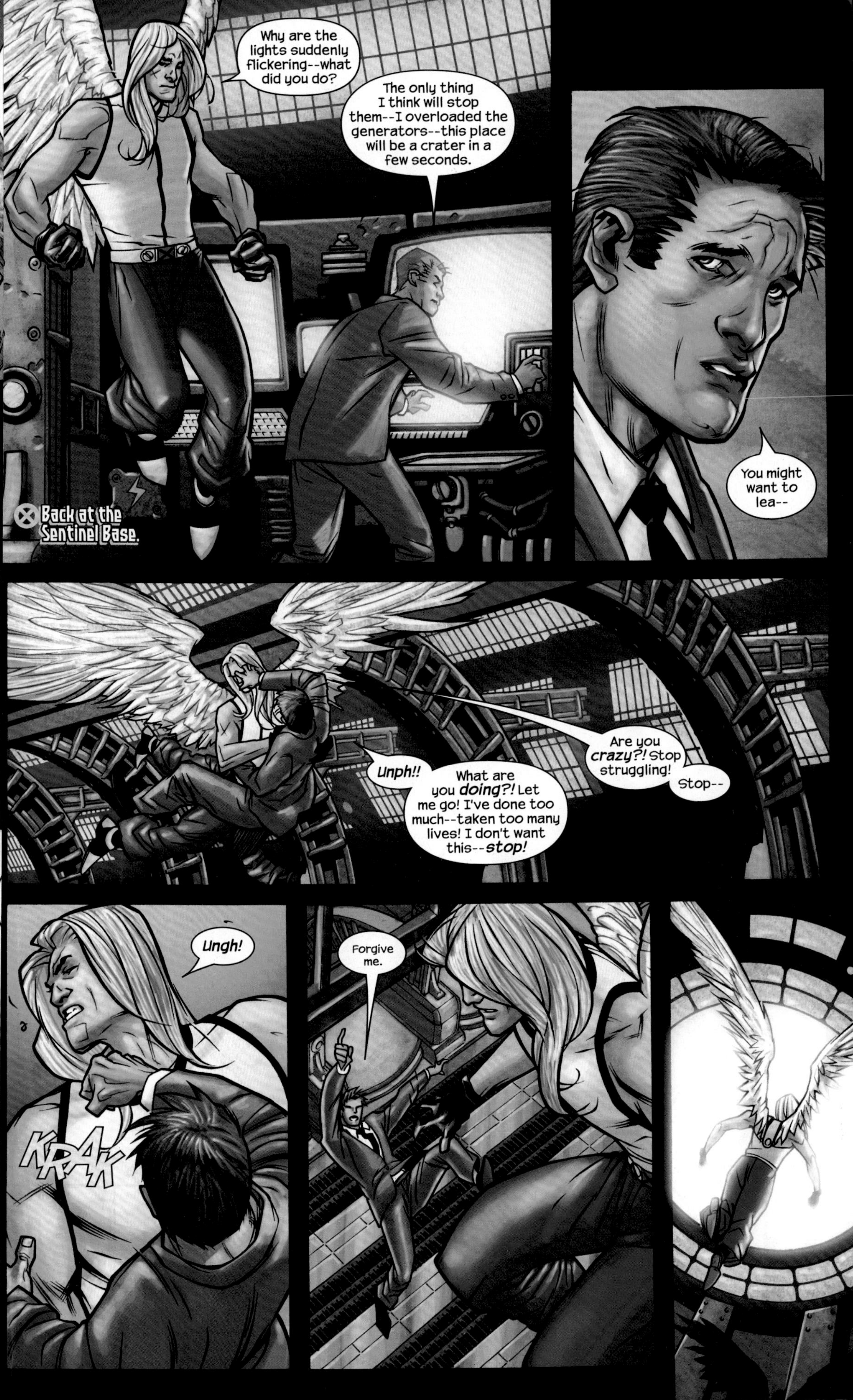
Why are the lights suddenly flickering--what did you do?
The only thing I think will stop them--I overloaded the generators--this place will be a crater in a few seconds.
Back at the Sentinel Base.
You might want to lea--
Are you crazy?! Stop struggling!
Stop--
Unph!!
What are you doing?! Let me go! I've done too much--taken too many lives! I don't want this--stop!
Ungh!
KRAK
Forgive me.

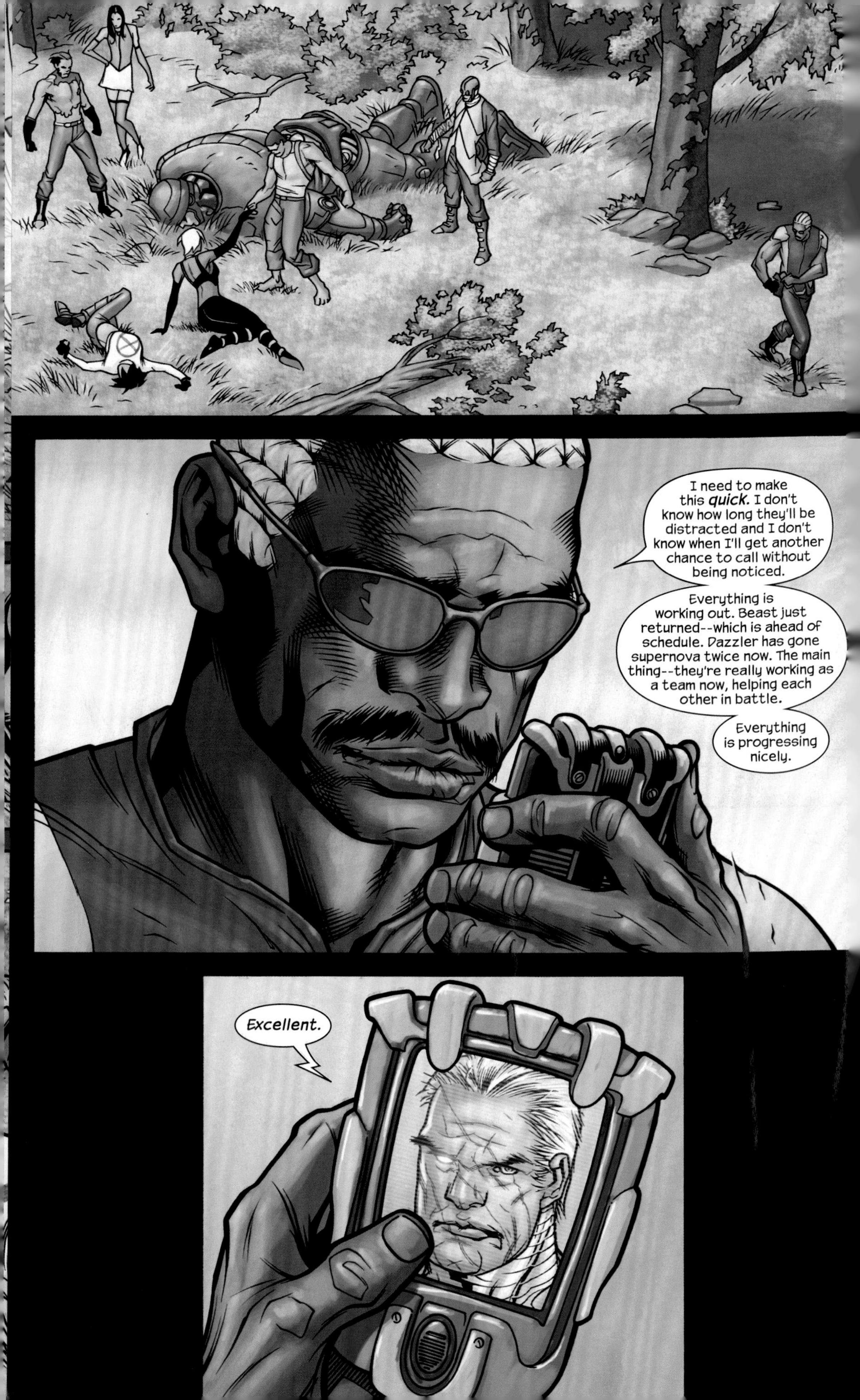
I need to make this *quick.* I don't know how long they'll be distracted and I don't know when I'll get another chance to call without being noticed.
Everything is working out. Beast just returned--which is ahead of schedule. Dazzler has gone supernova twice now. The main thing--they're really working as a team now, helping each other in battle.
Everything is progressing nicely.
Excellent.

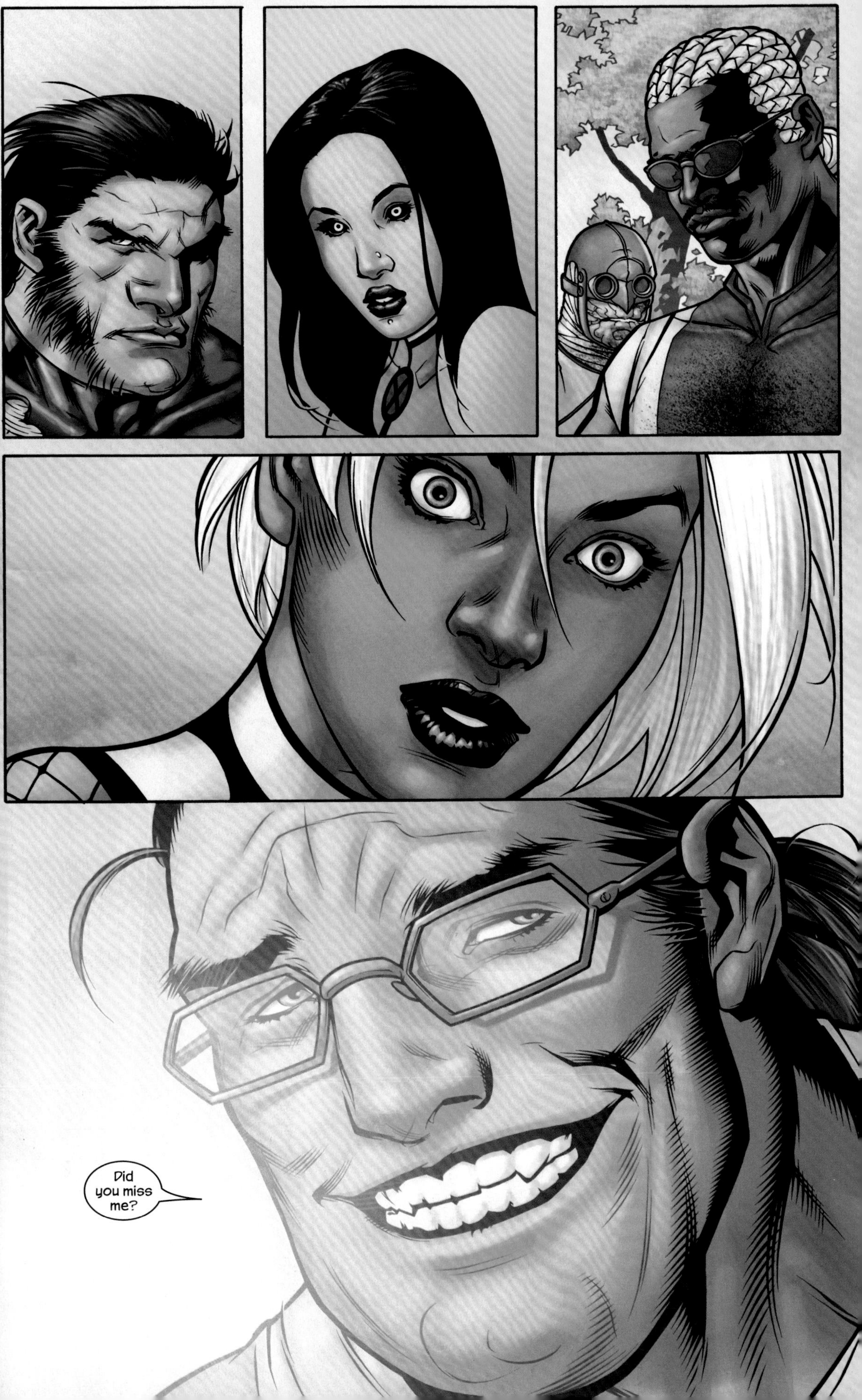
Did you miss me?

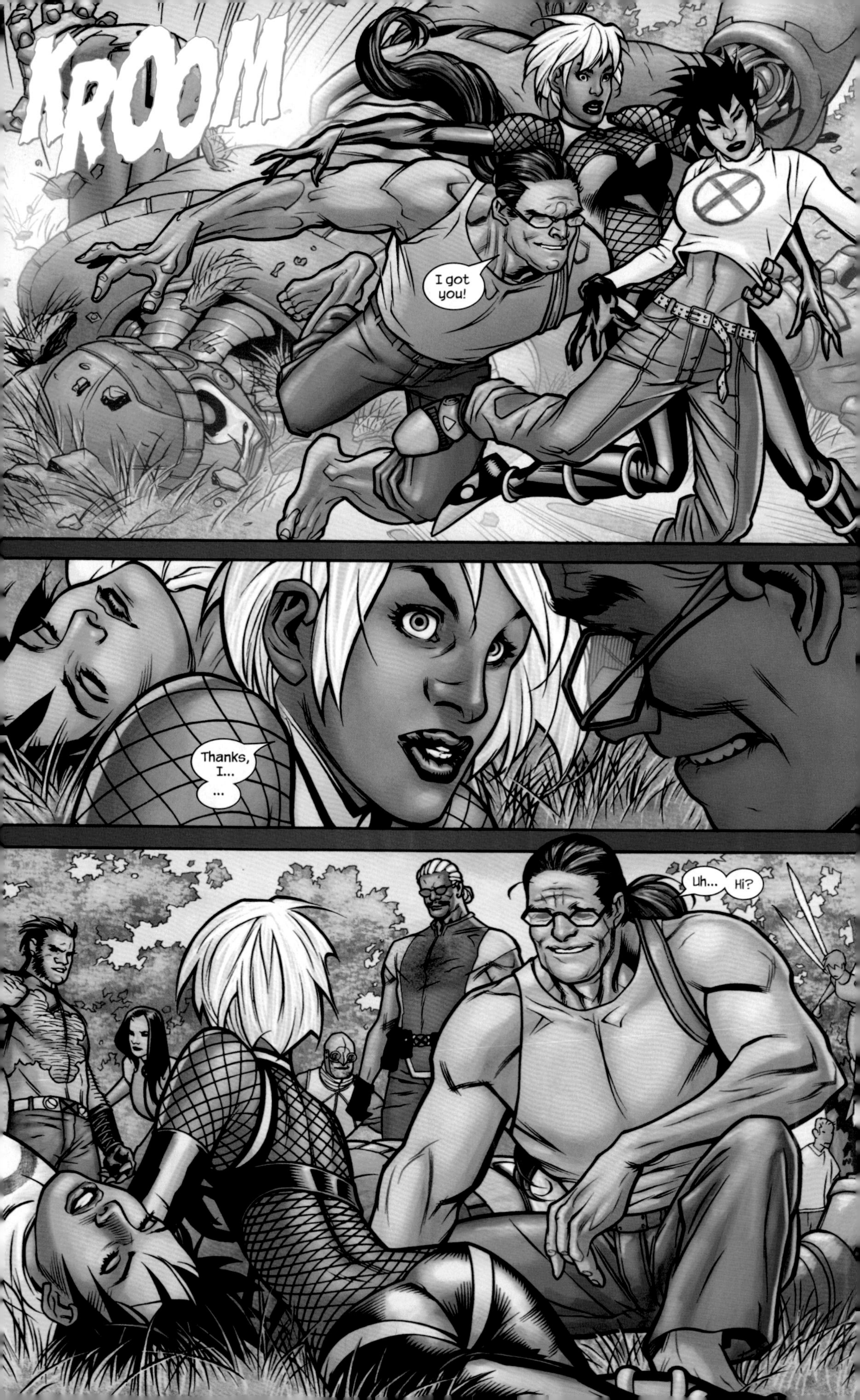
KROOM
I got you!
Thanks, I...
...
Uh...
Hi?

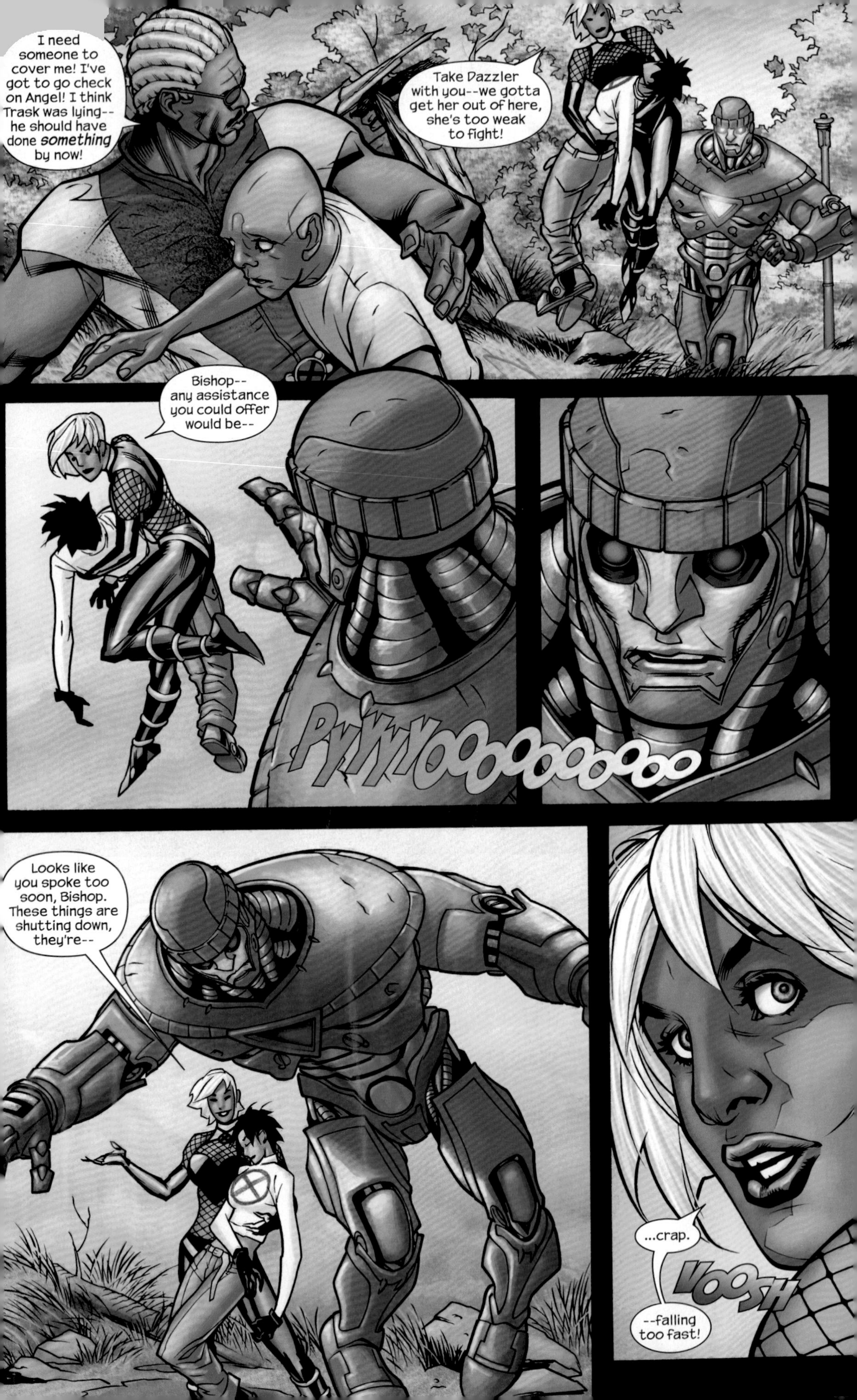
I need someone to cover me! I've got to go check on Angel! I think Trask was lying--he should have done *something* by now!
Take Dazzler with you--we gotta get her out of here, she's too weak to fight!
Bishop--any assistance you could offer would be--
PYWYOOOOOOOOOOOOO
Looks like you spoke too soon, Bishop. These things are shutting down, they're--
...crap.
VOOSH
--falling too fast!

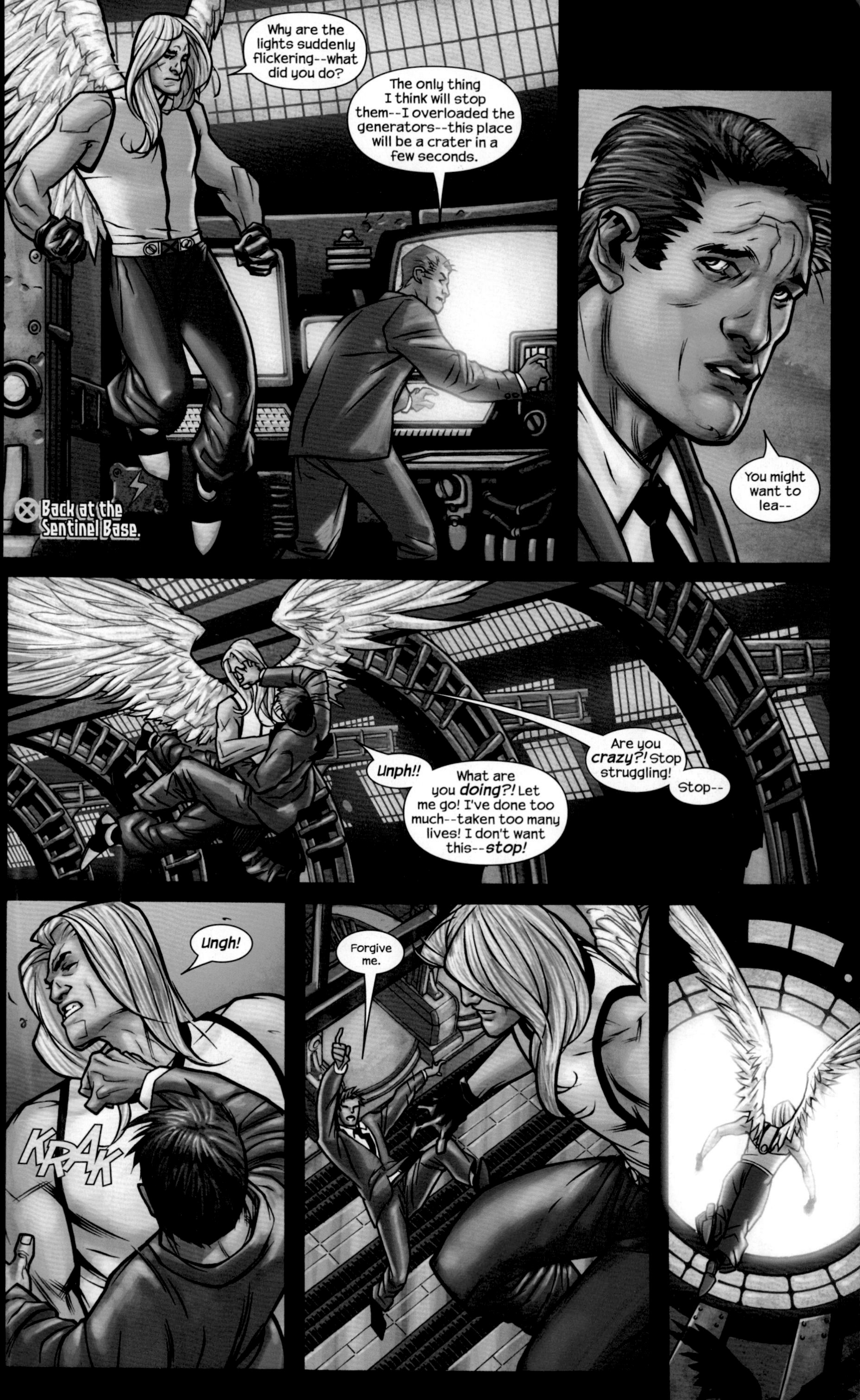
Back at the Sentinel Base.
Why are the lights suddenly flickering--what did you do?
The only thing I think will stop them--I overloaded the generators--this place will be a crater in a few seconds.
You might want to lea--
Unph!!
What are you doing?! Let me go! I've done too much--taken too many lives! I don't want this--stop!
Are you crazy?! Stop struggling!
Stop--
Ungh!
KRAK
Forgive me.

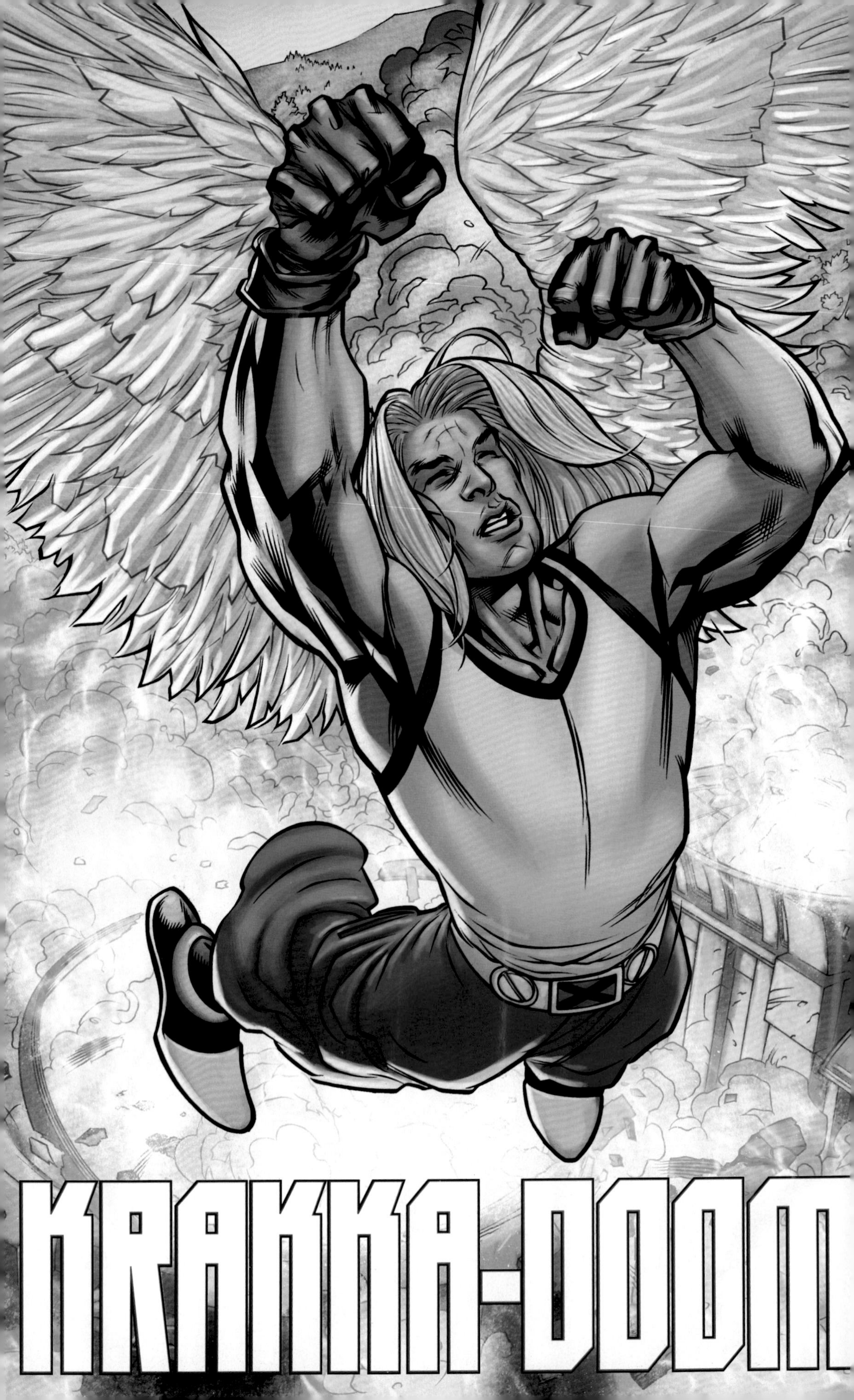
KRAKKA-DOOM

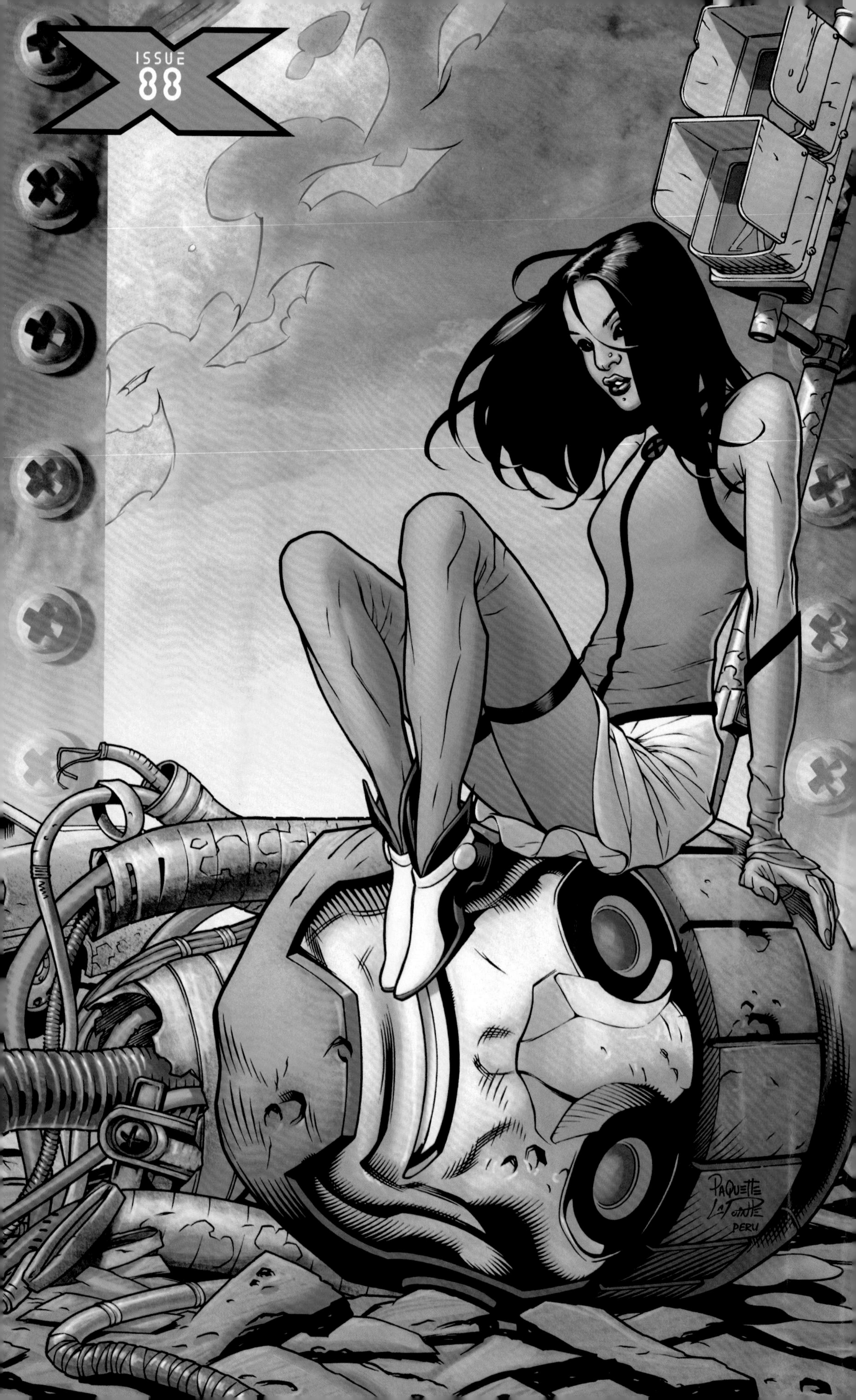

ISSUE
88
PAQUETTE
LaPOINTE
PERU

SENTINELS
EPILOGUE

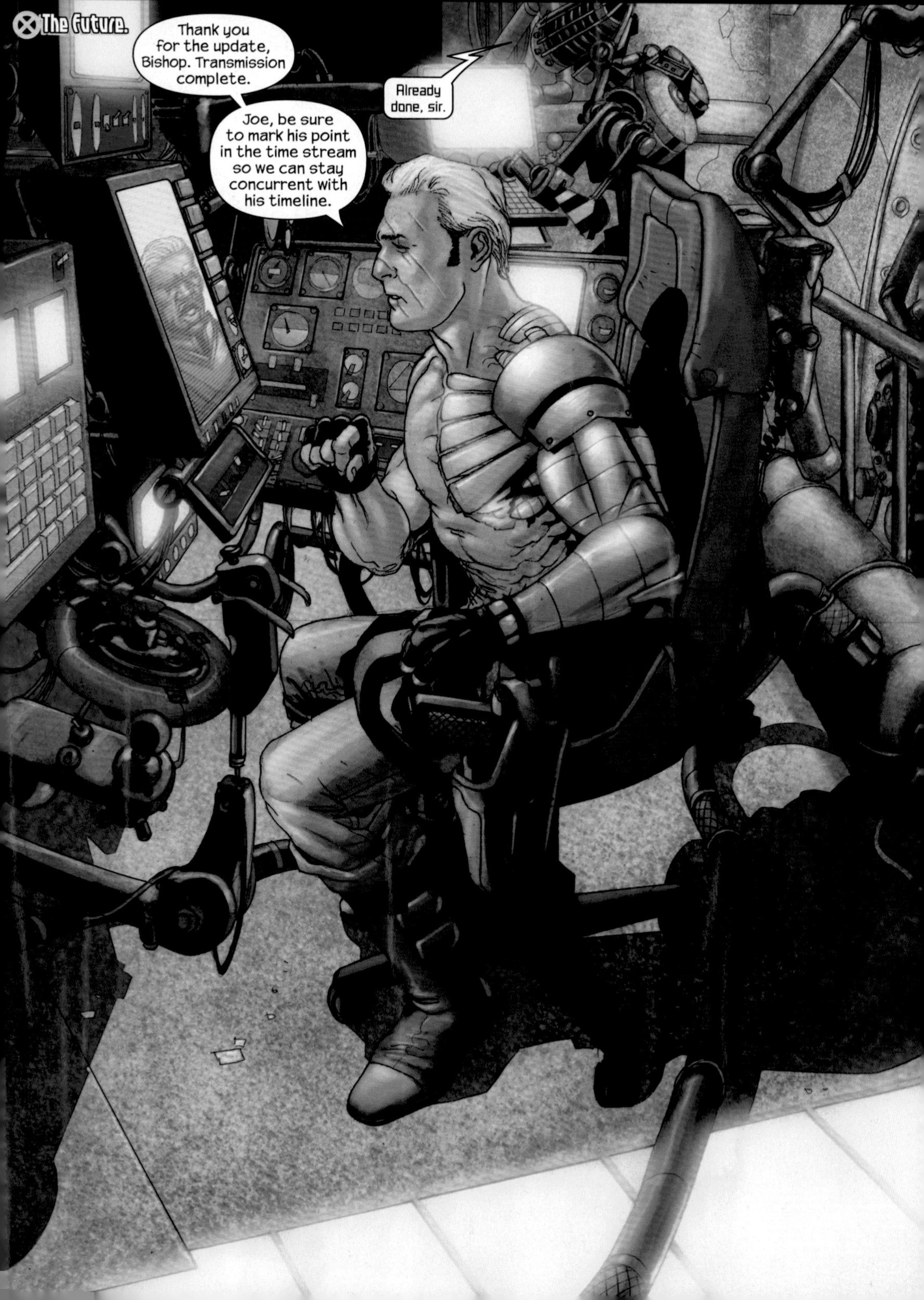
The Future.
Thank you for the update, Bishop. Transmission complete.
Joe, be sure to mark his point in the time stream so we can stay concurrent with his timeline.
Already done, sir.

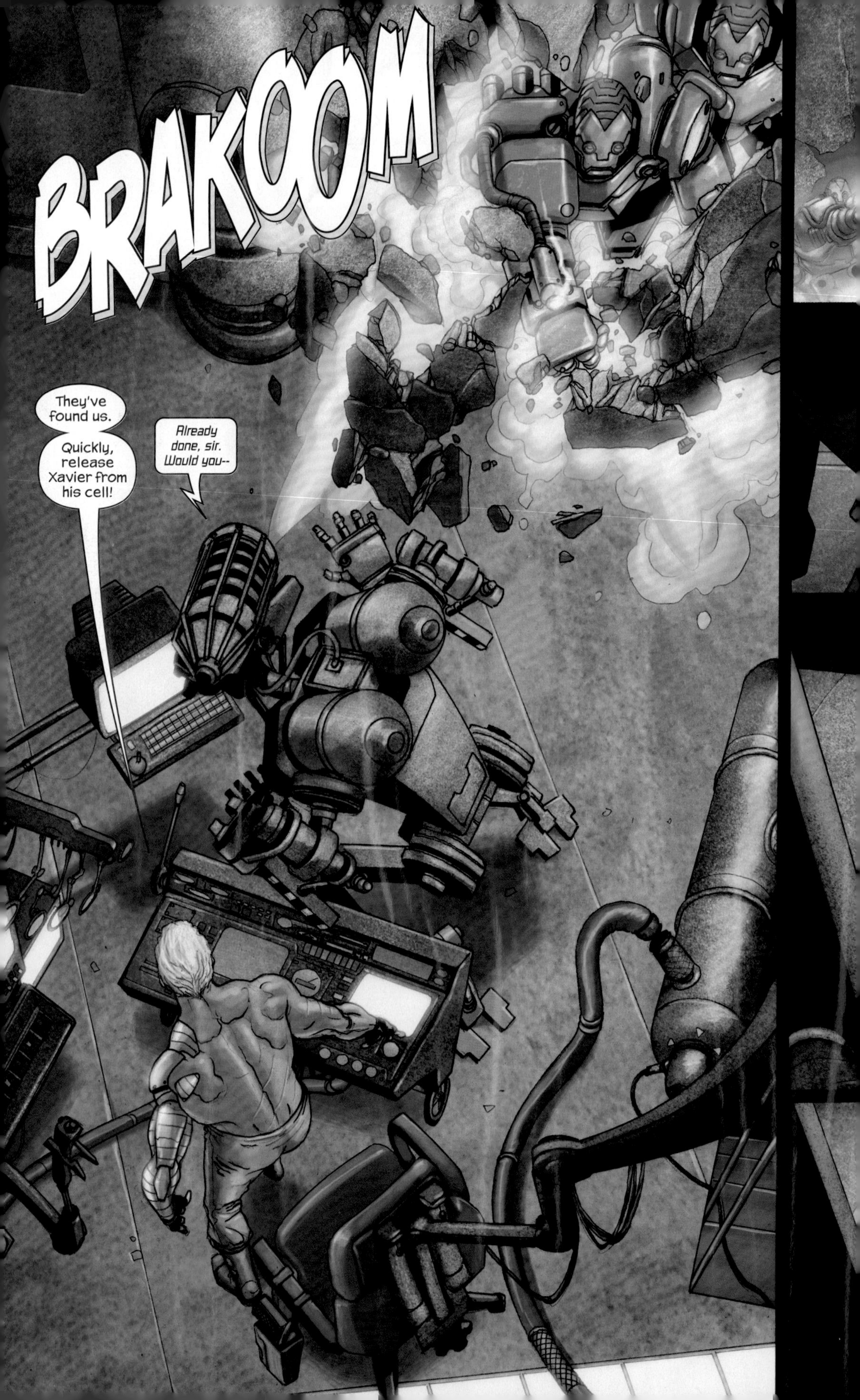
BRAKOOM
They've found us.
Quickly, release Xavier from his cell!
Already done, sir. Would you--

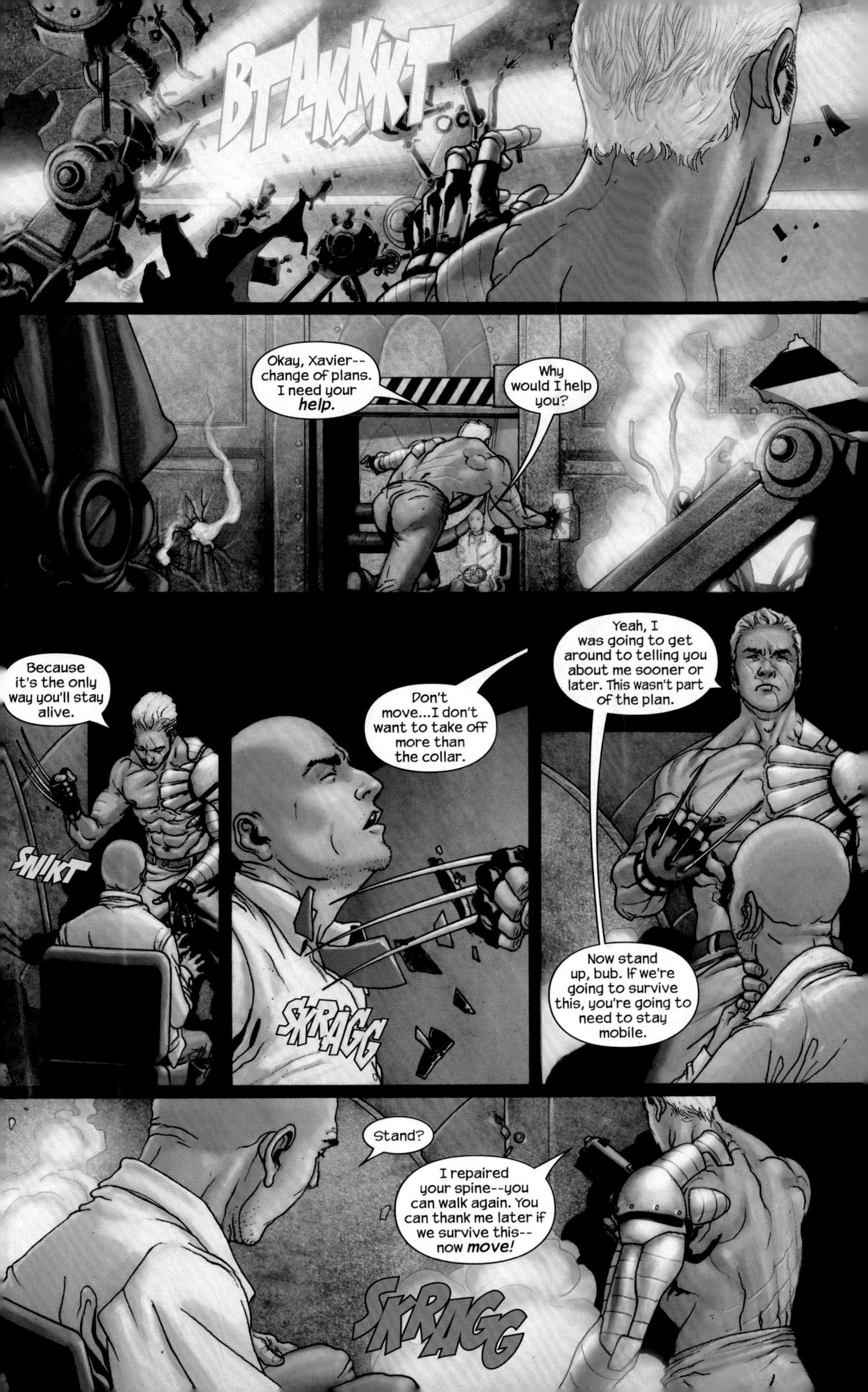

BTANKKT
Okay, Xavier-- change of plans. I need your *help.*
Why would I help you?
Because it's the only way you'll stay alive.
SNIKT
Don't move...I don't want to take off more than the collar.
SKRAGG
Yeah, I was going to get around to telling you about me sooner or later. This wasn't part of the plan.
Now stand up, bub. If we're going to survive this, you're going to need to stay mobile.
Stand?
I repaired your spine--you can walk again. You can thank me later if we survive this-- now *move!*
SKRAGG

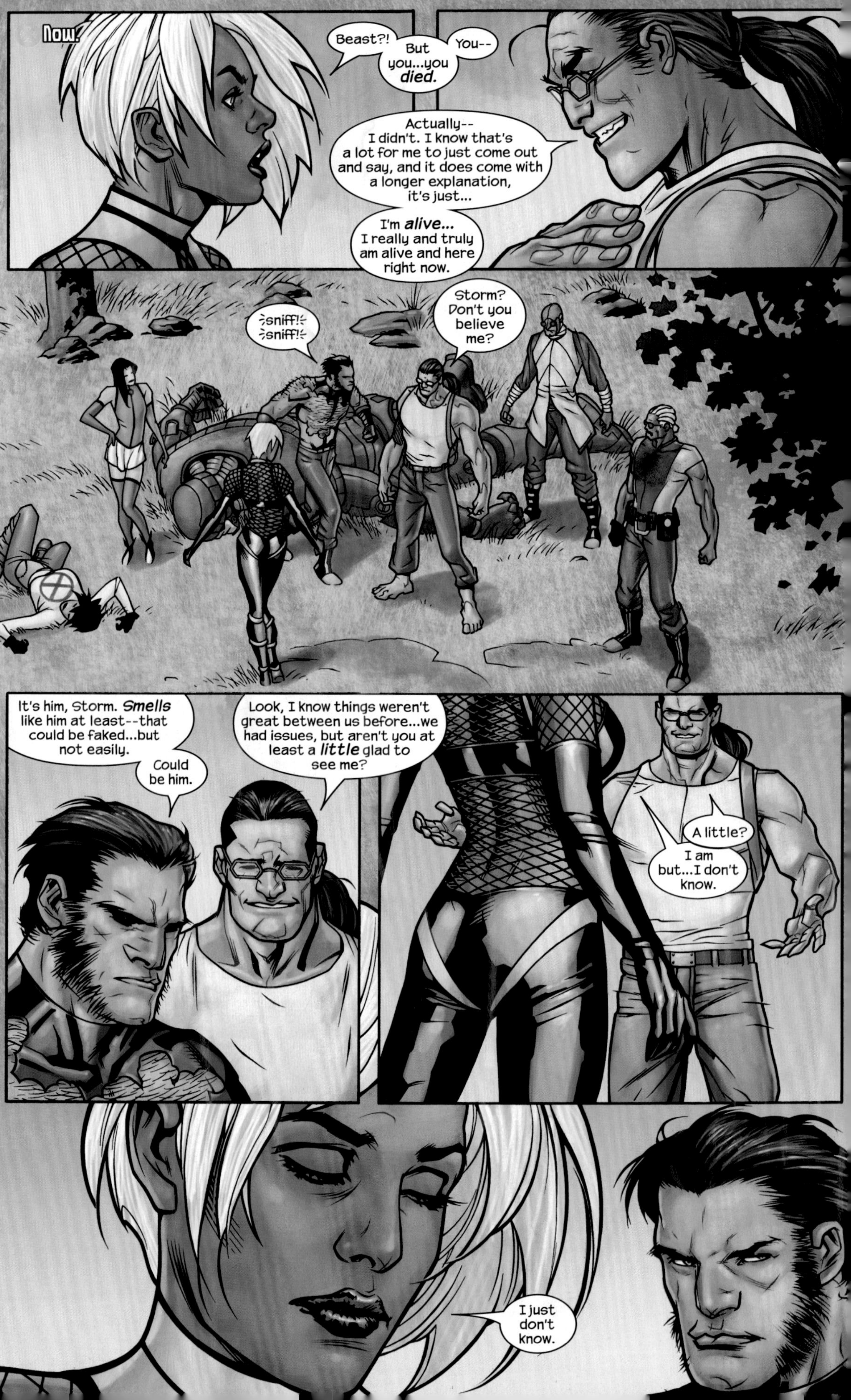
Now.
Beast?!
But you...you died.
You--
Actually-- I didn't. I know that's a lot for me to just come out and say, and it does come with a longer explanation, it's just...
I'm alive... I really and truly am alive and here right now.
:sniff!: :sniff!:
Storm? Don't you believe me?
It's him, Storm. Smells like him at least--that could be faked...but not easily.
Could be him.
Look, I know things weren't great between us before...we had issues, but aren't you at least a little glad to see me?
A little?
I am but...I don't know.
I just don't know.

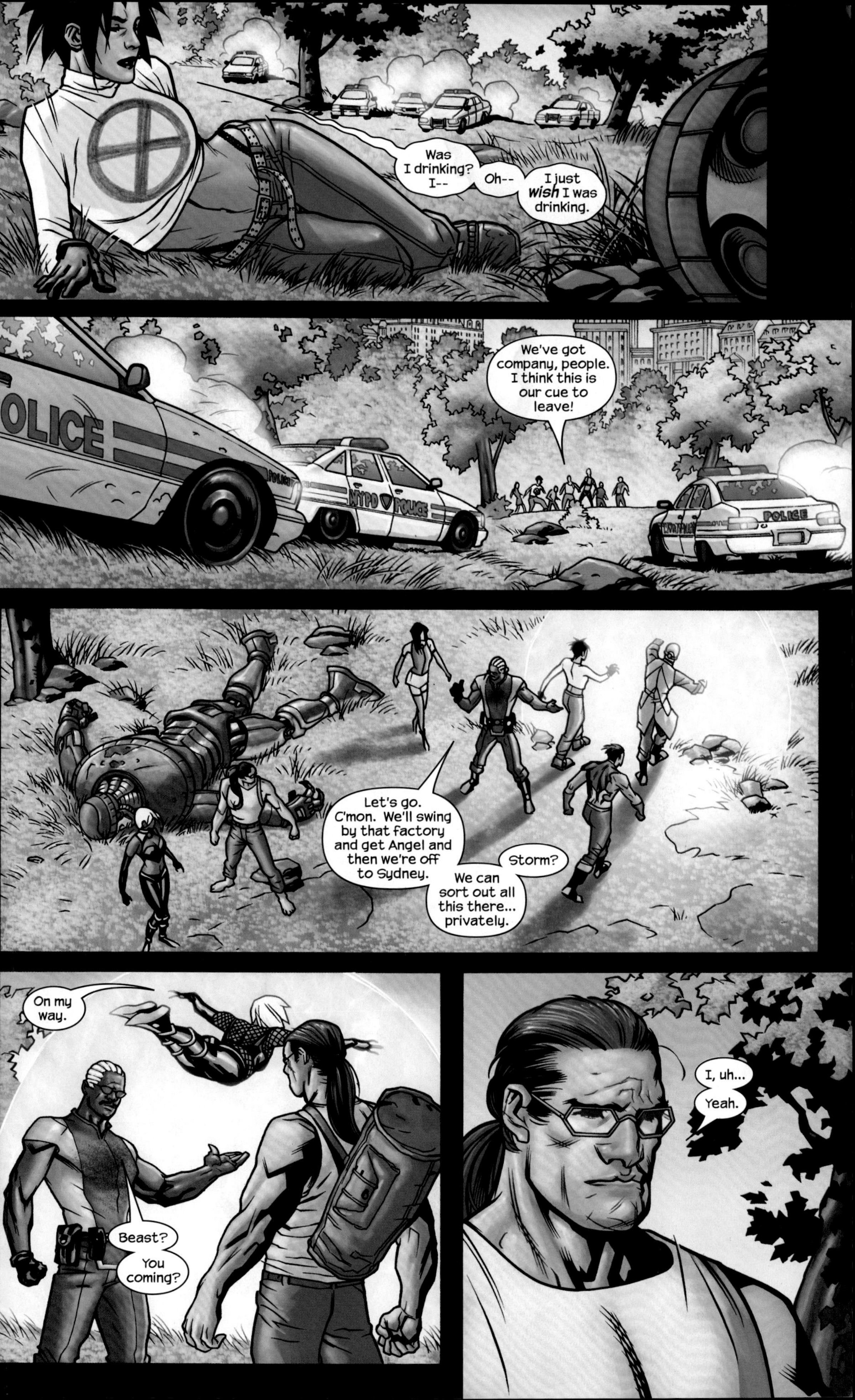
Was I drinking? I--
Oh--
I just *wish* I was drinking.
POLICE
NYPD POLICE
POLICE
We've got company, people. I think this is our cue to leave!
Let's go. C'mon. We'll swing by that factory and get Angel and then we're off to Sydney.
Storm?
We can sort out all this there... privately.
On my way.
Beast?
You coming?
I, uh...
Yeah.

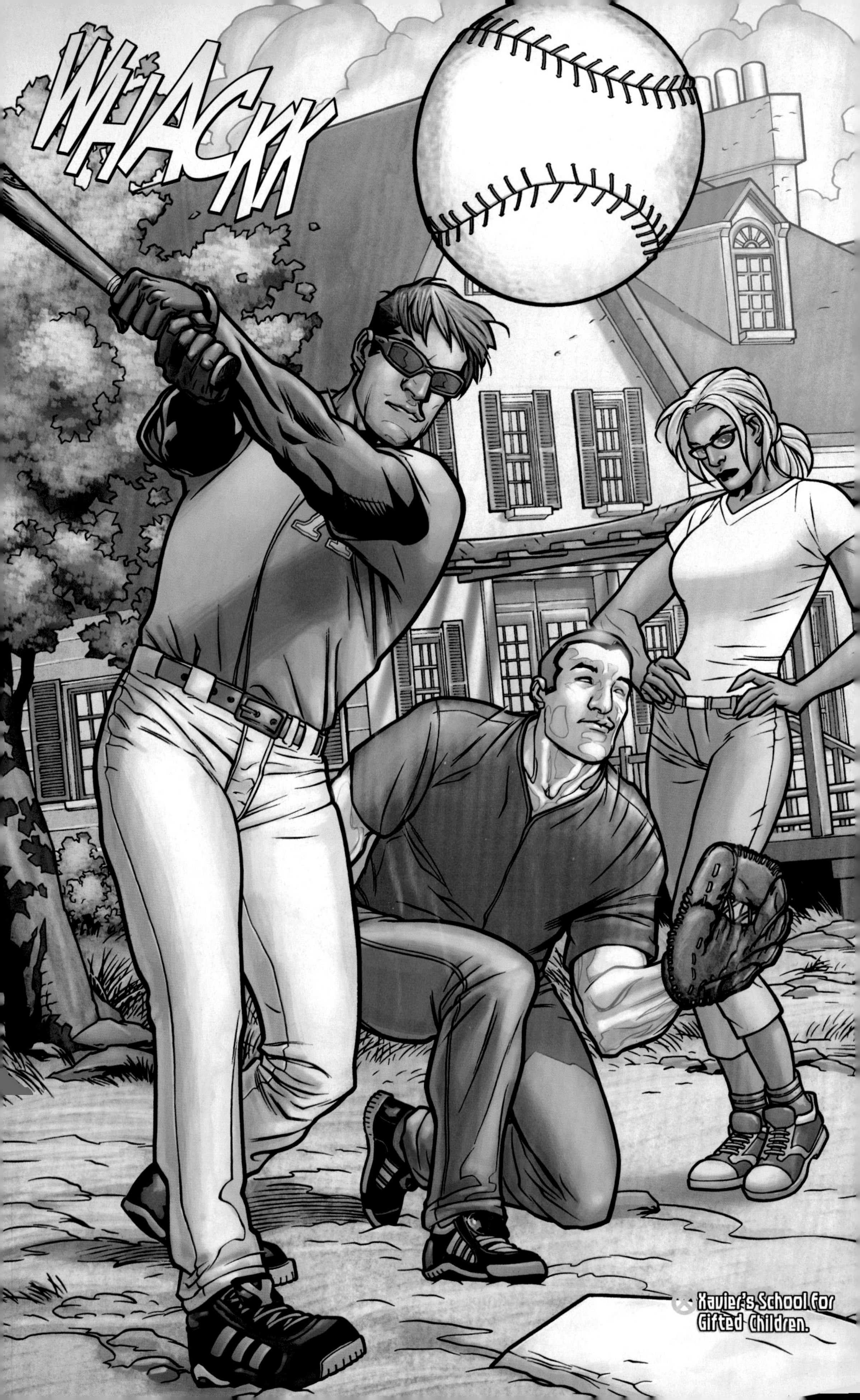
WHACKK
Xavier's School for Gifted Children.

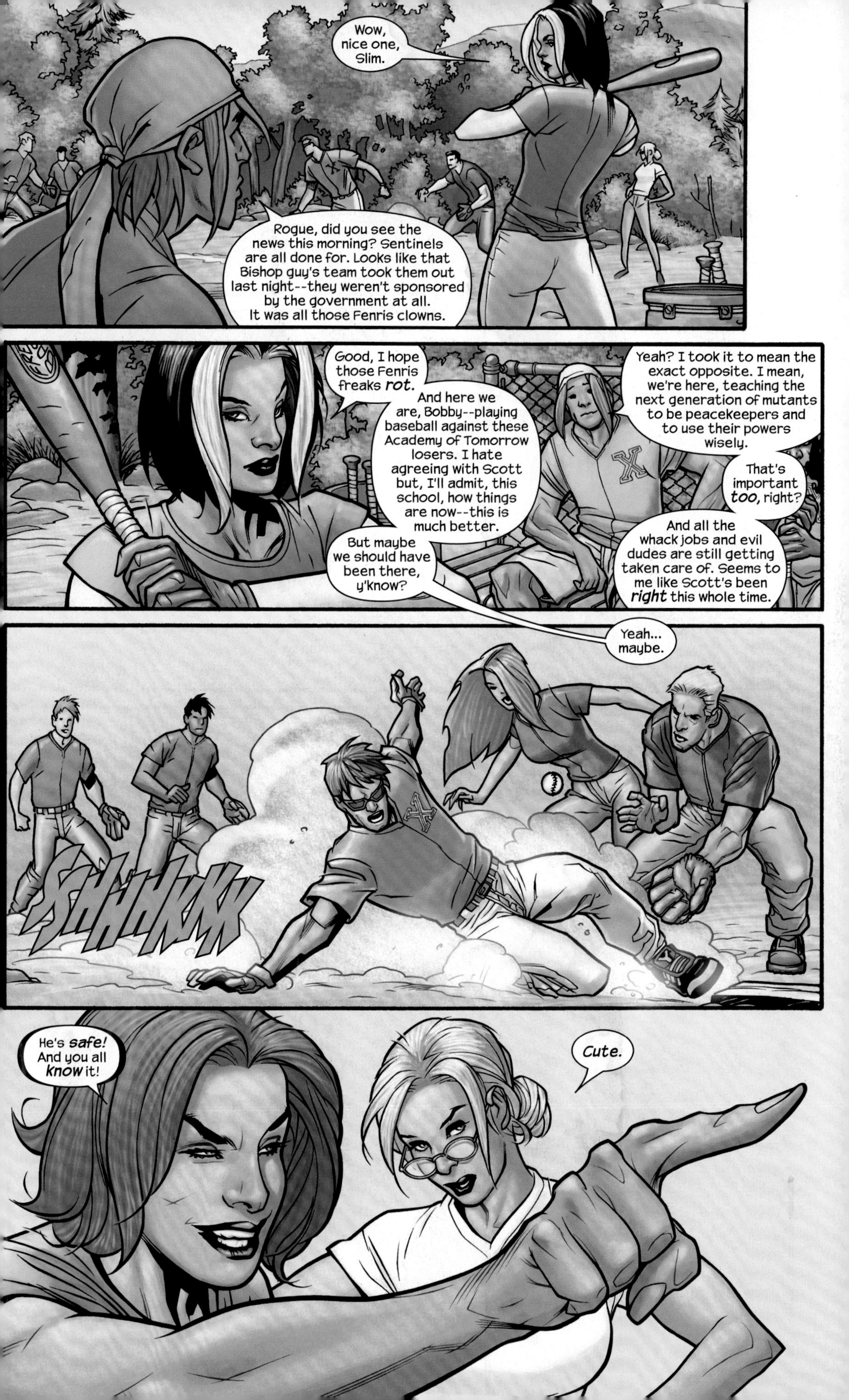
Wow, nice one, Slim.
Rogue, did you see the news this morning? Sentinels are all done for. Looks like that Bishop guy's team took them out last night--they weren't sponsored by the government at all. It was all those Fenris clowns.
Good, I hope those Fenris freaks rot.
And here we are, Bobby--playing baseball against these Academy of Tomorrow losers. I hate agreeing with Scott but, I'll admit, this school, how things are now--this is much better.
But maybe we should have been there, y'know?
Yeah? I took it to mean the exact opposite. I mean, we're here, teaching the next generation of mutants to be peacekeepers and to use their powers wisely.
That's important too, right?
And all the whack jobs and evil dudes are still getting taken care of. Seems to me like Scott's been right this whole time.
Yeah... maybe.
SHHHKKK
He's safe! And you all know it!
Cute.

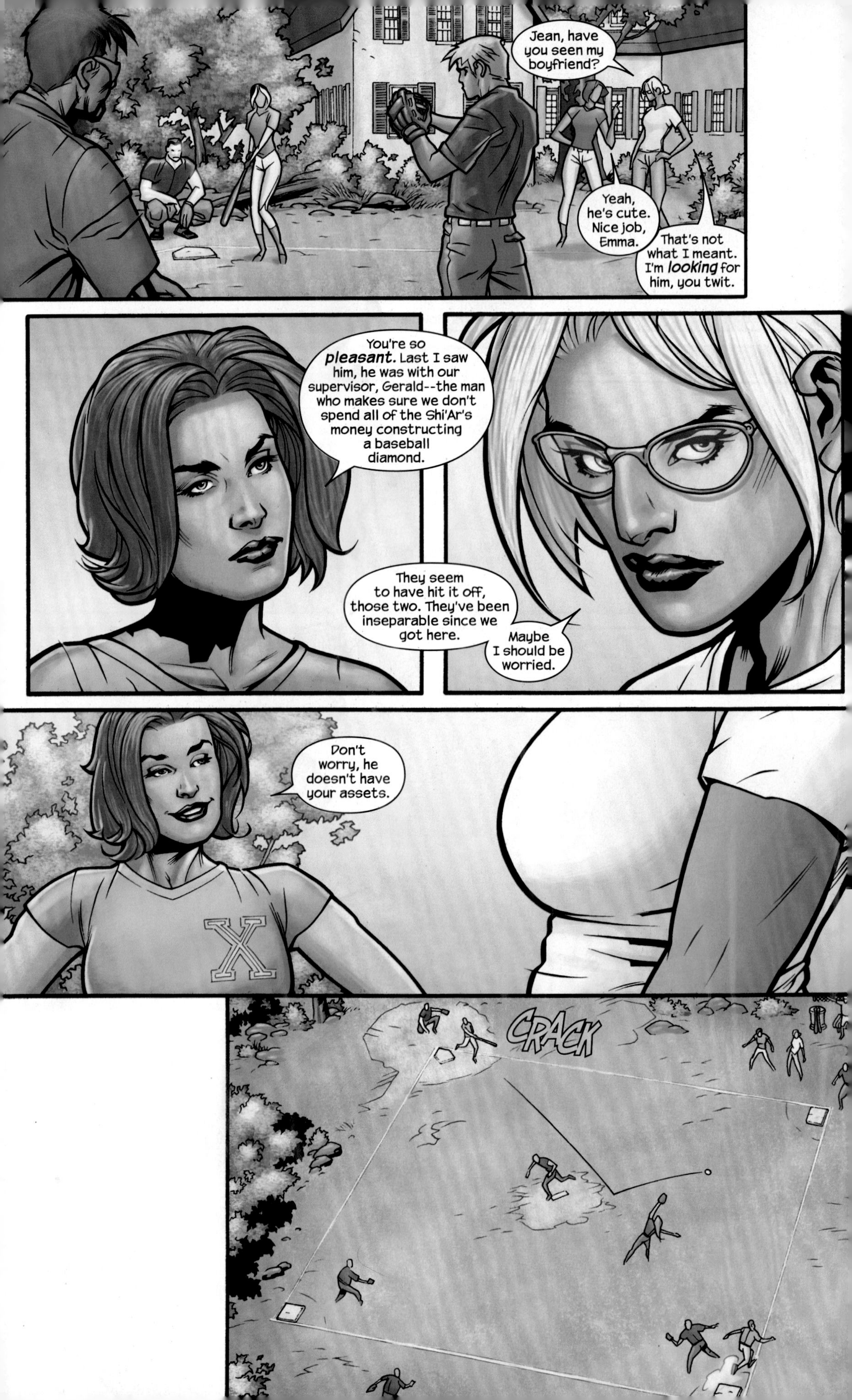
Jean, have you seen my boyfriend?
Yeah, he's cute. Nice job, Emma.
That's not what I meant. I'm looking for him, you twit.
You're so pleasant. Last I saw him, he was with our supervisor, Gerald--the man who makes sure we don't spend all of the Shi'Ar's money constructing a baseball diamond.
They seem to have hit it off, those two. They've been inseparable since we got here.
Maybe I should be worried.
Don't worry, he doesn't have your assets.
CRACK

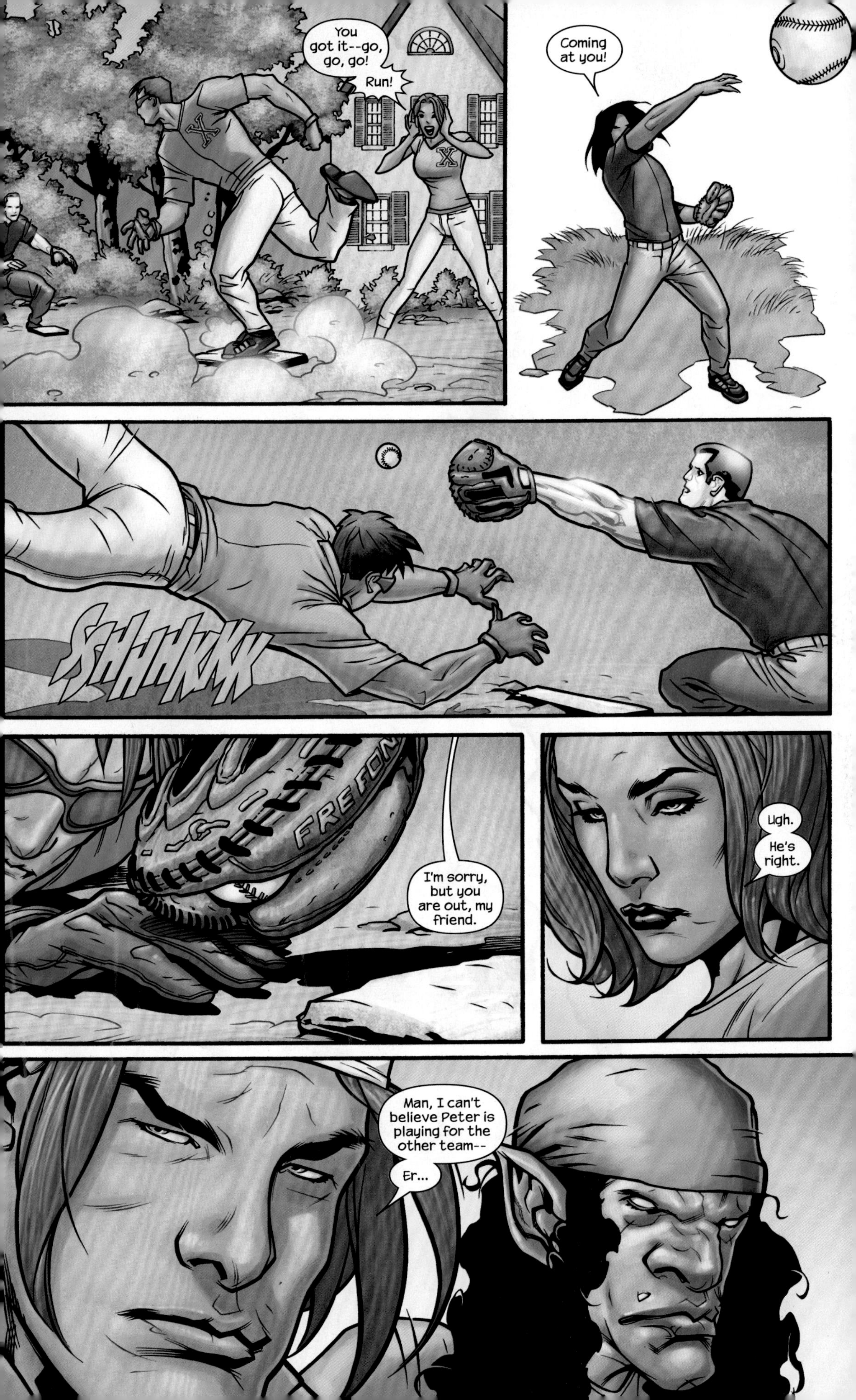
You got it--go, go, go!
Run!
Coming at you!
SHHHKKK
FREFON
I'm sorry, but you are out, my friend.
Ugh.
He's right.
Man, I can't believe Peter is playing for the other team--
Er...

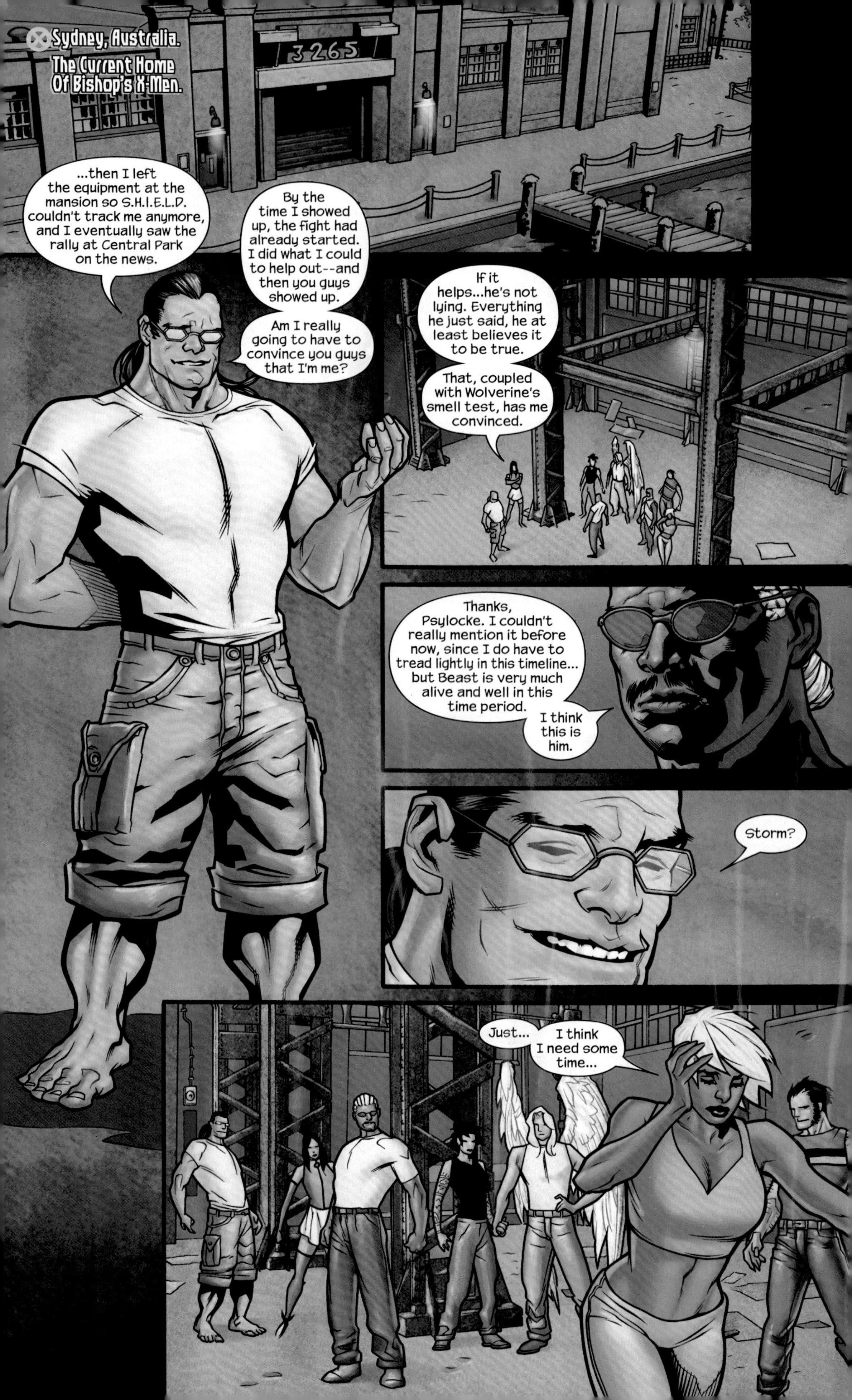
Sydney, Australia.
The Current Home Of Bishop's X-Men.
3265
...then I left the equipment at the mansion so S.H.I.E.L.D. couldn't track me anymore, and I eventually saw the rally at Central Park on the news.
By the time I showed up, the fight had already started. I did what I could to help out--and then you guys showed up.
Am I really going to have to convince you guys that I'm me?
If it helps...he's not lying. Everything he just said, he at least believes it to be true.
That, coupled with Wolverine's smell test, has me convinced.
Thanks, Psylocke. I couldn't really mention it before now, since I do have to tread lightly in this timeline... but Beast is very much alive and well in this time period.
I think this is him.
Storm?
Just...
I think I need some time...

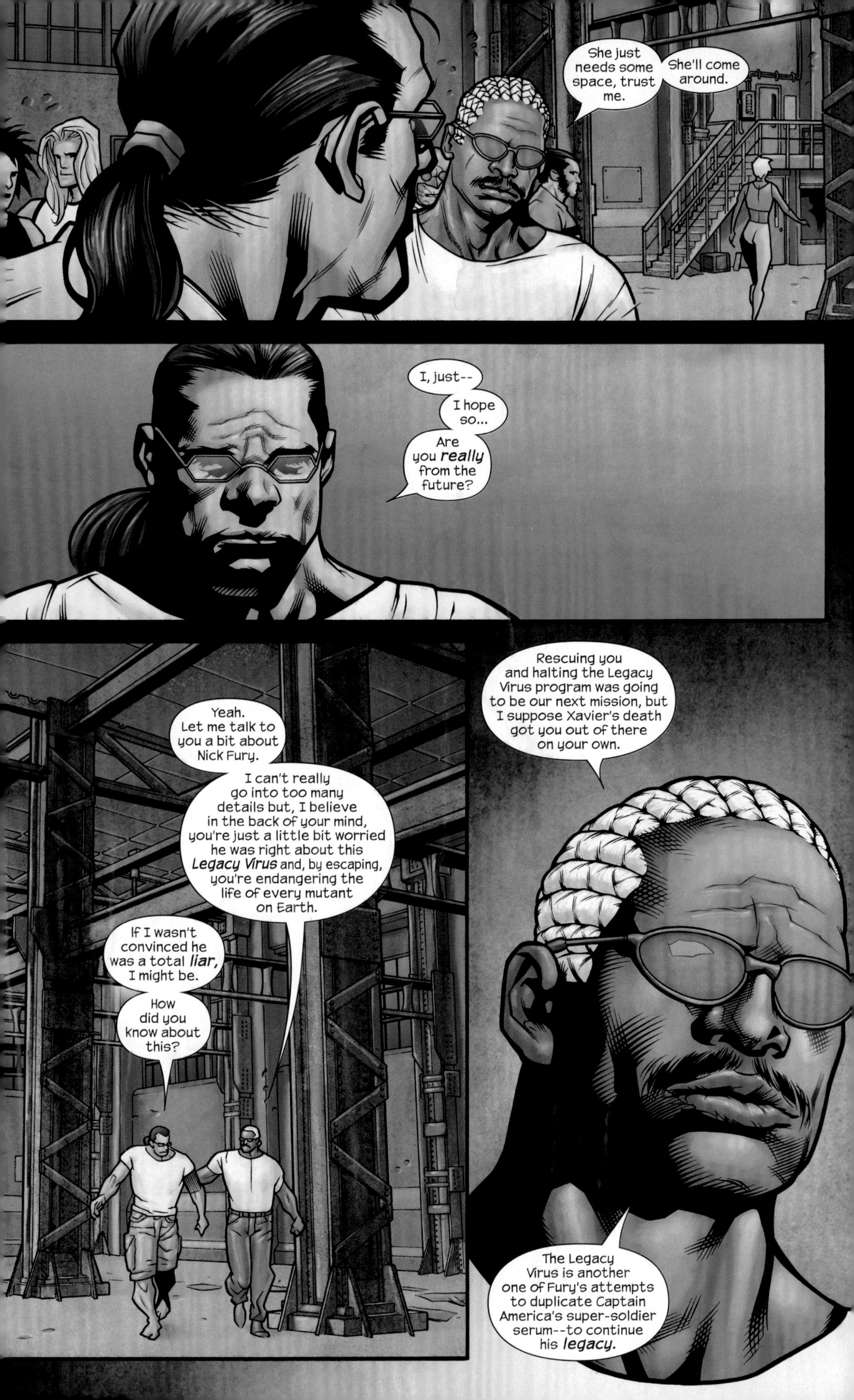
She just needs some space, trust me.
She'll come around.
I, just--
I hope so...
Are you *really* from the future?
Yeah. Let me talk to you a bit about Nick Fury.
I can't really go into too many details but, I believe in the back of your mind, you're just a little bit worried he was right about this *Legacy Virus* and, by escaping, you're endangering the life of every mutant on Earth.
If I wasn't convinced he was a total *liar,* I might be.
How did you know about this?
Rescuing you and halting the Legacy Virus program was going to be our next mission, but I suppose Xavier's death got you out of there on your own.
The Legacy Virus is another one of Fury's attempts to duplicate Captain America's super-soldier serum--to continue his *legacy.*

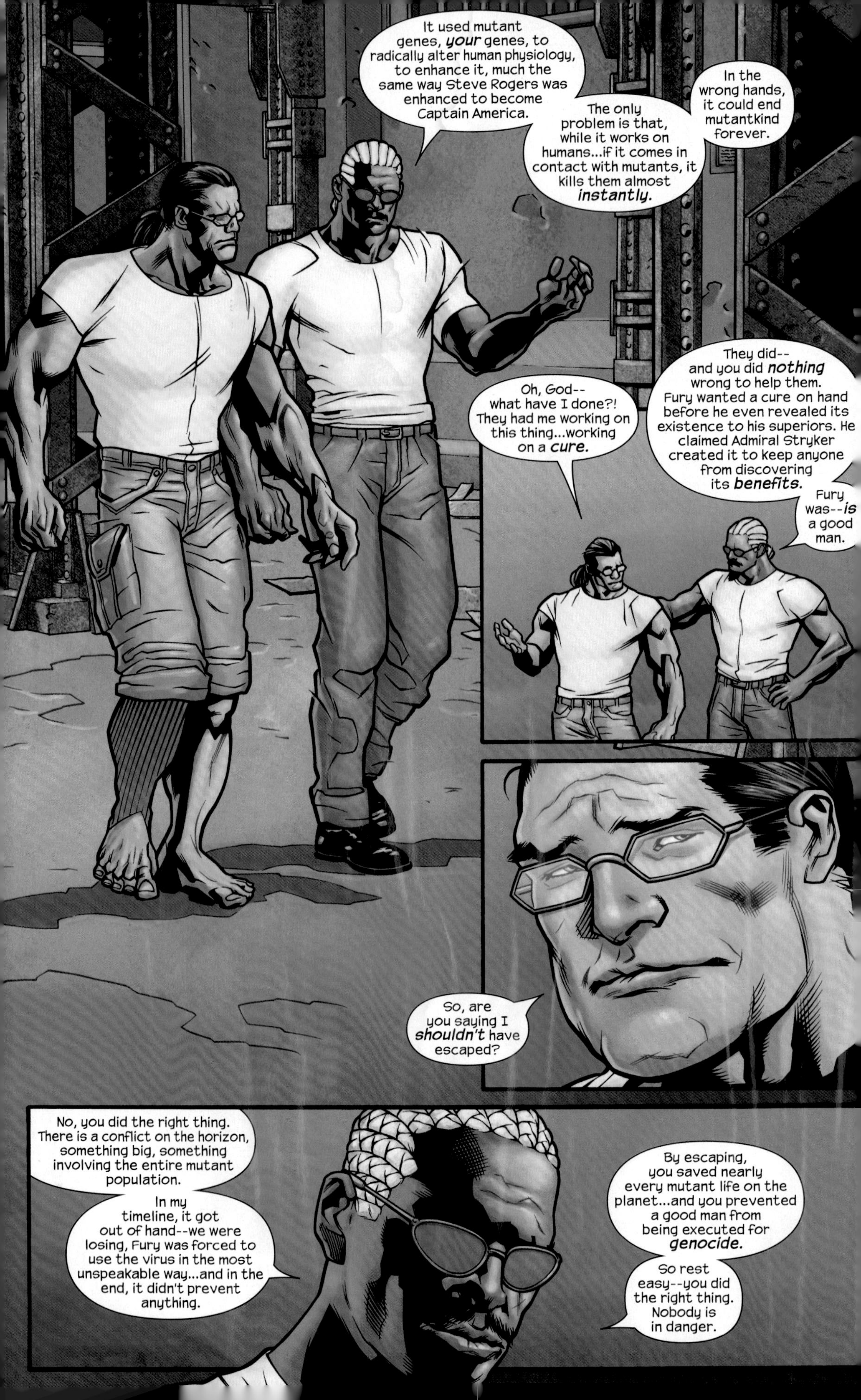
It used mutant genes, your genes, to radically alter human physiology, to enhance it, much the same way Steve Rogers was enhanced to become Captain America.
The only problem is that, while it works on humans...if it comes in contact with mutants, it kills them almost instantly.
In the wrong hands, it could end mutantkind forever.
Oh, God-- what have I done?! They had me working on this thing...working on a cure.
They did-- and you did nothing wrong to help them. Fury wanted a cure on hand before he even revealed its existence to his superiors. He claimed Admiral Stryker created it to keep anyone from discovering its benefits.
Fury was--is a good man.
So, are you saying I shouldn't have escaped?
No, you did the right thing. There is a conflict on the horizon, something big, something involving the entire mutant population.
In my timeline, it got out of hand--we were losing, Fury was forced to use the virus in the most unspeakable way...and in the end, it didn't prevent anything.
By escaping, you saved nearly every mutant life on the planet...and you prevented a good man from being executed for genocide.
So rest easy--you did the right thing. Nobody is in danger.

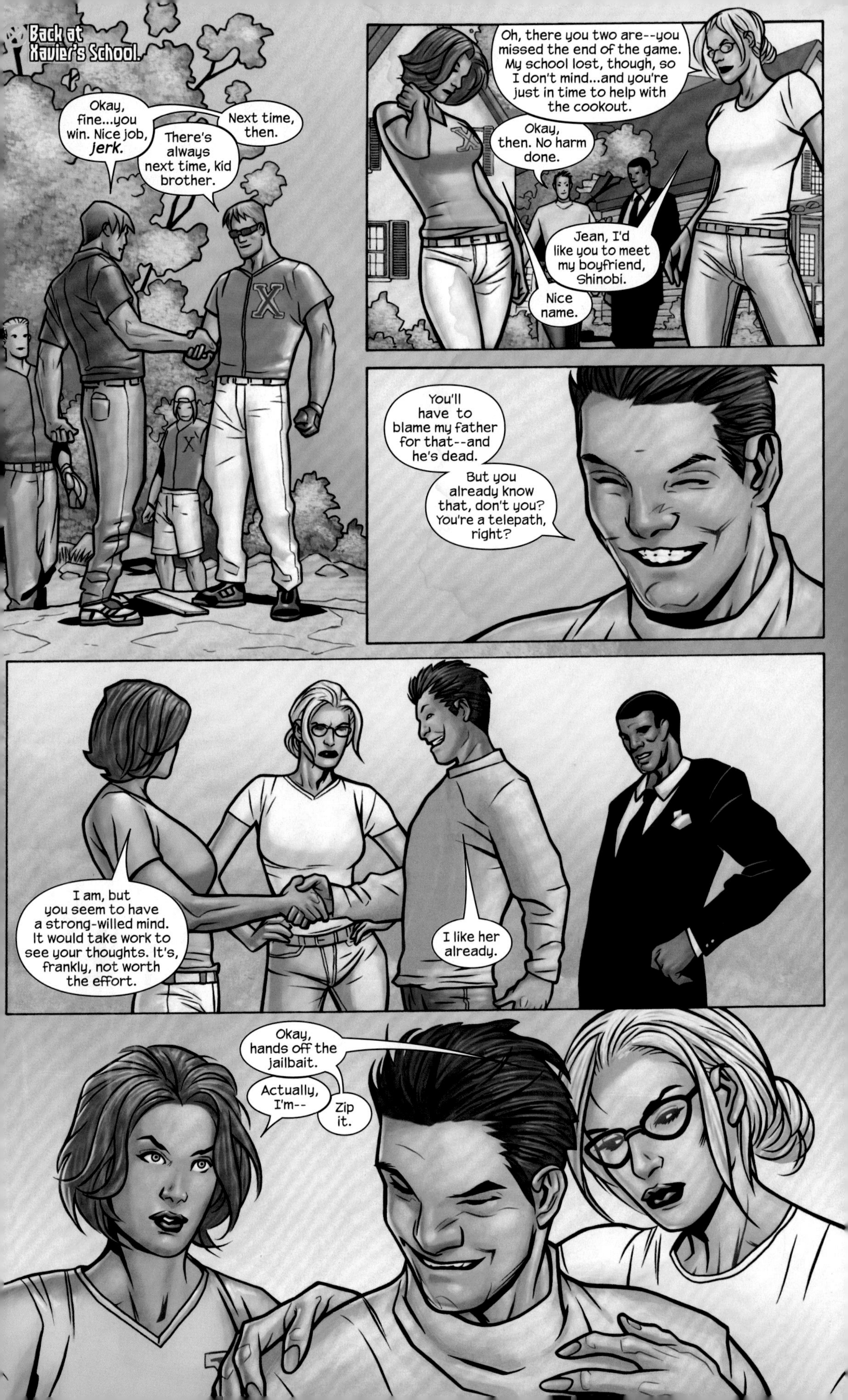
Back at Xavier's School.
Okay, fine...you win. Nice job, *jerk.*
There's always next time, kid brother.
Next time, then.
Oh, there you two are--you missed the end of the game. My school lost, though, so I don't mind...and you're just in time to help with the cookout.
Okay, then. No harm done.
Jean, I'd like you to meet my boyfriend, Shinobi.
Nice name.
You'll have to blame my father for that--and he's dead.
But you already know that, don't you? You're a telepath, right?
I am, but you seem to have a strong-willed mind. It would take work to see your thoughts. It's, frankly, not worth the effort.
I like her already.
Okay, hands off the jailbait.
Actually, I'm--
Zip it.

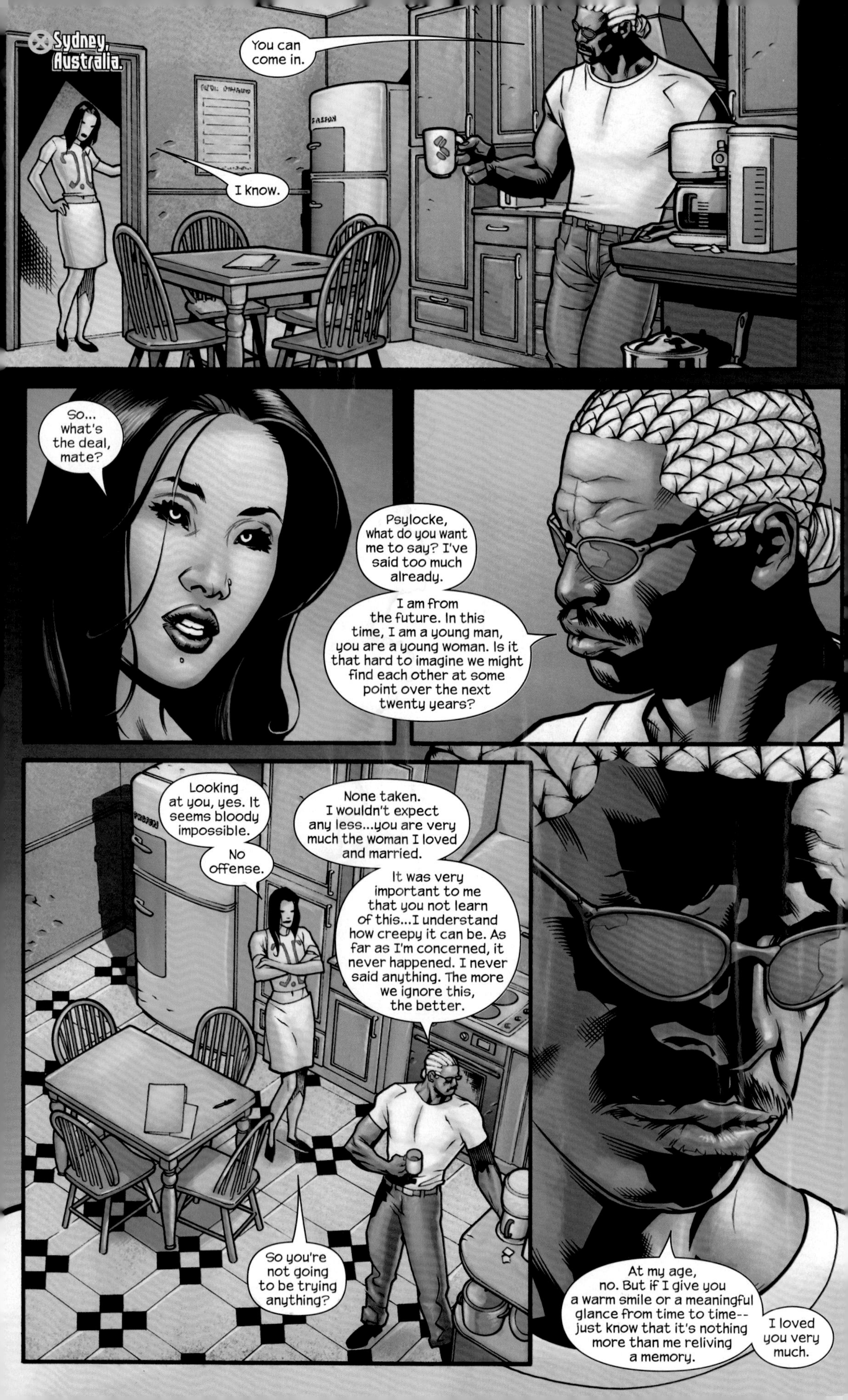
Sydney, Australia.
You can come in.
I know.
So... what's the deal, mate?
Psylocke, what do you want me to say? I've said too much already.
I am from the future. In this time, I am a young man, you are a young woman. Is it that hard to imagine we might find each other at some point over the next twenty years?
Looking at you, yes. It seems bloody impossible.
No offense.
None taken. I wouldn't expect any less...you are very much the woman I loved and married.
It was very important to me that you not learn of this...I understand how creepy it can be. As far as I'm concerned, it never happened. I never said anything. The more we ignore this, the better.
So you're not going to be trying anything?
At my age, no. But if I give you a warm smile or a meaningful glance from time to time--just know that it's nothing more than me reliving a memory.
I loved you very much.

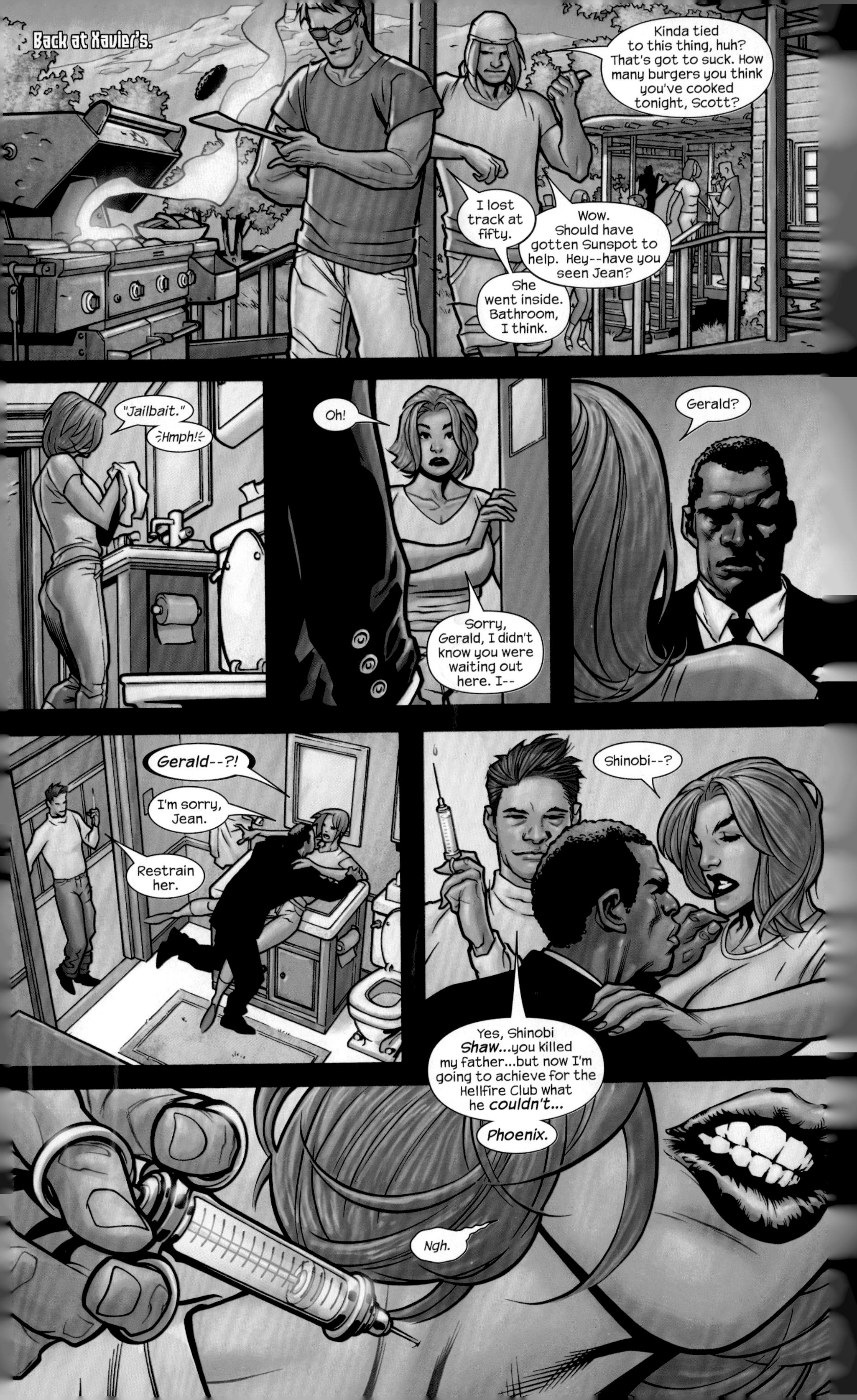
Back at Xavier's.
Kinda tied to this thing, huh? That's got to suck. How many burgers you think you've cooked tonight, Scott?
I lost track at fifty.
Wow. Should have gotten Sunspot to help. Hey--have you seen Jean?
She went inside. Bathroom, I think.
"Jailbait."
Hmph!
Oh!
Sorry, Gerald, I didn't know you were waiting out here. I--
Gerald?
Gerald--?!
I'm sorry, Jean.
Restrain her.
Shinobi--?
Yes, Shinobi Shaw...you killed my father...but now I'm going to achieve for the Hellfire Club what he couldn't...
Phoenix.
Ngh.

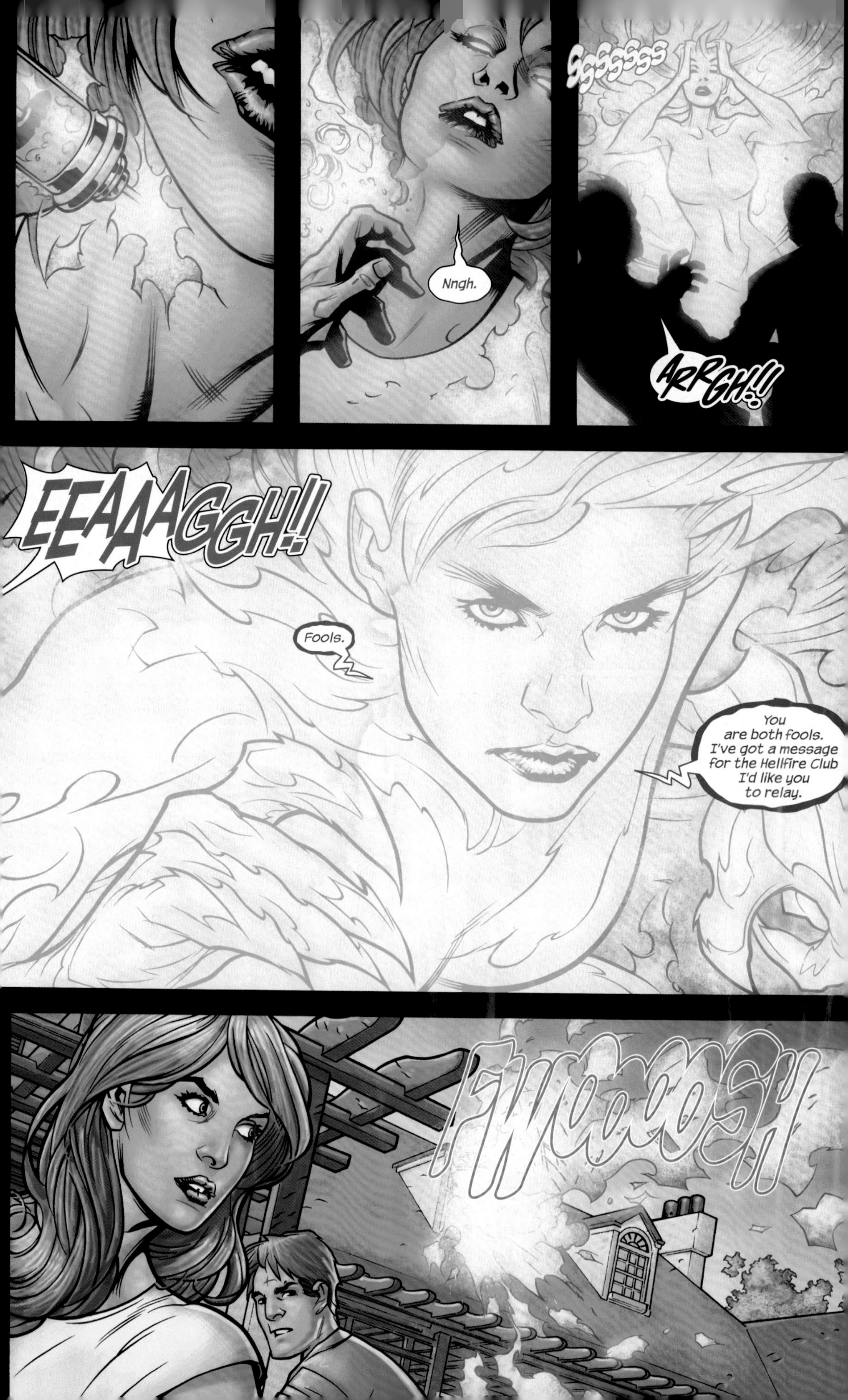
Nngh.
SSSSSSS
ARRGH!!
EEAAAGGH!!
Fools.
You are both fools. I've got a message for the Hellfire Club I'd like you to relay.
FWOOSH

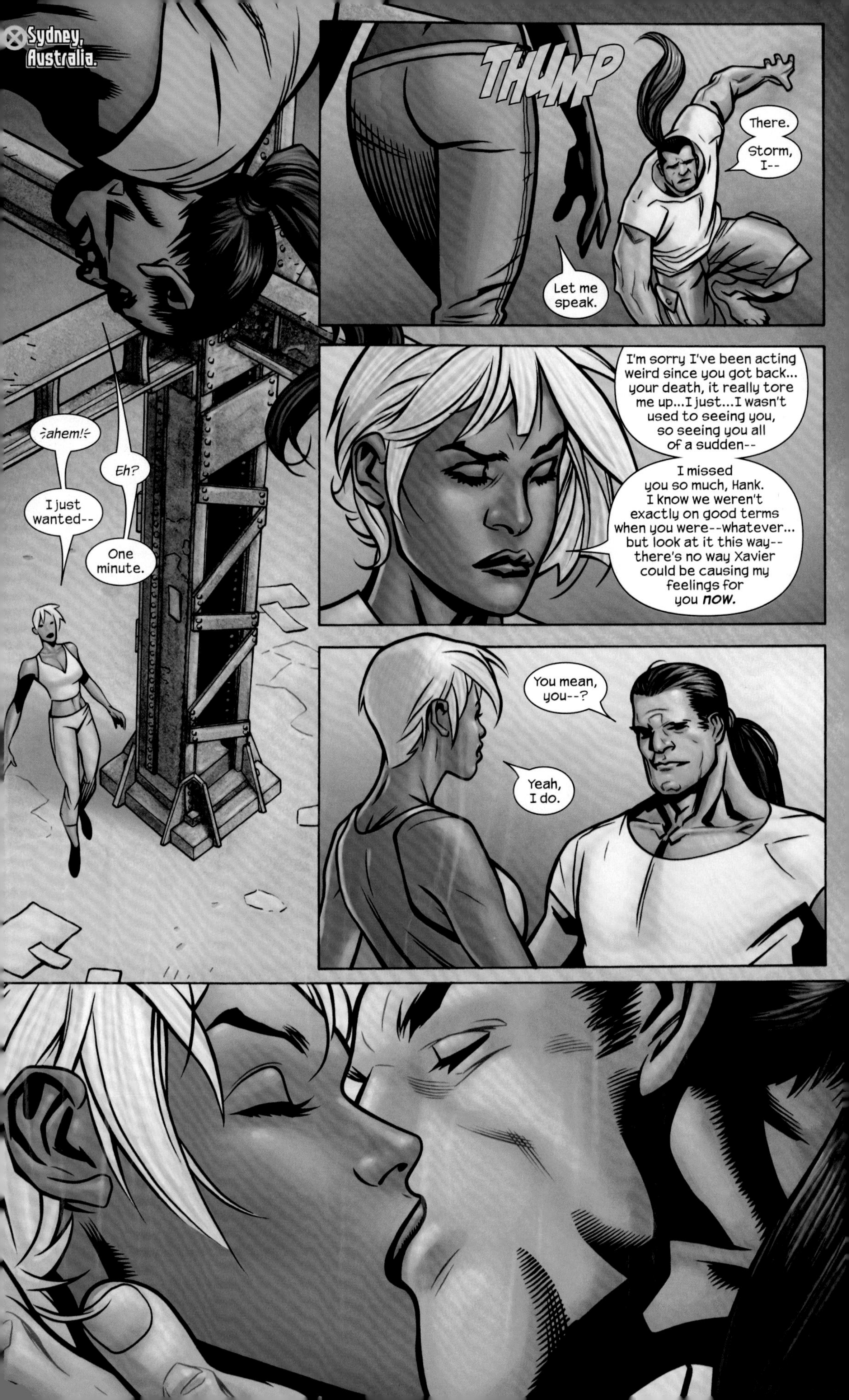
Sydney, Australia.
THUMP
There.
Storm, I--
Let me speak.
ahem!
Eh?
I just wanted--
One minute.
I'm sorry I've been acting weird since you got back... your death, it really tore me up...I just...I wasn't used to seeing you, so seeing you all of a sudden--
I missed you so much, Hank. I know we weren't exactly on good terms when you were--whatever... but look at it this way--there's no way Xavier could be causing my feelings for you *now.*
You mean, you--?
Yeah, I do.

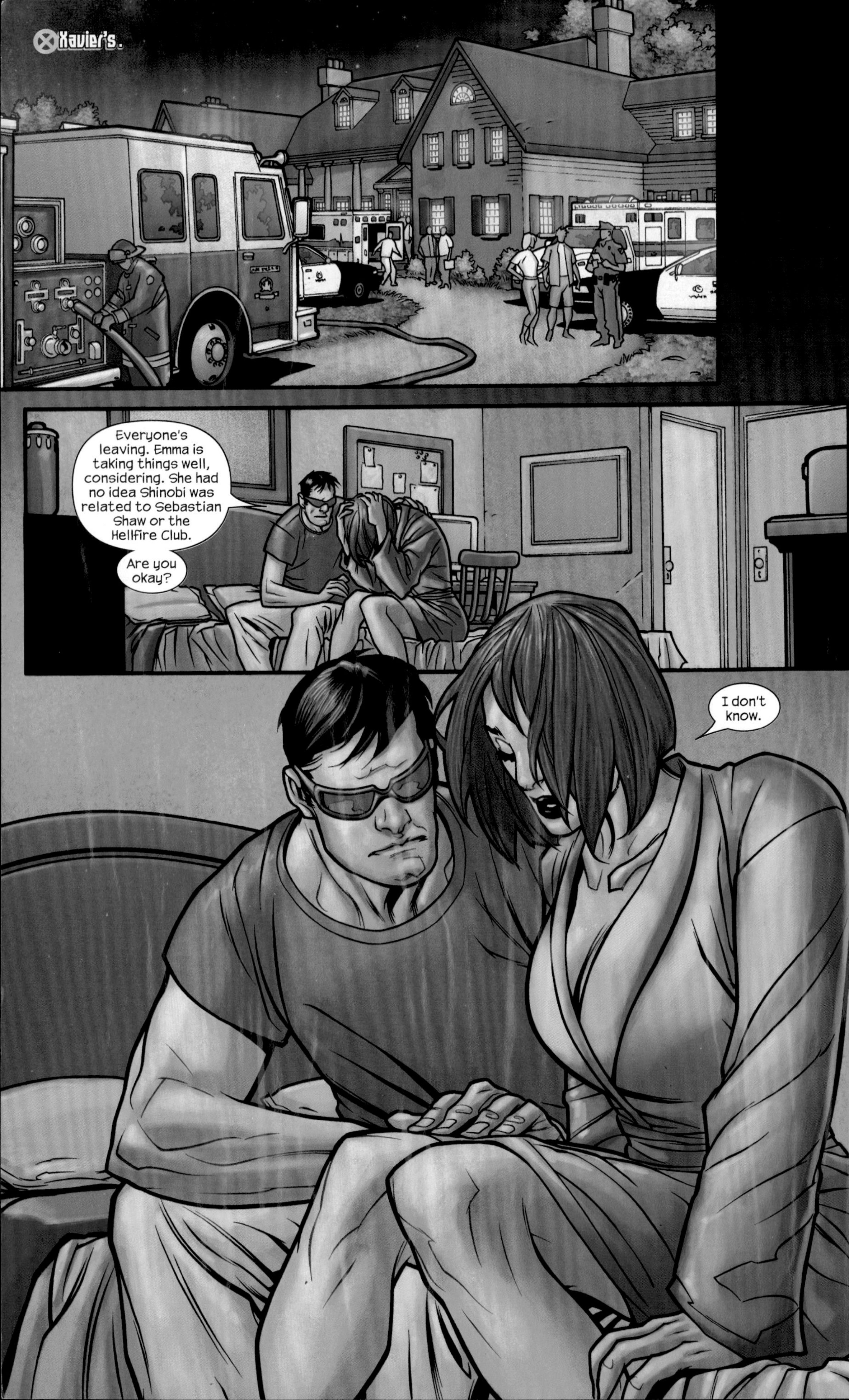
Xavier's.
Everyone's leaving. Emma is taking things well, considering. She had no idea Shinobi was related to Sebastian Shaw or the Hellfire Club.
Are you okay?
I don't know.

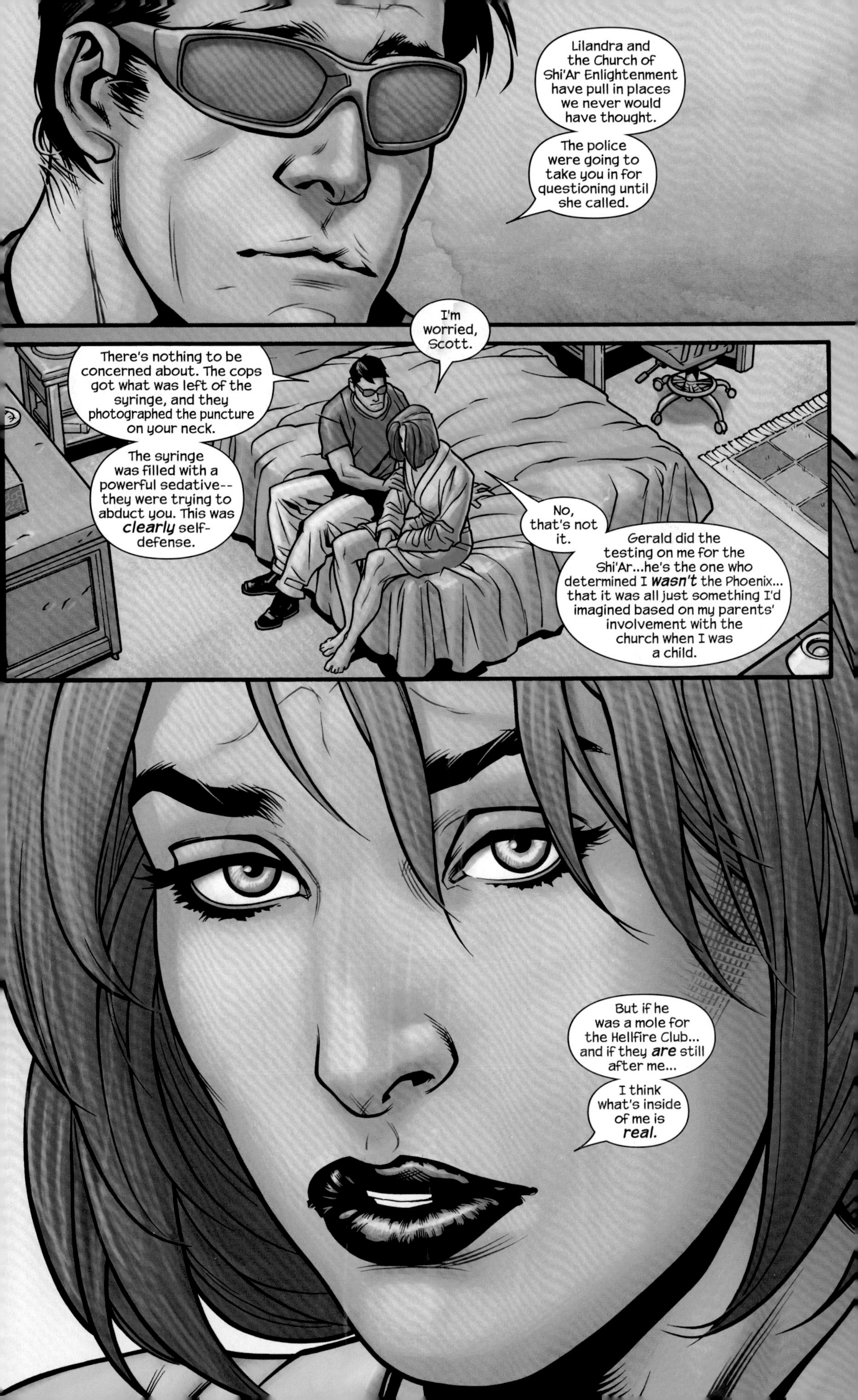
Lilandra and the Church of Shi'Ar Enlightenment have pull in places we never would have thought.
The police were going to take you in for questioning until she called.
I'm worried, Scott.
There's nothing to be concerned about. The cops got what was left of the syringe, and they photographed the puncture on your neck.
The syringe was filled with a powerful sedative--they were trying to abduct you. This was *clearly* self-defense.
No, that's not it.
Gerald did the testing on me for the Shi'Ar...he's the one who determined I *wasn't* the Phoenix...that it was all just something I'd imagined based on my parents' involvement with the church when I was a child.
But if he was a mole for the Hellfire Club...and if they *are* still after me...
I think what's inside of me is *real.*

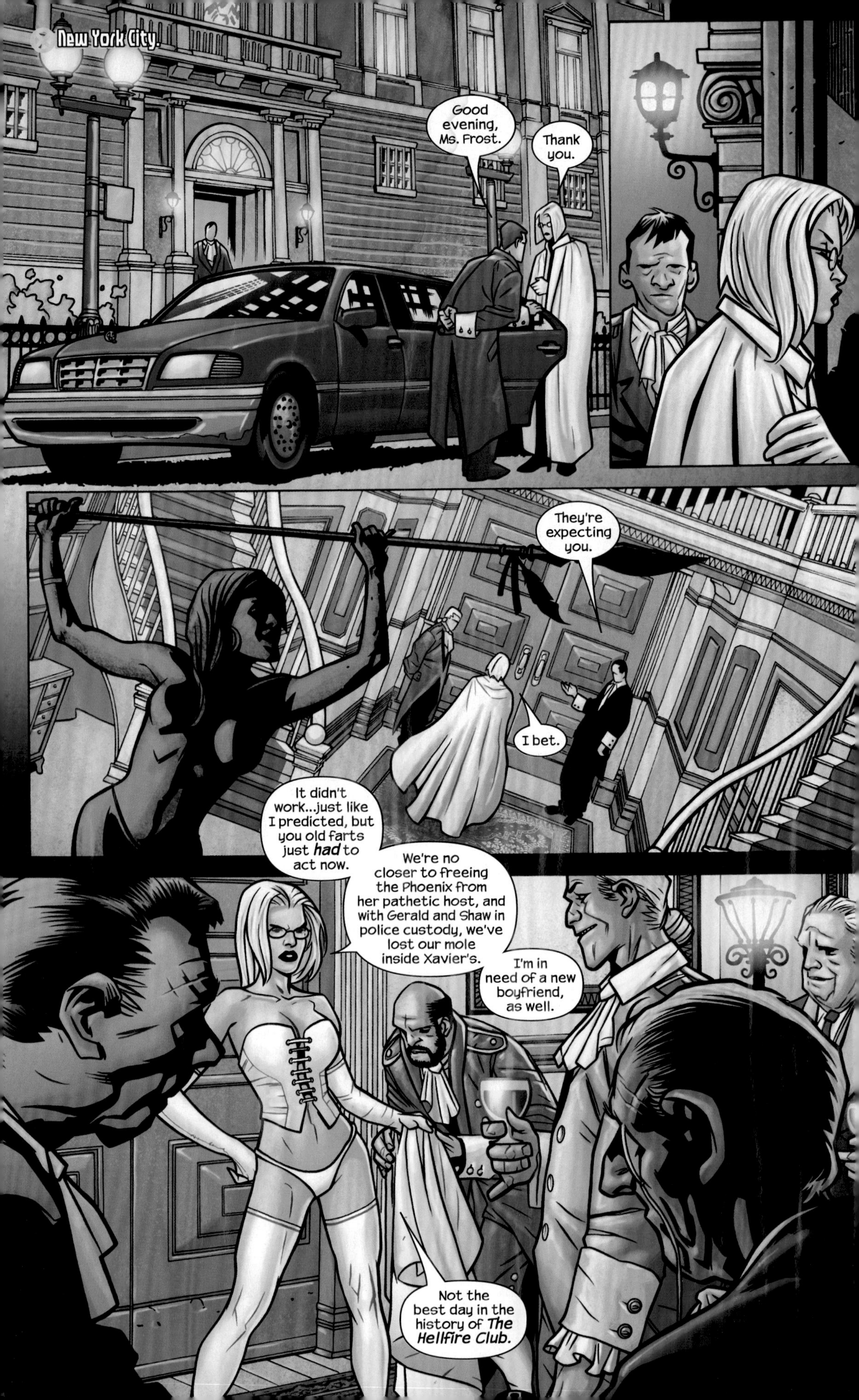
New York City.
Good evening, Ms. Frost.
Thank you.
They're expecting you.
I bet.
It didn't work...just like I predicted, but you old farts just *had* to act now.
We're no closer to freeing the Phoenix from her pathetic host, and with Gerald and Shaw in police custody, we've lost our mole inside Xavier's.
I'm in need of a new boyfriend, as well.
Not the best day in the history of *The Hellfire Club.*

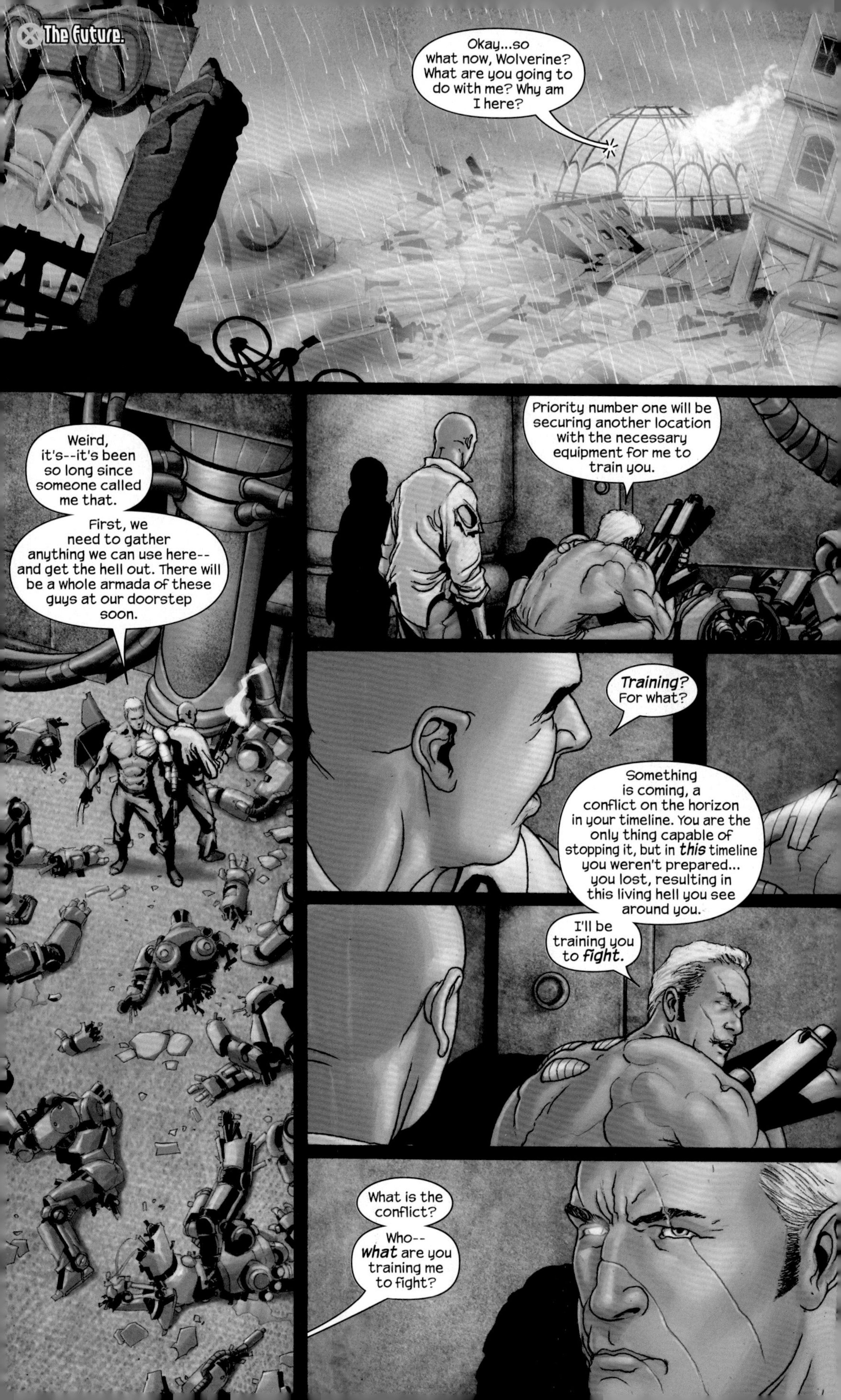
The Future.
Okay...so what now, Wolverine? What are you going to do with me? Why am I here?
Weird, it's--it's been so long since someone called me that.
First, we need to gather anything we can use here--and get the hell out. There will be a whole armada of these guys at our doorstep soon.
Priority number one will be securing another location with the necessary equipment for me to train you.
Training? For what?
Something is coming, a conflict on the horizon in your timeline. You are the only thing capable of stopping it, but in this timeline you weren't prepared... you lost, resulting in this living hell you see around you.
I'll be training you to fight.
What is the conflict?
Who--what are you training me to fight?

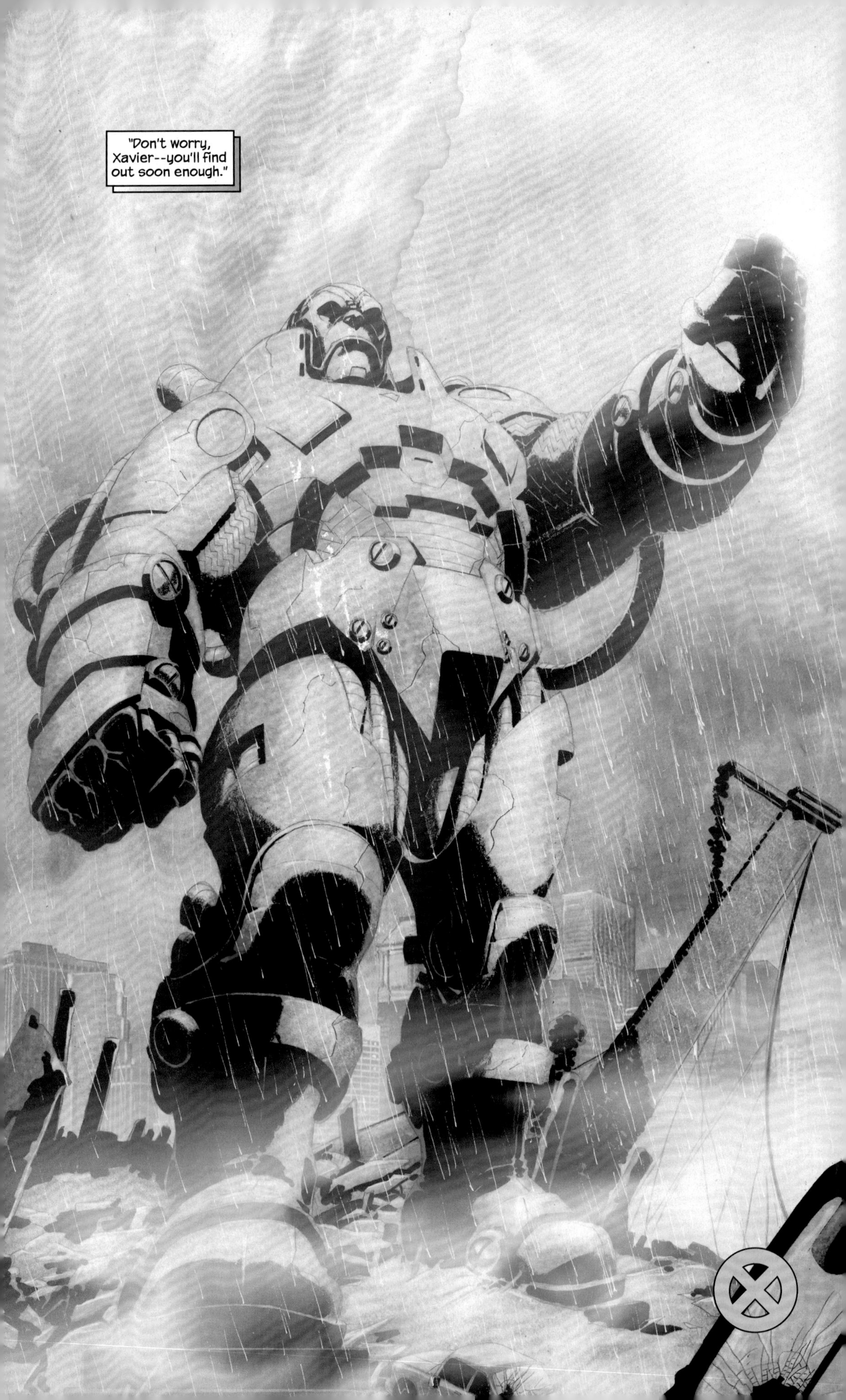
"Don't worry, Xavier--you'll find out soon enough."